Index
to the
Fairfax County
Virginia
Register of Marriages
1853 - 1933

Constance K. Ring
Craig R. Scott, CGRS

Willow Bend Books
Lovettsville, Virginia
1997

Willow Bend Books
39475 Tollhouse Road
Lovettsville, Virginia 20180-1817

Visit our bookstore at:

http://www.mediasoft.net/ScottC

or e-mail us at:

willowbend@mediasoft.net

Printed in the United States of America

ISBN: 1-888265-27-2

Introduction

The Fairfax County Register of Marriages, 1853-1933 is a treasure-trove of full of Fairfax County relationships. Housed in the Fairfax Circuit Court Archives, the Register consists of one oversized volume of 145 double pages containing more than 6500 chronologically arranged handwritten entries. Each entry spans two pages. The information includes : line number, date and place of marriage, names of parties, age and status before marriage (single, divorced, widowed), places of birth and residence, names of parents, occupation of husband, name of person performing the ceremony, and remarks. Each entry was made by the court clerk by date of marriage when the license was returned to his office. An incomplete file of licenses is also maintained by the Circuit Court Archives.

Occasionally discrepancies occur between the Register and the marriage license. An effort has been made to reconcile the Register with the license in cases of a difference in date, when the page in the Register is damaged or the writing is illegible, or when the given name in the Register is represented by initials only. The full name, as it appears on the license, is used in this book. While there is no separate column in the Register for race, the clerk beginning in 1911 entered the letters "c" and "w" (colored and white) in the age column. This was done sporadically prior to that year, as in 1884-1889, and appears from the handwriting to have been at the discretion of the clerk. The marriage licenses themselves consistently include race beginning in 1874. Racial information from the licenses has been included in this book when not provided by the clerk.

This index, arranged alphabetically by the surname of the groom, provides the user with quick access to the information in the Register. Each entry contains the names of the parties, their race when colored, marital status (divorced or widowed), date of marriage and the page in the Register on which the information can be found. An index to brides is provided in the back of the book.

Copies cannot be made of pages in the Register because of its size and fragile condition. The Library of Virginia has microfilmed the Register and it is available through interlibrary loan. However, copies can be made of the licenses, if available, by sending a money order for $2.50, payable to the Clerk of the Court, to the Circuit Court Archives, 4110 Chain Bridge Road, Fairfax, VA 22030. Include a stamped, self-address envelope and a brief note containing the marriage date and names of the parties whose license you are requesting. Mention also that you found the information in this book.

Dedication

During her tenure as the first archivist of the Fairfax County Circuit Court, from 1982 until her death, Constance K. Ring created numerous finding aids to improve researcher access to the records in her custody. Her death, on January 6, 1997, occurred before the work on this finding aid could be completed. Her death is a heartfelt loss to the entire Northern Virginia historical and genealogical communities. The Archives Room at the Circuit Court has been named in her memory. It is to her that this work is dedicated.

Index to the Fairfax County, Virginia, Register of Marriages
1853 - 1933

Groom	Bride	Date	Page
ABBOTT, Howard B /div	TAGGART, Martha J	8 Aug 1912	83
ACTON, Henry L	LLOYD, Annie G	15 Sep 1932	139
ACTON, John C	HUMMER, Martha F	26 Dec 1867	8
ADAMS, Alfred Lee	BRYANT, Maude V	29 Jul 1910	78
ADAMS, Arthur K	COBB, Dorothy	27 Dec 1919	97
ADAMS, Clarence /c	WILLIAMS, Hannah E /c	15 Apr 1925	111
ADAMS, Claude M	MATEER, Hattie A	5 Dec 1912	83
ADAMS, George /c	JOHNSON, Louisa /c	3 Sep 1920	98
ADAMS, Henry	MATTOCKS, Iola /wid	26 Feb 1924	108
ADAMS, Henry W	DORSEY, Mary H	20 Aug 1919	96
ADAMS, Ira W	STONE, Eudoxia V	30 Nov 1859	4
ADAMS, James H /wid	KINSMAN, Mary E /wid	29 Aug 1931	133
ADAMS, James Henry	BREEDEN, Clara M	1 Apr 1918	94
ADAMS, James R	HUNT, Jessie	19 Sep 1911	81
ADAMS, John William	ELTER, Mary Cecelia	27 Apr 1921	100
ADAMS, Lewis J	CLARKE, Annie L	14 Nov 1894	48
ADAMS, Nelson H /div	POWELL, Ella L	5 Sep 1931	133
ADAMS, Oscar	TRAMMELL, Belle	11 Apr 1877	22
ADAMS, Oscar	ADAMS, Gertrude T	26 Jun 1912	82
ADAMS, R L	ADAMS, Lottie	19 Nov 1885	35
ADAMS, Robert /c	SHORTS, Clara /c	2 Jan 1886	36
ADAMS, Robert Leo	ALDER, Agnes Jackson	7 Jul 1927	118
ADAMS, Roy /c	GEATOR, Lula /c	31 Jul 1916	90
ADAMS, Thomas E	FONDA, Mary L	3 Mar 1906	70
ADAMS, Thomas Edwin	KENNEDY, Agnes E	17 Jun 1919	96
ADAMS, Thomas W	GROH, Elizabeth S	20 Mar 1907	72
ADAMS, Truman	BURLEIGH, Allie M	20 Nov 1912	83
ADAMS, Vern T	BRADSHAW, Ona Virginia	15 Nov 1919	97
ADAMS, William /c	HONESTY, Lizzie /c	25 Nov 1893	47
ADAMS, William /c	BOWLES, Emma /c wid	24 Jul 1917	92
ADAMS, William Henry James /c	STOKES, Annie /c	26 Dec 1896	52
ADDISON, Joseph /c	FLETCHER, Annie /c	4 Jan 1885	34
ADRIAN, Carl A Jr	NUTLER, Elizabeth Louise	29 Sep 1931	133
ADRIAN, Floyd	FLEMING, Clara	8 Jun 1903	64
ADRIAN, Oscar M	DEY, Emma A	31 Oct 1900	59
AINSLEY, Robert H /wid	GAGGIANO, Maria M	29 Jan 1931	131
AKERS, Scott /c wid	BECKWITH, Hattie /c	21 Sep 1910	79

ALDER, Amos M	ROBERTSON, Mary E	3 Apr 1917	*91*
ALBERTSON, William F	MABEN, Nelly	6 Jan 1897	*52*
ALBOUGH, Fred G	SHEAR, Annie B /wid	21 Jan 1914	*86*
ALDEN, Harry L	POWELL, Maud	20 Apr 1892	*44*
ALDERTON, J Franklin	BURRISS, Mamie	14 Sep 1916	*90*
ALDERTON, O H	BRUMBACK, Mary E	14 Apr 1924	*108*
ALEXANDER, Albert H M III	FARMER, Inez	8 Feb 1932	*136*
ALEXANDER, Alfred Romley /c	SMACKUM, Christine Edna /c	17 Jul 1933	*143*
ALEXANDER, Arthur /c	WASHINGTON, Mary /c	16 Apr 1927	*117*
ALEXANDER, David	SHELNITZ, Rose L	5 Sep 1929	*125*
ALEXANDER, David C	LEE, Helen B	4 May 1921	*100*
ALEXANDER, Earl /c	WILLIAMS, Ora Bell /c	19 May 1915	*88*
ALEXANDER, Edward /c	PAYNE, Gertrude /c	20 Dec 1911	*82*
ALEXANDER, Eugene /c	PEARSON, Mary /c	18 Dec 1890	*42*
ALEXANDER, Frederick W	MATHES, Mary E	27 Dec 1899	*57*
ALEXANDER, James W	SMITH, Emily L /c	6 Feb 1884	*32*
ALEXANDER, Lewis W	HESTER, Frances G	19 May 1930	*128*
ALEXANDER, Sumner /c	FRENCH, Janie /c	16 Aug 1915	*89*
ALEXANDER, William	ROBERSON, Diana	28 Apr 1870	*12*
ALEXANDER, William /c	EVANS, Elephy /c	15 Jan 1880	*24*
ALLDER, Paul Fox	SWART, Edna May	3 Oct 1923	*106*
ALLDER, Roy B	SWART, Mary M	14 Jun 1923	*105*
ALLEN, A M /c	BROOKS, Mary E /c	13 Jul 1904	*66*
ALLEN, Albert W	LIGHTBOWN, Maud	17 Sep 1932	*139*
ALLEN, Alexander	ROBERSON, Ella	11 Dec 1870	*13*
ALLEN, Anthony /c	ALLEN, Maria E /c div	3 May 1917	*92*
ALLEN, Arvine	WEBSTER, Lucy /c	10 Mar 1926	*114*
ALLEN, Christopher	TRICKETT, Lottie	31 Jan 1881	*28*
ALLEN, E T	DOVE, Ruth M /wid	29 Dec 1920	*99*
ALLEN, Francis Jeff	BURRITT, Mary Frances	26 Sep 1921	*101*
ALLEN, George /c	HARRIS, Susie /c	23 Mar 1918	*94*
ALLEN, J Herbert	GUNNELL, Virginia B	12 Oct 1897	*53*
ALLEN, James F	SMITH, Mary Etta	7 Feb 1923	*104*
ALLEN, James W	CLARKE, Alice V	26 Apr 1877	*22*
ALLEN, John /c wid	HARRIS, Anna /c	8 Nov 1903	*65*
ALLEN, John G /c	TALIFERRO, Marion /c	12 Dec 1879	*26*
ALLEN, John H	NICHOLS, Emeline H	11 Jan 1870	*11*
ALLEN, Philip /c	PAYNE, Virginia /c	10 Sep 1924	*109*
ALLEN, Piercie Mansfield /div	LACY, Nina E	8 Aug 1932	*138*
ALLEN, Raymond Eugene	HUTCHINS, Elsie E	29 Mar 1919	*95*
ALLEN, William Henry /c	BARNETT, Mollie /c	26 Mar 1932	*136*
ALLISON, James G	ALLISON, Martha A /div	14 Oct 1857	*3*

ALLISON, James W	HOPE, Ann H /div	7 Oct 1932	139
ALLISON, John M	COLLINS, Annie Blanche	23 Dec 1908	76
ALNUTT, William T	RANNEBERGER, Mabel W	4 May 1920	98
ALRICH, William A	LOVE, Mary J	6 May 1869	11
ALTER, Jesse N	CASSELL, Mary B	25 Mar 1924	108
ALVORD, Henry E	SWINK, Martha S	6 Sep 1866	6
AMBLER, C F /wid	CROSON, Annie R /wid	7 Mar 1912	82
AMBLER, J C	CUNNINGHAM, Mary B	28 Mar 1901	60
AMBLER, James S	BEACH, Priscilla	26 Apr 1870	12
AMLIE, Thomas R /wid	BEYER, Gehrta F /div	7 May 1932	137
AMO, George J /div	SHARP, Catherine P /wid	17 Jun 1920	98
ANDERSON, Charles /c wid	BAILEY, Sallie /c wid	19 Dec 1880	27
ANDERSON, Charles /c wid	SHELTON, Josie /c	25 Jun 1891	43
ANDERSON, Ernest E	DETWILER, Beula Mae	8 Jul 1918	94
ANDERSON, George /c	DORSEY, Eliza /c	9 May 1906	70
ANDERSON, George W /c	TEBBS, Matilda	8 Sep 1878	24
ANDERSON, James E /c	BROWN, Edloe E S /c	28 Jun 1932	138
ANDERSON, John Luther /c	JOHNSON, Catharine Idella /c	3 Oct 1878	25
ANDERSON, Luther /c	STOTTS, Sarah /c	18 Jan 1914	86
ANDERSON, Luther H	MILLER, Catherine M	15 Jul 1932	138
ANDERSON, Milton	GOTT, Susette V	10 Apr 1926	114
ANDERSON, Peter /wid	OTIS, Mary /wid	7 Apr 1881	28
ANDERSON, Samuel C	RIGG, Beulah	24 Sep 1914	87
ANDERSON, Silas E /c wid	DAVIS, Mary Adaline /c	7 Jun 1903	64
ANDERSON, Stephen /c	ALLEN, Eliza /c	9 Dec 1890	42
ANDERSON, Thomas J	LEDMAN, Alcinda	19 May 1875	18
ANDERSON, Walter C	BAS, Gertrude	13 Jan 1919	95
ANDERSON, William A	SMALLWOOD, Mildred F	21 Nov 1867	8
ANDRE, George W Jr /div	WHEELER, Thelma	13 Sep 1929	126
ANDREAS, Otto F	KIDWELL, Daisy M	7 Feb 1900	58
ANDREWS, Warren H	GOETZ, Rosa A /div	5 Mar 1918	93
ANDRICK, Tobias V	ALLEN, Nellie G	6 Dec 1926	116
ANDRUS, Arthur J	LANHAM, Annie V	1 Nov 1896	51
ANKERS, J E	LLOYD, Sarah J	22 Apr 1895	49
ANKERS, Jonathan B	BLADEN, Olive R	24 Dec 1910	80
ANKERS, Jonathan E	MILSTEAD, Susan A	11 Apr 1881	28
ANKERS, Mahlon A	FLEMING, Mary L	10 Sep 1919	96
ANTHONY, William H	FLANIGAN, Mary F	6 May 1886	36
APGAR, Gillard W /div	CATES, Iola	31 Dec 1921	101
APPERSON, H N	KERSEY, Bessie W	27 Oct 1909	77
ARBELL, Harry S	PALMER, Elizabeth M	14 Nov 1924	110
ARCHIBALD, Frank E	GREER, Urith L	24 Apr 1933	142

ARENDES, Bernard H	JAVINS, Marie A R	25 May 1926	*114*
AREY, William L	BOTELER, Mildred M	5 Apr 1924	*108*
ARMACOST, Charles F	SISSON, Margaret C	31 Dec 1931	*135*
ARMENTROUT, John M	DOLLY, Martha	22 Oct 1868	*10*
ARMSTRONG, R H	ELGIN, Sarah E /wid	25 Jun 1913	*84*
ARNOLD, Albert H	REYNOLDS, Ida P /wid	3 Jun 1903	*64*
ARNOLD, Arthur /c	WILLIAMS, Amanda /c	28 Dec 1899	*57*
ARNOLD, Christian F	WRENN, Edna D	21 Jun 1899	*56*
ARNOLD, Edward C	SANDERS, Adelaide	4 Nov 1908	*75*
ARNOLD, George	RIVIERE, Addie O	3 Jun 1930	*128*
ARNOLD, Gilbert R	MOFFETT, Pauline R	27 Jun 1931	*132*
ARNOLD, John B	SCHOFIELD, Edna Lane	30 Dec 1933	*145*
ARNOLD, Marshall	FORD, Virginia	21 Feb 1882	*30*
ARNOLD, Warren	CRAIGG, Ruth	17 Sep 1921	*101*
ARNOLD, William Potter	MATHESON, Julia Torrey	29 Jun 1933	*142*
ARNUNGER, Robert H	HILTON, Ethel	21 Jan 1930	*127*
ARRINGTON, T T	DAVIS, Julia F	25 Jan 1876	*20*
ARTHUR, William K /wid	ROBINSON, Virginia	21 Nov 1866	*7*
ARUNDALE, John W	WHITE, Florence C	9 Nov 1929	*126*
ASH, Clifton P	BOUCHER, Cora F	12 Nov 1908	*75*
ASH, Eli J /c	DERRICK, Maggie /c	8 May 1894	*47*
ASHBURN, Pierce B /c	CLEMENTS, Ivy V /c	.5 Nov 1913	*85*
ASHBY, Benjamin /c	SKINNER, Mary /c wid	1 Mar 1877	*21*
ASHBY, Carroll W	WATKINS, Lillian E	21 Mar 1925	*110*
ASHBY, Edward Jos.	GRANIGAN, Ida V	21 Nov 1923	*106*
ASHBY, Isaac /c	CARY, Rosalie L /c	18 Jul 1886	*36*
ASHBY, Isaac /c wid	GRANT, Maria /c wid	14 Jun 1894	*48*
ASHBY, Samuel /c	JACKSON, Louisa /c	26 Jul 1883	*31*
ASHFORD, George S	MITCHELL, Cora L	11 Jan 1885	*34*
ASHFORD, J D	COCKERILLE, Edna L	25 Feb 1891	*43*
ASHFORD, James W	WOODYARD, Malvina F	21 Dec 1869	*11*
ASHFORD, John William	FAIRFAX, Fannie R	11 Sep 1909	*77*
ASHLEY, Frank	MORRIS, Virginia	30 Jan 1932	*136*
ASHMEAD, Benjamin W /div	AMBROSE, Valerie W /div	2 Jun 1932	*137*
ASHTON, Armistead	JOHNSON, Rachael	24 Jul 1870	*13*
ASHTON, Armistead /c	LEE, Mary /c	28 Jan 1877	*21*
ASHTON, Charles A /wid	BRYANT, Maggie May	16 Jan 1901	*58*
ASHTON, David G	WOODWORTH, Harriet	15 Oct 1853	*1*
ASHTON, Henry	CRANKUM, Nancy /wid	21 Dec 1867	*8*
ASHTON, S T [Dr.]	BARNES, Nina F	12 Dec 1888	*39*
ASPESLAGH, Louis M	HAVERTY, Beatrice L	18 Feb 1928	*121*
ATKINS, Addison B	STUART, Ellen C	19 Oct 1854	*1*

ATKINS, Winford B	ROGERS, Reba	1 Mar 1924	*108*
ATKINSON, Rollins J	SMITH, Mary M	15 Aug 1927	*119*
ATKINSON, William T */wid*	DAVIS, Katherine M	20 Aug 1929	*125*
ATWOOD, Raymond P	MORRISON, Lelure B	7 Feb 1918	*93*
AUCMOODY, Walter S */wid*	ERWIN, Julia L */wid*	10 Oct 1869	*11*
AUGUR, Cassius	BARNES, Juanita E	15 Apr 1873	*16*
AULD, George F	MARTIN, Elizabeth C	21 Apr 1892	*44*
AULD, James	BARNUM, Emma C */wid*	2 Nov 1892	*45*
AUSTIN, Benjamin M	SCHATZ, Hulda L	30 Jul 1927	*118*
AUSTIN, Frank A	ERLMEIER, Frances A M	22 Dec 1919	*97*
AUSTIN, William C */wid*	POYNER, Beatrice	11 May 1929	*124*
AVEILLIE, Jules B	BROCK, Lillian	16 Aug 1906	*71*
AWLBRETON, George W	MILLS, Susan	20 Jul 1858	*3*
AYRE, Elmer T	FERGUSON, Sarah C	3 Oct 1922	*103*
AYRE, William Jr	WALKER, Florence O	15 Jan 1878	*23*
AYRES, Bert	HARTBOWER, Mary L	30 Sep 1903	*65*
AYRES, Charles L	BURKE, Mildred M	27 Jan 1876	*20*
AYRES, David	RAMSDELL, Myrtle M	27 Aug 1921	*101*
AYRES, Henry C	WELSH, Vernnie O	28 Apr 1904	*66*
AYRES, John E Jr	PERONE, Audrey	24 Oct 1930	*130*
AYRES, John W	DOVE, Agnes M	11 Dec 1932	*140*
AYRES, Samuel	WILSON, Blanche	10 Apr 1902	*62*
AYRES, Warren L	DANIELS, Frances A	10 Feb 1886	*36*
BACHELDER, Frederick */div*	CARLSON, Hulda M */div*	14 Aug 1907	*73*
BAGGOTT, Harvey	KING, Ethel	15 Sep 1925	*112*
BAGGOTT, John W	ASHFORD, Martha J	23 Mar 1869	*10*
BAGGOTT, Townsend */wid*	DODSON, Ella Edwina	13 Aug 1933	*144*
BAILEY, Addison */c*	MILLINER, Clara */c*	23 Nov 1905	*70*
BAILEY, Charles */c*	ASHTON, Mary */c*	12 Apr 1888	*38*
BAILEY, Charles W	CAUDLE, Versie A	3 Sep 1930	*129*
BAILEY, Edgar G	WATKINS, Ida W	21 Apr 1897	*52*
BAILEY, Edward */c*	JACKSON, Rebecca */c*	15 Sep 1891	*43*
BAILEY, Elmer H Jr	HUGHES, Gertrude Marie	17 May 1924	*108*
BAILEY, Frank */c*	SCOTT, Clara M */c*	11 Mar 1923	*107*
BAILEY, Frank V	SONES, Ruth	21 Dec 1928	*123*
BAILEY, Henson */c*	JACKSON, Nora */c*	5 Dec 1889	*40*
BAILEY, Herbert	SPAULDING, Hilda	12 Sep 1925	*112*
BAILEY, Horace U	GORDON, Eliza D	3 Dec 1884	*34*
BAILEY, James	CRANKUM, Lucy	16 Sep 1871	*18*
BAILEY, Ray T	SHREVE, Alice	27 Oct 1869	*13*
BAILEY, Ray T	GORDON, Mary E	4 Dec 1878	*26*
BAILEY, Robert J	BROWN, Belle */c*	12 Aug 1897	*53*

BAILEY, Vernon F /c	WILLIAMS, Mattie /c	13 Jun 1931	*132*
BAILEY, W A Jr /c	TINNER, Elizabeth /c	17 Nov 1915	*89*
BAILEY, William /c	BRADLEY, Jennie /c	16 Jul 1882	*30*
BAILEY, William G	FEBREY, Ida I	8 Jan 1878	*23*
BAIN, Robert	BRADLEY, Rose	17 Mar 1856	*2*
BAINES, Bernard M	KREZELL, Marie A	7 Nov 1925	*113*
BAKER, David /wid	GARDNER, Ida /wid	15 Dec 1927	*120*
BAKER, Floyd J	HOYS, Catheryne	30 Jun 1926	*115*
BAKER, George R	DEAVERS, Effie	9 Jun 1898	*54*
BAKER, Henry T	BONDEY, Elizabeth C	28 Feb 1931	*131*
BAKER, Herbert John /wid	BURROUGHS, Mary Roberta	8 Jul 1896	*51*
BAKER, James /c	CARTER, Lizzie /c wid	12 Sep 1906	*71*
BAKER, James /c	LUCAS, Amanda /c	22 Mar 1932	*136*
BAKER, John /wid	ISENHOUR, Ruby Lee /div	17 Jun 1933	*142*
BAKER, John J /c	HARRIS, Jeanette E /c	14 Sep 1912	*83*
BAKER, Leroy	KEAN, Rosa B	13 Sep 1924	*109*
BAKER, Manny Davison	DUNN, Irene Matilda	7 Jun 1906	*71*
BAKER, Melvin /c	TYLER, Leola	26 Nov 1926	*116*
BAKER, R W	FOX, Eolene R	25 Oct 1905	*69*
BAKER, Thomas	RILEY, Mary	1 Jun 1871	*13*
BALDERSON, W C	FOLLIN, Annie B	12 Jun 1901	*60*
BALDERSTON, Walter C	DANIELS, Ivy D	14 Nov 1903	*65*
BALDWIN, A H	GREEN, Grace G	30 Nov 1910	*80*
BALDWIN, Raymond	FRAZIER, Lucille	16 May 1931	*132*
BALDWIN, Walter J /wid	KIDWELL, Lillian	1 Oct 1909	*77*
BALL, Arthur H	DAVIS, Harriet C	18 Nov 1884	*34*
BALL, Boolton F	MOHLER, Alma H	5 Mar 1902	*62*
BALL, Francis M	NOBLE, Alice	28 Nov 1906	*72*
BALL, Harry W	PECK, Edna M	8 Feb 1911	*80*
BALL, James A /c	HAMILTON, Mary E /c	17 Dec 1902	*63*
BALL, M M	GANTT, Charlotte P	30 Jun 1870	*12*
BALL, Samuel A /wid	COOKSEY, Cora F	17 Sep 1902	*63*
BALL, Simon /c	RUSSEL, Carrie C /c	4 Jul 1888	*38*
BALL, William A /c	COLE, Sylvia R /c	2 Oct 1917	*93*
BALL, William Asbury	ROWELL, Martha	29 Nov 1921	*101*
BALL, William Edward	CHAMBERS, Lillian O	13 Oct 1927	*119*
BALL, William S	BALL, Martha C T	10 Dec 1879	*26*
BALL, Wilmer C	CROSS, Edna	26 Apr 1905	*68*
BALLARD, George H	ROAT, Barbara	15 Jan 1931	*131*
BALLARD, James W	GOODWIN, Margaret Lewis	24 Nov 1908	*75*
BALLARD, John N	THRIFT, Lillie	22 Sep 1874	*20*
BALLARD, Joseph Robert	LILLARD, Rita Pauline	4 Nov 1933	*144*

BALLENGER, A J /wid	JAVINS, Emma J	27 Nov 1879	26
BALLENGER, Benjamin F	TURNER, Mary	7 Jan 1869	10
BALLENGER, Charles /wid	ROBERTS, Ann E	12 Apr 1870	12
BALLENGER, De Walton	MOON, Jessie F	10 Oct 1889	40
BALLENGER, E E /wid	BROOKS, Tillie W /div	10 May 1928	121
BALLENGER, Frank L	LYLES, Nellie E	6 Nov 1907	73
BALLENGER, Franklin S	WATKINS, Marion V	15 Jan 1890	41
BALLENGER, John W	REID, Margaret F	19 Nov 1867	8
BALLENGER, Julien	PULMAN, Frances H	12 Aug 1886	36
BALLENGER, Peyton /wid	SHEETS, Anna M /wid	10 Aug 1882	30
BALLENGER, Robert W	HUNTER, Jane F	3 Oct 1866	7
BALLENGER, Wesley	BALLENGER, Annie	14 May 1880	26
BALLOU, Frank M	STARR, Sarah E	2 Nov 1893	47
BALTIMORE, Lewis	WORMLY, Bell /c	23 Dec 1868	10
BAMFORD, George A	ENNIS, Annie D	14 Jun 1919	95
BANCROFT, Owen M	STONEBURNER, Bessie E	29 Dec 1909	78
BANKS, Franklin /c	BRENT, Harriet L /c	12 Aug 1875	18
BANKS, Richard /c	CORAM, Fannie /c	27 May 1897	52
BANKS, Ulysses J /c	JONES, Vernita E /c	24 Dec 1912	84
BANTER, Richard W	ANDERSON, Eva V	19 Nov 1927	119
BARBEE, Lawrence Edward	MOORE, Mildred E	15 Jun 1933	142
BARBER, E J /wid	STEPHENSON, Arabella	27 Jun 1877	22
BARBOUR, James /c	JOHNSON, Bettie /c wid	6 Jun 1915	88
BARDEN, Henry Thomas Jr	MCGUIN, Tacy Jane	16 Nov 1933	144
BARHAM, Grover C	ASKINS, Alverta B	28 Jun 1915	90
BARKER, Charles	KILLAM, Laura M	21 Apr 1869	11
BARKER, Harry B	NEWMAN, Mable E	3 Nov 1904	67
BARKER, Joseph L	DAINTY, Sophy A	18 Oct 1871	14
BARKER, William	WILLIAMS, Mildred	27 Sep 1857	3
BARNES, Alexander H	FERGUSON, Anna M /div	11 Nov 1933	144
BARNES, Briston E	NOLAND, Eleanor M	16 Sep 1926	116
BARNES, Griffin /c	CARTER, Susie /c	3 Feb 1907	72
BARNES, John Horace	THOMAS, Eula	18 Oct 1890	42
BARNES, John M	TARMAN, Virgie I	25 Mar 1919	95
BARNES, Joseph O /c	WOMBLE, Louise /c	12 Oct 1932	139
BARNES, Louis J	BOWMAN, Emma M /div	22 Jul 1930	128
BARNES, Orville	FORD, Mabel C	3 Dec 1926	116
BARNES, Thomas /c wid	BROOKS, Annie /c wid	15 Jun 1898	54
BARNES, William A	WRIGHT, Hannah L	14 Nov 1865	6
BARNHART, Jesse A	FIFER, Charlotte A	12 May 1922	102
BARNHILL, Eveleth	DENTY, Frances E	14 Aug 1906	71
BARNINGHAM, John W	SABIN, Grace	14 Sep 1905	69

BARNUM, H S /wid	WHALEY, Emma C	12 Jun 1882	30
BARNWELL, Carlton	HOOFF, Louise Tyson	4 Feb 1915	88
BARRINGTON, Wiley	DYER, Mary A	5 Jul 1926	115
BARROWS, H A	RIDEOUT, Grace E	19 Dec 1884	34
BARTHOLOMEW, Alfred B	STARK, Etta J	9 Dec 1908	76
BARTLETT, Eugene	BERKLEY, Atalanta	16 Jan 1856	2
BASTOW, Charles H	BLATCHLEY, Georgianna	5 Jun 1895	49
BASTOW, Richard /wid	MILLS, Ann Virginia	9 Jan 1872	14
BASTOW, William J	WELLS, Catherine E	18 Dec 1866	7
BATEMAN, Clarence A	LEWIS, Evangeline	2 Jul 1903	65
BATSON, George H /c	HARRIS, Costella C /c	10 Jan 1927	117
BATSON, Thomas E /c	STOKES, Winnie A /c	16 Dec 1929	127
BAUCHMAN, George Hay	HORSEMAN, Sadie	31 Oct 1925	113
BAUCKMAN, Aquilla	SCHORTER, Mary	13 Apr 1904	78
BAUGHART, John S /wid	KITCHEN, Naomi F /wid	22 Jul 1890	41
BAUGHMAN, C A	SCHUERMAN, Martha M	21 Feb 1911	80
BAUGHMAN, Harry C	BANCROFT, Albertine E	31 Dec 1912	84
BAUGHMAN, John	FRENZEL, Charlotte	30 Oct 1915	89
BAUGHMAN, W A	THOMPSON, L B	20 Dec 1905	70
BAUMANN, David M	HOFFMAN, Gene Louise	31 Dec 1927	120
BAXTER, George F Jr /wid	CLARKE, Eula May	11 Aug 1924	109
BAXTER, James M	MYERS, Dorothy M	28 May 1932	137
BAXTER, John L /wid	LANDRIAN, Palmyra M	24 Nov 1887	38
BAYEN, Malaku /c	HADLEY, Dorothy /c	29 Sep 1931	134
BAYLISS, George Arthur	DENTY, Mary Elizabeth	1 Jun 1910	78
BAYLISS, John E /div	SOUTHERLAND, Mary Elizabeth	21 Feb 1918	93
BAYLISS, John F /wid	MILLER, Annie /wid	12 Nov 1902	63
BAYLISS, Lester N	HAMPTON, Valeria Hester	23 Dec 1933	145
BAYLISS, N T Jr	TRAVERS, Virgie /wid	16 Dec 1922	104
BAYLISS, Richard H	WEBSTER, Elizabeth	4 Jan 1872	14
BAYLISS, Thomas /wid	CRUMP, Hannah	8 Feb 1857	2
BAYNES, Wade Hampton	MCPHERSON, Margaret Jeanne	6 Jun 1933	142
BEACH, A J	LEWIS, Jane M	17 Feb 1859	4
BEACH, Andrew J	SIMPSON, Hattie	16 Mar 1892	44
BEACH, Arthur	SENNE, Helen	13 Oct 1897	53
BEACH, Charles S	WELLS, Amelia	1 Sep 1858	3
BEACH, Charles S /wid	REEDY, Mary A	25 Feb 1911	80
BEACH, Charles T /wid	BICKSLER, Ann M	31 Jan 1878	23
BEACH, Charlie	RANDALL, Elsie	14 Nov 1933	144
BEACH, Clarence	MCINTOSH, Maud H	22 May 1889	40
BEACH, Colbert /wid	BEACH, Mildred /wid	14 Sep 1871	15
BEACH, Colvert	MAILEY, J A /wid	9 Nov 1879	25

BEACH, D Solomon /wid	CARSON, Edith M	27 Dec 1906	72
BEACH, David M	BUTLER, Margaret /wid	1 Jul 1885	35
BEACH, Ernest T	LEAPLEY, Bessie R	14 Apr 1900	58
BEACH, Frederick W	BEACH, Sarah E	27 Feb 1873	16
BEACH, John R	TRICE, Louisa V	21 Dec 1871	14
BEACH, John S	WILEY, Emma M	8 Feb 1881	28
BEACH, Richard W	DOVE, Virginia	22 Oct 1867	8
BEACH, Samuel	WENZEL, Lizzie	18 Dec 1900	59
BEACH, Sandford	PETTITT, Ann R	21 Dec 1871	14
BEACH, Sullivan	WILEY, Birdie	14 Jan 1915	88
BEACH, Thomas R	FORBES, Mary A	8 Oct 1878	24
BEACH, William H	STEELE, Mary J	2 Feb 1887	37
BEACH, William Thomas	HOLLY, Mary E	26 Apr 1870	12
BEAHM, George W	CROSON, Anna E	26 Dec 1894	48
BEAHM, Thomas W	JENKINS, Annie L	19 Mar 1905	68
BEALE, Guy Gilbert	HILL, Lois D	26 Oct 1925	112
BEALE, John W /wid	BENSON, Elizabeth M /wid	17 Jul 1913	84
BEALL, George H	ROBERTS, Ruby V	1 Dec 1930	130
BEAMER, George B	DODD, Florence	21 Nov 1925	113
BEAN, C N	MARTIN, Velma J	5 Oct 1918	94
BEAN, Charles H /wid	HUMMER, Ketturah L	19 Sep 1867	8
BEAN, H H	GLADDEN, Lillie	24 Jul 1898	55
BEAN, Mellen F /wid	KERR, Edith M L	25 Apr 1894	47
BEANS, Aaron T	KEARNS, Martha	16 Feb 1874	17
BEANS, Charles E	HURST, Florence I	24 Dec 1901	62
BEANS, J E	MCKEARNS, Hattie	14 Mar 1888	38
BEANS, Marshall C	LEEDS, Lydia	28 Dec 1892	45
BEANS, Theodore A	KEARNS, Margaret A	19 May 1878	23
BEARD, Carl Miller	LEE, Lillian Mary	26 Nov 1919	97
BEARD, Eugene E	WOODS, Mary M	27 Dec 1906	72
BEARD, George W	SISK, Bertha Lee	2 Mar 1921	100
BEATTY, James Robert	RIGG, Irene	5 Aug 1892	46
BEATTY, Albert R	OWEN, Elizabeth G	2 Jun 1925	111
BEAVERS, Abraham	HATTON, Sarah C	6 Mar 1856	2
BEAVERS, Charles H	TOWN, Hannah H	2 Oct 1901	60
BEAVERS, Earl	COOK, Rosa	24 Dec 1925	113
BEAVERS, Elmer L	CROUCH, Ida	24 Feb 1908	74
BEAVERS, G H	HURST, Jane A	4 Jun 1902	62
BEAVERS, James William	CAMPBELL, Sarah Catherine	15 Jun 1892	45
BEAVERS, John	ENNIS, Rebecca A /div	12 Jan 1926	113
BEAVERS, John Thomas	KIDWELL, Mary Ann	19 Nov 1868	10
BEAVERS, Joseph T	KIDWELL, Ida	24 Dec 1901	61

BEAVERS, Thomas E	CATON, Bettie M	8 Sep 1896	*51*
BEAVERS, Thomas L */wid*	BUTLER, Frances	23 Dec 1869	*11*
BECK, Richmond J	TUCKER, Madge B	15 Jul 1920	*98*
BECKLEY, Lawrence	GREHAN, Harriet L	27 Nov 1906	*71*
BECKTON, James */c*	FOLKS, Maggie */c*	10 Aug 1902	*63*
BECKTON, John Thomas	HARRIS, Sally	17 Oct 1867	*8*
BECKWITH, Albert */c*	HARRIS, Sarah */c*	8 Dec 1870	*13*
BECKWITH, Alfred */c wid*	CURTIS, Fannie */c*	5 Apr 1881	*28*
BECKWITH, Everett D	DERBYSHIRE, Fay Virginia	17 Jan 1929	*124*
BEDORE, Edward L	HENKE, Viva L	23 Mar 1927	*117*
BELCHER, Charles K	GENTRY, Eliza	6 Aug 1922	*103*
BELL, Frank */c*	JACKSON, Lavenia */c*	10 Jan 1877	*21*
BELL, George Ray	GRIMSLEY, Katherine Lee	10 Oct 1924	*109*
BELL, Hugh	BASTOW, Hattie E	29 Dec 1891	*44*
BELL, Joseph M	SIMMS, Mary R	6 Nov 1872	*15*
BELL, Louis Clark	COE, Madeline D	17 Jul 1926	*115*
BELL, Moses */c*	JOHNSON, Eliza */c*	21 Dec 1886	*37*
BELL, William	PHILLIPS, Jennie */c*	13 Feb 1890	*42*
BELL, William A */c*	POSEY, Lulie */c*	12 Apr 1185	*34*
BELL, William McNeill */c*	LEE, Harriette Louise */c*	12 Sep 1933	*143*
BELT, Walter	PACE, Marie	30 May 1933	*142*
BENDER, George T	TAYLOR, May G	20 Oct 1925	*112*
BENNER, Charles W	GRAY, Doris V	19 Oct 1931	*134*
BENNETT, Frank A	BRUNNER, Emma V	2 Jun 1902	*62*
BENNETT, Frank L	JOHNSON, Arminta G */wid*	24 Jun 1903	*64*
BENNETT, Glen W	THOMPSON, Fedora	6 Jun 1918	*94*
BENNETT, John	MONCH, Mary	19 Apr 1882	*30*
BENNETT, John C	TOBAN, Lillie S	28 Nov 1888	*39*
BENNETT, John E W	CROCKER, Sarah D	6 Feb 1856	*2*
BENNETT, Joseph F	FOX, Bettie	23 Jan 1877	*21*
BENSTED, William F	CRUMBAUGH, Maud	15 May 1906	*71*
BENTON, B G	HUTCHINSON, Bessie F	2 Oct 1907	*73*
BENZLER, Arthur Charles	PIERSON, Mary Florence	26 Jan 1910	*78*
BERG, William G	WRENN, Delfina	16 Apr 1890	*41*
BERKLEY, Edward Armstead */c*	NALLS, Ann */c*	8 May 1881	*28*
BERKLEY, Harrison */c*	WILLIAMS, Susan */c*	26 Apr 1877	*22*
BERKLEY, Thomas */c*	BROWN, Daisy */c*	30 Aug 1930	*129*
BERRY, Dallas	SWETNAM, Roberta Randolph	26 Oct 1910	*79*
BERRY, George	THOMAS, Sally	9 Jun 1870	*12*
BERRY, J Gilbert	ORRISON, Frances E	20 Sep 1928	*122*
BERRY, J Owens	GUNNELL, Mary J	15 Nov 1860	*5*
BERRY, John Kenyon	STOY, Dorothy Virginia	24 Aug 1921	*101*

BERRY, Richard Edgar	KENYON, Alma	20 Apr 1899	56
BESLEY, Harry E G	MONEY, Sallie A	16 Oct 1907	73
BESLEY, James Leonard	WATT, Jessie Gannie	13 Apr 1904	66
BESS, LeRoy /c	BRADLEY, Katherine /c wid	2 Jul 1932	138
BEST, Marvin J	ALEXANDER, Billee	16 Sep 1928	122
BETHUNE, Neleigh /wid	WALDVOGEL, Lucy B /div	5 Sep 1931	133
BETSON, Rodolph /c	LIONS, Mary /c	26 Dec 1896	52
BETTS, S J	BARTON, Fanny J	5 Jan 1881	28
BEVAN, Frank A	MCGROARTY, Alma G	17 Jun 1926	115
BEVERLY, Ezekiel /c	HARRIS, Sally /c	19 Oct 1875	19
BIAS, Benjamin /c wid	DAY, Ella /c	8 Jan 1878	23
BIAS, Selden /c	HARRIS, Bettie /c	12 Aug 1880	27
BICKSLER, C H	WADDELL, Mary Eva	12 Jan 1909	76
BICKSLER, Eugene P /div	STANARD, Ida F	24 Dec 1930	130
BICKSLER, F D	COULTER, Ida J	5 Dec 1882	31
BICKSLER, John F	HOUGH, Sallie J	2 Mar 1882	30
BICKWELL, George C	MILLARD, Lillian M	1 May 1903	64
BIESTER, William H /wid	SMITH, Jennie M	1 Dec 1897	53
BIGGS, James H	GASH, Martha C	3 Dec 1930	130
BINDER, Christopher /wid	OSGOOD, Blanche P	1 Aug 1933	143
BING, William /c wid	GARRETT, *Mary Virginia* /c	19 Apr 1919	95
BINNIX, Edward C	ROBINSON, Julia /wid	23 Jul 1912	82
BINNS, Charles	RICHARDS, Mary E /wid	11 Oct 1854	1
BINNS, Charles /wid	CANNON, Frances G /wid	1 Feb 1899	56
BIRCH, E	DAVIS, Mary C	29 Feb 1860	5
BIRCH, Edward J	SHREVE, Mary C	26 Apr 1872	14
BIRCH, Frank L	CROSSMAN, Flora B	14 Dec 1882	31
BIRCH, George C	WITSON, Margaret M	4 Apr 1900	58
BIRCH, James	LEE, Pearl C	3 Jan 1900	58
BIRCH, R Wilber	BIRCH, Agnes	4 Feb 1885	34
BIRD, Ampy /c	MILLER, Julia /c	4 Sep 1873	16
BIRD, Charlie	ROBEY, Elsie Ellen	7 Jan 1926	113
BIRD, Elijah /c	FLETCHER, Lucy F /c	18 Feb 1897	52
BIRD, Ernest /c	FAIRFAX, Eliza /c	2 Apr 1895	50
BIRD, Frank /c	HONESTY, Pearl /c div	23 Sep 1912	83
BIRD, Hugh R	GILLEN, Mary A	22 Oct 1927	119
BIRD, John W	WYNKOOP, Stella	9 Oct 1904	67
BIRD, Samuel /c	CARROLL, Ellen /c	24 Apr 1873	16
BIRGE, Harry C	RILEY, Jeanne E	3 Jun 1896	51
BISCHOFF, John E /wid	HICKS, Grace E	5 Jun 1923	105
BISHOP, Grover C Jr	STANTON, Barbara L	21 Sep 1932	139
BISHOP, Harold M	MUMFORD, Mary Elizabeth	9 Jul 1931	132

BISHOP, William L	BALL, Ida N	7 Mar 1905	68
BLACK, William A	KIDWELL, Rosa A	7 Jan 1886	36
BLACKBURN, James T	HOWELL, Elizabeth V	18 Apr 1892	44
BLACKBURN, LaFayette E /c	GROOMES, Sophronia /c	27 Jun 1910	78
BLACKBURN, W H /c	FISHER, Catherine /c	18 Jun 1879	25
BLACKFORD, Launcelot Minor	AMBLER, Eliza C	5 Aug 1884	33
BLACKLOCK, D R /wid	GODWIN, G W	19 Apr 1859	4
BLACKMAN, Raymond	PETTITT, Bertha	19 Aug 1911	81
BLACKMON, James Albert /wid	NEAVER, Effie Belle	19 Aug 1933	143
BLACKWELL, H Elmer /c	THOMPSON, Helen B /c wid	13 Dec 1929	126
BLACKWELL, Peter /c	DICKSON, Martha Ann /c	16 Dec 1875	19
BLADEN, A F	BLACK, Martha Ellen	21 Dec 1904	67
BLADEN, A G	DAVIS, Edna V	16 Aug 1905	69
BLADEN, C N	CROSS, Barbara A	1 Jan 1914	86
BLADEN, Charles N	TURNER, Annie A	28 Apr 1881	28
BLADEN, Ernest L	CRUMP, Effie B	25 Apr 1888	38
BLADEN, Frank E	COCK, Nannie R	17 Apr 1895	49
BLADEN, Thomas	O'MEARA, Beatrice	22 Sep 1903	65
BLAKE, John R	SHERMAN, Martha T	24 Jun 1925	111
BLAKE, Lemuel C /c	CHOLSON, Anna E /c	19 Feb 1932	136
BLALOCK, Elgin H	HAINES, Dorothy H	1 Sep 1910	79
BLANCHARD, Charles	GRIMSLEY, Bessie	1 Jun 1929	124
BLANCHARD, Ed B /wid	COLLINS, Mary A	5 May 1880	26
BLANCHARD, H W	KILLAM, Susan	1 Aug 1874	17
BLANCHARD, John	ROGERS, Maggie	8 Jan 1930	127
BLANCHARD, William St.John	SIMONDS, Anna M	5 Dec 1900	59
BLAND, William M	LUTZ, Ethel	22 Sep 1919	96
BLATCHLEY, Charles	GINNELLEY, Mabel	22 Sep 1897	53
BLEASE, Marion H	MILLER, Charlotte M	27 Apr 1922	102
BLEIGHT, A C	TERRETT, Grace A	26 Sep 1877	22
BLOCK, Milton	KEPLER, Kathryn	10 May 1930	128
BLOOMSBURG, Harry E	FRISTOE, Mary E	27 Sep 1924	109
BLOXHAM, John L	YATES, M J	24 Jan 1883	31
BLOXHAM, William P	VEITCH, Georgia B	10 Oct 1883	32
BLOXTON, C P /wid	SPARKS, Blanche E	2 Dec 1913	85
BLUNDY, John Eugene	CASSELL, Reba Kathleen	6 Jan 1933	141
BLUNT, Charles T	STONNELL, Bessie L	27 Dec 1899	57
BLUNT, Henry H	PULMAN, Janet L	6 Nov 1895	50
BOADMAR, George	RHIEL, Margaret	12 Nov 1855	1
BOATNER, Mark Mayo Jr	GUNNELL, Emily Nelson	25 Jun 1920	98
BODMER, L H	HUTCHISON, Lillian C	14 Jun 1904	66
BODMER, Thomas E	HUTCHISON, Effie May	28 Sep 1904	67

BOHM, Harry	LEVY, Helen	11 Mar 1931	*131*
BOLDIN, C E	LINFOOT, Laura T /div	2 Jul 1912	*82*
BOLES, Robert /c	LEE, Elizabeth I /c	25 Apr 1878	*23*
BOMAR, Thomas P /c wid	FREELAND, Jeanette M /c	1 Aug 1932	*138*
BONEBRAKE, DuWalt E	GALTON, Inez M /div	24 Mar 1932	*136*
BOOKER, Henry /c wid	RUKER, Carrie /c	12 Feb 1903	*64*
BOOKER, Lavega	PEACOCK, Bertha	24 Nov 1919	*97*
BOONE, Robert T	PATTERSON, Florida O	1 Jul 1933	*142*
BOONE, William Kyle	LOWRY, Irvel E	15 Jun 1932	*137*
BOOTHE, Gardner Lloyd	MONCURE, Margaret Elizabeth	5 Jun 1923	*105*
BORLEAN, Walter	MILLER, Claudia	5 Jun 1922	*102*
BOROUGHS, W L /wid	CORNELL, Roberta	5 Feb 1908	*74*
BOSS, Trixton	MARTIN, Louise E	1 Dec 1932	*140*
BOSTON, J B /c	BROWN, Irene /c	23 Jun 1923	*105*
BOSWELL, A J	DICKEY, Mary F	8 Apr 1858	*4*
BOTELER, Lemuel I /wid	WASHBURN, Sallie	15 Dec 1897	*54*
BOTT, Earle E	PETER, Ellen Eugenia	26 Nov 1928	*123*
BOTTS, James /c	MANDLEY, Maggie /c	21 Dec 1902	*63*
BOTTS, John Minor /c	FORD, Ida V /c	28 Jun 1900	*58*
BOTTS, M C	HAMILTON, Bridget A	27 Dec 1888	*39*
BOTTS, Melvin A	BAGGERLY, Minnie O	18 Mar 1927	*117*
BOTTS, Peter	MITCHELL, Nora O	22 May 1895	*49*
BOTTS, John W	SMITH, Mildred D	1 Sep 1932	*139*
BOUSHEE, Franklin	MARTIN, Clelia B	2 Jun 1917	*92*
BOUSHEE, Franklin Pearce /wid	CARPENTER, Carrie Belle	20 May 1916	*91*
BOVIS, William Rapley	POTTER, Sarah Alice	20 Dec 1888	*39*
BOWELL, Harry	TRUAS, Ora Anna	1 Jul 1931	*132*
BOWERMAN, George Shannon	TROUT, Minna Mae	11 Nov 1933	*144*
BOWIE, James W /wid	DAVIS, Martha E	17 Jun 1896	*51*
BOWIE, Philip B /c	ROBINSON, Rose C /c	22 Nov 1922	*104*
BOWIE, Samuel /c	FOSTER, Emma J /c wid	27 Mar 1894	*47*
BOWIE, Thomas M /wid	CARROLL, Fannie /wid	27 Sep 1923	*106*
BOWLER, Thomas C /c	TAYLOR, Narcina /c	3 Mar 1927	*117*
BOWLES, Artis /c	GASKINS, Iris P /c	13 Oct 1931	*134*
BOWLES, Johnie /c	KINES, Bettie /c	20 Oct 1897	*53*
BOWLES, Robert S /c div	COOK, Emma /c	14 Feb 1897	*52*
BOWLES, Rozier /c	FOLKS, Lola /c	2 Aug 1929	*125*
BOWLES, Walter /c	CLARKE, Susie /c	9 Jun 1907	*73*
BOWLING, Arthur M	TALBOTT, Nellie A	20 Dec 1911	*82*
BOWLING, Charles S /wid	RYAN, Genevieve A	22 Oct 1916	*91*
BOWMAN, Albert /c	CARROLL, Milly /c	10 Aug 1876	*20*
BOWMAN, Edward /c	PIERSON, Flora /c	22 Jun 1914	*86*

BOWMAN, George	ROY, Delia	25 Jun 1868	9
BOWMAN, Harry A	KENYON, Ida	4 Oct 1887	38
BOWMAN, Josiah B /wid	RUMSEY, Hannah	12 Sep 1895	49
BOWMAN, William H	COMMINS, Effie A	25 May 1886	36
BOYCE, Benjamin F	JONES, Edith H	3 Mar 1928	121
BOYCE, George W	GINNELLEY, Lizzie H	5 Dec 1893	47
BOYD, John D /wid	MOORE, Ella	1 Sep 1880	27
BOYD, John J	RUSSELL, Virginia M	30 Sep 1933	143
BOYER, Charles M	LARGENT, Mary	20 Nov 1929	126
BOYER, Joseph O	MATTHEWS, Fannie F	10 Jun 1904	66
BOYER, Murray H /div	HOOVER, Doris H /div	16 May 1932	137
BOYER, William G	TILLETT, Willella	4 Jun 1891	43
BOYLE, Isaiah (Charles I.)	FITZHUGH, Meek E	16 Apr 1911	80
BOYLE, Robert H	MOORE, Minnie L /wid	17 Sep 1932	139
BRADFIELD, George W	GRAY, Irene	24 Dec 1930	130
BRADFIELD, James F	CHICHESTER, Martha H	18 Dec 1884	34
BRADFORD, Howard F	WHEELER, Sarah E	26 May 1885	35
BRADFORD, Webster E	JENKINS, Mary E	5 May 1870	12
BRADLEY, Harry	WILHAITE, Margueritte M	24 Nov 1897	53
BRADLEY, Horace E	STONE, Lorena	30 Nov 1892	45
BRADLEY, John H /wid	CATON, Artemesia	3 Dec 1874	18
BRADLEY, Robert /c wid	NEWMAN, Tessie /c wid	9 Nov 1922	104
BRADLEY, William /wid	STODDARD, Elizabeth P /wid	30 Aug 1876	20
BRADSHAW, Asa E	CHAMBLIN, Ruth E	29 Sep 1915	89
BRADT, Isaac H	BASTOW, Ann E	22 Sep 1859	4
BRADWAY, Judson H	CROUNSE, Jennie	21 Jul 1897	53
BRADY, Herman	HALL, Naomi	14 Nov 1929	126
BRADY, William H	RUSSELL, Vashti B	23 Aug 1920	98
BRADY, William T	LESTER, Ida	17 Sep 1932	139
BRAMBLEE, H W	DELANY, E J /wid	3 Dec 1879	26
BRANDAN, Adam G	NIXDORFF, Frances S	24 Dec 1932	140
BRANDON, George R	MALONE, Mary T	15 Nov 1883	32
BRANHAM, Herman /c	BURKE, Ida /c	31 Jul 1914	86
BRANHAM, Robert /c	SIMMS, Fanny M /c	28 May 1911	80
BRANNAN, Jefferson /c	WORMLY, Harriet /c	29 May 1882	30
BRAWNER, Charles Edward	RUSH, Mable	18 Jul 1904	66
BRAWNER, John A	MERO, Mary E	12 Feb 1890	41
BRAWNER, John P /wid	STONNELL, Ida	21 Dec 1880	27
BRAXTON, Frank /c	JORDAN, Henrietta /c	26 Sep 1911	81
BRAXTON, J T /c	GASKINS, Sally A /c	6 Oct 1885	35
BRAXTON, Wilton /c	DAGGS, Mary /c	23 Dec 1875	19
BRAY, M L	THOMPSON, Maud C	9 Sep 1903	65

BRAYMAN, D Everett	CARR, N E Maude	25 Nov 1896	*51*
BRAYMAN, Milton E	STEWART, Jennie	16 Jun 1906	*71*
BREADY, Benjamin H	NORDSTROM, Hattie */wid*	22 Dec 1890	*42*
BREADY, George Albaugh	GALT, Emily Hornet	26 Dec 1924	*110*
BREADY, William W	ALBAUGH, Annie J	14 Dec 1898	*55*
BREEDEN, Charles M	ROYSTON, Dorothy	2 Apr 1918	*94*
BREEDLOVE, Charles */div*	WOOSTER, Annie L	6 Dec 1932	*140*
BREEN, Joseph	BUCKLEY, Gertrude	4 Jan 1911	*80*
BRENIZER, F L	FOWLER, Mary F	26 Oct 1898	*55*
BRENIZER, W F	THORNE, Maud G	17 Oct 1893	*46*
BRENNER, John E */wid*	DEAR, Mary V	2 Sep 1874	*17*
BRENT, George	CARTER, Isabella	18 Dec 1870	*13*
BRENT, Hobert */c*	DIXON, Nettie */c*	1 Feb 1917	*91*
BRENT, James */c*	PARKER, Sarah */c*	2 Nov 1896	*51*
BRENT, Logan */c*	WILLIAMS, Alberta */c*	25 Nov 1909	*78*
BRENT, Richard	JONES, Margaret	10 Nov 1870	*13*
BRENT, Richard */c wid*	PAYNE, Arina */c*	27 Apr 1882	*30*
BRICE, Albert */c*	BRISCOE, Mamie */c*	24 Jun 1913	*84*
BRICE, Arthur T	ESTERLY, E Alyce	30 Aug 1930	*129*
BRICE, Henry */c*	THOMPSON, Bettie */c*	15 Feb 1897	*54*
BRICE, Jacob E */c*	WILLIAMS, Patsey */c*	24 Aug 1876	*20*
BRIDGE, Rixey John	CARROLL, Margaret Elizabeth	18 Feb 1928	*121*
BRIDGEFORTH, E J	JOHNSON, Roberta M	23 Sep 1903	*65*
BRIDGEFORTH, George B	QUIGG, Mary Elizabeth	4 Nov 1922	*103*
BRIDWELL, Eliphalet	WINEGARDNER, Ella */wid*	23 Apr 1906	*70*
BRIGGS, Frederick	JERMAN, Annie E	20 May 1891	*43*
BRIGGS, J Edson	MASON, Annie L	26 Jun 1882	*30*
BRIGGS, Nathan */c*	TURNER, Lucy */c*	24 Jun 1868	*9*
BRIGHT, Alvah E	CLARK, Evelyn M	27 Nov 1929	*126*
BRINDLEY, Earl F	WAKEMAN, Mollie C	30 Jun 1926	*115*
BRINKERHOFF, M H	BURTON, Mary C	7 Jan 1869	*10*
BRINKERHOFF, M H */wid*	BERKSHAW, Mary	30 Nov 1915	*89*
BRINKLE, William D	MONCURE, Anna Hull	26 Jun 1901	*60*
BRINKLOW, Howard K	NEVINS, Leotta E	3 Mar 1920	*97*
BRITT, Walter Lee */wid*	SISK, Lillie B */wid*	30 Apr 1930	*127*
BRITTON, Joseph F */wid*	TURNER, Sarah Ann */wid*	8 May 1927	*118*
BROADUS, Jefferson D	TOBIN, Elsie J	16 Oct 1926	*116*
BROADUS, Marion */c*	ADAMS, Mary */c*	6 Dec 1904	*67*
BROCK, C L R	HENSEN, Edna M	27 Apr 1909	*76*
BROCK, Franklin W	KEITH, Mary R	17 Sep 1927	*119*
BROENING, Joseph J Jr	CLATCHEY, Mary E	7 Sep 1932	*139*
BROGDEN, William */wid*	MIDDLETON, Hannah V	26 Nov 1919	*97*

BROMWELL, Berton Allen /div	BRAHLER, Edith Mary	21 Jan 1933	*141*
BRONAUGH, Charles /c	GREEN, Adaline /c wid	26 May 1880	*26*
BRONAUGH, Daniel /c	GREEN, Lucretia /c	14 Dec 1890	*42*
BROOKE, Eppa H	STELY, Katie S	13 Dec 1893	*47*
BROOKE, John O	WAGNER, Addie	13 May 1915	*88*
BROOKE, P A	REID, Rosa B	26 Nov 1901	*61*
BROOKS, Arthur /c	HARRIS, Ophelia /c	16 Mar 1884	*33*
BROOKS, C E	SIMMS, Bessie	2 Feb 1914	*86*
BROOKS, C W	HALL, Mabel V	5 Apr 1911	*80*
BROOKS, Charles Windsor /c	WALLER, Frances E /c	25 Aug 1874	*17*
BROOKS, Clinton /c	HORTON, Eliza /c	11 Feb 1892	*44*
BROOKS, Edgar O	TRENANY, Dixie Lee	20 Feb 1907	*72*
BROOKS, Edward /c wid	GIBSON, Sarah A /c wid	3 Aug 1868	*9*
BROOKS, Frank /c	BUTLER, Isabella Jr /c	1 Nov 1904	*67*
BROOKS, Henry /c	NICKENS, Carrie /c	23 Jul 1874	*17*
BROOKS, Henry T	HOAG, Helen J	16 Mar 1858	*3*
BROOKS, J F /c	JACKSON, Augusta /c	26 Nov 1904	*67*
BROOKS, James /c wid	FLETCHER, Mary /c	31 Dec 1888	*39*
BROOKS, James /c	TAYLOR, Lucinda A /c	9 Jan 1900	*58*
BROOKS, James E /c wid	GROOMS, Sarah /c wid	28 May 1925	*111*
BROOKS, James W /c	HARRIS, Aurina /c	15 Jan 1899	*56*
BROOKS, Joseph /c wid	HENDERSON, Rita /c wid	3 Dec 1922	*104*
BROOKS, Lester L	STROBLE, Virginia Mae	19 Sep 1931	*133*
BROOKS, Lucius J /wid	WOODYARD, Frances E	29 Sep 1912	*83*
BROOKS, Samuel A	SMITH, Mary E	15 Nov 1869	*11*
BROOKS, Thomas /c	HORTON, Elizabeth /c	27 Dec 1882	*31*
BROOKS, William /c	PEARSON, Annie E /c	1 Jul 1890	*41*
BROOKS, William A	EGLIN, Mary K	25 Sep 1915	*89*
BROSIUS, Samuel M /wid	WILKINSON, Anna M	1 Jun 1911	*81*
BROWDER, Nelson	CARICO, Emily	11 Jul 1899	*56*
BROWN, Alexander /c	CRANKUM, Martha /c wid	27 Dec 1877	*23*
BROWN, Alexander G	COOKSEY, Fannie A	6 Jan 1859	*4*
BROWN, Bernard	DANIELS, Charlotte L	2 Apr 1927	*117*
BROWN, Charles E	DAVIS, Janie M	16 Oct 1894	*48*
BROWN, Charles R	SHERWOOD, Anna E	22 Dec 1891	*44*
BROWN, Chester A /c	CHASE, Frances A /c	7 Apr 1897	*52*
BROWN, Clinton A	CREWS, Mabel L	6 Feb 1932	*136*
BROWN, David /wid	SHERWOOD, Rebecca	12 Jul 1877	*22*
BROWN, Denton J	ELY, Ottie V	12 Sep 1910	*79*
BROWN, Edward	HOGAN, Grace S	14 Nov 1878	*24*
BROWN, Everett C	DAVIS, Lula E	18 Mar 1929	*124*
BROWN, Frank Godfrey /wid	GORDON, Emma M /div	20 Nov 1928	*123*

BROWN, Frederick /c	DAVIS, Maria /c	27 Dec 1877	23
BROWN, Frederick /c wid	WALKER, Martha /c wid	31 May 1900	58
BROWN, George /wid	MALORY, Harriet C	17 Apr 1872	15
BROWN, George Cleverland	SHEETS, Johny Colene	5 Apr 1923	105
BROWN, Gerard C	BARCROFT, Caroline V	8 Feb 1872	15
BROWN, Harry J	YOUNG, Alberta H	16 Jul 1928	122
BROWN, Harry L	JONES, Mary E	28 Nov 1911	81
BROWN, Hartley H /c wid	LUCAS, Ethel H /c	20 Oct 1921	101
BROWN, Irving	CUNNINGHAM, Mary	30 Oct 1879	25
BROWN, J L /c wid	HUNTER, Mattie /c wid	1 Apr 1926	114
BROWN, J W	ELGIN, M C J	6 Mar 1879	25
BROWN, J W	COMPTON, R F	8 Nov 1899	57
BROWN, James Deane	DE ARMOND, Ethel S	14 Nov 1917	93
BROWN, James W	WILLIAMS, Lizzie	16 Mar 1880	26
BROWN, Jefferson /c	HARRIS, Florida /c	22 Sep 1881	29
BROWN, John	PIERSON, Belinda /wid	23 Jul 1870	13
BROWN, John /c	ROY, Sarah /c	15 Jun 1907	73
BROWN, John C H	BIRCH, Maggie K	28 Dec 1883	32
BROWN, John K	ELGIN, Anna S	12 May 1874	17
BROWN, Joseph W	HOLLIDGE, Lola E	30 Jul 1896	51
BROWN, Julian M	WHEELER, Sue C	15 Oct 1917	93
BROWN, Kennie R /c	MCCURRY, Bernice /c	24 Feb 1923	104
BROWN, Lawrence M	FITZHUGH, Abigail Thorn	18 Oct 1919	96
BROWN, Lemuel /c	BANKS, Lizzie /c	26 Sep 1894	48
BROWN, Leo Dennis	FORD, Gertrude Thomas	11 Jul 1925	112
BROWN, Louis /c	COLES, Annie /c	2 Jun 1919	95
BROWN, Neil	BUSHROD, Mary C	6 Apr 1867	7
BROWN, Oliver /c	SMITH, Julia /c	22 Apr 1874	17
BROWN, Peter /c	SHELTON, Martha A /c wid	8 Aug 1889	40
BROWN, Rev. Benjamin W /c	WHALEY, Mollie E /c	10 Oct 1877	22
BROWN, Richard Theo	BLEVINS, Virgie P	21 Nov 1933	144
BROWN, S E /wid	BUCKLEY, Cora L /wid	14 Dec 1930	130
BROWN, Samuel	TYLER, Rosa Belle	8 Jul 1896	51
BROWN, Samuel /c	GRAY, Ada /c	25 Apr 1906	70
BROWN, Samuel E /wid	CORNWELL, Mrs. Richard /wid	21 May 1902	62
BROWN, Seth L	DETWILER, Elizabeth	22 Aug 1923	105
BROWN, Sigel	MCDONOUGH, Nina	8 Oct 1884	33
BROWN, Thomas P /div	FISHER, Hilda Jane	14 Jul 1919	96
BROWN, Ulysses /c	ROBINSON, Louisa /c	13 Feb 1889	39
BROWN, Walter /c	CARTER, Mary E /c	23 Oct 1902	63
BROWN, Wilbert P /c	FORD, Florence E /c	16 Sep 1908	75
BROWN, William /c	HUNTER, Cecelia /c wid	11 Oct 1909	77

BROWN, William /c div	GASKINS, Mattie O /c	16 Oct 1919	96
BROWN, William E	COCKERILLE, Katie M	20 Nov 1894	48
BROWN, William J /c	SHARPER, Mary C /c	29 Dec 1991	44
BROWN, William L	AMBLER, Gabrielle L	25 Apr 1899	56
BROWN, William M	STUDDS, Jeannette	23 May 1900	58
BROWNLEE, James	HAYNES, Dianna	25 Nov 1856	2
BROY, Charles Clinton /div	SISSON, Cecil /wid	25 Jul 1924	109
BRUCE, Albert W	SCHULZ, Katherine L	28 Aug 1930	129
BRUIN, Cola	ROSE, Sarah Rebecca	17 Jun 1858	4
BRUNNER, George A	BIRCH, Carrie D	24 Nov 1880	27
BRUNNER, James Howard	DAWSON, Margaret A	8 Mar 1899	56
BRUNNER, Joseph E	HIGGINS, Louise B	19 Oct 1916	91
BRYAN, Albert Vikers	GASSON, Marie Elizabeth	1 Dec 1923	106
BRYAN, George Keith /div	BRAWNER, Hester L	6 Jun 1931	132
BRYAN, James William	BURGESS, Blanche	11 Dec 1915	89
BRYANT, A M	HAASE, Rosie N	30 Apr 1918	94
BRYANT, Bertram	THOMPSON, Ella L	2 Nov 1911	81
BRYANT, Clifton R /c	MADDEN, Geneva R /c	1 Jul 1932	138
BRYANT, Frank /c	QUANDER, Minnie /c	2 May 1876	20
BRYANT, John H	PAYNE, Bettie B	25 Dec 1878	24
BRYCE, Lyman H	STEWART, Fannie	27 Sep 1904	67
BRYCE, Stewart L	KIDWELL, Thelma Josephine	22 Jun 1931	132
BUBB, Edwin S	COLEMAN, Clara V /wid	9 Jun 1909	77
BUCHANAN, Travis /c	BRYANT, Marietta /c	2 Apr 1874	17
BUCHANAN, William G	MOORE, Eugenia M	27 Apr 1912	82
BUCHER, George P	KANE, Laura A	5 Feb 1903	64
BUCHWALD, Paul R /wid	KLEIN, Emma M /wid	1 Dec 1898	55
BUCK, John H /wid	BEACH, Alice	6 Feb 1890	41
BUCKLEY, Charles Robert	ELGIN, Helen Wickliff	22 Jun 1929	125
BUCKLEY, Clarence E	SANDERS, Martha H	17 Dec 1914	87
BUCKLEY, Clarence V	WELK, Nora V	26 Mar 1923	104
BUCKLEY, D W	DETWILER, L E	28 Jan 1905	68
BUCKLEY, D W	HITT, Delia M	8 Oct 1927	119
BUCKLEY, J Frank	FAIRFAX, Leah A	27 Apr 1913	84
BUCKLEY, James	KIDWELL, Waneta M	18 Oct 1933	144
BUCKLEY, John W	ROBY, Wesleyena	6 Dec 1875	19
BUCKLEY, Joseph L	ANDERSON, Geneva T	12 Oct 1910	79
BUCKLEY, Robert A /wid	CROUCH, Eveline J	27 Mar 1901	60
BUCKLEY, Robert R	DETWILER, Bessie	9 Dec 1896	51
BUCKLEY, Rush	WEST, Ella M	30 Apr 1910	78
BUCKLEY, Samuel W	DAVIS, Lucy V	26 Dec 1883	32
BUCKLEY, W S	DAVIS, Harriet L M	27 Dec 1893	47

BUCKLEY, William T	MURTAUGH, Anna	4 Sep 1879	25
BUCKLEY, Wilton	CARPER, Cora L	21 Jan 1885	34
BUCKMAN, Elliott M	FINKS, Frances S	4 Oct 1930	129
BUCKMAN, Horace Dillworth	COX, Christine Hughes	1 Sep 1927	119
BUCKNER, Frederick M /c	LOTT, Ida M /c div	13 Oct 1932	139
BUCKNER, George /c wid	BEAL, Mary A /c wid	17 Nov 1896	51
BUCKNER, Thornton /c wid	HAIGHT, Eliza /c wid	7 Nov 1917	93
BUDD, Philip H	STONE, Mary G	26 Jul 1930	129
BULL, Robert L Jr	SMITH, Elizabeth W	25 Sep 1930	129
BULLOCH, William Gaston	REICH, Liley Wood	14 Jul 1923	105
BULLUCK, James Fred	ROACHE, Ella Beatrice	1 Apr 1933	141
BUNNEL, Dallas	DAVIS, Amanda C	23 Feb 1880	26
BUNYON, James /c	CARY, Mary /c	30 Aug 1924	110
BURDETTE, Edward A	STEELE, Frances C	6 Oct 1909	77
BURGER, Leonard L	ADRIAN, Marie	6 Jul 1929	125
BURGESS, Alpheus H	MILSTEAD, Lou E	10 Nov 1900	59
BURGESS, Arthur	WALKER, Clara C	25 Jan 1899	56
BURGESS, George Martin /wid	ROBERTS, Stella Marie	3 Nov 1928	123
BURGESS, John F	GRAY, Thelma	4 Sep 1916	90
BURGESS, M C /wid	BLAKE, Mamie G	2 Oct 1920	99
BURGNOINE, Alfred /c	HONESTY, Mary /c wid	25 Oct 1894	48
BURKE, Augustus /c	ASHTON, Elizabeth F /c	14 Sep 1902	63
BURKE, Bernard G	HUTCHINS, Emma F	27 Jun 1933	142
BURKE, Charles M	SAFFOLD, Ruth E	27 Apr 1910	78
BURKE, Forest /c	WYATT, Agnes /c wid	25 Aug 1917	93
BURKE, Forrest /c wid	LEE, Mary /c wid	17 Aug 1921	101
BURKE, George /c	MORGAN, Anna /c	21 Dec 1877	22
BURKE, Henry C	BEDORE, Joyce J	20 Jul 1931	132
BURKE, J F	MAY, Ida	27 Dec 1923	107
BURKE, Jesse /c	HARRIS, Maria /c	28 Dec 1876	21
BURKE, Julian L	BUCKLEY, May V	9 Aug 1905	69
BURKE, Luther M	SMITH, Carrie A	6 Oct 1904	67
BURKE, Richard A	CROUCH, Clementine	30 Jan 1873	16
BURKE, Thomas T	BUCKLEY, Julia	14 Feb 1867	6
BURKE, William /c	HARRIS, Catherine /c	6 Jan 1887	37
BURKHOLDER, Lloyd B	FRENZEL, Bertha C	26 Oct 1912	83
BURKS, John Franklin	FISHER, Elizabeth P	20 Sep 1898	55
BURLEIGH, D H	HEFFRON, Cassie	12 Nov 1919	97
BURLEY, Reuben /c wid	QUEEN, Lucy /c wid	4 Jun 1893	46
BURNAUGH, Charles /wid	NELSON, Nancy	26 Jan 1869	10
BURNE, James Edward Fowler	BEST, Dorothy	31 May 1922	102
BURNETT, Norman	DUGE, Edna May	26 Dec 1929	127

BURNETT, Raymond J	SAVIDGE, Helen M	15 Feb 1922	*102*
BURNS, Howard M	WEST, Joyce */wid*	3 Sep 1931	*133*
BURNS, Thomas A	THOMPSON, Chloe V	7 Aug 1916	*90*
BURNS, William Henry	BAYLISS, Julia F	22 Feb 1887	*37*
BURNS, Winfield B	AUSTIN, Ragina Adele	25 Jan 1933	*141*
BURNSLEY, James M	HAWES, Eugenia M	30 Dec 1929	*127*
BURR, Charles N	CAYLOR, E A G	7 May 1872	*14*
BURR, Everett	KING, Annie	2 Nov 1922	*103*
BURR, Henry Eppa Hunton	SNIDER, Lavenia	24 Nov 1897	*53*
BURR, Howard E	TWOMBLY, Eunice B	16 May 1925	*111*
BURROUGHS, Harmon P	SUMMERS, Alice M	2 Jan 1868	*8*
BURTON, Charles M	HOWARD, Anna Dell	26 Sep 1872	*15*
BURTON, George C	HUTCHISON, Lena Z	10 Jul 1906	*71*
BURTON, Henry M	CRIPPEN, Arlie M	10 May 1905	*68*
BURTON, Willis */c*	BROWN, Mary */c*	17 Oct 1876	*21*
BUSH, Aaron */c wid*	BUSH, Mary B */c*	22 Jul 1907	*73*
BUSH, Henry */c wid*	STEWART, Maria */c div*	9 Dec 1928	*123*
BUSH, J H H */c*	HAMILTON, M A */c*	27 Oct 1895	*50*
BUSH, James D */c*	WILLIS, Mary M */c*	5 Jan 1899	*56*
BUSH, James D */c wid*	HARRIS, Kate */c wid*	26 Aug 1914	*87*
BUSH, Jesse */c*	JOHNSON, Susan */c*	3 Jun 1875	*18*
BUSH, Louis A */c*	HENDERSON, Mattie M */c*	20 Dec 1911	*82*
BUSHROD, John */c*	WILLIAMS, Sarah */c*	20 Jun 1895	*49*
BUSHROD, William */c*	WINGFIELD, Idella */c*	27 Aug 1896	*51*
BUTLER, Arthur */c*	ROBINSON, Marie */c*	29 Jun 1923	*105*
BUTLER, C H	HARRIS, Bertha	6 Feb 1897	*54*
BUTLER, Ferdinand */c wid*	LEE, Malinda */c*	23 Oct 1890	*42*
BUTLER, George */c*	WHEELER, Bella */c*	26 Dec 1888	*39*
BUTLER, John */c*	WARNER, Cora */c*	30 Mar 1903	*64*
BUTLER, Mahlon	POWELL, Ophelia	31 Dec 1868	*10*
BUTLER, Spencer */c*	WILLIAMS, Isabel */c*	4 May 1911	*80*
BUTLER, William B	ARUNDLE, Sarah E	1 Feb 1872	*15*
BYRNE, Claude Smith	DEAN, Florence M	5 Sep 1925	*112*
BYRNE, F Lambert Jr	BALLARD, Varina Katherine	9 Apr 1913	*84*
BYRNE, George F	RECTOR, Dorothy V	22 Feb 1929	*124*
BYRNE, George W	NASH, Catherine Virginia	5 Apr 1928	*121*
BYRNE, Samuel G	JOHNSON, Sallie	8 Aug 1894	*48*
BYRNE, Sydner B	HUMMER, Emma E	7 Dec 1904	*67*
BYRNE, Thomas Adams	BAYLISS, Ethel Virginia */wid*	8 Aug 1932	*138*
BYRNE, Thomas W	HARRISON, Lule	13 Feb 1890	*41*
BYRNES, Bernard P	BECROFT, Ruth U	27 Aug 1917	*93*
BYRNES, Joseph W	LLOYD, Frances V	5 Mar 1878	*23*

BYRNES, Peyton A	MUDD, Ethel A	30 Jun 1924	*108*
BYWATER, T R /wid	POINDEXTER, Laura /wid	3 Jun 1921	*100*
CALLAR, D	DETWILER, Blanche R	28 Aug 1915	*89*
CALTRIDER, Arthur E	PURDUM, Frieda L	14 Jan 1932	*136*
CAMERON, Ashby	HORNBECK, Effie	29 Aug 1912	*83*
CAMERON, James Hunter	ROW, Susie Grace	23 Jun 1904	*66*
CAMP, Botsford	BARCROFT, Rachael	7 Jun 1860	*5*
CAMPBELL, Frederick L	BAUMAN, Mildred E	17 Jul 1926	*115*
CAMPBELL, H C	KLINGSBURY, Dorothy H	6 May 1924	*108*
CAMPBELL, James	KIDWELL, Angelina	3 Sep 1856	*2*
CAMPBELL, James /wid	KIDWELL, Martha V	23 Jul 1874	*17*
CAMPBELL, Sanford	ROSS, Elsie Ann /div	16 Dec 1930	*130*
CAMPBELL, Thomas	BAYLOR, Susannah	16 Apr 1889	*40*
CAMPHER, Frank E /c	FINKER, Ireatha /c	14 Nov 1929	*126*
CANAVAN, Patrick	JONES, Elizabeth E	20 Jun 1886	*36*
CANAVAN, Patrick /wid	JONES, Frances	21 Dec 1898	*55*
CANDLER, William M /wid	FOSTER, Juliet /wid	1 Oct 1910	*79*
CANNON, Albert	MITCHELL, Effie	12 Oct 1898	*55*
CANNON, Alfred D /wid	HAYDEN, Lauretta A	15 Jun 1892	*45*
CANNON, Arthur P	WOODVILLE, Margaret	9 Apr 1928	*121*
CANNON, George M	KIDWELL, Mary E	25 Oct 1859	*4*
CANTER, Albert D	THOMAS, Esther E	7 Nov 1933	*144*
CAPLINGER, John W	ROBEY, Frances V	6 Jan 1923	*104*
CARD, John F	NOURSE, Ella J	2 Oct 1883	*32*
CAREY, Elisha /c wid	JACKSON, Lillian H /c wid	22 Dec 1923	*107*
CARL, C W	EDWARDS, Ruth L	4 Sep 1926	*116*
CARL, Orville T	ALFRED, Kate Ann	8 Jul 1906	*71*
CARLIN, William M	CRIMMINS, Mary A	19 Nov 1902	*63*
CARLISLE, Charles A	JENKINS, Mary L	25 Aug 1917	*93*
CARMEN, Frederick A /c wid	HALL, Annie M /c	28 Oct 1925	*113*
CARMODY, Raymond L	MCGRATH, Grace A	3 Apr 1924	*108*
CARNE, Richard L Jr	DOVE, Ruth	5 Sep 1933	*143*
CARNEY, James L	STAHL, Emily L	29 May 1930	*128*
CARNEY, John S /wid	TOBIN, Lola T	6 Feb 1900	*58*
CARPENTER, Frank A Jr	LESTER, Melissa	10 Jun 1920	*98*
CARPENTER, John	MALONEY, Beulah /wid	2 Jul 1927	*118*
CARPENTER, W H /c wid	PEARSON, Caroline /c wid	21 Dec 1927	*120*
CARPENTER, William /c	ADAMS, Kizzie /c	10 May 1897	*52*
CARPENTER, William A	READE, Mary W	20 Dec 1924	*110*
CARPER, B Miller	LOGAN, Dorothea V	8 Oct 1930	*129*
CARPER, Hailman H	WATSON, Rena Anne	6 Jun 1923	*105*
CARPER, Stanley Thomas	RECTOR, Vera Evelyn	16 Oct 1926	*116*

CARPER, T J	DALTON, Laura	4 Oct 1913	85
CARPER, Thomas E	LOWE, Lucretia	18 Oct 1881	29
CARPER, Thomas S	PHILLIPS, Laura V	1 Nov 1888	39
CARR, Ernest F	GUNNELL, Mary A	15 Sep 1921	101
CARR, Grover L	BLEVINS, Clyde	21 Aug 1923	106
CARROLL, Charles /wid	PEARSON, Ann /wid	25 Nov 1856	2
CARROLL, John H /c	TAYLOR, Della B /c	12 Sep 1894	48
CARROLL, John H /c wid	SHEPHERD, Willie Alice /c wid	13 Jun 1929	125
CARROLL, John W	CHRISTIE, Estelle /wid	12 Nov 1879	25
CARROLL, Michael	ROURKE, Maggie T	12 Sep 1897	53
CARROLL, Walter R	BLAHA, Ruth R	11 Aug 1931	133
CARSON, Charles	SMALLWOOD, Ada	18 Aug 1909	77
CARSON, Henry T /wid	VOLLAND, Louise M C	15 Aug 1901	60
CARTER, A J /c	TURNER, Sarah E /c	27 Feb 1880	26
CARTER, Alexander /c	FORD, Martha E /c	25 Jun 1891	43
CARTER, Alfred /c	DIXON, Mary S /c	19 Dec 1882	31
CARTER, Alfred /c	JACKSON, Susan /c	22 Sep 1883	32
CARTER, Archie N	MARTIN, Nellie A	15 Nov 1898	56
CARTER, Augustus /c	DENNEY, Susan	8 Dec 1867	8
CARTER, Benjamin /c	JAMES, Geneva /c	2 May 1907	72
CARTER, C H /c	THOMPSON, Martha A /c	21 Dec 1882	31
CARTER, Cassius	CARTER, Pauline	19 Jul 1882	30
CARTER, Charles H /c	NEAL, Carrie A /c	12 Feb 1891	43
CARTER, Claude R	SPINKS, Dorothy	9 Sep 1930	129
CARTER, Colvin H	HOSKINS, Hulda P	9 Oct 1932	139
CARTER, Cyrus /c wid	LEE, Malany /c wid	13 Apr 1872	14
CARTER, Emmett	FLETCHER, Margaret E	1 Aug 1929	125
CARTER, Giles A	TYERS, Mary	12 Sep 1883	32
CARTER, Herbert /c	NEWLON, Dora /c	4 Aug 1925	112
CARTER, Howard /c	WEBB, Ida /c	27 Jan 1902	62
CARTER, James /c	ODRICK, Annie /c	2 Jan 1881	28
CARTER, James E /c div	WINES, Elsie D /c	12 Apr 1923	105
CARTER, James L Jr	RICHARDS, Viola L	8 Sep 1921	101
CARTER, Jeff /c wid	FAIRFAX, Rosa /c	15 Oct 1868	10
CARTER, John /c	FRY, Minnie /c	4 Mar 1886	36
CARTER, John /c	CARROLL, Lucy /c	15 Mar 1923	104
CARTER, John B	CRUMP, Ella E	8 Oct 1896	51
CARTER, John T /c	FAIRFAX, Lydia L /c	13 May 1879	25
CARTER, Joseph N /c	HARROD, Hazel F /c	17 Aug 1933	143
CARTER, Landon E	CARTER, Rose M	16 Jun 1874	17
CARTER, Linwood	LIGHT, Carrine	3 Dec 1927	120
CARTER, M L	FINNELL, Violett	23 Aug 1905	69

CARTER, Paul /c	THOMAS, Odessa A /c	12 Dec 1928	*123*
CARTER, Richard C	FITZHUGH, Ellen L	14 Oct 1897	*53*
CARTER, Richard C	FINN, Mary C	31 Oct 1919	*96*
CARTER, Robert /c	BURGESS, Alice /c	18 Jul 1876	*20*
CARTER, Robert	CARTER, Louisa T	15 Jun 1882	*30*
CARTER, Robert R /c	ROBERSON, Fanny /c	21 May 1875	*18*
CARTER, Russell	SHEPHERD, Vivian L	3 Dec 1929	*126*
CARTER, Starr V	SWIFT, Ellen E	20 Oct 1891	*44*
CARTER, Thomas G /wid	WELLER, D K	19 Oct 1895	*50*
CARTER, Willard	CORNELL, Alice	23 Aug 1928	*122*
CARTER, William /c	CARTER, Effie J /c	2 Sep 1903	*65*
CARTER, William /c	POLLARD, Estella K /c	31 Dec 1908	*76*
CARY, Edmund /wid	COLEMAN, Julia	10 Jun 1866	*6*
CARY, Walter M	HARRISON, Gertrude A	23 Nov 1904	*67*
CASE, Boyd Albert	ENSOR, Violette Murman	15 Apr 1933	*142*
CASEY, Francis B /div	CASSIDY, Margaret M	7 Sep 1927	*119*
CASEY, J Wesley /c	ADAMS, Ada /c	20 Oct 1897	*53*
CASEY, Thomas J /div	SHAVER, Thelma B	27 May 1930	*128*
CASH, John /wid	KELLY, Mary A /wid	4 Feb 1869	*10*
CASHATT, Ivey Wesley	FRISTOE, Sadie Young	1 Sep 1921	*101*
CASS, Lewis /c	SAWYER, Lizzie /c	3 Apr 1881	*28*
CASSADY, James H	SHREVE, Maggie	11 Nov 1874	*17*
CASSADY, Robert Idleman	MCKINNEY, Margaret	16 May 1913	*132*
CASSADY, Charles E	HOLLIS, Sadie E	25 Feb 1931	*131*
CASSELL, Robert C /wid	HAISLIP, Ella V	20 Dec 1876	*21*
CASTEEL, B Lazelle	NELSON, Cora E	19 Sep 1908	*75*
CATLER, Harry L	POWELL, Mary Vivian	16 Dec 1913	*85*
CATON, George C /wid	STEPHENS, Sarah L	28 Dec 1915	*89*
CATON, George T	BURROUGHS, Nellie L	6 Oct 1891	*43*
CATON, John Russell	SATTERFIELD, Audrey O	13 Aug 1929	*125*
CATON, Milton E	MULHOLLAND, Emma	9 Sep 1903	*65*
CATON, Earl W	SATTERFIELD, Sarah I	22 Oct 1922	*103*
CATTS, John H	PULMAN, Gracie B	29 Apr 1886	*36*
CAUDLE, Robert L	POWELL, Irma M	26 Feb 1931	*131*
CAUSER, William P /div	DORSEY, Mabel R	4 Dec 1907	*74*
CAWMAN, John Wesley	TYLER, Minnie F	30 Mar 1901	*60*
CAYLOR, George F	DIXON, Edith	28 Jul 1909	*77*
CAYLOR, Joseph J	COCKERILLE, Edith	24 Mar 1885	*34*
CHADWICK, J P	BALLENGER, Janie P	15 Jan 1910	*78*
CHAMBERS, Daniel	CAMPBELL, Maggie	27 Dec 1870	*13*
CHAMBERS, Luther /c	BRIGGS, Margaret /c	26 Jun 1887	*38*
CHAMBERS, William J /c	SMITH, Ida /c	10 May 1910	*78*

CHAMBERS, William J /c div	OVERTON, Georgie /c	14 Jun 1916	90
CHAMBLIN, Thomas O	IVES, Demis A	17 Apr 1867	7
CHAMPAGNE, Harold Joseph	MCCLURE, Margaret M	14 May 1930	128
CHANDLER, John M	WOOD, Katherine	3 Apr 1933	141
CHANEL, Orson J	PAYNE, Bertha L	24 Oct 1901	61
CHANEY, Edwin L	STEELE, Gladys G	12 Jul 1917	92
CHAPIN, Charles J	HARRISON, Carrie S	30 Sep 1890	42
CHAPMAN, Joseph L	GREENWOOD, Leahbell	10 Nov 1909	77
CHAPMAN, Thomas P Jr	TAYLOR, Elizabeth I	4 Sep 1928	122
CHAPMAN, Wilford Lee	COON, Edna Grace	10 Dec 1927	120
CHAPMAN, William	RUFFNER, Esther	2 Apr 1923	105
CHASE, Henry /c	CARTER, Evelyn /c	15 Jun 1927	118
CHASE, Howard G /wid	MULHERON, Helen	29 Apr 1933	142
CHASE, Samuel /c	TURLEY, Vida /c	21 Sep 1911	81
CHASE, Theodore L	MASON, Kora	14 Feb 1871	13
CHASE, Winfield S /wid	SPEER, Georgiana V	19 May 1874	17
CHAUNCEY, Julien F	STUDDS, Gennetta	14 Oct 1884	33
CHAUNCEY, Julien F /wid	COWLING, Annie H	5 Dec 1893	47
CHAVIS, Wellington /c	SCOTT, Norma C /c	9 Jun 1917	92
CHEEKS, George /c	JACKSON, Sophy /c	28 Nov 1878	24
CHEEKS, Samuel /c	BROWN, Mary /c	19 Nov 1880	27
CHESHIRE, Henry L	BUTLER, Elizabeth M	7 Aug 1913	84
CHESLEY, J H	SMITH, Claudia W	10 Jul 1878	23
CHESLEY, O W	RICE, Hattie Alice	5 Oct 1909	77
CHESTON, Henry C	HUNTER, Grace	29 Jun 1893	46
CHEW, Addison /c	LOWE, Betsy /c	20 Feb 1889	39
CHICHESTER, George /wid	CORSE, Mary R	12 Jul 1857	3
CHICHESTER, John C	CORSE, R V	2 Aug 1860	5
CHICHESTER, John H	DULANY, Sarah Ellen	29 Nov 1854	1
CHICHESTER, Richard Moncure	COCKERILLE, Nannie Lee	19 Apr 1876	20
CHILCOTT, Amos H	HUDDLESON, Elizabeth	25 Nov 1925	113
CHILD, Stephen Jr	SWEENEY, Terry	29 May 1926	114
CHILDRESS, James T	LYNCH, Mary V	30 Oct 1889	40
CHINN, John Stretchley /wid	THOMAS, Carrie Elton	7 Sep 1898	55
CHLOE, William H /c	NAYLOR, Columbia /c	27 Dec 1877	23
CHLOE, Rhoda /c	ROBINSON, Edna /c	6 Oct 1928	122
CHOATE, Columbus D	BITZER, Ella V	2 Oct 1884	33
CHOATE, Conrad B	DETWILER, Ruth	7 Apr 1917	91
CHRISTIAN, Rufus L /wid	FANT, Frances Howard /wid	21 Jun 1932	138
CHURCH, C A	SETTLEMYER, Irene	29 May 1930	128
CHURCH, Merton E	NORTHROP, Carrie B	14 Feb 1884	33
CLAGGETT, Hammett S	VAN SICKLER, Margaret Lee	2 Jul 1915	88

CLAGGETT, Herbert M	RATHBURN, Cora T	25 Sep 1894	*48*
CLAIR, Charles	CONROW, Emma	30 Nov 1871	*14*
CLAIR, William	DEAVERS, Frances	19 Nov 1879	*25*
CLAPP, Howard D	TERRETT, Nettie L	21 May 1902	*62*
CLAPP, Schuyler L	PARKER, Florence	11 Nov 1929	*126*
CLARKE, Austin	HANTT, Hilda	16 Sep 1933	*143*
CLARK, Benjamin F /wid	CROSSMAN, Annie F	1 Jan 1895	*49*
CLARKE, Carlton Lee	DAWSON, Margaret L	1 May 1926	*114*
CLARK, Charles /wid	MCVEIGH, Cornelia	5 Nov 1885	*35*
CLARK, Daniel	GESSFORD, Lois M	16 Jul 1932	*138*
CLARKE, Edward F	MILLARD, Goldie V	25 Dec 1906	*72*
CLARKE, Ellsworth E	BARKER, Elizabeth	5 Sep 1888	*39*
CLARKE, Fayette	CLARKE, Bessie	15 Sep 1919	*96*
CLARK, G S	PARMALEE, Lee A /div	17 Apr 1909	*76*
CLARK, Herbert E	FAIRFAX, Mary Ann	26 Oct 1928	*123*
CLARK, Jesse /c wid	NELSON, Margaret /c	12 Feb 1882	*29*
CLARK, John	HICKOCK, Caroline Augusta	27 May 1857	*3*
CLARKE, John D	HENEKE, Marie Storch /div	21 Sep 1927	*119*
CLARK, Lawrence J	BUELL, Dorothy W	29 Jun 1918	*94*
CLARK, O F	DAWSON, Lillian H	12 Sep 1899	*57*
CLARK, Ollie Raymond	FERGUSON, Esther R	24 Aug 1933	*143*
CLARKE, Overton L	SAUNDERS, Virgie	7 Feb 1905	*68*
CLARK, Percy E	ATKINS, Alma L	6 Jul 1929	*125*
CLARK, Pomeroy P	HUNTER, Mary D	12 Jul 1905	*69*
CLARKE, Robert F	HUNTT, Emma B	6 Sep 1888	*39*
CLARKE, Robert J	CORNEAL, Mary E	1 Jun 1926	*114*
CLARKE, Roscoe	WADDELL, Viola	2 Aug 1926	*115*
CLARK, Seth L /div	LANHAM, Mary E	12 Mar 1907	*72*
CLARKE, Thomas I	HUNTT, Martha V	23 Dec 1873	*16*
CLARK, Thomas I /wid	BARRS, Bessie	5 Oct 1904	*67*
CLARK, Thomas P	SINCLAIR, Kate L	15 May 1898	*54*
CLARK, W L	HOWDERSHELL, M M	2 Jul 1902	*62*
CLARK, Walter B	BROWN, Laura Catherine	3 Jul 1933	*143*
CLARK, Walter C	SYLVESTER, Camilla M	15 Jun 1932	*137*
CLARK, Wilbar Fisk	SUMMERS, Sally J	12 Dec 1866	*7*
CLARK, William /c	BOWLES, Mary /c	8 Sep 1878	*24*
CLARKE, William	MACK, Grace Hamilton	3 Oct 1907	*73*
CLARK, William A	SHIPMAN, Virginia F	16 Oct 1890	*42*
CLARK, William E	TWOGOOD, Marjorie Olive Amy	14 Nov 1917	*93*
CLARK, William F Jr	MARCHANT, Elizabeth	4 Sep 1931	*133*
CLARK, William M	WALKER, Laura M	8 Jun 1881	*28*
CLARKSON, James W /wid	ROWE, Julia A /wid	16 May 1928	*121*

CLAY, Willie L	BRADBURG, Hertha	22 Dec 1925	*113*
CLEARY, Michael S	HARRISON, Jennie	23 Oct 1895	*50*
CLEM, Carroll M	BOWIE, Dora V	20 Nov 1921	*101*
CLEMENTS, Robert /c	BATES, Harriet /c	30 Nov 1880	*27*
CLEMENTS, Robert /c	WHITE, Hattie B /c	7 Jun 1919	*95*
CLEMMONS, Samuel	HARRIS, Martha I	27 Dec 1866	*7*
CLEVELAND, Bernard	BRANZELL, Virginia	20 Jun 1922	*102*
CLICK, William L	MATHIAS, Mary Maud	31 Oct 1905	*69*
CLIFFORD, James W	WATSON, Martha	31 Dec 1931	*135*
CLIFTON, Otis /c	BARNES, Alma /c	10 Jun 1927	*118*
CLIFTON, Ralph R	WITT, Effie A	22 Oct 1928	*123*
CLINE, F H /wid	MOORE, Florence O	16 Jan 1907	*72*
CLINGGEMPEEL, Cecil Lee /wid	GHEEN, Mary P /div	9 Sep 1933	*143*
CLINTON, Winfield A	DAVIS, Pauline	20 Jun 1922	*102*
CLISBY, Robert L /c wid	BROWN, Mary E Rich /c div	16 Dec 1923	*107*
CLOTWORTHY, Harris A /div	KLEIN, Violet E S	13 Jun 1923	*105*
CLOUD, Etenna L	BALL, Dorothy M	1 Jun 1931	*132*
COAKLEY, Horace A	CATTS, Lillian L	19 Apr 1893	*46*
COATRIGHT, Lewis	GUNNELL, Linton Virginia	13 Sep 1883	*32*
COATS, Charles /c	TINNER, Frances /c	30 Oct 1913	*85*
COATS, Frank /c	BECKWITH, Martha /c	28 Jun 1905	*69*
COATS, George /c	HOGAN, Betty /c	6 Mar 1895	*49*
COATS, Howard	SUTTON, Alice M	9 Jan 1872	*14*
COATS, James /c	WALKER, Alice /c	19 Apr 1879	*25*
COATS, James Henry	CRANKUM, Maria	8 Dec 1870	*13*
COATS, John /c	WATSON, Martha /c wid	20 Dec 1899	*57*
COATS, John E /c	TAYLOR, Lucy	31 Dec 1874	*18*
COATS, John E /c wid	TURNER, Agnes /c wid	28 Mar 1917	*91*
COBB, Gray Moore	ALSOP, Ethel Clara	22 Jul 1925	*112*
COBB, James O	SPEER, Sarah M	12 May 1921	*100*
COBURN, Thomas	MANN, Edith	22 Oct 1918	*95*
COCK, Ambrose Jr	SWEENY, Sarah E	21 Dec 1859	*4*
COCK, Thomas S	PADGETT, Ellen M	1 Feb 1872	*15*
COCK, William W	COCK, Lora V	7 Nov 1889	*40*
COCKERHAM, Craft E	KLINE, Sallie M	17 Jun 1918	*94*
COCKERILLE, C E	SNYDER, Lillie	29 Oct 1919	*96*
COCKERILLE, Charles B	STONNELL, Margaret A L	17 Dec 1878	*24*
COCKERILLE, Charles William	WRENN, Sarah A	17 Oct 1871	*14*
COCKERILLE, Clarence C	SPRAKER, Norfa C	11 Sep 1915	*89*
COCKERILLE, George B	CORNWELL, Fern E	30 Dec 1914	*87*
COCKERILLE, George William	STONNELL, A B C	16 Jan 1879	*24*
COCKERILLE, H C	SANDERS, Margaret E	10 Mar 1896	*50*

COCKERILLE, Harvey W	HUTCHISON, Mary E	30 Dec 1904	*66*
COCKERILLE, Henry E	MILLARD, Sarah C	10 Dec 1895	*50*
COCKERILLE, James	COLEMAN, Annie E	21 Feb 1856	*2*
COCKERILLE, James	BUELL, Mary Elizabeth	17 May 1910	*78*
COCKERILLE, James F	COLE, Sarah A	15 Jul 1880	*27*
COCKERILLE, Jeremiah W	PEARSON, Florence R	1 Dec 1897	*53*
COCKERILLE, Jonathan	BOSWELL, Sarah A	16 Jan 1859	*4*
COCKERILLE, Mark	MOXLY, Maud C B	16 May 1889	*40*
COCKERILLE, Philip	BUCKLEY, Marchie	28 Oct 1903	*65*
COCKERILLE, Robert	ROBY, Bertie	22 Dec 1917	*93*
COCKERILLE, Samuel W	KIRBY, Nettie L	21 Nov 1894	*48*
COCKERILLE, Stonewall	TRACY, Sarah J	31 Oct 1893	*47*
COCKERILLE, Stonewall J /wid	DIMSEY, Julia D	5 Jul 1903	*65*
COCKERILLE, Benjamin F	HUMMER, Laura B	24 Jan 1884	*32*
CODARR, Salmon A	JENKINS, Jessie F	8 Jun 1904	*66*
COE, Lowry N	GRAY, Edith H	1 Sep 1923	*106*
COE, Spencer	THORN, Maggie B	13 May 1869	*11*
COFFEE, Michael C	JOYCE, Annie	12 Aug 1883	*31*
COFFEE, Watson C /wid	DAVIES, Mary E	7 Aug 1927	*119*
COFFER, Joshua	SIMPSON, Huldah V	21 Sep 1858	*4*
COFFMAN, Jack T	DE PLANTER, Catherine	21 Dec 1931	*135*
COFFMAN, John B /wid	SEIBERT, Mary B	10 Aug 1917	*92*
COFFREN, Richard H	ELLIS, Margarite	18 Aug 1924	*109*
COHEAN, Ray B Jr	RICHARDS, Mary Ellen /wid	1 Jun 1931	*132*
COHEN, Robert S	STALEY, Genevieve M	12 Aug 1929	*125*
COHN, Edmund M	LEONARD, Winifred Borck /div	2 Jun 1926	*114*
COLBERT, Clarence W /c	GREEN, Mary L /c	16 Aug 1919	*96*
COLBERT, William /c	HARRISON, Isabella /c	14 Oct 1884	*33*
COLE, Elijah /c wid	WILLIAMS, Nellie /c wid	9 Sep 1922	*103*
COLE, Frank	PECK, Mary Ellen	4 Apr 1893	*46*
COLE, Jacob	KIDWELL, Annie B	20 Dec 1894	*48*
COLE, James Edward	JOHNSON, Jane W	22 Apr 1933	*142*
COLE, James Samuel /c	CHLOE, Magy R /c	20 Sep 1920	*99*
COLE, John T	LEE, Ann E	28 Apr 1886	*36*
COLE, Mortimer	JACOBS, Essie	22 Apr 1933	*142*
COLE, William	KIDWELL, Harriet C	9 Mar 1856	*2*
COLEMAN, Charles C	PLASKETT, Clara V	9 Oct 1901	*61*
COLEMAN, Edward /c	BUTLER, Dorothy /c	20 Jun 1929	*125*
COLEMAN, Eustace /c	DODSON, Leaster /c	22 Oct 1907	*73*
COLEMAN, Fred R /wid	STAGE, Catherine O /wid	10 Apr 1933	*142*
COLEMAN, Henry D	MOORE, Kate W	8 Dec 1897	*53*
COLEMAN, John /c	THOMAS, Hilda /c wid	10 Nov 1930	*130*

COLEMAN, Richard	ROESER, Thekla	25 Jan 1883	31
COLEMAN, Robert L	SLACK, Mary Edith B	4 Apr 1905	68
COLEMAN, Robert Mc	BOYER, Mary	13 Oct 1917	93
COLEMAN, Samuel	DAILEY, Elnora	16 Sep 1896	51
COLEMAN, Watson E	MOSBY, Victoria S	12 Dec 1894	48
COLEMAN, William Henry /c	WASHINGTON, Mary /c	27 Aug 1895	49
COLES, Benjamin R /div	FAVORITE, Grace L	22 Jun 1909	77
COLLIER, Clarence L	GOODSPEED, Grace	3 Jul 1926	115
COLLIER, James H	KEYS, Sarah J	11 Apr 1917	91
COLLINGSWORTH, Rob	HIX, Georgie /wid	25 Jan 1870	12
COLLINS, Douglas /c	ROBINSON, Jennie /c	28 May 1895	49
COLLINS, James	CRONIN, Maggie E	27 Apr 1881	28
COLLINS, Linwood McCroy	LACY, Ramona A	28 Jun 1916	90
COLLINS, Marshal /c	THOMPSON, Margaret /c	20 Mar 1890	41
COLLINS, Owen J /wid	PIGGOTT, Martha V	21 Feb 1912	82
COLLINS, Patrick	LEE, Delilah	28 Jan 1886	36
COLLINS, Richard A	BYRNE, Cordelia L	15 Apr 1908	74
COLLINS, Stephen R	GILL, Aurelia Bingham /wid	23 Oct 1895	50
COLLINS, W G	ROLLINS, Britania	14 Sep 1885	35
COLLINS, Willard	ARNOLD, Daisy	25 Feb 1924	108
COLLINS, William /c wid	HUDNALL, Hattie B /c	1 Nov 1899	57
COLLINS, William H /c	WILLIAMS, Betsy /c	12 Oct 1899	57
COLMAN, Wallace	MARTIN, Frances	21 Nov 1929	126
COMBS, Lawrence R	JACOBS, Mary R	21 Nov 1883	32
COMERFORD, Bert M	EASTER, Aurora A	10 Nov 1914	87
COMMINS, James H	WALKER, Jane E	7 Feb 1878	23
COMPHER, Joseph	WARNER, Elta	22 Jan 1913	84
COMPTON, Charles B	CONROY, Sarah DeSalle	7 Jul 1898	54
COMPTON, Eppa	MARSHALL, Minnie	21 Feb 1900	58
COMPTON, Felix	FAIRFAX, Eloise	14 Dec 1871	14
COMPTON, P F	JONES, Sallie /wid	12 Apr 1904	66
COMPTON, William A	GILBERT, Blanche B /div	15 Aug 1910	79
CONGDON, Clem	MEISSEL, Amelia V /div	11 Jan 1923	104
CONNER, A N	WILLIAMS, Fannie	12 Feb 1890	41
CONNER, Robert S /wid	JENKINS, Mary F	27 Nov 1917	93
CONRAD, Philip Fuller	ECKER, Nora Jeanette	6 Jan 1923	104
CONSTABLE, Jonathan /wid	SPEER, Elizabeth	15 Oct 1857	3
CONWAY, James W	KESTNER, Margaret M	6 Feb 1933	141
COOK, A L	BURDHAM, Elva	17 Jan 1928	121
COOKE, Clifford C	GALLMAN, Beulah	17 Jul 1922	103
COOKE, Corpl. J S	HUMMER, Dorothy Mae.	6 Mar 1920	97
COOK, Enoch	HAISLIP, Martha A	24 Sep 1868	10

COOK, Ernest	HORSEMAN, Janie	7 Aug 1904	*67*
COOK, Frederick */c*	WILLIAMS, Louisa */c*	20 Nov 1870	*13*
COOK, Frederick */c*	PEARSON, Mattie */c*	15 Dec 1908	*76*
COOK, George	STRUDER, Josephine	15 Aug 1925	*112*
COOK, George A */c*	BROWN, Eva Wilkerson */c*	13 Mar 1907	*72*
COOK, George G	PETTITT, Isabella	7 Oct 1890	*42*
COOK, George G */wid*	MATTHEWS, Annie E	8 Jun 1904	*66*
COOK, George W	TAYLOR, Helen M	15 Nov 1932	*140*
COOK, Hayes	SHIRLEY, Mary G	15 Dec 1931	*135*
COOK, James F */c*	THOMPSON, Emma V */c*	28 Dec 1893	*47*
COOK, John Henry */wid*	STAFFORD, Mary J	24 Apr 1870	*12*
COOK, John R	FULLER, Mary E	12 Jul 1898	*54*
COOK, Leak	SCHULTZ, Bessie */wid*	25 Apr 1929	*124*
COOK, Luther M */c*	HENDERSON, Gracie M */c*	22 Sep 1901	*60*
COOK, Marcus M	ROSS, Hanna F	20 Jul 1887	*38*
COOK, Merlin Carl	FISHER, Hermorin C	21 Jan 1933	*141*
COOK, Robert E */c*	ISRAEL, Lillian */c*	7 Jun 1928	*121*
COOK, Thomas R	BRADSHAW, Mary D	28 Oct 1922	*103*
COOK, William P */c*	SMITH, Mamie M */c*	11 Jun 1910	*78*
COOKSEY, James W	BURKE, Frances Lena	11 Jun 1867	*7*
COOKSEY, Sanford W	CROUCH, Minnie Lee	15 Dec 1885	*35*
COOKSEY, Thomas H	CROUCH, Margaret H	29 Jan 1874	*17*
COOLEY, Milton Stanley	ESTERLY, Dorothy Mae	22 Sep 1921	*101*
COOLEY, William M */wid*	RALEIGH, Helen C */div*	4 Aug 1923	*105*
COOMBE, Albert T	PRICE, Madeline P */div*	21 Sep 1927	*119*
COOMBE, Albert Thompson	HUNT, Alice Ives	14 Oct 1886	*36*
COOMBE, W A	HENESSY, Blanche K */wid*	28 Nov 1925	*113*
COOMBS, Lewis J	BRYANT, Elizabeth B	25 Apr 1890	*41*
COON, Clark	LADUE, Margaret Ann	7 Nov 1854	*1*
COOPER, Arthur	BRADY, Martha E */wid*	24 Aug 1923	*106*
COOPER, Bernard H	HOLDEN, Virginia F	2 Oct 1925	*112*
COOPER, Charles O */div*	PETER, Willy E	31 Oct 1906	*71*
COOPER, Charles S	FULTON, Lula O	24 Jun 1908	*75*
COOPER, Julian W */c*	POE, Anna L */c wid*	16 Apr 1927	*118*
COPPERTHITE, Charles	HELLBACK, Phyllis	18 May 1926	*114*
COPPERTHITE, Chester A	CARTWRIGHT, Susan E	11 Sep 1932	*139*
CORCORAN, John	BRUFF, Mary E	17 Jan 1931	*131*
CORDOVA, Henry W	ARONE, Alleen Lane	2 Nov 1931	*134*
CORE, John T	WILEY, Virginia M	30 Nov 1899	*57*
CORNELIUS, Joseph	SANSONE, Bernedeta J	27 Jan 1913	*84*
CORNELL, Frank M	DOHNER, Rosemary	15 Jan 1930	*127*
CORNELL, George W	BORDEN, Virginia E	28 Jun 1926	*115*

CORNELL, Harvey	JEWELL, Annie	3 Feb 1903	*64*
CORNELL, John R	GUNNELL, Julia A /wid	21 Feb 1864	*5*
CORNELL, Theodore	BLINCOE, Eliza E	6 Dec 1859	*4*
CORNELL, William C /wid	THOMPSON, Laura T	10 Oct 1888	*39*
CORNISH, James E	WEBB, Alice	6 Mar 1884	*33*
CORNWALL, James G	REID, Frances S	28 Feb 1867	*7*
CORNWELL, Daniel D /wid	GOODE, Alice E /wid	6 Jul 1927	*118*
CORNWELL, Ernest	PEARSON, Myrtle	10 Oct 1925	*112*
CORNWELL, Harvey	BRUMBACK, Blanche Oliver	9 Jun 1931	*132*
CORNWELL, Jacob	KIDWELL, Martha	10 Mar 1857	*3*
CORNWELL, Thornton	BEDAKER, Mary	22 Jul 1920	*98*
CORNWELL, William	COOK, Emily	4 Aug 1859	*4*
CORRIDON, James D	FITSPATRICK, C Louise	8 Jun 1929	*125*
CORSE, Charles Samuel	BLAKE, Emily K	17 Oct 1931	*134*
CORSE, J Douglas	SMITH, Lucy E	14 Jun 1856	*2*
CORUM, Moses	CRAVEN, Janie	1 Jun 1907	*73*
COSTA, Joseph James	FLANNAGAN, Margaret R	26 Aug 1933	*143*
COSTELLO, Ernest	ROUSE, Mary L	12 Jun 1926	*115*
COSTELLO, Samuel /wid	BEAHM, Annie /wid	8 Jul 1922	*103*
COSTER, Albert H	WOOD, Olea Moulton	20 Nov 1923	*106*
COTTON, Myron S	BRONSTEIN, Zelda Jean	24 Jan 1930	*127*
COTTON, Preston H /c	HOLLAND, Rhoda B /c	6 May 1912	*82*
COTTRELL, E C	MONEY, Mary E	7 Jun 1882	*30*
COTTRELL, E C /wid	BICKSLER, Emma	3 Jan 1894	*47*
COUBER, Arthur E	BROWN, Elsie	27 Sep 1926	*116*
COUCHMAN, Lawrence K	LINDSAY, Evelyn R	23 Apr 1930	*127*
COULBY, Edgar M /wid	STINE, Irene A	3 May 1932	*137*
COULTER, Thomas A	BRADFORD, Emma J	21 Jun 1892	*45*
COURTNEY, Marvin M	SUIT, Clara V	15 Jul 1925	*112*
COURTNEY, Robert /c	GARRIES, Rachel /c	26 Dec 1925	*113*
COVINGTON, W E	WAGSTAFF, Helen	19 Oct 1929	*126*
COWHERD, Henry Hill	MILLER, Evelyn /wid	14 Jun 1921	*100*
COWLING, Edward	CRUX, Mary	18 Jan 1855	*1*
COWLING, Edward W	STUDDS, Araminta	3 Jul 1895	*49*
COX, A Melville	TILLEY, Anita I	17 May 1930	*128*
COX, Burton E	KLOCK, Loretta M	24 Sep 1925	*112*
COX, Claibourn	MAYHUGH, Ruth	19 Oct 1898	*55*
COX, Francis Augusta	MONCURE, Mary Pemberton	3 Aug 1921	*101*
COX, Granville Claude	KACHE, Virginia	26 Aug 1933	*143*
COX, Herman J	DIKES, Elsie F	6 Aug 1931	*133*
COX, John W	POWELL, Annie	11 Nov 1873	*16*
COX, William Archer /div	JOHNSON, Minnie Elizabeth	19 Jan 1925	*110*

COXEN, James	BURNSIDE, Josie	29 Apr 1897	*52*
COXEN, Millard Filmore	RIGHTER, Emma J	29 May 1925	*111*
COYLE, James J	PATTERSON, Ida E	16 Nov 1889	*40*
CRABILL, Collieta L /div	BECKER, Mabel E	13 Nov 1930	*130*
CRAGG, T Mark	HUNTER, Mabel Isable	7 Jul 1910	*79*
CRAGUN, John Wiley	CABBARD, Hazel	31 Jul 1931	*133*
CRAIG, David N	CASTLEMAN, Frances F	14 Jun 1930	*128*
CRAIG, G W	ROLLINS, Edna May	25 Mar 1924	*108*
CRAIG, James Henry	SPEER, Martha Mary	22 Nov 1911	*81*
CRAIG, Russell S /wid	GLASSCOCK, Eunice L	9 Sep 1926	*116*
CRAIG, Scott /c	GROOMS, Mary /c	31 Mar 1902	*62*
CRAIG, W N	BYRNE, Rena /wid	31 Dec 1903	*65*
CRAIGHEAD, Lee D	MOORE, Geneva V	18 Jan 1932	*136*
CRANE, John /c	TATE, Pearl /c	23 May 1917	*92*
CRANE, T Seymour Jr	THOMPSON, Anna S	21 May 1917	*92*
CRANFORD, James H	HARROVER, Priscilla	18 Oct 1860	*5*
CRANFORD, Wesley H	GRIMSLEY, Ella M	25 Feb 1903	*64*
CRAVEN, Charles /c wid	RATCLIFFE, Maria L /c	21 Sep 1876	*20*
CRAWFORD, Clifford	SHOTROFF, Edna	20 Oct 1927	*119*
CRAWFORD, Philip M	BODMER, Marjorie	20 Jul 1927	*118*
CRAWFORD, Stanley C	ALLEWALT, Margaret Viola	18 Jun 1932	*138*
CREED, John Thomas	DE JESUS, Hilda	22 Jul 1927	*118*
CREEL, James	GRIFFITH, Janie	20 Oct 1909	*77*
CREIGHTON, Frank C /wid	MARSHALL, Helen B	7 Sep 1910	*79*
CRIDER, Howard C	WINE, Elsie Leigh	27 Oct 1926	*116*
CRIM, James A Jr	PHILLIPS, Mamie E /wid	11 Jul 1931	*132*
CRIPPEN, Asa M	WHITACRE, Hettie J	23 Dec 1891	*44*
CRIPPEN, Henry A	LLOYD, Lavinia V	16 Jan 1875	*18*
CRIPPEN, Samuel /c	KNIGHT, Maria E /c	5 Nov 1892	*45*
CRISE, John F /wid	WILLIAMS, Louise M	30 Apr 1902	*62*
CRISSMAN, William Arthur	WALTERS, Regina A	10 Nov 1933	*144*
CROCKER, William	FETZER, Hester Jane	20 Dec 1855	*2*
CROMWELL, Daniel F	KENNEDY, Audress	17 May 1930	*128*
CRONIN, Michael	DESMOND, Margaret	2 Jun 1908	*75*
CRONK, Greenberry M	THOMPSON, Sarah	24 Nov 1874	*17*
CROPP, Jacob A	THOMPSON, Ida J	21 Mar 1883	*31*
CROSON, E F	SAFFER, Annie R	17 Nov 1897	*53*
CROSON, E W	KIDWELL, Nancy	24 Nov 1887	*38*
CROSON, George H	GHEEN, Martha W	9 Mar 1891	*43*
CROSON, James Burr	SHAW, Raydelle B	3 Aug 1905	*69*
CROSON, James I	PETTITT, Nellie	1 Jan 1888	*38*
CROSON, John H	ROBY, Levinia	5 Oct 1871	*14*

CROSON, Joseph	PETTY, Eva	9 Sep 1903	65
CROSON, L J	KEARNS, Eva	7 Jan 1903	64
CROSON, Peyton W	WELLS, Eva L	19 Mar 1884	33
CROSON, Rice	ELLIS, Maria C	4 May 1856	2
CROSON, William E	SUTPHIN, Rachel M	25 Jan 1907	72
CROSON, William Fenton	PETTITT, Nancy A	8 Dec 1870	13
CROSON, Charles	LYNN, Ann E	21 Feb 1878	23
CROSS, A Judkins	MCDONOUGH, Willie May	14 Apr 1886	36
CROSS, Arthur L	GINNELLEY, Ida J	25 Jan 1893	46
CROSS, Benjamin	COATES, Virginia Lucinda	29 Mar 1857	3
CROSS, Eugene A Jr	TAYLOR, Alverta R	22 Aug 1932	139
CROSS, George P	GRIFFIN, Nancy E	28 Aug 1910	79
CROSS, Glenn J	WEST, Edith S	2 Apr 1932	137
CROSS, H M	SHIFFLETT, Annie B	20 Feb 1911	80
CROSS, James B	CANFIELD, Bella	3 Jun 1885	35
CROSS, John P	BUCKLEY, Emily Ann	13 Jan 1870	12
CROSS, Roger W	CAMPBELL, Julia Coles	9 Dec 1922	104
CROSS, William D	MCDONOUGH, Addie	2 Jan 1881	28
CROSS, William W	ALLDER, Eunice M	3 Jun 1914	86
CROSSMAN, George G	DODGE, Nellie M	7 Apr 1892	44
CROSSMAN, John M	HARNDEN, Anner F /wid	10 Oct 1877	22
CROUCH, Arthur V	BROOKS, Elizabeth M	21 Mar 1912	82
CROUCH, John J	BUCKLEY, Ida	17 Jan 1871	13
CROUCH, Ralph S	SMITH, Olive L	5 Sep 1900	59
CROUCH, S F	KINCHELOE, Jannie	13 Oct 1875	19
CROUCH, William A	WELLS, Susan	15 Apr 1869	11
CROWELL, Lawrence L	COCKERILLE, Mary Jane	15 Oct 1918	94
CROWELL, Michael	MULHOLLAND, Alice	16 Apr 1876	20
CROWELL, Thomas E	COCKERILLE, Ruby A	29 Jan 1913	84
CROWELL, Thomas E /wid	JENKINS, Alma J	9 Sep 1918	94
CROWLEY, Barney	TANSELL, Mary Ann	15 Jan 1866	6
CROWLEY, Franklin F /wid	WHITESIDE, Ruth N	6 Jun 1923	105
CROWLEY, Myles A /div	KIATTA, Marie /div	18 Nov 1933	144
CRUMBAUGH, Alfred R	AMBLER, Rita B	10 Jun 1933	142
CRUMBAUGH, Clark	BEAVERS, Lorena	17 Sep 1924	109
CRUMBAUGH, William C	MUNDAY, Bertha	7 Apr 1897	52
CRUMMEY, Thomas /c	LARKIN, Lottie /c	26 Nov 1902	63
CRUMP, Charles W	STUDDS, Harriet	- Feb 1856	2
CRUPPER, John S	WATKINS, Belle H	4 Apr 1877	22
CRUX, James	SWEENY, Gwinetta K	22 Oct 1872	15
CUDLIP, Frank /wid	MARTIN, Anna D	1 Aug 1930	129
CULINANE, John	FLINN, Ann	26 Jul 1868	9

CULLEMBER, Ernest B	WEAVER, Ethel M /wid	19 Aug 1922	*103*
CULLIN, John T	PEYTON, Annie E	4 Nov 1896	*51*
CULLISON, B Franklin	HARTLE, Gertrude E	6 Feb 1932	*136*
CUMBERLAND, Clarence C	CARRINGTON, Flora	20 Dec 1918	*95*
CUMBERLAND, J W	BACHELDER, Ada R /wid	2 Jun 1917	*92*
CUMBERLAND, John R /div	CRICKENBERGER, Anna M	19 Jul 1930	*128*
CUMMINGS, George W	THOMAS, Sarah A	5 May 1870	*12*
CUMMINGS, George W /wid	ROGERS, Maggie May	7 Oct 1896	*51*
CUMMINS, Charles F	DYER, Edith S	6 May 1896	*51*
CUMMINS, George W	STALLINGS, Sarah A	19 Jun 1866	*6*
CUMMINS, Henry /wid	MILSTEAD, Ida M /wid	1 Jul 1903	*64*
CUMMINS, Paul K	FOWLER, Ruth A	30 Mar 1918	*94*
CUNNINGHAM, Frederick B	MILLER, Etta V	25 Aug 1920	*98*
CUNNINGHAM, H F	MERRY, Catherine D	16 Apr 1907	*72*
CUNNINGHAM, Howard L	MILLARD, Vennie T	25 Mar 1888	*38*
CUNNINGHAM, Joseph P	MILLS, Mary L	2 Jan 1930	*127*
CUNNINGHAM, Neil	RYAN, Mabel St Clair	15 Nov 1913	*85*
CUNNINGHAM, R S	MONEY, Mary L	23 Dec 1885	*35*
CUNNINGHAM, Robert H	HODGKIN, Mary A	2 Mar 1875	*18*
CUNNINGHAM, Silas H	AMBLER, Ruby B	28 Apr 1909	*76*
CUNNINGHAM, William G	MILLER, Lenna K	15 Oct 1925	*112*
CURLEY, George W	WALTERS, Marietta V	11 Jun 1870	*12*
CURRY, George /c	BROOKS, Ellen /c	31 May 1874	*17*
CURRY, George /c	SMITH, Alice /c	9 Jul 1882	*30*
CURRY, Hobart /c	HARRIS, Sadie /c	10 May 1918	*94*
CURRY, Randolph /c	BRANNON, Annie /c	22 Jul 1879	*25*
CURRY, Spencer B /div	KRAEMER, Lillian E	29 Jan 1931	*131*
CURRY, William John	KINSLER, Willetta A	19 Sep 1931	*133*
CURTICE, Kolbe	AUD, Jeanne Louise	23 Oct 1917	*93*
CURTICE, Sanger C	DEMOSLAWSKA, Lillian Valeria	4 Jul 1922	*102*
CURTIS, Edwin F	THOMPSON, Barbara S	5 Mar 1885	*34*
CURTIS, James /c wid	PARKER, Martha /c	26 Aug 1880	*27*
CURTIS, Philip /c	LACKSEY, Lucretia /c	28 Dec 1880	*27*
CURTIS, Thomas	STEERS, Anna Maria	4 Sep 1855	*1*
CUSHMAN, Robert Asa /wid	MCLEOD, Emma Laura King /wid	1 Jul 1922	*102*
D'ARCY, D T	RUSH, Mary E	7 Jul 1923	*105*
DADE, Charles /c wid	SMITH, Eliza /c wid	14 Feb 1883	*31*
DADE, Nace /c wid	CLEMENTS, Harriet /c wid	24 Nov 1904	*67*
DADE, Thomas /c	WYATT, Minnie /c	6 Nov 1887	*38*
DADE, Thomas /c	WILSON, Florence /c	29 Dec 1908	*76*
DAIGER, Charles Walter	WHITING, Coral R	16 Feb 1925	*110*
DAILEY, Thomas J	FISCHER, Martha E	26 Jun 1926	*115*

DAILEY, W A	JAMESSON, Jean K	31 Dec 1867	8
DAILEY, Henry W	WOODS, Mary I	27 Jul 1921	101
DALTON, P S	CARPER, Ida B	2 Apr 1914	86
DALZIEL, Gilbert J	ROBEY, Hazel	28 Nov 1921	101
DANGERFIELD, Julian /c	JENKINS, Lillie /c	27 Jun 1930	128
DANGERFIELD, Lloyd M	FLAHERTY, Beatrice Marie	24 Nov 1933	144
DANIEL, Ellis	WILLIAMS, Rachel	8 Oct 1867	8
DANIEL, James Thomas	JERMAN, Annie B	17 Mar 1886	36
DANIEL, John Moncure Jr	MICON, Margaret	15 Dec 1908	76
DANIEL, Leonard P	DE PUTRON, Lillian C	12 Jun 1901	60
DANIEL, R L	AMORNETT, Dora	7 Jun 1911	81
DANIEL, Ray R	DANIEL, Lucy M	10 Nov 1923	106
DANIEL, William T	TRAMMELL, Alice	8 Dec 1881	29
DANIELS, George E /div	MARSHER, Emma V	2 Jan 1908	74
DANIELS, Henry L	DOVE, Mary	19 Apr 1897	52
DANIELS, Orlando H /wid	HODGKIN, Alice Jane	25 Dec 1898	55
DANIELS, Owen H	WILLINGHAM, Myrtle Woodrow	5 Jan 1933	141
DANIELS, William T /wid	BEACH, Susan	9 Apr 1868	9
DANLEY, Joseph W /wid	WAKEFIELD, Oneita G	7 Jun 1899	56
DARCAS, Daniel /wid	BENNETT, Angelina /wid	20 Apr 1868	15
DARCEY, Hiram H	BOARMAN, Florence T	19 Aug 1910	79
DARNE, Leonard Lee	DONALDSON, Florence Gray	29 Nov 1905	70
DARNE, Lorenzo	ALLEN, Alice	29 Jun 1904	66
DARNE, Nelson Page	WALKER, Mary N	26 Jun 1878	23
DARNE, Samuel W	BALL, Edith C	30 Mar 1904	66
DARNE, W Meade	FUNSTEN, Susie Meade	30 Sep 1869	11
DARR, James W	LLOYD, Rebecca A	13 Apr 1876	20
DARST, Thomas Campbell	WISE, Florence Newton	24 Jul 1902	63
DASHIEL, T Grayson	SPARROW, Wilhelmina	18 Jul 1854	1
DAVES, Lewis /c wid	WHEELER, Laura /c	6 Sep 1911	81
DAVIDSON, Clarkson W	LEISTER, Evelyn B	17 Feb 1932	136
DAVIDSON, Hunter	YIRKA, Anna T	18 Oct 1933	144
DAVIDSON, John C	CHICHESTER, Mary R	29 Nov 1889	40
DAVIDSON, William B	CRICKENBERGER, Helen	24 Dec 1930	130
DAVIES, Acquila C	HENDERSON, Vera B	1 Jan 1902	62
DAVIES, George M	CRIMMINS, Catherine L	7 Oct 1907	73
DAVIES, George U	DUNN, Mary E	19 Dec 1931	135
DAVIS, Albert Maurice	ADAMS, Josephine B	29 Dec 1925	113
DAVIS, Arthur	CATON, Sallie D	30 Dec 1884	34
DAVIS, Benjamin F	STEELE, Ann M	24 May 1899	56
DAVIS, Calvin H	LEWIS, Amanda E	12 Feb 1891	43
DAVIS, Charles Frederick	DODSON, Ellen	5 May 1881	28

DAVIS, Clarence W	HOFFMASTER, Camille R	7 Jan 1929	*124*
DAVIS, Claude W	FAIRFAX, Mary C	5 Jul 1905	*69*
DAVIS, Clifton	FLOYD, Margaret M	22 Aug 1925	*112*
DAVIS, Cover N	SMITH, Adria M	27 Jun 1925	*111*
DAVIS, Daniel E	COMPTON, Virginia	12 Mar 1911	*80*
DAVIS, Edward L	TYRELL, Ella L	28 Jun 1913	*84*
DAVIS, Francis E	MARSHALL, Mary A	23 Dec 1875	*19*
DAVIS, Fred M	DENTY, Annie L	9 Apr 1890	*41*
DAVIS, George C	COMPTON, Lucy	22 Apr 1903	*64*
DAVIS, George Jr /wid	LEWIS, Jane S /wid	17 Jun 1886	*36*
DAVIS, George Samuel	PLASKETT, Mary E	10 May 1899	*56*
DAVIS, Gilbert B	GREENLEASE, Beulah F	7 Jun 1903	*64*
DAVIS, H M /wid	ARUNDLE, Ann V	23 Mar 1870	*12*
DAVIS, Haywood	STONE, Fanny F	24 Dec 1867	*8*
DAVIS, Haywood /wid	ROSENHAMMER, Theresa C	12 Dec 1894	*48*
DAVIS, Henry	WOODYARD, Mary J	14 Dec 1893	*47*
DAVIS, Henry E /wid	DAVIS, Catharine	6 Jan 1870	*11*
DAVIS, Henry E /wid	LEWIS, Kate	7 Feb 1895	*49*
DAVIS, Henry T	WOODYARD, Eva V	21 Aug 1901	*60*
DAVIS, Herman W	OTTERBACK, Emma J	7 Jun 1877	*22*
DAVIS, Irving	JAMES, Virginia E	26 Dec 1932	*140*
DAVIS, James B	FORCE, Edna	15 Feb 1893	*46*
DAVIS, James F	GARNER, Harriet E	19 Dec 1865	*6*
DAVIS, James T J	TALBERT, Hazel Elizabeth	17 Nov 1926	*116*
DAVIS, John A	BRADLEY, Catharine H	3 Dec 1868	*10*
DAVIS, John A	MARSHALL, Nona E	26 Dec 1902	*65*
DAVIS, John C /wid	WHALEY, Alice L	20 Aug 1879	*25*
DAVIS, John F	MAYHUGH, Fanny A	27 Dec 1882	*31*
DAVIS, John F	MAYHUGH, Laura L	10 Apr 1888	*38*
DAVIS, John F	CURRIER, Rosa L	29 Sep 1909	*77*
DAVIS, John H	TAYLOR, Elizabeth	13 Nov 1860	*5*
DAVIS, John H /c	CROSBY, Mary E /c	27 Dec 1887	*42*
DAVIS, John H	MOORE, Zerita O	1 Jul 1922	*102*
DAVIS, John I	THOMPSON, Lottie A	12 Oct 1897	*53*
DAVIS, John Nicholas	NEWMAN, Josephine	30 Jan 1932	*136*
DAVIS, John W	BAYLISS, Sarah	3 Nov 1868	*10*
DAVIS, Kenneth I	WADDELL, Elizabeth E	10 Dec 1932	*140*
DAVIS, Lemuel J /wid	MALEY, Nellie V	25 Dec 1922	*104*
DAVIS, Lovell M	BRADLEY, Mary L	30 Jan 1894	*47*
DAVIS, Lucien	FAIRFAX, Ada	25 Dec 1898	*55*
DAVIS, M Van B	WOODYARD, Nancy Ann	6 Jan 1859	*4*
DAVIS, Mahlon M	MARSHALL, May V	25 Dec 1907	*74*

DAVIS, Marshall /c	BECTON, Mag /c	23 Jul 1905	69
DAVIS, Marshall /c wid	SUMMERS, Amelia /c wid	18 Feb 1920	97
DAVIS, Marshall Earl	HAISLIP, Margaret Louise	29 Oct 1919	96
DAVIS, Matthew	DAVIS, Ann E	4 Sep 1855	1
DAVIS, Matthew C	HAMILTON, Kate M	30 Jan 1889	39
DAVIS, Meredith R	MAKELY, Grace S	18 Jan 1927	117
DAVIS, Millard F	HOOD, Myrtle B	14 Nov 1916	91
DAVIS, Moses	LEE, Alice	31 Dec 1868	10
DAVIS, Oliver S	WOODYARD, Emma J	31 Dec 1879	26
DAVIS, Persival F	DAVIS, Sarah C	6 Nov 1890	42
DAVIS, Philip A	FAULKNER, Mary E	27 Apr 1880	26
DAVIS, R M	MAYHUGH, H V	10 Feb 1881	28
DAVIS, R M	DAVIS, Huldah J	9 Oct 1881	29
DAVIS, R Morrison	HAMPTON, Nellie C	18 Apr 1931	131
DAVIS, Raymond A	BROWN, Margaret Ellen	27 Apr 1929	124
DAVIS, Redmond	DAVIS, Harriet L	25 Dec 1884	34
DAVIS, Reginald F	GILL, Rosie E	27 Mar 1910	78
DAVIS, Richard M /wid	DAVIS, Idella F	17 Oct 1894	48
DAVIS, Robert F	MAYHUGH, Rena	29 Dec 1892	45
DAVIS, Roy E /wid	SESSIONS, Maude	15 Nov 1930	130
DAVIS, Samuel /c	JACKSON, Fannie /c	26 Sep 1878	24
DAVIS, Samuel Arthur	WRIGHT, Julia Elizabeth	1 Aug 1920	98
DAVIS, Thaddeus	MAYHUGH, Ella L	27 Dec 1893	47
DAVIS, W A	KEYS, F V	21 Dec 1882	31
DAVIS, W W	POWELL, Hazel M	1 Mar 1915	88
DAVIS, Wallace /c	WRIGHT, Irene /c	16 Jun 1917	92
DAVIS, Warren I	ROWELL, Mary R	20 Jun 1925	111
DAVIS, William C	MARTIN, Mollie	7 Jun 1905	68
DAVIS, William D	ARUNDLE, Mary F	21 Dec 1855	1
DAVIS, William Humphrey /c	DAY, Sarah Isabella /c	22 Oct 1878	24
DAVIS, Willie /c	GIBSON, Adeline /c	10 Dec 1905	70
DAVIS, Wilmer	DAVIS, Mary S	25 Dec 1877	23
DAW, George Wilson	WINE, Carrie Lee	6 Oct 1921	101
DAWSON, Eldridge A	SMALLWOOD, Mary Ellen	23 Dec 1875	19
DAWSON, Henry C	STEERS, Margaret E	29 Sep 1870	13
DAWSON, J W	YOUNG, Hattie	16 Aug 1892	45
DAWSON, James T	NELSON, Roberta L	9 Apr 1884	33
DAWSON, John E	HALL, Jennie B	24 Dec 1926	117
DAWSON, John W	COCKERILLE, Ada M	27 Sep 1876	20
DAWSON, Nicholas	COOPER, Virginia M	28 Oct 1873	16
DAWSON, William H /wid	ROBEY, Jennie H	11 Dec 1907	74
DAY, Alexander /c	VASS, Ella /c	18 Oct 1894	48

DAY, Allie E /wid	DEAN, Katie E	10 Oct 1899	57
DAY, Faust	SLACK, Gertrude Aurelia	29 Oct 1902	63
DAY, Frank /c	DIXON, Lucy /c	9 Jun 1887	38
DAY, Robert E Jr	GOSWELL, Margaret E	23 Dec 1926	117
DAY, Robert F	LANGSTON, Eleanor	8 Oct 1929	126
DAY, William Benjamin	YATES, Ruth V	30 Jan 1926	113
DE BELL, John T	TURBERVILLE, Mary C	7 Jan 1914	86
DE BRIM, Louis	CATON, Mary Estelle	6 Oct 1923	106
DE BUCK, Clyde E	MAKELY, Virginia L	7 Sep 1922	103
DE BUTTS, S Wesley	BOHRER, Ruth E	11 Apr 1914	86
DE CHANNY, Pierre /wid	ERASO, Cecile	28 Jul 1925	112
DE COSS, J W	CROUCH, Elzira	17 Oct 1877	22
DE GIULIAN, Attilie Peter	AYRE, Inez A	26 Dec 1931	135
DE PUTRON, Jacob C	SHERWOOD, Mary E	26 Apr 1866	6
DE VENISH, Oliver W /wid	POOLE, Edith W /wid	27 Dec 1933	145
DE YOUNG, Daniel	KELLY, Helen	4 Dec 1922	104
DEAN, Alfred R	TRAMMELL, Bertha V	7 Oct 1929	126
DEAN, Elwood J	WILLIAMS, Rena Virginia	8 Sep 1928	122
DEAN, James D /c	SMITH, Lillian A /c	3 Jul 1901	60
DEAN, John /wid	HARROVER, Frances	26 Nov 1874	17
DEAN, John A	DEAVERS, P A	5 Feb 1874	17
DEAN, John Edward	DANIELS, Hattie	16 Oct 1906	71
DEAN, Morris /c	MARTIN, Mary /c	1 Dec 1897	53
DEAN, Robert A	DUNBAR, Alice L	11 Aug 1923	105
DEAN, William E	GARVY, Annie C	2 Dec 1886	37
DEARDORFF, Clair B	HOSTELLER, LaRue	15 Feb 1930	127
DEATS, William	ENNIS, Lillian	27 Nov 1906	72
DEAVERS, Albert	BEAVERS, Edith	17 Jun 1932	138
DEAVERS, Barny	HALL, Mary J	5 Aug 1866	6
DEAVERS, Benjamin F	CRAGG, Lizzie H	4 Nov 1880	27
DEAVERS, Edward E	CLAIR, Mamie E	10 Nov 1900	59
DEAVERS, George Otis	JAVINS, Rebecca	28 Oct 1903	70
DEAVERS, Hiram	JOHNSTON, Virginia	22 Jun 1875	18
DEAVERS, Ira	LYLES, Elizabeth /wid	31 Jan 1867	7
DEAVERS, Lafayette	DEAVERS, Osie R	2 May 1901	60
DEAVERS, Lambert	DEAN, Emma	3 Dec 1895	50
DEAVERS, Lewis E	WILLIAMSON, Ruth	30 Apr 1885	35
DEAVERS, Lewis E /div	PETTIT, Anna J	2 Jul 1891	43
DEAVERS, Simeon	TAYLOR, Effie May	6 Feb 1902	62
DEAVERS, Theo E	OWENS, Nellie	24 Apr 1926	114
DEAVERS, Thomas	SIMMS, Ann V	15 Jan 1860	4
DEAVERS, Uriah	TYLER, Susanna	26 Jul 1857	3

DECKER, Andrew J	HOLLISTER, Mary C	5 Jan 1854	*1*
DELAMARTER, De Witt C	MILLER, Ella	7 Dec 1886	*37*
DELANEY, Rufus /c	COOK, Laura T /c	18 Nov 1880	*27*
DELLA, Edward L /div	LUDERS, Bertie M /div	13 Apr 1928	*121*
DELOZIER, Walter E	LANDMAN, Lydia	9 Mar 1925	*110*
DEMORY, Fred J	MOCK, Mabel R	12 Sep 1931	*133*
DEMORY, Roger A	REID, Rowena M	30 May 1931	*132*
DEMPSEY, Ed Leith	HARRIS, Daisy Dean /wid	24 Oct 1925	*112*
DEMPSEY, John T	SUMNER, Charlotte	30 May 1931	*132*
DENISON, Charles A	PEARSON, Simie	16 Dec 1878	*24*
DENNY, Anthony /c	WILLIAMS, Cora /c	14 Dec 1899	*57*
DENNY, Raymond /c	PARKER, Julia /c	8 Jun 1927	*118*
DENNY, Roland /c	HUNTER, Madge /c	31 Mar 1925	*111*
DENT, Edgar M	HUTCHISON, Maggie	24 Sep 1907	*73*
DENT, Edgar M /wid	MOORE, Oga	19 Oct 1911	*81*
DENT, Mackwood H	BROOKS, Eva R	29 Sep 1909	*77*
DENTON, Nathaniel W	DUNCAN, Ruby A	11 Oct 1905	*69*
DENTY, Luther A	VIOLETT, Maud	9 Aug 1899	*57*
DENTY, Simeon	ROTCHFORD, Janapher P	27 Apr 1873	*16*
DESKINS, Hiram T	QUICK, S Christine	20 Jul 1910	*79*
DESKINS, Rippin	LEE, Eliza	10 Jul 1870	*13*
DESKINS, Robert /c	SIMMS, Nettie E /c	22 Dec 1898	*55*
DESKINS, William H /c	THORNTON, Lucy E /c	6 Nov 1895	*50*
DETWILER, Benjamin B	ROTCHFORD, Roberta L	22 Oct 1890	*42*
DETWILER, Daniel L	THOMPSON, Thelma L	21 Oct 1925	*112*
DETWILER, Frank /div	MITCHELL, Sarah J /wid	12 Oct 1933	*144*
DETWILER, John H	MOORE, Margaret A	1 Feb 1899	*56*
DETWILER, John L	LEWIS, Amanda E	20 Dec 1923	*107*
DETWILER, Oscar L	FAIRFAX, Annie F	28 Mar 1900	*58*
DETWILER, Wilbur B	FORESTER, Catherine F	27 Oct 1929	*126*
DEUTERMANN, Charles Jr	CLEVELAND, Carrie Virginia	17 Feb 1919	*95*
DEUTERMANN, William B	BILLSBOROUGH, Irene Gladys	2 Sep 1920	*98*
DEVEREUX, Francis N	GHEEN, Caroline E	1 May 1866	*6*
DEWEY, Albert A	FAIRFAX, Rebecca Ann	25 Nov 1858	*4*
DEWEY, Alton J	MILLS, Sarah F	28 Dec 1880	*27*
DEWEY, David C	JAVINS, Bessie A	2 Jun 1920	*98*
DEWEY, L A	SISSON, Alma E	18 Jun 1913	*84*
DEY, Edward S	JARRETT, Elizabeth M	12 Oct 1898	*55*
DEY, Winfield S	HARRISON, Lucy W	25 Dec 1900	*59*
DI DOMANICO, John	SULLENS, Ruth N	2 Oct 1931	*134*
DI VECCHIA, Frederick	LORIA, Ann Barbara	27 May 1927	*118*
DICKENS, Leslie R L	MURRAY, Margaret Lee	22 Dec 1910	*80*

DICKENSON, Thomas B	PIERCY, Marion W /wid	28 Feb 1926	*114*
DICKERSON, Frederick /wid	WEBB, Blanche /wid	29 Aug 1909	*77*
DICKEY, J N	GRIMES, Sarah E	15 Jun 1882	*30*
DICKEY, John Victor	DANIELS, Marion E	14 Apr 1933	*142*
DICKEY, Ray E	TURNER, Bertie	11 Dec 1924	*110*
DIGGS, John M /c	PENDLETON, Annie /c	14 Sep 1876	*20*
DIGGS, Roscoe A	FOX, Louise S	5 Oct 1931	*134*
DIGGS, Thomas /c	BAILEY, Alice /c	26 Jan 1882	*29*
DILL, Norman B	JOINES, Jettie E	13 Mar 1929	*124*
DILLON, William L	BROWN, Melva	4 Nov 1911	*81*
DIMSEY, Charles W	FRIDDELL, Eva J	18 Oct 1882	*30*
DIMSEY, Charles W /wid	KIDWELL, Sallie	5 Jun 1895	*49*
DIMSEY, George Frank	KIDWELL, Lillie	8 Mar 1883	*31*
DIMSEY, Guy Otis	COCKERILLE, Pearl Elizabeth	22 Oct 1919	*96*
DINGES, William H	HUNSBERGER, Annie M	17 Oct 1907	*73*
DISNEY, Lewis H	CRAGGS, Sally J	5 Feb 1879	*24*
DIXON, Alfred /c	HONESTY, Virginia /c	14 Oct 1897	*53*
DIXON, Ernest /c	BALL, Mary /c	21 Nov 1900	*59*
DIXON, Henry /c	THOMAS, Mary /c	11 Jun 1889	*40*
DIXON, Henry /c wid	WILLIAMS, Lue /c wid	24 Dec 1899	*57*
DIXON, Turner /c wid	BRADLEY, Martha /c wid	24 Feb 1891	*43*
DOBLERE, Eugene W	RIVERS, Augustine C	5 Aug 1932	*138*
DOBSON, Charles /c	JOHNSON, Rachael /c	6 Mar 1871	*15*
DOBSON, J Fielder	LATCHFORD, Debbie	12 Sep 1883	*32*
DOBSON, William M	PETTITT, Phebe A	26 Mar 1879	*25*
DOCKSTAEDER, Arthur B (alias Arthur B BARRINGER) /div			
	STAATS, Clara V	26 Oct 1907	*73*
DODD, F Frank	SMITH, Catherine L	30 Jun 1909	*77*
DODD, J Mosley	HEAD, Rose A	19 Apr 1900	*58*
DODD, Luther Alexander	GODFREY, Sallie Elta	29 May 1905	*68*
DODD, Luther C	PEARSON, Artie B	18 Dec 1912	*83*
DODD, William Howard	PETTITT, Virginia Ellen	27 Jun 1931	*132*
DODSON, Albert	SHEPHERD, Myrtle	23 Aug 1906	*71*
DODSON, Christopher C	HALL, Melvina	24 Dec 1885	*35*
DODSON, Jacob /c	WILLIAMS, Katherine /c	14 Apr 1925	*111*
DODSON, James	KING, Ruth	26 Oct 1923	*106*
DODSON, James E	BARKER, Virginia C	7 Aug 1929	*125*
DODSON, John T	DEAVERS, Sarah	26 Sep 1857	*3*
DODSON, M A	MCWEEDON, Alice J	21 Jan 1886	*36*
DODSON, Ollie J	DOOLEY, Ella	2 Nov 1906	*71*
DODSON, Osha	BERLO, Lillian D /div	2 Jul 1925	*112*
DODSON, S E	SIMPSON, Lena	20 Dec 1906	*72*

DODSON, W W /wid	REID, Anna A	24 Dec 1872	15
DODSON, Walter	HARROVER, Sarah	1 May 1865	6
DODSON, Walter	DEAVERS, Lucy	28 May 1930	128
DODSON, William	TAYLOR, Ella J	27 Sep 1894	48
DODSON, William S	HALL, Eva V	12 Sep 1925	112
DODSON, William W /wid	YOUNG, Mary J	10 Sep 1895	49
DOELGER, Richard J	DOHERTY, Eileen Martha	6 May 1933	142
DOLLY, Lawrence B	UTTERBACK, Minnie F	18 Mar 1912	82
DONALDSON, Armistead M	BIRCH, Mildred J	20 Jan 1870	12
DONALDSON, Edward	REID, Estelle	12 Mar 1924	108
DONALDSON, J M	WALKER, Kate	27 Dec 1882	31
DONALDSON, Martin F	SHREVE, Martha A	24 Mar 1868	9
DONALDSON, Wilber Franklin	BOUCHER, Alma	19 Apr 1905	68
DONALDSON, William E	BEAVER, Olive Irene	4 Dec 1920	99
DONALDSON, Willis	LENT, Maggie I	14 Mar 1914	86
DONEY, Carletos H /div	FULLER, Edna L	21 Oct 1933	144
DONOHOE, C E	AYRES, Mattie S	6 Jan 1870	11
DONOHOE, Stephen Roszel /wid	MOORE, Susan L	20 May 1884	37
DONOHOE, William F	MURTAUGH, Rose	6 Jun 1906	71
DONOVAN, James A	HAWKINS, Dortha V	6 Feb 1932	136
DOOLEY, Joseph W	TRUMBLE, Jane	9 Nov 1881	29
DOOLEY, Joseph W Jr	THOMPSON, Minnie E	30 Jun 1915	88
DOOLEY, Timothy L	FLOWERS, Eva Rebecca	8 Jun 1917	92
DORDEN, Dave /c	FREST, Elorna /c	14 Apr 1933	142
DORION, Emile A	JONES, E Dora	21 Oct 1933	144
DORSEY, Basil /c	STUART, Elizabeth /c	14 Jul 1881	28
DORSEY, C W /wid	GHEEN, Virginia /wid	9 Oct 1898	56
DORSEY, Charles W /c	HONESTY, Mary /c	8 Sep 1892	45
DORSEY, Ira /c	JOHNSON, Hattie M /c wid	4 Dec 1920	99
DORSEY, R B	AYRE, M L	27 Jan 1881	28
DOTERY, Charles /c	HOLLAND, Cora /c	9 Jan 1906	70
DOTSON, Francis T /c wid	DAVIS, Pocohontas /c	24 Dec 1874	18
DOTSON, John /c	EDMUNDS, Vidie /c	25 Dec 1876	21
DOUGLAS, George /c wid	BOTTS, Julia /c	27 Dec 1877	23
DOUGLAS, Robert B	RICHARDSON, Madge H	26 Apr 1876	20
DOVE, A K	DEAVERS, Lizzie	26 Noc 1884	34
DOVE, Charles F	MILLS, Laura S	30 Oct 1893	47
DOVE, Charles L	DEAVERS, Rebecca A /wid	2 Mar 1903	64
DOVE, Earl F	CLEM, Marguerite E	28 Nov 1928	123
DOVE, Fenton D	WELLS, Caroline	23 Dec 1865	6
DOVE, Fenton D /wid	HITCHCOCK, Rebecca	4 Aug 1886	36
DOVE, H E	KERNS, Nellie M	14 Jul 1912	82

DOVE, Halley C	COLE, Ellen E	23 Dec 1919	*97*
DOVE, Howard	BIGGS, Sadie	25 Jun 1919	*96*
DOVE, Hugh Fletcher	DODSON, Agnes C	25 Apr 1932	*137*
DOVE, James H	TRUMBLE, Dollie	30 Jul 1924	*109*
DOVE, Jether	THOMPSON, Edna Lee	3 Dec 1918	*95*
DOVE, John	POOL, Ann E	27 Mar 1860	*5*
DOVE, Kenneth	CAMPBELL, Myrtle	26 May 1917	*92*
DOVE, M L	GOODSPEED, Loretta	30 Dec 1913	*85*
DOVE, Mack Edward	MONCH, Ethel Vetura	26 Sep 1923	*106*
DOVE, Robert H	BURGESS, Blanche /div	16 Dec 1915	*89*
DOVE, Robert H /wid	TRUMBLE, Bessie	22 Feb 1923	*104*
DOVE, Samuel	DANIELS, Mary E	29 Dec 1869	*11*
DOVE, Samuel Lufton	TAYLOR, Mamie V	14 Feb 1905	*68*
DOVE, Sylva V	BELLER, Barbara E	20 May 1925	*111*
DOVE, Thomas	NEWMAN, Lydia	1 Aug 1878	*23*
DOVE, W E	BEACH, Sarah Jane	1 Nov 1906	*71*
DOW, Scott Heisey	KNAPP, Brenda	24 Jun 1925	*111*
DOWDEN, Emmett D	ANDERSON, Susie Lee	6 Feb 1931	*131*
DOWDEN, Lemuel T	CAMP, Maud H	13 Feb 1901	*60*
DOWDEN, Russell C /wid	WHALEY, Alma O	19 Mar 1924	*108*
DOWELL, Ernest L	SMITH, Mildred E	10 Jun 1908	*75*
DOWNING, F Winslow /c	JONES, Lucinda A /c	30 Nov 1908	*76*
DOWNS, Aubrey L /wid	WILTSHIRE, Edna Lee	30 Oct 1929	*126*
DOWNS, George	WRENN, Florence E	25 Jul 1893	*46*
DOWNS, Henry /wid	CLEM, Dora Violett /wid	29 May 1933	*142*
DOWNS, James R	SHERWOOD, Gladys L	28 Apr 1925	*111*
DOYLE, Carl M	LYLES, Leon	16 Mar 1922	*102*
DOYLE, R C	NEWELL, Elizabeth C	7 Nov 1916	*91*
DRAKE, Clarence H	KEYS, Ida	15 Oct 1879	*25*
DRAKE, Reginald P	SANDERS, Maude	4 Nov 1908	*75*
DRANE, B D	ASHFORD, S	2 Jul 1857	*3*
DREW, Richard H /c	COATS, Malinda /c	30 Dec 1897	*54*
DRIGGERS, Jackson	WOOSTER, Jennie R	9 Oct 1901	*61*
DRISCHLER, Carl S	MOORE, Rebecca L	26 Jul 1922	*103*
DRISH, G W	SUIT, Ethel I	12 Nov 1923	*106*
DRITLER, Carl L	JOHNSON, Ruby C /div	3 Jul 1930	*128*
DRYDEN, Martin T	BRASHEARS, Bessie	17 Jun 1905	*69*
DUDLEY, Edward B	REMSBURG, Pansy B	7 Jan 1906	*70*
DUDLEY, Philip Dana	LEE, Winifred F	20 Mar 1924	*108*
DUERSON, Lawrence S /wid	DOYLE, Beulah Virginia	14 Apr 1931	*131*
DUFF, Edward E	CECIL, Gertrude G	11 Oct 1932	*139*
DUFF, Guy Rush	HOCKMAN, Doris Evelyn	6 Feb 1932	*136*

DUFFIELD, Andrew J /c	MARSHALL, Luana /c	15 Jul 1925	*112*
DUGAN, Robert A	CROWN, Margaret /wid	15 Feb 1921	*100*
DULEY, William C	MOONEY, Lucie Ann	19 Feb 1879	*25*
DULIN, Ralph F	WILLIS, Louise V	12 Mar 1927	*117*
DUNBAR, Henry Steiner Jr	RANDOLPH, Margaret Duncan	2 Nov 1926	*116*
DUNCAN, Allen	WILLIAMS, Bertie	7 Nov 1922	*103*
DUNCAN, Cain /c wid	EWELL, Nannie /c	15 Apr 1896	*50*
DUNCAN, Gabriel /c	HARRIS, Bettie /c	31 Jan 1923	*104*
DUNCAN, McKinley /c	PORTER, Nealy /c	30 Nov 1916	*91*
DUNCAN, Robert /c	SCOTT, Bernice /c	27 Jan 1926	*113*
DUNCAN, William /c	COOK, Eassie /c	31 Dec 1879	*26*
DUNDAS, Samuel /c	MURRAY, Rosa B /c	25 Jun 1913	*84*
DUNDAS, Walter William /c	JACKSON, Lillian /c	22 Nov 1921	*101*
DUNDORE, Harry A Jr	GREEN, Marion L	7 Mar 1931	*131*
DUNN, C M	GARNER, Helen L	8 Oct 1927	*119*
DUNN, Charles Livingston	VINCENT, Virginia Louise	3 Oct 1931	*134*
DUNN, Elbert M	TAYLOR, Julia M	23 Feb 1920	*97*
DUNN, Frank Otis	GROSECLOSE, Elizabeth P	23 Jun 1923	*105*
DUNN, James F Jr	MITCHELL, Emma V	30 Apr 1932	*137*
DUNN, Martin H	TAYLOR, Dora C	18 Feb 1897	*52*
DUNN, Martin H /wid	DEAVERS, Lizzie A /wid	26 Jul 1924	*109*
DUNNE, Paul Raoul	RYAN, Madeline E	20 Mar 1933	*141*
DUNN, Thomas DeWitt	BIDDISON, Elva Dell	27 May 1922	*102*
DURBIN, Joseph W	CHENOWETH, Elsie M	17 Mar 1931	*131*
DUSON, William /c	SMITH, Janine B /c	26 Apr 1923	*105*
DUSON, William /c wid	STEWART, Mary /c wid	9 Apr 1930	*127*
DUTROW, Charles G	ROGERS, Birdie E	29 Oct 1884	*33*
DUTROW, J H	NEWMAN, Virginia	4 May 1879	*25*
DUTROW, J T	READSHAW, Mrs. L A or A L /wid	22 Feb 1887	*37*
DUVALL, Frank E	PALMER, Virginia R	18 Jun 1907	*73*
DUVALL, James G	JACOBS, Sadie D	21 Aug 1919	*96*
DUVALL, Peter W	DOWNING, Esther	4 Sep 1929	*125*
DWYER, Thomas	LACY, Ella V	24 Dec 1919	*97*
DYCUS, Charles Baxter /wid	WHITACRE, Elizabeth Luke	16 Mar 1926	*114*
DYER, Asa (John Asa)	BRYANT, Minnie	19 Dec 1894	*48*
DYER, Fred H	GIBSON, Mamie	27 Dec 1911	*82*
DYER, Hammond L	KIDWELL, Goldie A	17 Nov 1920	*99*
DYER, Herbert	FOLLIN, Ann E	22 Dec 1891	*44*
DYER, John /wid	FAIRFAX, Virginia C	2 Nov 1856	*2*
DYER, John C /wid	THOMPSON, Sallie /wid	13 Sep 1900	*59*
DYSON, James T	BURROUGHS, Emma J	25 Aug 1915	*89*
EADIE, Thomas	WATKINS, Janet	15 Apr 1932	*137*

EAGER, Thomas Haywood	CUMBERLAND, Elizabeth Mae	29 Dec 1933	*145*
EAGLE, Robert E	BUTTS, Ruth E	3 Apr 1926	*114*
EARLE, Charles Thomas /wid	WOODARD, Marion E	25 Nov 1914	*87*
EARLY, Howard H /c	PYLES, Katherine C /c	31 Dec 1928	*123*
EARLY, Winston	GOLDEN, Sarah	22 Dec 1868	*10*
EASLEY, George Gilmer	MASON, Josephine Beverly	15 Oct 1916	*91*
EASTERWOOD, Henry W	CHAUNCEY, Nettie H	28 Sep 1921	*101*
EATON, Allen /c wid	MURRAY, Pearl /c	20 Aug 1932	*138*
EATON, Leonard F /wid	POLTON, Emma R	20 Apr 1927	*118*
EATON, N A Jr	MILLER, Gladys	29 Oct 1927	*119*
EATON, Samuel J	THOMPSON, Ruth E	15 Mar 1911	*80*
EBAUGH, Paul	CARRILL, Elizabeth M	28 May 1932	*137*
ECHOLS, John Warnock /div	HINE, Katrina	10 Oct 1906	*71*
ECKER, Samuel E	DORSEY, Helen E	31 Jan 1929	*124*
EDGE, Charles N	REYNOLDS, Elsie E	4 Sep 1926	*115*
EDINGER, Samuel O	FLETCHER, Elvira J	5 Mar 1902	*62*
EDMONDS, William Fitzhugh	NOWLAN, Maud Moss	18 May 1907	*73*
EDMONDSON, Henry W	SPENCER, Dora A	4 Jun 1921	*100*
EDMONDSON, Thomas L	SUMNER, Pearl G	5 Sep 1928	*122*
EDMUNDS, Philip M	SLADE, Salina M	25 Oct 1877	*22*
EDWARDS, Abraham /c	LEE, Hannah /c	16 Apr 1874	*17*
EDWARDS, Albert J	CRITZER, Doris E	15 Oct 1930	*130*
EDWARDS, Charles L T	FLAGG, Aveline I	20 Mar 1918	*94*
EDWARDS, Henry /c	DIXON, Georgie /c	27 Dec 1883	*32*
EDWARDS, James William	JENKINS, Mary Jane	19 Jan 1881	*28*
EDWARDS, John W	MOORE, Irene B	14 Jun 1917	*92*
EDWARDS, Joseph R /div	CATON, Pearl E	2 Apr 1924	*108*
EDWARDS, Paul L	STANDISH, Olive R	17 Feb 1932	*136*
EDWARDS, Russell F	VAN VOORHIS, Anna E	17 Jul 1926	*115*
EDWARDS, Samuel Erwin	MANVELL, Dorothy Cecilia	25 Feb 1933	*141*
EDWARDS, Taylor E /c	POWELL, Carrie E /c	27 Aug 1914	*87*
EELLS, Rev. Edward Jr	AUCKMOODY, Annie	24 Dec 1891	*44*
EGGLESTON, J D	LE MAT, Eugenia	5 Jan 1923	*104*
EGLIN, Benjamin	THOMAS, Annie	18Dec 1872	*15*
EICHELBERGER, J Elmer	STRAYER, May L	24 Dec 1933	*145*
EISENBEISS, Adolph J	NYMAN, Vienna M	26 Jul 1900	*58*
ELMORE, Derrill G	HARTIG, Katherine	20 Aug 1917	*92*
ELLMORE, Samuel F	COCKERILLE, Mary E	21 Dec 1869	*11*
ELLMORE, W H	MIDDLETON, Minnie H	16 Nov 1904	*67*
ELDRED, Byron E /div	BRATTON, Mary L /wid	22 Apr 1911	*80*
ELGIN, Charles M	BEACH, Zarah	27 Jan 1859	*4*
ELGIN, Charles T	JACKSON, Laura R	26 Jan 1892	*44*

ELGIN, James C	SMITH, Pauline	30 May 1917	92
ELGIN, John W /wid	DAVIS, Bettie	11 Dec 1906	72
ELITON, T H	EINSTEIN, Kate	28 Dec 1917	93
ELLIOTT, Anderson /c	SIMPSON, Catherine /c	21 May 1874	17
ELLIOTT, John N	GARRETT, Fannie	3 Jun 1895	49
ELLIOTT, Joseph C	HARRISON, Martha E	9 Dec 1873	16
ELLIOTT, Robert B	LANDICK, Ruth E	4 Aug 1930	129
ELLIOTT, Sargent Charlton	STEPHENS, Ruth Elizabeth	6 Nov 1920	99
ELLIS, Benjamin /wid	MATHERS, Catharine /wid	21 Sep 1855	1
ELLIS, Benjamin /c	COOPER, Amanda /c	11 Oct 1896	51
ELLIS, Benjamin /c	HENRY, Evelyn /c	17 Apr 1915	88
ELLIS, Benjamin F	JAVINS, Ada V	28 Dec 1870	13
ELLIS, Charles /c	BROWN, Jennie /c	19 Feb 1929	124
ELLIS, Claude /c	WHITE, Lydia /c	14 Nov 1907	74
ELLIS, Henry L /wid	LLOYD, Elizabeth	29 Aug 1858	3
ELLIS, James B	LEWIS, Mary J	12 Jan 1882	29
ELLIS, John H	LEWIS, Cora A	20 Jan 1881	28
ELLIS, Joseph /c	PAGE, Ida /c	15 Aug 1929	125
ELLIS, Joshua /wid	WATKINS, Mary C /wid	22 Jun 1892	45
ELLIS, Orrison C	JERMAN, Mary L	1 Mar 1887	37
ELLIS, Samuel /c	BOWIE, Emma J /c wid	9 Jan 1929	124
ELLIS, Solomon /c	SIMMS, Eliza /c	15 Feb 1896	50
ELLIS, Walter H	BEATTIE, Pauline	4 Apr 1923	105
ELLISON, Frederick K	SCHNEIDER, Pauline K	22 Dec 1923	107
ELLISON, William M	BALL, Lillian	21 Nov 1883	32
ELLSWORTH, Clarence J	RIDGEWAY, Edna B	12 Aug 1931	133
ELLZEY, Millard Fillmore /c div	BUTLER, Carrie /c	26 Nov 1892	45
ELMS, Howard	MYERS, Blanch	11 Jun 1922	102
ELTING, Philip L F /wid	WATKINS, Olive C	25 Apr 1885	35
EMIGH, Jerome S	LYDECKER, Lavinia	2 Jan 1869	10
EMIGH, Thomas /wid	CURTIS, Harriet C	16 May 1860	5
ENGLISH, Garland	HILL, Louise /wid	2 Sep 1931	133
ENGLISH, George H	KERNS, Kate M	24 Jun 1907	73
ENNES, William	SYSSOCK, Fannie	7 Sep 1890	41
ENNIS, Charles	PENDLETON, Lillie A	29 Nov 1892	45
ENNIS, Middleton Smoot	WILEY, Catherine M	20 Jun 1894	48
ENNIS, William J	LACEY, Alma	20 Feb 1926	114
EPPARD, William T	LACEY, Mary Helen	27 Dec 1933	145
EPPES, Charles Henry	RICHARDSON, Rose	26 Jul 1911	81
ERSKINE, George E	GARNER, Jennie A	25 Dec 1915	89
ERWIN, George L	ELLIOTT, Ida R	31 Oct 1900	59
ESHLEMAN, Walter B	THOMPSON, Virginia E	15 Jun 1927	118

ESTES, William W	TAVENNER, Mary E /wid	8 Mar 1929	124
ETTER, Joseph	HALL, Frances	11 Jul 1931	132
EVANS, Charles S /wid	LUDLOW, Phebe A	8 Jan 1890	41
EVANS, Daniel R	CRUMP, Hattie C	30 Jan 1877	21
EVANS, E D	LINDAWOOD, Birtie F	21 Mar 1910	78
EVANS, Francis M /wid	HUNTER, Nina C /wid	24 Oct 1922	103
EVANS, George A	LOCRAFT, Lucile E	20 Mar 1926	114
EVANS, Ralph	DEAHL, Audrey Leigh /div	13 Jan 1923	104
EVANS, Rev. John E /wid	ROBERTS, Esther O /wid	8 Mar 1875	18
EVANS, William A	GHEEN, Delina A	22 Sep 1881	29
EVERITT, Charles M	SMITH, Bertha L	28 Apr 1910	78
EVETT, William A /div	REINBECK, Della M /div	20 Jul 1929	125
EWELL, Fred /c	LOMAX, Susie /c	22 Oct 1900	59
EWELL, Henry /c	CRAGG, Sarah /c	20 Aug 1902	63
FACCHINA, Dante Vincent	COOPER, Mildred M	26 Dec 1933	145
FADELEY, George B	RICE, Marian	6 Jun 1893	46
FAIRBAIRN, Clifford A	STONE, Jessie H	17 Mar 1928	121
FAIRFAX, Archie F	DAVIS, Lou E	20 Dec 1891	44
FAIRFAX, Arthur W	ARUNDLE, Lucy Jemima	10 Nov 1870	13
FAIRFAX, Ernest	DAVIS, Beatrice	5 Feb 1919	95
FAIRFAX, Ferdinand W	RICHARDS, Nancy A Catherine	27 Dec 1870	13
FAIRFAX, Herbert S	HARRISON, Annie G	11 Dec 1889	40
FAIRFAX, J D	HAMPTON, Maud M	27 Dec 1904	66
FAIRFAX, James	WOODYARD, Margaret	8 Jun 1856	2
FAIRFAX, James Thomas	FINACOM, Mary E	17 Oct 1914	87
FAIRFAX, John /c	PINN, Hattie A /c	18 Jun 1919	95
FAIRFAX, John F /c	JACKSON, Martha	10 Jul 1879	25
FAIRFAX, John H	LANGDEN, Ann Maria	19 Aug 1867	8
FAIRFAX, John H	REID, Mary Alice	4 Feb 1891	43
FAIRFAX, John Thomas	STEEL, Mary Elen	9 Apr 1857	3
FAIRFAX, Luther E /wid	DAVIS, Alice	24 May 1904	66
FAIRFAX, Nicholas P	BUCKLEY, Hattie A	27 Dec 1911	82
FAIRFAX, Norman B	DAVIS, Bessie R	26 Feb 1917	93
FAIRFAX, Thomas M	DAVIS, Lucinda	21 Dec 1866	7
FAIRFAX, Thomas N	DE COSS, Katie	24 Dec 1910	80
FAIRFAX, Wellington	DAVIS, V P	19 Dec 1867	8
FAIRFAX, William Smith	MARSHALL, Sarah V	17 Jul 1882	30
FAIRFAX, Willie E	BEAVERS, Winnie E	28 Jul 1932	138
FAIRFAX, Winfred	FAIRFAX, Bessie V	24 Dec 1905	70
FALKENSTINE, Niles G	KLINEFELTER, Harriett A	1 Feb 1930	127
FANT, Charles C /wid	HATHAWAY, Mary V	27 Dec 1894	48
FARR, Bain /div	BERRYHILL, Lorene	10 Sep 1927	119

FARR, Jackson /c	RATCLIFFE, Virginia /c	9 Mar 1909	76
FARR, John /c	SMITH, Judy /c	21 Mar 1881	28
FARR, John D	REID, Sallie C	8 Jun 1882	30
FARR, Maurice W /c	BRADFORD, Marion /c	26 Dec 1914	87
FARR, Richard Ratcliff	MERIGOLD, Viola Louise	12 Dec 1928	123
FARR, William N	GARDNER, Rosana	15 Jun 1891	43
FARR, Wilson Mahone	WILEY, Edith Regeina	24 Nov 1915	89
FARRAR, Green /c wid	JENKINS, Harriet /c	30 Nov 1871	14
FARRAR, James S	SMITH, Grace P	12 Jan 1929	124
FARVER, Harry Robert	STORM, Della Virginia	22 Apr 1916	90
FARVER, Robert T /div	HALE, Nellie	4 Jul 1928	121
FENEY, Hezekiah /c	GAINES, Lillis V /c	29 Dec 1914	87
FEENEY, James Leon	BALL, Lela /div	30 Oct 1926	116
FEENEY, John W Jr	WALLOCH, Ruth C	18 Aug 1926	115
FEASTER, James William	MILLS, Marjoria	30 Aug 1928	122
FEBREY, Ernest J	PAYNE, Grace W	10 Sep 1889	40
FEBREY, James E	ADAMS, Emma B	25 Oct 1882	30
FEEHAN, John A	CUNNINGHAM, Mary A Rourke	26 Jan 1894	47
FEEHAN, Joseph R	GOODSPEED, Catherine E	28 Nov 1924	110
FELL, Abner Garrett	GILLINGHAM, Mary McK	28 Dec 1892	45
FELTNER, Charles M	SHERWOOD, Hattie B	2 Jun 1909	77
FELTON, Isaac /c	JOHNSON, Harriet /c	7 Jun 1874	17
FENDALL, Stratford	MOLINARD, Nannie Robinson /wid	14 Sep 1875	18
FENLEY, Albert Q	JONES, Julia E /wid	14 Jul 1928	122
FENTON, Frank T	SHOCKEY, Catherine J	7 Jun 1930	128
FENWICK, Edward Taylor	GULAGER, Clara L	3 Sep 1895	49
FENWICK, Thomas	STELL, Alice	18 Dec 1855	2
FENWICK, Thomas J /wid	WRENN, Sarah H	3 Sep 1867	8
FERGUSON, Alfred /c	BARNES, Iva /c	16 Nov 1911	81
FERGUSON, George W /c	STEWART, Isabella /c wid	3 Aug 1898	55
FERGUSON, Horace Isaac /c	CHASE, Isabell /c	22 Feb 1922	102
FERGUSON, James /c wid	JACKSON, Susan /c	13 Nov 1887	38
FERGUSON, John W /c	TINNER, Louisa /c wid	12 Aug 1908	75
FERGUSON, Milton C /c	QUANDER, Alice M /c	10 Sep 1925	112
FERGUSON, Norman /c	GRIMES, Mary /c	25 Jan 1926	113
FERGUSON, Robert /c	JENKINS, Martha /c	15 Oct 1919	96
FERGUSON, Robert M	BEACH, Mary B	7 Jun 1877	22
FERGUSON, Uriah M	SHEID, Martena E	23 Jan 1868	9
FERRALL, John /c	TAYLOR, Amanda /c wid	3 May 1904	66
FERRIS, Warren W	BRANSON, Bernice M	2 Mar 1923	104
FERTNEY, Charles T	HUNTT, Marcilla R	1 Jan 1860	4
FICKAS, Melville P	BLACK, Frances R	7 Aug 1911	81

FIELDS, Frank	CLARK, Ann Maria	22 Jan 1893	46
FIELDS, Peter	DOVE, Edith	20 Sep 1908	75
FIFER, Lurty E	WEASE, Carrie E	26 Sep 1928	122
FIGGINS, Robert L	FINISECY, Eva E	8 Mar 1930	127
FINCH, John /wid	CASH, Mary	17 Jan 1858	3
FINDLEY, Charles J	MOHLER, Fay L	17 Jan 1930	127
FINIKE, Henry A	JONES, Emma	22 Jul 1925	112
FINISECY, William O	DANIELS, Martha A	9 Nov 1907	74
FINNEL, R A /wid	HOLDEN, Phoebe	26 Nov 1890	42
FINNELL, H A	HERRELL, Ruth M	7 Oct 1914	87
FINNEY, Thomas /c	MAGRUDER, Nancy /c wid	27 Dec 1883	32
FISCHER, Walter	ALLEN, Isabelle	25 Oct 1907	73
FISH, Francis /wid	RATRIE, Isabel	6 Nov 1873	16
FISHER, Charles /c	GORDON, Eliza /c wid	18 Mar 1883	31
FISHER, S T	SUTHERLAND, Amanda	24 Nov 1912	83
FISHER, Wilbar F	MOHLER, Sallie M	29 Jun 1930	129
FISHER, William E /wid	BURKETT, Edna J /wid	1 Sep 1931	133
FITZGERALD, Edward	SIMERING, Helen M	6 Feb 1932	136
FITZGERALD, Gerald	SAGER, Geraldine M	15 May 1928	121
FITZHUGH, Gibbon /c	CORBIN, Harriet /c	16 Sep 1877	22
FITZHUGH, Samuel M	MARSHALL, Margaret E	1 Feb 1876	20
FLANAGAN, John J	CROWELL, Annie	17 Jun 1919	95
FLANAGAN, Matthew	LYNCH, Elizabeth	22 Jul 1858	4
FLEISCHER, Joseph	HAMRICK, Irene	20 Nov 1931	134
FLEMING, Aubrey Blakemore	NICKELL, Hallie S	28 Jun 1926	115
FLEMING, Clarence L	HOLDEN, Mariana	16 Oct 1902	63
FLEMING, Harry Jr	STALLINGS, Ethel R /div	14 Jan 1920	97
FLETCHER, Archibald /c	JORDAN, Hannah /c	28 Jan 1883	31
FLETCHER, John B	GARRETT, Lillie Maud	18 Sep 1901	60
FLETCHER, Joseph G /wid	TANNER, Mary E	28 Mar 1925	111
FLETCHER, Lewis R	TOBIN, Esther	30 Oct 1926	116
FLETCHER, Robert /c	BOWMAN, Fanny /c	5 Sep 1878	24
FLETCHER, Robert /c wid	HENDERSON, Ida Belle /c	29 Oct 1918	95
FLETCHER, Robert E	SWARTZ, Pearl E /wid	9 Mar 1915	88
FLICKINGER, L E	TAIT, Mrs. O C /wid	17 Jun 1901	60
FLING, Richard K	PLASKETT, Margaret A	25 Jun 1929	125
FLINN, Dallas F	GARNER, Harriet E	25 Apr 1900	58
FLINN, James B	HUNTER, Rachael P	3 Oct 1866	7
FLINN, M J	CLARK, Elvira E	25 Apr 1880	26
FLOOD, Henry Hamilton	CLARKE, Julia Loretta	5 Sep 1931	133
FLYNN, Guy	FUNKHAUSER, Ruby	30 May 1925	111
FOELLER, Adam H /div	HINKLEMAN, Marie E /div	24 Aug 1927	119

FOLEY, Raymond W	JOHNSON, Lillian M	15 Nov 1920	99
FOLKS, Dennis /c	GREEN, Eddie /c	20 Feb 1897	54
FOLKS, William /c	CLARKE, Mamie /c	10 Feb 1906	70
FOLLIN, Andrew R ·	LANHAM, Idella	29 Mar 1896	50
FOLLIN, Benjamin F	LYNN, Minerva E	22 Dec 1886	37
FOLLIN, Fletcher	LEE, Namie	22 Nov 1905	69
FOLLIN, Gabriel A	DICKEY, Rosa Lee	25 Dec 1900	59
FOLLIN, Harry L	SANDERS, Amy E	20 Jan 1909	76
FOLLIN, Harvey H	CONNORS, Margaret J /div	3 Jul 1923	105
FOLLIN, Howard	LANHAM, Hattie	24 Jan 1900	58
FOLLIN, John T	COCKERILLE, Sarah Ann	10 Jan 1854	1
FOLLIN, Mandaville	THOMPSON, Alice	15 Sep 1881	29
FOLLIN, Richard	HENDERSON, Mary F	26 Sep 1871	14
FOLLIN, Richard H	COCKERILLE, Ann E	11 Dec 1855	1
FOLLIN, Richard H /wid	ADAMS, Jane	3 Dec 1884	42
FOLLIN, Richard J /wid	MCDANIEL, Alice	21 Jan 1885	34
FOLLIN, S M	FOX, Susie J	18 Dec 1901	61
FOLLIN, Walter A	REID, Katie M	5 Apr 1892	44
FOOTE, Charles W	SUTTON, Mamie	30 Jan 1932	136
FOOTE, Frederick /c wid	CARTER, Margaret /c	7 Jan 1864	5
FORD, Amzi C	DALTON, Ethel R	14 May 1932	137
FORD, C Humphrey	MAKELY, Martha Zell	23 Oct 1907	73
FORD, Eugene G	COOKSEY, Isabella	22 Nov 1854	1
FORD, Frederick M	ROGERS, Fanny	20 Jan 1874	17
FORD, Frederick M /wid	SIMPSON, Mary C	9 Jul 1895	49
FORD, James /c	POSEY, Grisian /c wid	6 Mar 1870	12
FORD, James S /c	WEBB, Carrie B /c	18 Jun 1911	81
FORD, Joseph /c wid	ANDERSON, Harriet /c	22 Dec 1874	18
FORD, Joseph /c wid	DESKINS, Pennie /c wid	31 Oct 1885	35
FORD, Robert /c wid	TURNER, Georgeana /c	28 Dec 1881	29
FORD, W F Jr	BUCKLEY, Leota	2 Nov 1915	89
FORD, William F	PAYNE, Annie	2 Jun 1885	35
FORD, William Vernon	SWETNAM, Elizabeth J	12 Apr 1921	100
FORMER, M E	GREELEY, Anna R	22 Mar 1924	108
FORSTER, William /c	DIXON, Gertrude /c	1 Apr 1905	68
FORSYTH, Charles Edward	COOPER, Fannie Burgess	10 Aug 1892	45
FORSYTH, Rev. Robert W	SMITH, Madge W	12 Dec 1883	32
FORSYTH, Samuel	CLOVER, Mary A	21 May 1866	6
FORTNEY, Bernard G	RYAN, Viola J	10 Nov 1926	116
FORTNEY, John B	MONEY, Mary Virginia	8 Jan 1874	17
FORTUNE, Abraham	DUVALL, Ethel M	21 Jul 1915	88
FORTUNE, Randolph F /c	JOYCE, Dickie /c	4 Sep 1904	67

FOSTER, Charles F /wid	MILLER, Helen /wid	10 Apr 1926	114
FOSTER, Dowe A	ARNOLD, Maude C	15 Oct 1931	134
FOSTER, Frank	CRONIN, Edith B /wid	16 Aug 1913	84
FOSTER, Nelson J	JAVINS, Hazel E	15 Jan 1927	117
FOSTER, Waldo L	CASSIDY, Berta L	19 Apr 1917	92
FOUCHE, George H	TAYLOR, Pauline	14 Sep 1931	133
FOULKROD, Linton H	THOMAS, Verna M /div	25 Feb 1933	141
FOURNIER, Roland C	LOEB, Marion	4 Jul 1922	102
FOUST, Henry /c	WASHINGTON, Lena /c	24 Jan 1905	68
FOWLER, Herman George	SIMPSON, Virginia L	4 Oct 1930	129
FOX, Alfred M	FOX, Alma	1 Jun 1909	77
FOX, Bernard J	HUTCHISON, Julia F	22 Apr 1908	74
FOX, Charles A	ELLMORE, Mae Elizabeth	5 Jul 1930	128
FOX, Charlie	CROUCH, Helen	24 Dec 1927	120
FOX, Dr. C Albert	GUNNELL, Annie	9 Mar 1869	10
FOX, George Montgomery	TAYLOR, Sarah F	16 Mar 1887	37
FOX, Isaac N	STUDDS, Annie	7 Oct 1891	44
FOX, Leonard J	THOMPSON, Dorothy E	4 Dec 1931	135
FOX, Lisle M	RIGG, Hattie A	15 Feb 1872	14
FOX, Maurice W	SMITH, Wilhelmina A	25 Jan 1910	78
FOX, W I	THOMPSON, Ona May	26 Nov 1913	85
FOX, Willie E	KORZENDORFER, Lena	22 Dec 1904	67
FOX, Zachariah	CROSON, Lucy Alice	25 Jan 1877	21
FRAME, William P	SPICER, Annie L	26 Mar 1908	74
FRANCE, Isaac C /wid	PETTITT, Martha F	18 Dec 1889	40
FRANCIS, Henry /c	KNIGHT, Lavinia	14 Feb 1879	25
FRANK, Clements E	KEENER, Eulah E	14 Dec 1933	145
FRANKLIN, John /c	WILLIAMS, Pearl /c	29 Dec 1926	117
FRANKLIN, Lewis /c	CARNICK, Alice /c	7 Apr 1898	54
FRANZONI, Joseph D	FARR, Margaret Helen	20 Aug 1917	102
FRAZEE, Robert S	FERGUSON, Mary E V	4 Jul 1865	6
FRAZER, W G /wid	MOUNTS, Lena	29 Aug 1912	83
FRAZIER, C Leslie /c	HOPKINS, Gertrude C /c	8 Dec 1931	135
FRAZIER, Gilbert E	FISSELL, Rachel I	2 Sep 1909	77
FRAZIER, Raymond T	PANHOLZER, Lillian J	26 Aug 1916	90
FRAZIER, Walter F	DORSEY, Mary A	24 Mar 1932	136
FREDERICK, Edgar R /wid	HUNT, Elizabeth	27 May 1919	95
FREED, Clifton Henry	DONOVAN, Doris T	6 Feb 1932	136
FREEMAN, De Graphen	KOON, Jane S	28 Sep 1886	36
FREEMAN, George D /wid	LOVE, Jessie M	19 Aug 1903	65
FREEMAN, Leon L	CROCKER, Hattie Belle	30 Oct 1894	48
FREEMAN, Lewis H	COCKERILLE, Hattie L	13 Sep 1877	22

FREEMAN, William R /c	BRADLEY, Martha Ann /c	5 Oct 1878	24
FRENCH, Frederick /c wid	JACKSON, Henrietta /c	20 Oct 1886	37
FRENCH, John F	CULLINAN, Mary A /div	7 Jul 1930	128
FRENCH, Joseph E /c	JACKSON, Carrie /c	7 Sep 1905	69
FRENCH, Leon L L	KEELER, Beatrice R	5 Jun 1898	54
FRENCH, Welby J	BUCKLEY, Minnie M	25 Sep 1890	42
FRENZEL, Edward William	BEACH, Mary Elizabeth	26 Apr 1893	46
FRENZEL, Ernest E	CROUCH, Clara	29 Jun 1904	66
FREUND, W J	SHEA, Nellie T	12 Oct 1910	79
FREY, Alfred /c	WALKER, Mary E /c	1 Oct 1888	39
FREY, Alfred /c wid	HUNTER, Nannie /c	24 Jul 1902	63
FREY, Daniel /c	RILEY, Sarah F /c	16 May 1928	121
FREY, John C	KILLIAN, Grace I	22 Jul 1911	81
FRINKS, Charles /wid	GARRETT, Roena /wid	24 Mar 1904	66
FRISTOE, Luther S	BLOSS, Cora A	4 Sep 1882	30
FRITSCH, John F	SAMOY, Simone	26 Apr 1932	137
FRITTER, James E	KIDWELL, Margaret J	2 Nov 1891	44
FRIZZELL, A J	ANDERSON, Grace M	17 May 1922	102
FULLER, Archie /c	BANKS, Beatrice /c	25 Jun 1908	75
FULLER, James G /c	CHAMP, Pearl /c div	14 Dec 1931	135
FULLER, John Resley	ROGERS, Velma Pauli	1 Apr 1933	141
FULLERTON, Peter P /wid	CATON, Elizabeth	12 Feb 1873	16
FULLERTON, William Rudd	TILLETT, Fannie N	6 Mar 1902	62
FULLMER, Franklin E	FITZGERALD, Goldie C	9 Mar 1915	88
FUNKHOUSER, Oscar R	LA SALLE, Aldona Zerta	12 Sep 1925	112
FURLONG, Edward P	DOBSON, Isabella	18 Jan 1877	21
FURR, Buckner M	MAFFETT, Annie E W	6 Jun 1906	71
FURR, Joseph	LUSKEY, Annie	12 Aug 1931	133
FURR, Philip /c	BOWMAN, Eve /c	11 Feb 1879	24
GADD, A S Jr	BRAWNER, Ruth M	26 Jul 1924	109
GAGE, Charles E	RILEY, Kathleen M	21 Dec 1908	76
GAINES, George W	WILT, Elizabeth	22 Feb 1859	4
GAINES, J W	WILLIAMS, Della B	1 Feb 1887	37
GAINES, John E /c	BROWN, Eleanora /c	26 Dec 1890	42
GAINES, John Jr /c	CARROLL, Gertrude /c	1 Jun 1915	88
GAINES, Robert S	MARKS, Eva M	5 Nov 1896	51
GAITHER, George W	LANHAM, Alpha C	27 Sep 1899	57
GAITHER, John R	PACKMAN, Edith I	7 Mar 1931	131
GALL, John C	ROSENBERGER, Elsie G	4 Oct 1924	109
GAMBLE, Thomas C /c	WOOD, Emma E /c	16 Oct 1931	134
GANTT, Charles R /wid	JOHNSON, Mary L	2 Oct 1922	103
GANTT, D B	DE BELL, Annie V	2 Oct 1901	60

GANTT, Floyd M	MACK, Edith L	30 Aug 1930	*129*
GANTT, George E	LOWE, Eleanor C	28 Jan 1915	*88*
GANTT, Horace	ROBEY, Alice	2 Jun 1920	*98*
GANTT, John R	O'MEARA, Lillie A	23 Dec 1901	*61*
GANTT, Joseph M	DISNEY, Juliet	6 Sep 1860	*5*
GARBER, C M /wid	SANGER, Bettie M	28 Oct 1902	*63*
GARCIA, Blas G	HUNTER, Virginia Blake	7 Mar 1931	*131*
GARDES, Arthur H	VAN HERBULIS, Melanie	27 Nov 1915	*89*
GARDES, George W	FERN, Loretta G	31 Dec 1926	*117*
GARDNER, James S	REID, Anna A	16 May 1870	*12*
GARDNER, R A	CHAKIR, Syida /div	7 Dec 1929	*126*
GARLAND, Ralph I	BRUNNER, Mabel H	6 Oct 1914	*87*
GARNER, Hezekiah /wid	MILSTEAD, Daniza J	27 Dec 1877	*23*
GARNER, James H /wid	SIMPSON, Ada E	29 Oct 1899	*57*
GARNER, James M	PAYNE, Rachel V	25 Dec 1912	*84*
GARNER, John H	REID, Thedie	18 Mar 1880	*26*
GARNER, John W	FREEMAN, Lily R	16 Oct 1884	*33*
GARNER, Warren /c	ADAMS, Mary /c	2 May 1889	*40*
GARNER, Werten E	DAVIS, Harriet A	9 Nov 1876	*21*
GARRETSON, Carlton S	BOOTH, Minnie E	22 May 1903	*64*
GARRETT, David /c	TATE, Adelaide /c	18 Oct 1899	*57*
GARRETT, Edwin M	MILLAN, Mary Page	28 Sep 1932	*139*
GARRETT, P Y	MANKIN, Mattie E	4 Jun 1903	*64*
GARRETT, Thomas	DUCKET, Martha	20 Oct 1867	*8*
GARRETT, William Marshall	DOWNING, Sadie	16 Oct 1883	*32*
GARRISON, Clarence M	EDMUNDS, Mary	15 May 1901	*60*
GARRISON, F Ashby	HARMON, Ruby J	15 Dec 1909	*78*
GARRISON, John H /div	WEBSTER, Evelyn Mae /div	27 Jun 1925	*111*
GARRISON, Loren E	TRUMBLE, Roberta Hazel	28 Nov 1919	*97*
GARRISON, W T	HARMON, Elizabeth	29 Dec 1906	*72*
GARRISON, William E	MILLER, Annie A	29 Dec 1880	*27*
GARVEY, Richard B	DYER, Agnes E	6 Dec 1911	*81*
GASKINS, Arthur /c	HORTON, Ella J /c	2 Mar 1905	*68*
GASKINS, Henry /c	SNYDER, Malinda /c	31 May 1877	*22*
GASKINS, James W /c	SEALS, Mary V /c	14 Mar 1883	*31*
GASKINS, John H /c	LAMBERT, Laura /c	15 Nov 1921	*101*
GASKINS, Joseph /c	KNIGHT, Maggie /c	24 Dec 1884	*34*
GASKINS, Joseph /c	HORTON, Willie May /c	7 Sep 1904	*67*
GASKINS, Leroy /c	LAZENBERRY, Alice /c	20 May 1915	*88*
GASKINS, Nathaniel /c	BURKE, Elizabeth /c	8 Jun 1879	*25*
GASKINS, Oliver /c	CURRY, Adaline /c	15 Dec 1870	*13*
GASKINS, Raymond /c	JOHNSON, Bertha /c	30 Aug 1924	*109*

GASKINS, Richard /c	FEENEY, Louise /c	6 Jul 1910	79
GASKINS, Tasco /c	ALLEN, Catharine /c	4 Feb 1869	10
GATES, James F	SWEENY, Leittie K	27 Sep 1916	91
GATES, Joseph G	WALKER, Annie E	6 Jan 1909	76
GAYLE, Thomas	HURLEY, Katherine C M	3 May 1911	80
GAYNOR, Norman J	PAGE, Betsey B	16 Apr 1914	86
GEIB, John A /wid	BAYLISS, Theo	19 Feb 1873	16
GENELLA, Charles F	REGAL, Minnie M	18 Apr 1911	80
GENNS, William /c	BALL, Ella /c	13 Dec 1899	57
GENTRY, Harry	DAVIS, Virginia	17 Mar 1927	117
GEORGE, Edwin B	BAKER, M Louise	17 Jun 1928	121
GERDINE, Thomas G /wid	ROWELL, Marguerite N	1 Feb 1923	104
GERMAN, Hes	SCOTT, Minnie Agnes	20 Apr 1890	54
GERMAN, James	FERGUSON, Mary W	14 Apr 1925	111
GERSDORF, Wilbur A	HEIDENREICH, Elsie C	25 Nov 1923	106
GHEEN, Bernard L	MCGARITY, Margaret M	27 Jun 1923	105
GHEEN, Davis	RANDALL, Jennie Peppers /div	5 Jan 1910	78
GHEEN, E W	AUGER, Jone L	31 Jan 1872	15
GHEEN, Edward F	GAINES, Susie	1 Jan 1901	60
GHEEN, George Franklin	BUCKLEY, Eugenia	4 Jan 1870	11
GHEEN, John H /wid	BIRCH, Ruth A	31 Oct 1866	7
GHEEN, John T	RECTOR, D Ann	15 May 1862	7
GHEEN, Thomas Jackson /wid	RICHARDSON, Eliza C	24 Jun 1855	1
GHEEN, Thomas Jackson	ROBY, Alice	30 Dec 1886	37
GHEEN, William W	KIDWELL, Laura E	29 Jan 1889	39
GIBBONS, George A	WHALEY, Laura A	2 Jul 1873	16
GIBBONS, William	TURLEY, Eliza /wid	30 Jun 1920	98
GIBBS, John /c	TYLER, Rosetta /c	26 Nov 1902	63
GIBBS, Joseph Norman	HARRISON, Margaret N	27 May 1886	36
GIBSON, Brooke /c	BANKS, Minta /c	17 Apr 1884	33
GIBSON, Edmond /c wid	WILLIAMS, Ellen /c wid	24 May 1868	9
GIBSON, Edward /c	HUGHES, Cora /c	27 Dec 1905	70
GIBSON, Frank C	MARKS, Wenna	30 Nov 1899	57
GIBSON, Frank H	OLIVER, Georgie R	16 Nov 1898	55
GIBSON, George H	GRIMSLEY, Mattie E	4 Aug 1923	105
GIBSON, Henry H	WALKER, Lizzie F	25 Sep 1879	25
GIBSON, Isaac /c wid	RUTLEDGE, Louise /c	2 Oct 1922	103
GIBSON, Jerome M	SWAYZE, Marie M	17 May 1927	118
GIBSON, Jessie M	JOHNSON, Sarah Jane	5 Sep 1867	8
GIBSON, John N	BIRCH, Jennette	21 Oct 1886	36
GIBSON, Powell /c	HORTON, Hattie B /c .	27 Nov 1903	65
GIBSON, Robert C	NOEL, Renee C	7 Oct 1931	134

GIBSON, Samuel /c	GASKINS, Elizabeth /c	18 Jun 1874	17
GIBSON, Strother	WEIR, Martha	12 Jul 1868	9
GIBSON, Walter Ernest	FORD, Nina S	8 Sep 1928	122
GIBSON, Wesley /c wid	VASS, Courtney /c	22 Sep 1897	53
GICKER, Franklin S Jr	FOLLIN, Eleanor Ethel	29 Jun 1926	115
GIESE, Oscar W	BUELL, Virginia	4 Oct 1929	126
GILBERT, Dawson /c	BROOKS, Victoria /c	23 Apr 1876	20
GILBERT, George D	BOND, Norma Lee	2 Jan 1911	80
GILCHRIST, Arthur R	THIERBACH, Clara L	10 Sep 1912	83
GILES, Clinton A /div	FORD, Mabel Inez /div	28 May 1927	118
GILES, Dennis /c wid	JEFFREY, Ruth E /c div	26 May 1925	111
GILL, John F /wid	OGDEN, Ann /wid	9 Oct 1890	42
GILL, John H /wid	STAHLMAN, Carrie K	27 Feb 1910	78
GILLAM, Peter /c	WILLIAMS, Aletha /c wid	6 Jun 1878	23
GILLAM, Peter /c wid	BRADLEY, Sarah /c	14 Oct 1891	44
GILLEY, Charles D	JOHNSON, Mildred C	31 Jul 1924	109
GILLINGHAM, George Chalkley	TROTH, Martha Rebecca	12 Feb 1908	74
GINGELL, Madison U	WEEKLEY, Eunice M	7 Jun 1924	108
GINGELL, Reginald J	STODDARD, Elizabeth	29 Oct 1918	95
GLASCOE, David F /wid	FRENZEL, Rosetta	12 Jun 1928	121
GLASCOE, Lafayette /c	CRAVEN, Daisy A /c	3 Feb 1926	113
GLAZER, Louis	HAMMOND, Virginia	17 Oct 1933	144
GLENN, Marshall	DEFFENBAUGH, Helen	22 Aug 1928	122
GLICK, Medford Daniel	WILLIAMS, Lucille M	26 Sep 1933	143
GLIDER, Gentry P	GELINER, Grace E	28 Dec 1931	135
GODFREY, Gordon J	STEELE, Effie May	30 Dec 1917	89
GODFREY, Irving N	SMITH, Vallie D	19 Aug 1914	87
GOENS, Walter W /c	SCOTT, Lenora /c	7 Feb 1925	110
GOHEENS, Bernard W	KUKE, Juanita E	29 Jul 1933	143
GOLDEN, Frank Rowe	SMITH, Lydia Alice	24 Nov 1927	120
GOLDEN, William Samuel	NELSON, Grace	22 Jul 1927	118
GOLDSTEIN, Henry H	WEINBERG, Kate	15 Jun 1926	115
GOODE, Allen H /wid	GUNNELL, Alice E /wid	15 Jun 1917	92
GOOD, Willie J	THOMPSON, Esther S	15 Jul 1922	103
GOODAL, P Everheart /c	JONES, Allegra /c	29 Oct 1930	130
GOODING, Arthur W	ROBINSON, Sybilla	10 Jan 1870	12
GOODING, Charles F	MILLS, Alice M	3 Feb 1880	26
GOODING, Isaiah	KIDWELL, Sarah J /wid	5 Jan 1873	16
GOODING, J R	DOVE, Nettie E	18 Jan 1905	68
GOODING, James B	OWEN, Virginia E	25 Nov 1931	134
GOODING, Ray P	HURST, Bessie D	10 Dec 1913	85
GOODLEY, George	PEARSON, Mary	20 Feb 1868	9

GOODMAN, William S	OURAND, Elizabeth F	26 Mar 1927	*117*
GOODWICH, Thomas W	FULLER, Jennie E	3 Apr 1931	*131*
GOODWIN, Edward L	SMITH, Maria L	11 Jan 1881	*28*
GOODWIN, William T	BUCKLEY, Mary J */wid*	5 Feb 1879	*24*
GORDON, Albert	SHEPHERD, Eliza */wid*	21 May 1871	*16*
GORDON, Alexander */wid*	TIEFENTHALER, Daisy */wid*	2 Oct 1929	*126*
GORDON, Maurice M */c*	CAMPBELL, Jean Frances */c wid*	2 Oct 1933	*144*
GORDON, Willis L	RAWLING, Lillian	3 Jun 1890	*41*
GORGE, William T Jr	BOYLES, Louise	26 Oct 1929	*126*
GORHAM, Albert E	BRADFORD, Ethel M	11 Jun 1932	*137*
GORHAM, C F	LACEY, Alice	24 Jun 1929	*125*
GORHAM, Clarence M */div*	POWELL, Alice V	29 Sep 1927	*119*
GORHAM, Edward	MONEY, Narcissa R	7 Jun 1905	*68*
GORHAM, George */c wid*	CARTER, Emma */c*	9 Feb 1903	*64*
GORHAM, George Amos	VAUGHAN, Annabelle	5 Jan 1932	*136*
GORHAM, Harry B	STAATS, Elsie M	3 Jan 1906	*70*
GORHAM, Robert L	WELLS, Catherine E	8 Oct 1932	*139*
GORMES, Oden */c*	FURR, Hattie */c*	29 Dec 1923	*107*
GORMLEY, James H	STRATMEYER, Everett	22 Nov 1923	*106*
GOSLIN, Lewis	GREENWOOD, Sarah	9 Oct 1856	*2*
GOSSOM, John H */wid*	RILEY, Jane */wid*	27 Aug 1884	*33*
GOTT, Hugh G	ENSOR, Janice	26 Jun 1926	*115*
GOTTHARDT, Charles W	SHREVE, Viola L	28 Nov 1930	*130*
GOULD, James B	DOWNING, Mary C	16 Dec 1884	*34*
GOULD, James B */wid*	KUHN, Harriett */wid*	6 Jun 1932	*137*
GOULD, R B	MILLER, F J	9 Feb 1857	*2*
GRADY, Donald A	BENSON, Ethel Eugenia	25 Mar 1933	*141*
GRADY, Seymour	TUCKER, Behethlan A	23 May 1900	*58*
GRAHAM, Ashby M	BARNES, Helen Ashton	2 Nov 1910	*79*
GRAHAM, D M */wid*	WILCOX, Dora C	8 Jan 1920	*97*
GRAHAM, Ernest E	WHEELER, Maud Barlow */wid*	16 May 1908	*74*
GRAHAM, John W Jr	SMITH, Rose B	4 Jun 1890	*41*
GRAHAM, Lloyd S */wid*	SAUNDERS, Bertha H */wid*	11 Sep 1929	*126*
GRAHAM, Robert H	SULLIVAN, Grace E	11 Jan 1894	*47*
GRAHAM, William E	CANFIELD, Frances J	7 Jun 1887	*38*
GRAMMER, Julius E	SPARROW, Elizabeth Ann	20 Dec 1855	*2*
GRANGER, Walter R	DANIEL, Corinne L	23 Apr 1930	*127*
GRANIGAN, L M	WILLIAMS, Estelle	27 Apr 1904	*66*
GRANT, N B	DEAN, M E	19 Dec 1872	*15*
GRAPER, Lawrence F	SPRINKLE, Dorothy E	26 Sep 1931	*133*
GRAVEL, Charles W	WOODWORTH, Luella R	18 Jun 1914	*86*
GRAVES, William */wid*	LOWRY, Ella */wid*	9 Sep 1926	*116*

GRAY, Ernest /c	LUCAS, Ellen /c	10 Sep 1905	69
GRAY, Hamilton /c	COTTRELL, Carrie /c	24 Sep 1884	33
GRAY, Herbert L	BEARD, Hattie V	10 May 1922	102
GRAY, Hiram Thomas /c	GORDON, Sylvia May /c	28 Aug 1931	133
GRAY, I W /c	JASPER, Frances /c	25 Feb 1915	88
GRAY, Ira /c	BROWN, Lettie /c	27 Oct 1909	77
GRAY, Ira /c wid	GRIMPLES, Mary E /c wid	12 Dec 1922	104
GRAY, John /c	POWELL, Lucy /c	15 Aug 1881	29
GRAY, John H /c	WEBB, Bessie C /c	27 Apr 1916	90
GRAY, John T	KINCHELOE, Mabel L	2 Jun 1930	128
GRAY, William H /c	WRIGHT, Jella /c	26 Jan 1927	117
GRAY, William R	PALMER, Louisa	5 May 1898	54
GRAYBILL, Harry W	ROWELL, Dorothy B	24 Dec 1913	85
GRAYSON, Joseph /c wid	JONES, Jane /c wid	5 Sep 1917	93
GREEN, Alex	TAYLOR, Lillian R	3 May 1933	142
GREEN, Andrew /c wid	CAMPBELL, Louisa /c wid	4 Nov 1877	22
GREEN, Beverly /c wid	GREEN, Jane /c wid	5 Dec 1885	35
GREEN, Edward Allen	BARNARD, Mary Kathryn	9 Jul 1921	100
GREEN, Frank C	BEACH, Victoria E /wid	14 Jan 1910	78
GREEN, Fred /c	PARKER, Laura /c	9 May 1914	86
GREEN, Harman	WESTCOTT, Marion L	12 Nov 1920	99
GREEN, Robert /c	NELSON, Louisa /c	25 Dec 1890	42
GREEN, Thomas J /wid	FENSTERMAKER, Helen M /div	18 Oct 1928	123
GREEN, Washington /c	BRIGGS, Lillian /c	28 Dec 1890	42
GREEN, Washington /c wid	JACKSON, Lillian /c	11 Nov 1911	81
GREEN, William H /c	COLE, Mary C /c	9 Feb 1888	38
GREEN, William I	DAY, Sarah W	19 Dec 1872	15
GREENE, Elwyn	BABBITT, Agnes C	13 Dec 1894	48
GREENE, George W /wid	KING, Margaret L /wid	30 Nov 1931	135
GREENE, John W	FOLLIN, Kathryn O	5 Aug 1933	143
GREENLEASE, James H	DODD, Charlotte C	24 Nov 1892	45
GREENWELL, James A	BALDWIN, Margaret M	25 Jun 1932	138
GREER, Samuel m	HUEY, Margaret A	4 Apr 1872	15
GREGG, Johnie M	EVANS, Alice	4 Dec 1926	116
GREHAN, Joseph I	BRODERS, Hannie R	2 Jan 1872	14
GREHAN, William	MEGEATH, Effie F	30 Nov 1916	91
GREWE, John	MULLEN, Grace C	24 Dec 1930	130
GREY, Robert	MCKNIGHT, Amanda	10 Dec 1868	10
GRIFFIN, John T /div	HAWLEY, Ella G	18 Dec 1900	59
GRIFFIN, M J	KIRBY, Virginia N	11 Jun 1889	40
GRIFFIN, Presley	HUGHES, Kate	30 Aug 1905	69
GRIFFIN, William /c wid	ROBINSON, Henrietta /c	6 Jun 1926	114

GRIFFITH, Bladen Dulany	HAWES, Rosa Corinne	2 Mar 1904	66
GRIFFITH, H M	MUNDAY, Ouida	3 Aug 1920	98
GRIFFITH, Paul	JOHNSON, Nellie	4 Mar 1930	127
GRIFFITH, Richard R	BOND, Eleanor More	5 Aug 1933	143
GRIGSBY, William J	COOLBAUGH, Loretta M	20 Aug 1930	129
GRIMES, E William	TRICE, Sarah Jane	8 Feb 1894	47
GRIMES, Franklin P	HUNTER, Mary V	9 Sep 1874	17
GRIMSLEY, Norman	LAVINUS, Marguerite Louise	2 Nov 1931	134
GRIMSLEY, Thomas	CARTER, Dorothy V	1 Oct 1921	101
GRIMSLEY, William	HARRISON, Virginia	26 Nov 1919	97
GROFF, Anton E	MUTERSBAUGH, Alma L	6 Jun 1921	100
GROFT, Newton S	LEE, Lillian C	4 Nov 1908	75
GROH, Jacob D	BURTON, Anna May	22 Dec 1904	67
GROH, William S S	ARNOLD, Minnie A /wid	14 Aug 1895	49
GROOMS, Nelson /c wid	EARLY, Sarah /c wid	22 Feb 1903	64
GROOMS, Roland O /c	CLEMENS, Alice /c wid	3 Mar 1933	141
GROSEBECK, W H	DONALDSON, Annie Z	24 Feb 1869	10
GROVES, Milton	HARRISON, Hattie	16 Sep 1920	99
GRUBB, Claude A	BRADSHAW, Mary O	7 Jun 1905	68
GRUBB, Ralph Andrew	SLADE, Mary Fitzhugh	2 Jun 1933	142
GRYMES, William A	DICKEY, Eliza	7 Mar 1880	26
GUENTHER, Fred Laing	BICKSLER, Laura M	16 Apr 1889	40
GUERTLER, Arthur B	GUERTLER, Marie C	28 May 1930	128
GUINANE, Edward P	MORGAN, Estell M	10 Jan 1927	117
GULICK, Allen	THOMPSON, Myrtle	19 Sep 1923	106
GULICK, S E	NEWCOMB, Kate C	24 May 1860	5
GUNN, Alan P /wid	GLENN, Mary Elizabeth	29 Aug 1913	85
GUNNELL, Albert	JACKSON, Martha Alice	24 Feb 1857	3
GUNNELL, Amos F	MATEER, Mattie	23 Feb 1891	43
GUNNELL, Carberry	SMITH, Annie L	17 Dec 1885	35
GUNNELL, George W	GUNNELL, Matilda	16 Jan 1872	15
GUNNELL, George W /wid	BALTZER, Fannie	10 Aug 1881	28
GUNNELL, Hammond J	WOOD, Maude E	21 May 1929	124
GUNNELL, Hugh West	GUNNELL, Mary F	24 Dec 1878	24
GUNNELL, J N /wid	BREDY, E A /wid	20 Sep 1905	69
GUNNELL, James N	THOMPSON, Maggie	29 Jan 1884	32
GUNNELL, John H	WILEY, Anna	10 Apr 1883	31
GUNNELL, John M	WALKER, Florence E	29 Apr 1895	49
GUNNELL, John R	GUNNELL, Catherine V /wid	27 Sep 1868	10
GUNNELL, Luther	MILLS, Amy A	21 Nov 1878	24
GUNNELL, Luther /wid	THOMPSON, Frances	3 Mar 1881	28
GUNNELL, William H /div	CAWOOD, Amanda	9 Feb 1858	3

GURNS, Robert Ray /wid	UNGER, Lillie M /wid	26 Aug 1916	90
GUTHRIE, Reuben E	BAILEY, Addie W /wid	24 Mar 1928	121
GWALTNEY, Burl	DE BUSK, Bessie	8 Aug 1928	122
GWALTNEY, Hurshel	HALL, Nettie B /div	24 Dec 1921	101
HAAS, Gilbert H	BAXTER, Elvie V	24 Oct 1928	123
HAGAN, James A	BRODERS, Virginia	28 Dec 1905	70
HAGAN, S L /div	SMALL, G E	1 Apr 1914	86
HAGEMAN, Ezra Bertram /div	METZGER, Pearl H /div	14 Oct 1932	139
HAGER, Frederick	SHERIDAN, Florence	7 Jun 1926	114
HAINES, George Jackson /wid	FRENCH, Caroline H /wid	24 May 1919	95
HAINES, Robert D	JERMAN, Rosa May	5 Jun 1883	31
HAINES, Wilmer	WEAKLEY, Georgie	14 Sep 1911	81
HAIR, Paul W	KENNEDY, Edna M	20 Jan 1930	127
HAISLIP, John /wid	GARRISON, Annie R	20 Feb 1896	50
HAISLIP, John T	HAISLIP, Minnie	24 Feb 1897	52
HAISLIP, Thomas H	TRICE, Delila	10 Oct 1867	8
HAISLIP, Thomas H /wid	VIOLETT, Mary J	7 Jul 1870	13
HALBERT, H S /wid	MILLER, Elizabeth H	8 Nov 1871	14
HALE, Robert B /c	JACKSON, Martha F /c	27 Dec 1875	19
HALL, A J	KERBY, Ann V	19 Jan 1875	18
HALL, Adolphus /div	HARMON, Maggie	12 Dec 1907	74
HALL, Arch	DODSON, Amanda	18 Jan 1866	6
HALL, Arthur /c	PINKETT, Martha /c	26 Apr 1911	80
HALL, Arthur /div	SCHNEIDER, Wilhelmina M	15 Jun 1928	121
HALL, Arthur J L	JOHANSON, Ruth H	14 Mar 1918	93
HALL, Caleb /wid	DAWSON, Hattie J /wid	27 Sep 1911	81
HALL, D M	BEACH, Nellie	16 Nov 1905	69
HALL, Edward G	ANDERSON, Florence /div	17 Mar 1931	131
HALL, Everett T	HALL, Alma	29 Jul 1929	125
HALL, George Vernon	FAULKNER, Margaret A	19 Jul 1926	115
HALL, George W /wid	DAVIS, Florence	16 Apr 1890	41
HALL, Harvey H	FARR, Elsie M	19 Dec 1922	104
HALL, James	HARRISON, Rosanna	19 Sep 1895	50
HALL, James N	WRENN, Sarah A	6 Aug 1868	9
HALL, James N /wid	DAVIS, Annie Lee /wid	15 Sep 1909	77
HALL, John Q	HALL, Emeline	14 Aug 1873	16
HALL, John W	BRADLEY, Alice	10 mar 1885	34
HALL, John W	TRUSSELL, Florence	21 Jun 1905	69
HALL, John W /wid	HATTON, Ida Virginia	30 Aug 1916	90
HALL, L C /wid	CROSON, Mary	26 May 1907	73
HALL, Lawrence C	MASON, Hazel R	13 Aug 1930	129
HALL, Lindsay D	PEGELOW, Elsie Virginia	20 Sep 1922	104

HALL, Luther	DEAVERS, Flora	19 Feb 1921	100
HALL, M D	COFFER, Ella A	8 Jun 1881	28
HALL, Moses M /c	SUMMERS, Mary /c	26 Dec 1889	40
HALL, R B /wid	MCINTYRE, Allene	29 Apr 1931	132
HALL, Robert O /c	HARRISON, Mary J /c	23 Jun 1887	38
HALL, Robert P /c	LOMACK, Alice W /c	25 Nov 1931	134
HALL, Walter /c	DAGGS, Fanny /c	9 Feb 1875	18
HALL, Walter H	HALL, Nancy Coffer	18 Feb 1919	95
HALL, Warren Gifford	SWART, E Gwyndolyn	24 Jun 1929	125
HALL, William /c	WALLACE, Martha /c	26 Oct 1893	47
HALL, William A	LAMP, Princess G	2 Aug 1932	138
HALL, William E	BUTLER, Gertrude V	18 May 1932	137
HALL, William Edward	THOMPSON, Mary V /wid	7 Nov 1888	39
HALL, William Withers	BEASLEY, Helen Veronica	27 Dec 1916	91
HALLETT, Harley J /wid	BORTREE, Helen M	21 Dec 1932	140
HALLEY, Jeremiah /wid	HUTCHISON, Laura	27 Dec 1874	18
HALLEY, William F	HOWARD, Susan	22 Feb 1866	6
HALLORAN, Charles E	DOHERTY, Beatrice	8 Feb 1921	100
HALLORAN, Francis D /wid	PLAUT, Adelle J	30 Mar 1929	124
HAMELL, John J	MURNANE, Alice	9 Jun 1881	28
HAMELL, Thomas M	HAIGHT, Elizabeth B	9 Jun 1920	98
HAMMELL, Bernard T	KEYS, Genevieve E	6 Jun 1917	92
HAMMELL, Zackariah Taylor	BEACH, Mary C	1 Apr 1872	14
HAMILTON, Clayton S	SPENCER, L Pauline	19 Dec 1933	145
HAMILTON, James H /wid	NEISH, Mamie	20 Mar 1926	114
HAMILTON, Jerry M /c	JONES, Alice V /c	8 Nov 1905	69
HAMILTON, Joseph E /c	BECKWITH, Adalaide I /c	21 Dec 1899	57
HAMILTON, Leslie	WHITE, Blanche	11 Nov 1933	144
HAMILTON, Percival Y /c	BRATTON, Lulilla /c	3 Jul 1922	102
HAMILTON, W F	WASHINGTON, Rosetta /c?	19 Dec 1867	8
HAMILTON, Walter /c	PINN, Nellie /c	19 Apr 1905	68
HAMILTON, William S /c	BECKWITH, Elnora /c	21 Jun 1898	54
HAMMERS, Donald M	BUTERHAUGH, Rhoda L	7 Jul 1930	128
HAMMON, Morris /c	SCOTT, Willins /c	3 Dec 1905	70
HAMMOND, Harry	CATTS, Mary Etta	15 Jan 1896	50
HAMMOND, Lee Norris	YINGER, Valletta E	31 Oct 1931	134
HAMPTON, A A	DAVIS, Maggie M	2 Dec 1906	72
HAMPTON, Benjamin /c	PEYTON, Fannie /c	29 Dec 1898	56
HAMPTON, Napoleon E	PEARSON, Mary P	25 Dec 1901	61
HAMPTON, W H	MARSHALL, Anna	24 Dec 1867	8
HAMPTON, Wade L	FAIRFAX, Susie /wid	8 Feb 1905	68
HANCOCK, Harry L	KIRK, Grace K	5 Nov 1932	139

HANCOCK, John F	O'MADIGAN, Cecelia	21 Oct 1931	*134*
HANDY, Walter K	KERFOOT, Grace B	29 Apr 1908	*74*
HANES, Robert H	MAKELY, Mary H	18 Nov 1903	*65*
HANES, Stanley B	CRIPPEN, Helen L	21 Jun 1932	*138*
HANEY, Fleming	ROBINSON, Mary	2 Oct 1868	*9*
HANEY, Walter Scott /c	POLLARD, Clara Bell /c	7 Apr 1904	*66*
HANKINS, Stanley E	BOWMAN, Mildred	28 Mar 1931	*131*
HANNA, Duvey L	DELLINGER, Beulah M	11 Sep 1922	*103*
HANNON, Ernest /c	SCOTT, Gracie /c	31 Jul 1910	*79*
HANRAHAN, Thomas	HASSETT, Margaret	25 Apr 1880	*26*
HANSBOROUGH, Howard	BONTZ, Beauregard	12 Jan 1881	*28*
HANSEN, Howard T	DOLL, Dorothea D	15 Feb 1933	*141*
HARDEN, Randolph T	CLEVELAND, Alice E	30 Dec 1902	*63*
HARDING, Donald M	KRAHNKE, Cleone	10 Apr 1933	*142*
HARDING, Edgar W	BUCK, Grace	29 Nov 1886	*37*
HARDY, John M Jr	KING, Dorothy A	17 Sep 1932	*139*
HARE, Edward T /wid	HOCKMAN, Ethel L	24 Jun 1908	*75*
HARGETT, John A	MILLS, Blanche W	7 Aug 1916	*90*
HARMAN, John R	COLLINS, Mary E	10 Dec 1878	*24*
HARNSBERGER, Reynolds T	BERRIEN, Mary Elizabeth	16 Sep 1927	*119*
HAROLD, Harry /c	HINES, Julia /c	11 Sep 1910	*79*
HAROLD, James	TRICE, Sarah J /wid	24 Jul 1878	*23*
HARPER, Douglas B	JENKINS, Louise M /div	2 Aug 1933	*143*
HARPER, George /c wid	WEBSTER, Veronica /c	24 Sep 1930	*129*
HARPER, Harold E /c	PIERRE, Alice /c	22 Apr 1931	*132*
HARPER, James /c wid	LOMAX, May /c wid	24 Jan 1909	*76*
HARPER, Jerry /c	BRADLEY, Alice /c	27 Sep 1905	*69*
HARPER, Lawrence /c	JACKSON, Lucinda /c	27 Nov 1923	*106*
HARPER, Sydney E	HOUSE, Leona P	25 Nov 1930	*130*
HARPER, William S	CLASBY, Lillian /wid	30 Jul 1899	*57*
HARRELL, John C /div	HARRELL, Julia S /div	30 Apr 1900	*58*
HARRELL, John Wade	BROWN, Ivy Adell	6 Jun 1901	*60*
HARRELL, Maurice Wayne	BOZATTA, Sophia	2 Mar 1923	*104*
HARRIMAN, Charles C	JORDAN, Georgianna	21 Dec 1931	*135*
HARRINGTON, Richard D	THOMAS, Marion W	8 May 1917	*92*
HARRIS, Edward	BIRD, Jane E	1 Aug 1868	*9*
HARRIS, Edward /c wid	GRAY, Sarah /c	8 Oct 1897	*53*
HARRIS, Aaron	OVENSTEIN, Shirley	23 Feb 1931	*131*
HARRIS, Alphonso /c	MARTIN, Virginia /c	30 Apr 1927	*118*
HARRIS, Arthur /c	CARTER, Annie /c	17 Mar 1891	*43*
HARRIS, Arthur /c	SAUNDERS, Effie /c wid	28 Aug 1928	*122*
HARRIS, Benjamin /c	DOWLING, Amanda /c	26 Dec 1895	*50*

HARRIS, Charles /c wid	WALKER, Lottie /c	30 Apr 1903	64
HARRIS, Charles /c	HARRIS, Alice /c	25 Aug 1913	85
HARRIS, Charles William	BEAVERS, Anna Elizabeth	3 Jun 1933	142
HARRIS, Edgar /c	ROBINSON, Judy /c wid	16 Dec 1912	83
HARRIS, Edward /c	COLE, Mahala /c wid	25 Aug 1874	17
HARRIS, Edward /c	MURPHY, Margaret /c	3 Jun 1889	40
HARRIS, Edwin H	SPEER, Carrie B	7 Dec 1904	67
HARRIS, Ellsworth /c	HENDERSON, Malinda /c	9 Jan 1893	46
HARRIS, Frank /c wid	MOULDEN, Mary /c	25 Oct 1913	85
HARRIS, George /c	SCOTT, Kate /c	22 Dec 1908	76
HARRIS, George /div	LINDAWOOD, Margaret	25 Mar 1916	90
HARRIS, George W /c	ALLEN, Narcissa /c	19 Feb 1890	41
HARRIS, George W	ROW, Annie W	4 Dec 1898	55
HARRIS, Henry /c wid	GRAY, Louisa /c	16 Dec 1900	59
HARRIS, Henry /c	HARPER, Gertie /c	18 Oct 1905	69
HARRIS, James Robert	HARRISON, Nellie V	23 Oct 1933	144
HARRIS, James T /c	WEBSTER, Clara E /c	14 Apr 1892	44
HARRIS, Jerome /c	ROBINSON, Aloynsia /c	2 Dec 1906	72
HARRIS, Jesse /c wid	LEE, Lucy /c wid	24 Mar 1887	37
HARRIS, John /c	HARRIS, Lucretia /c	24 Dec 1884	34
HARRIS, Joseph /c	ALLEN, Nancy /c	30 Jan 1886	36
HARRIS, Joseph /c wid	MORARITY, Alice /c wid	26 Oct 1933	144
HARRIS, Joseph Vannes /c	BOWLES, Virginia /c	1 Oct 1920	99
HARRIS, Levi /c	JORDAN, Matilda /c	15 Jun 1884	33
HARRIS, Lushion /c	BOWLES, Doris /c	10 Jul 1933	143
HARRIS, Moses /c wid	HARRIS, Elizabeth /c wid	3 May 1910	78
HARRIS, Obed R /c	STEWART, Minnie /c	18 Feb 1891	43
HARRIS, R T	EMBRY, Daisy	10 Apr 1920	97
HARRIS, Rosier /c	LONG, Pearl /c	10 Oct 1927	119
HARRIS, Shedrick /c	NAILOR, Lena /c	6 Apr 1905	68
HARRIS, Thomas /c	MURPHY, Lizzie /c	19 Dec 1888	39
HARRIS, Thomas P /c	QUANDER, Emma J /c	2 Dec 1890	44
HARRIS, Ulysses /c	HARRIS, Gertrude /c	17 Aug 1908	75
HARRIS, Wilbur /c	BROOKS, Nina /c	6 Nov 1909	77
HARRIS, William /c	SMITH, Florence E /c	20 Nov 1883	32
HARRIS, William /c wid	MOORE, Harriet A /c	16 Oct 1892	45
HARRIS, William /c	ROBISON, Jennie /c	13 Feb 1895	49
HARRIS, William /c wid	HARRIS, Jannie /c	29 Dec 1904	68
HARRIS, Willie /c	HARRIS, Nettie /c	30 Aug 1922	103
HARRISS, Charles /wid	DAVIS, Jennie /wid	22 Oct 1868	10
HARRISS, Elijah /c	MILES, Sarah /c	7 Jan 1869	10
HARRISS, Joseph /c wid	CAMBRIDGE, Henrietta /c wid	18 Nov 1926	116

HARRISON, Arthur B	BENNETT, Rosa A	28 Dec 1881	29
HARRISON, Asberry S	HOLDEN, Nancy Clinton	10 Apr 1896	50
HARRISON, Charles D	RICE, Mary L	22 Jun 1903	64
HARRISON, Clyde D	KNISELY, Edna	7 Jun 1929	124
HARRISON, Ernest P	SWETNAM, Bettie Keith	15 Sep 1910	79
HARRISON, George /wid	CANS, Mary E /wid	14 Dec 1868	10
HARRISON, George	DAVIS, Annie	15 May 1912	82
HARRISON, George F	AYRE, Ida D	1 Sep 1880	27
HARRISON, George W	SUTPHIN, Ann E	8 Nov 1869	11
HARRISON, Henry H /c wid	WEAVER, Ella M /c	14 Dec 1919	97
HARRISON, Holden S	RUCKER, Clara L	8 Jun 1929	125
HARRISON, James E	RICHARDS, Mildred	24 Feb 1855	1
HARRISON, James Ernest	VOWLES, Fannie Field	30 Dec 1907	74
HARRISON, James M	ASHFORD, Hannie	26 Oct 1879	25
HARRISON, John L	FORD, Amanda F	18 Dec 1901	61
HARRISON, R Townsend	AMBLER, Dorothy	3 May 1930	128
HARRISON, Robert B	BUCKLEY, Elizabeth C	25 Sep 1867	8
HARRISON, Robert L	DETWILER, Mary E	14 Dec 1898	55
HARRISON, Thomas J	KIDWELL, Caroline V /wid	21 May 1872	15
HARRISON, William	CLAPDORE, Mary J /wid	18 Jan 1869	10
HARRISON, William F /wid	ROBEY, Malinda /wid	5 Oct 1904	67
HARRISON, William G	MOCK, Joanna W	14 Jan 1880	24
HARRISON, William R	MUNSON, Mary Jasper	1 Oct 1895	50
HARROD, George H /c wid	BUTLER, Roberta /c wid	2 Aug 1906	71
HARROD, Simon /c wid	SHEPHERD, Nancy /c	12 Aug 1886	36
HARROD, William J /c	LEWIS, Martha /c	14 Feb 1885	34
HARROD, Arthur A /c	SINKFIELD, Laura V /c	6 Feb 1887	37
HARROVER, Alex /wid	WILEY, Sarah	30 Jul 1868	9
HARROVER, Hiram C	PRIDMORE, Martha A	15 Jun 1854	1
HARROVER, Jackson	DEAVERS, Rebecca A	1 Jan 1880	26
HARROVER, Robert L	MCCAULEY, Elsie	30 Jan 1906	70
HART, William L	SAGAR, Emma N	18 Oct 1886	36
HARTFIELD, Louis C /c	MALLETTE, Jennie J /c	30 Sep 1914	87
HARTLEY, Hugh V	BERNTSEN, Ruby H	18 Jun 1932	138
HARTLEY, Milton E	GASTEN, Gladys L	1 Oct 1925	112
HARTMAN, Henry /c div	CARROLL, Margaret E /c	6 Oct 1913	85
HARTMAN, John	SMITH, Jane	22 Mar 1870	12
HARTMAN, John E	GALPIN, Mamie E	24 Apr 1889	40
HARTMAN, Walter E /div	OREN, Myrtle F /div	11 Aug 1927	119
HARVELL, Charles W	TRUSSELL, Eva M	29 May 1933	142
HARVEY, Herbert N	FUCHS, Ellen M	19 Nov 1923	106
HASKAS, Thomas J	FISK, Eunice E F /div	17 Sep 1928	122

HASSALL, Albert R	OGLE, Aileen I	28 Apr 1926	*114*
HASTINGS, Leighton Burford	BUTLER, Lilian Frances	20 Apr 1920	*98*
HATCHER, Samuel T	MAFFETT, Lillian M	26 Dec 1906	*72*
HATCHER, William /c wid	BROWN, Mary C /c wid	21 Dec 1921	*101*
HATTON, Charles	SHELTON, Rosa	17 Aug 1905	*69*
HATTON, Charles /wid	LOWE, Edith	7 Apr 1908	*74*
HATTON, John	KIDWELL, Jennie	29 Nov 1899	*57*
HAUSER, William E	PAYNE, Olive A	29 Sep 1917	*93*
HAUSER, William E /wid	SCHULTZE, Eva M /wid	2 Jun 1932	*137*
HAVENER, Alonzo	SHAW, Mattie	10 Feb 1904	*66*
HAVENER, R H	HUMMER, Mary E	5 Nov 1867	*8*
HAWES, John T	SCHNEIDER, Christine A	6 Sep 1911	*81*
HAWES, M E	VOWLES, Garnett N	23 Dec 1903	*65*
HAWLEY, B M /wid	AMBLER, Hulda C	30 Mar 1913	*86*
HAWLEY, J G	BEACH, Delila	2 Jan 1867	*7*
HAWXHURST, George White /wid	QUICK, Ida J	22 Sep 1897	*53*
HAWXHURST, Henry	SMITH, Margery L	28 Jan 1902	*62*
HAYCOCK, George S	DORSEY, Elizabeth N	28 Dec 1904	*68*
HAYDEN, John F Jr	DARBY, Julia	8 Aug 1900	*59*
HAYES, Edward L /c	PEARSON, Mary L /c	2 Jun 1931	*132*
HAYES, George	RINKER, Mary G	5 Oct 1929	*126*
HAYES, George E C /c	ADAMS, Louise A /c	15 Nov 1924	*110*
HAYES, Oscar E	COCKERILLE, Georgia A	31 Oct 1925	*113*
HAYES, Robert /div	HOFFMAN, Emily E /div	10 Aug 1925	*112*
HAYNES, Marshall J /div	YAROCH, Mary	7 Oct 1922	*103*
HAYWOOD, Philo W	MAHONY, E A	27 Nov 1856	*2*
HEAD, Cameron	CROSS, Mary Lena	10 Dec 1908	*76*
HEAD, George	RILEY, Mary T	22 Oct 1868	*10*
HEATH, Edward	FAULKNER, Elizabeth	7 Sep 1910	*79*
HEATH, John H	ROBY, Lillie	26 Oct 1898	*55*
HEATH, Spencer A	PAYNE, Selinda A	14 May 1874	*17*
HEDGES, Hargest Marion	TETLOW, Ida Marguerite	21 Jan 1933	*141*
HEFFRON, Robert	GALLAHAN, Foncie	15 Aug 1921	*101*
HEFLIN, Alger Robert	PEERY, Inez Virginia	4 Nov 1933	*144*
HEGLAR, E Jerome	MCGUIRE, Edith Virginia	13 Jul 1933	*143*
HEIMENDAHL, Werner Edward	BIRD, Bessie	8 Jun 1895	*49*
HEISHMAN, Charles L	SILEY, Elma Virginia	5 Jul 1933	*143*
HEISLEY, Frank C	FAGANS, Rosanna E	20 May 1903	*64*
HEITMULLER, Albert H	HUTCHISON, Susie W	21 Sep 1898	*55*
HELBIG, Oscar A	WILCOX, Mary Jane	28 Sep 1919	*96*
HELENN, Raleigh /c	BRANHAM, Jeanette /c	20 Dec 1911	*82*
HELFENSTEIN, Edward Trail	NELSON, Grace F	8 Apr 1890	*41*

HELMAN, John G	NICHOLS, Pauline V	12 Nov 1932	*140*
HELMES, Henry	NARRINGTON, Louise	24 May 1924	*108*
HELMLING, Leon Willis	TITLOW, Elizabeth Hazelton	14 May 1921	*100*
HELT, Frank R	POWER, Phoebe L */wid*	5 Feb 1927	*117*
HEMING, George R */wid*	SACRISTE, Alice G */wid*	27 Oct 1913	*85*
HENDERSON, Benjamin H */c*	NICKENS, Marie D */c*	3 Sep 1924	*109*
HENDERSON, Charles E */wid*	HULETT, Altie	15 Apr 1926	*114*
HENDERSON, Charles F	FOLLIN, Emma V	10 Nov 1886	*36*
HENDERSON, Charles W	THOMAS, Lucretia R	18 Nov 1865	*6*
HENDERSON, Charles W */wid*	MONROE, Kate	9 Apr 1874	*17*
HENDERSON, Frank */c wid*	LEE, Birdie */c*	26 Dec 1889	*40*
HENDERSON, James H	WALKER, Elizabeth V	21 Jul 1872	*15*
HENDERSON, James H */c*	REEVES, Martha Jane */c*	15 Apr 1873	*16*
HENDERSON, James McKonkey	RICHARDSON, Virginia Fairfax	25 Jun 1925	*111*
HENDERSON, John */c*	NAYLOR, Jennie */c*	15 Aug 1878	*23*
HENDERSON, John R */wid*	MILSTEAD, Emma V	22 Dec 1886	*37*
HENDERSON, Joshua W */c*	STYLES, Gracie Anna */c*	18 Apr 1917	*91*
HENDERSON, Raymond C	CLAYTON, Rosalie E	22 Jul 1922	*103*
HENDERSON, Samuel Jr */c*	BUTLER, Emma */c*	5 Nov 1888	*39*
HENDERSON, Stephen S	CUMMINS, Martha A	11 Oct 1899	*57*
HENDERSON, Tyler	BROOKS, Grace	24 Nov 1870	*13*
HENDERSON, William */c*	SMITH, Maggie */c*	27 Dec 1898	*56*
HENDERSON, Willis	HALL, Dixie	24 Feb 1927	*117*
HENDRYX, Dexter J	KEENE, Clair Frances	11 Feb 1928	*121*
HENFORD, James S	CHICHESTER, Jenny P	27 Jan 1874	*17*
HENRY, Harold P	MECHLING, Emma A	21 Jun 1927	*118*
HENRY, Robert C	KIDWELL, Sallie E	7 Jan 1909	*76*
HENRY, Thomas T	PULLIN, Elizabeth L	29 Oct 1929	*126*
HENSHAW, Fayette	HOLDEN, C R	26 Feb 1857	*3*
HENSON, Edward C */div*	EVERETT, Margaret E	18 May 1933	*142*
HERBERT, Albert S	BURKE, Annie E	29 May 1904	*66*
HERBERT, Charles R */div*	FAIRFAX, Essie H	4 Mar 1906	*70*
HERDER, Fred C	SHEPHERD, Mary */wid*	3 Dec 1895	*50*
HERDER, John C */wid*	JOHNSON, Mary E	7 Apr 1895	*49*
HEREFORD, T J	JEFFRIES, Lottie	21 Feb 1927	*117*
HERFURTH, Oscar G	GAINES, Sadie I	14 Jan 1914	*86*
HERNDON, Francis M	GERARD, Agnes P */div*	29 Mar 1933	*141*
HERNDON, Paul T	BROWN, Effie	3 Jul 1930	*128*
HERNS, Robert */c*	TERRELL, Lucinda */c div*	19 Mar 1817	*91*
HERRELL, Charles I	ROBEY, Millie A	18 Jan 1894	*47*
HERRELL, Frank	THOMPSON, Annie M	6 Nov 1884	*34*
HERRING, William Mayo	SWETNAM, Nelle Franklin	25 Feb 1922	*102*

HERRITY, Walter B	GORHAM, Sallie Mae	10 Oct 1931	*134*
HESS, Stephen C /wid	EVANS, Catherine F	7 May 1932	*137*
HESS, William Boyer	SHOWALTER, Kathryn B	2 Jan 1932	*136*
HEWEY, G Austin	EGGERT, Daisy Catherine	28 May 1921	*100*
HEWLETT, Frank L /wid	SPARKS, Mary H	30 Jun 1932	*138*
HEYDRICK, George K	DAWSON, Adelaide V	21 Jun 1911	*81*
HIATT, John E	JOHNSON, Anna M	15 Sep 1931	*133*
HICKERSON, Herman /c	MACK, Adelaide /c	20 Dec 1914	*87*
HICKS, Albert E /div	DARNE, Vera D /div	30 Nov 1932	*140*
HICKS, Freeland O	WALKER, Ella R	25 Dec 1895	*50*
HICKS, Preston E	WRIGHT, Gladys G	26 Aug 1925	*112*
HIGDON, Clayton Ignatius	HARRIS, Margaret Pritchard	24 Mar 1919	*95*
HIGGINS, George L	BOTTS, Barbara	13 Jan 1876	*20*
HIGGINS, Richard /div	HATTON, Charlotte J	2 Jan 1929	*124*
HIGGS, Benjamin F	ORRISON, Lucy R	12 Oct 1876	*22*
HILEMAN, Ernest A	HEATH, Irene E	18 Jun 1924	*108*
HILL, Charles	HUNTER, Eugenia	5 Oct 1867	*8*
HILL, Charles Hawley	LAWRENCE, Marie V Z	19 Nov 1904	*67*
HILL, Joseph A	GILBERT, Katherine B	17 Sep 1932	*139*
HILL, Mac A	FLAHERTY, Sylvia Marie	5 Feb 1926	*113*
HILL, Marvin /c	TAYLOR, Lillian /c	7 Mar 1928	*121*
HILL, Rex R	HOUTZ, Edith V	1 Feb 1925	*110*
HILLS, John /c	TERRELL, Mary /c	17 Dec 1908	*76*
HILLYARD, Leo	HEAD, Bernedett	24 Nov 1904	*67*
HINCHLIFFE, Virgil J	BURNHAM, Katheryn	20 Aug 1932	*138*
HINES, Clifford G	PAULY, Eleanor C	18 Oct 1922	*103*
HINES, Ezell /c	QUANDER, Alcinda A /c	18 Apr 1931	*131*
HINKEL, Edward A	GOODALL, Ruth V	4 Jun 1927	*118*
HINSON, George A	MCLEAN, Mae /wid	1 Oct 1931	*134*
HINTON, Raymond	ARNOLD, Elenora	4 May 1931	*132*
HINTON, William C	ELLETT, Olive	26 Mar 1921	*100*
HIRSHAWITZ, Nathan	FRAZIER, Eleanor R	1 Aug 1917	*92*
HIRST, John E	PAYNE, Virginia	19 Mar 1868	*9*
HIRTH, Phil	LIPCOM, Edith D /wid	31 Jul 1910	*79*
HISER, Oscar Kervit	MCWAVEE, Mabel E	19 Apr 1927	*118*
HITAFFER, Charles	DEAVERS, Nellie M	22 Sep 1928	*122*
HITAFFER, Pierce H	SHIPMAN, Elizabeth	29 Oct 1907	*73*
HITCHCOCK, William H	STORM, Fannie S	16 Dec 1912	*83*
HITCHINGS, Francis	SIMS, Matilda F	9 Sep 1855	*1*
HITE, Newton McI /wid	SMITH, Evelyn Burton	2 Jan 1929	*124*
HITE, W H	SHOCKEY, Mary E	6 Jul 1915	*88*
HITE, William Fowler	LOVE, Isabella Fairfax	9 Jun 1892	*44*

HITT, Lawrence W	BROOME, Anne B	20 Sep 1917	*93*
HOBBS, Floyd S	PROSISE, Augusta E	26 Jul 1930	*129*
HOBBS, James L */wid*	ECHISON, Florence B */wid*	5 Aug 1922	*103*
HOCKNEY, George William	LATHAM, Etta Jane */div*	27 Mar 1933	*141*
HODGE, Clifton F */div*	DAWSON, Jean	20 Sep 1916	*90*
HODGES, J H Stancill	MOON, Cora Myrtie	29 Jun 1904	*66*
HODGES, William Henry	WYATT, Edith Rodgers */wid*	4 Aug 1928	*122*
HODGES, William Thomas	WALTON, Euphemia Lee	24 Nov 1910	*80*
HODGKIN, James O	DAY, Roberta	20 Nov 1878	*24*
HOEMILE, William A	REIF, Lottie P	27 Sep 1924	*109*
HOFFLINGER, Walter	WHITEHEAD, Virginia	3 Aug 1931	*133*
HOFFMAN, Edwin H	LACY, Lyda M	25 Dec 1915	*89.*
HOFFMAN, Frank M	KERNS, Marjorie A	7 Sep 1932	*139*
HOGAN, Burpee E */wid*	SIMPSON, Rosa M	20 Jan 1905	*68*
HOGANS, Samuel */c*	LUCAS, Mattie */c*	24 Oct 1906	*71*
HOGARTH, William N	FALCONER, Mary C	27 Mar 1926	*114*
HOGELAND, John B	GREEN, Virginia	18 Dec 1878	*24*
HOLBROOK, Elton R	WILEY, Martha Wagner	2 Oct 1901	*60*
HOLBROOK, Stockton S	SCOTT, Minnie B	14 Sep 1910	*79*
HOLBROOK, Thomas Henry	RICHARDSON, Elmira V	9 Aug 1861	*6*
HOLDAWAY, John W	MCGLINCY, Laura B	5 Jun 1930	*128*
HOLDEN, Thomas	SUMMERS, Bell	28 Feb 1872	*14*
HOLDERITH, Aloysius	McCONVEY, Agnes M	6 Nov 1907	*73*
HOLDSTOCK, Henry B	SMALL, Apphia E	8 Oct 1928	*123*
HOLLAND, Cornelius */c wid*	STEWARD, Malessa */c wid*	26 Nov 1925	*113*
HOLLAND, Frank */c*	QUANDER, Susie */c*	12 Oct 1904	*67*
HOLLAND, Robert L */c*	GIBSON, Grace */c*	26 Feb 1880	*26*
HOLLAND, William H */c*	DODSON, Annie */c*	29 Sep 1909	*77*
HOLLENBEAK, O A	STOUT, Alice R	29 Jan 1896	*50*
HOLLEY, Emile */c*	EIGLUNIE, Alice */c*	6 Apr 1929	*124*
HOLLIDAY, Edward	CUMMINS, Pearl	9 Nov 1926	*116*
HOLLIS, F A	DOVE, Mattie	10 May 1893	*46*
HOLLIS, Lawrence S	NASH, Alice L	9 Oct 1906	*71*
HOLLISTER, Frank W */div*	HALL, Rosa	22 Sep 1915	*89*
HOLLISTER, Frank W */div*	ROBINSON, Janie */wid*	25 Nov 1924	*110*
HOLLISTER, Franklin W	MITCHELL, Florence	20 Jan 1875	*18*
HOLMAN, Herbert P */wid*	STEWART, Anna A	17 Dec 1927	*120*
HOLMES, Atchley J	RICHARDSON, Dorothy E	25 Aug 1921	*101*
HOLMES, Bertram L */c*	HORTON, Blanche L */c*	28 Jun 1900	*58*
HOLMES, Matthew */c*	JEFFREY, Creasey */c*	15 Nov 1880	*27*
HOLMES, Walter E */div*	ALEXANDER, Ruby C	22 Jul 1930	*129*
HOLMES, Wildon */c*	THOMAS, Harriett */c*	31 Jul 1930	*129*

HOLSCLAW, J W /wid	KIDWELL, Mary V	31 Mar 1903	64
HOLT, Robert Pegram	HERBERT, Nora Carlyle	3 Jun 1908	75
HOLTZCLAW, W L	WELCH, Hanorah E	22 Feb 1897	52
HOMMEDIEN, John W L	ADAMS, Ruth	5 Mar 1927	117
HONESTY, Asbury /c	BRYCE, Amanda /c	1 Jan 1878	23
HONESTY, Charles /c	JOHNSON, Lula /c	12 Dec 1900	59
HONESTY, Columbus C /c	DORSEY, Laura V /c	23 Mar 1884	33
HONESTY, Frank /c	WILLIAMS, Kate /c	12 Nov 1882	30
HONESTY, Harry A /c	HORTON, Lucyetta /c	28 May 1902	62
HONESTY, Howard /c	ADAMS, Hazel /c	5 Jul 1921	100
HONESTY, Hudey /c	ROBINSON, Catherine /c	26 Mar 1908	74
HONESTY, John /c	TYLER, Bertie /c	4 Mar 1890	41
HONESTY, Maurice /c	TINNER, Elmira /c	24 Nov 1908	75
HONESTY, Raymond /c	BAILEY, Hattie /c	29 Jan 1913	84
HONESTY, William /c	JACKSON, Martha /c	8 Jan 1880	26
HONESTY, William /c wid	POLES, Lizzie /c	13 Jan 1898	54
HONESTY, William E /c	WAYNES, Esther L /c	8 May 1907	73
HONESTY, William Henry /c	DIXON, Louisa /c	15 Jun 1891	43
HONESTY, William S /c	JOHNSON, Sarah Ann /c	9 Jan 1878	24
HOOD, Isaiah /c	WASHINGTON, Irene /c	5 Nov 1902	63
HOOE, John Daingerfield	HERBERT, Maria	4 Jun 1890	41
HOOE, John R	FARR, Mary V	30 Jan 1860	5
HOOFF, E L	GLADDEN, Victoria V /wid	30 Oct 1884	33
HOPKINS, Charles A /wid	KIDWELL, Roberta	21 Jun 1866	6
HOPKINS, Charles H /c wid	HARRIS, Maria G /wid	30 Sep 1930	129
HOPKINS, J Bryan Jr /c	DAVIS, Mae Iris /c	19 Oct 1929	126
HOPKINS, James A	RIDGEWAY, Laura E	18 Apr 1931	131
HOPKINS, John W	JACOBS, Mary	26 May 1920	98
HOPKINS, Ludwood A	WALSH, Leo	10 Nov 1902	63
HOPKINS, Thomas J Jr /c	WARE, Marjoria V /c	29 May 1925	111
HOPKINS, W A	FAIRFAX, Sallie R	23 Apr 1902	62
HOPKINS, Warriner B	KEISTER, Eveline M	20 Jan 1926	113
HOPPE, Henry J	BUCKLEY, Martha H /wid	9 May 1925	111
HOPPER, Guy S	DILLON, Julia H /wid	21 Apr 1929	124
HOPPIN, Ray Minor	BARNES, Lola Rebecca	5 Aug 1924	109
HORN, R B	FINCH, Ivy H /wid	7 Jun 1926	114
HORNBECK, Charles W	KIDWELL, Sarah C	1 Mar 1877	21
HORNBECK, Nelson S	THOMPSON, Olive	4 Jan 1877	21
HORNBECK, Nelson S	GANTT, Ann R	20 Jan 1886	37
HORNER, William G	JEWELL, Ann Eliza	5 Mar 1884	33
HORSEMAN, James C	ROBINSON, Katie	12 Mar 1903	64
HORSEMAN, Milton	LAWSON, Eva	10 Aug 1920	98

HORTON, D D	CHAPMAN, Carrie	11 Feb 1873	*16*
HORTON, Francis M	CRIMMINS, Marie M	5 Aug 1933	*143*
HORTON, James /c	BROOKS, Lucinda /c	15 Jun 1873	*16*
HORTON, Snowden /c	EDWARDS, Winnie T /c	20 Jan 1901	*60*
HORTON, William /c	BROOKS, Hester Ann /c	31 Dec 1876	*21*
HORTON, William /c	BROOKS, Hester Ann /c	31 Dec 1876	*23*
HORTON, William H H	SIMMS, Annie L	7 Nov 1913	*85*
HOSKINS, Andrew /c	WRIGHT, Annie /c	29 Dec 1907	*74*
HOUCHINS, Claude M	STEWART, Rose A	30 Nov 1916	*91*
HOUCHINS, Walter Lee	LEATHERMAN, Vida Naomi	30 Aug 1916	*90*
HOUGH, A Lincoln /wid	DAVENPORT, Fannie A	20 Nov 1915	*89*
HOUGH, Robert W	RAUB, Ida A	22 Nov 1876	*21*
HOUGH, Samuel W	ALLISON, Anna L	8 Mar 1912	*82*
HOUSE, Louis B	BRENT, Margaret O	23 Oct 1933	*144*
HOUSE, Richard	SCHOFIELD, Catherine A	30 Oct 1932	*139*
HOUSTON, Henry W	DICKINSON, Ruth H	15 Jan 1921	*100*
HOUSTON, James L	LEWIS, Jessie M	28 May 1932	*137*
HOUSTON, Samuel F /wid	BROWN, Charlotte /wid	8 Apr 1902	*62*
HOUTZ, Edward	BINNS, Blanche A	11 Aug 1902	*63*
HOUZE, Charles Percy	KEITH, Hannah Morris	19 Mar 1927	*117*
HOWARD, A F /wid	DOVE, Margaret	7 Sep 1892	*45*
HOWARD, A Clarence	TRICE, Laura	17 Feb 1892	*44*
HOWARD, B /c	BOTTS, Narcissa /c	28 Sep 1898	*55*
HOWARD, Ernest L	MCKEAN, Minnie N	29 Apr 1884	*33*
HOWARD, Forrest K	HALL, M Bernice	28 Jun 1922	*102*
HOWARD, Henry B	CASSIDY, Lena May	2 Jun 1919	*95*
HOWARD, John /c	LEWIS, Alcinda /c	24 Dec 1901	*62*
HOWARD, John Randolph	HARRIS, Ora Virginia	9 Jun 1917	*92*
HOWARD, Lee	DANIELS, Emma	2 Dec 1927	*120*
HOWARD, Peter	SWART, Jane	13 Jan 1897	*52*
HOWARD, Philip	GRAHAM, Kate B	12 Apr 1876	*20*
HOWARD, Samuel T	PATTERSON, Ellen R	7 Oct 1884	*33*
HOWDERSHELL, George W /div	TAUGHINBAUGH, Anna V /div	1 Jul 1927	*118*
HOWE, Robert L	BEACH, Bessie M	9 Dec 1933	*145*
HOY, Franklin W	HURSH, Georgia M	18 Apr 1931	*131*
HOYT, Edward N	MALCOLM, Fannie H	22 Apr 1891	*43*
HUBBARD, J Troy	TAYLOR, Thelma I	28 Nov 1929	*126*
HUBBEL, Carter C	LOWELL, Elizabeth B	28 Feb 1931	*131*
HUBER, Karl /wid	SCHMIDT, Bertha /wid	30 Aug 1898	*55*
HUDNELL, James H /c wid	BRUCE, Rosa /c	8 Jun 1898	*54*
HUDSON, Aubrey W	PAYNE, Ellie L	11 Jul 1929	*125*
HUDSON, Charles C /wid	OLSEN, Gladys I /wid	27 Feb 1932	*136*

HUDSON, Herbert	SHEPHERD, Nettie	31 Jul 1926	*115*
HUDSON, Taylor	PETTITT, Mary E	23 Aug 1924	*110*
HUFFMAN, Elbie Stage	MONEY, Fannie	1 May 1920	*98*
HUGHES, George A	DOUGHERTY, Mary A	24 Dec 1904	*66*
HUGHES, John W	GILLINGHAM, Adrienne	8 Nov 1930	*130*
HUGHES, Lewis /c	ELLIS, Martha /c	4 Feb 1912	*82*
HUGHES, Philip E /c	BROOKS, Mary E /c	27 Jun 1900	*58*
HUGHES, Philip E /c wid	BECKWITH, Minnie /c	15 Oct 1902	*63*
HUGHES, William L	OGDEN, Estella C	14 Oct 1922	*103*
HULL, Maynard D	MUMMAW, Geneva	16 Mar 1911	*80*
HULL, Truman P	BARTLETT, Eliza C	30 Sep 1857	*3*
HUMMER, Benjamin A	BRUNNER, Ida M	16 Oct 1883	*32*
HUMMER, Beverly T	HOWDERSHELL, Lucille H	30 Jun 1919	*96*
HUMMER, Braden E /wid	ORRISON, Ellen E	21 Mar 1876	*20*
HUMMER, Joseph F	LOHMAN, Anna C	20 Dec 1876	*22*
HUMMER, William A	STROTHER, Mary L	24 Jul 1912	*83*
HUMPHRIES, Frank	HALGETT, Nellie	30 Nov 1917	*93*
HUMPHRIES, George C	RITCHIE, Jannie A	11 Jan 1871	*13*
HUMPHRIES, Howard F	DAVIS, Frances J	2 Oct 1933	*144*
HUMPHRIES, William A /c	FORREST, Elizabeth /c wid	21 Jun 1903	*64*
HUNNINGTON, Haven	YOUNG, Alice L	16 Dec 1878	*24*
HUNSBERGER, A W	KEENE, Lucy E	18 Jan 1905	*68*
HUNT, Albert J	CRONIN, Maggie	16 Apr 1895	*49*
HUNT, Charles A	SINCLAIR, Mary	3 Sep 1927	*119*
HUNT, Fenton /c	NORTON, Lottie /c	22 Dec 1898	*55*
HUNT, John	CAMPBELL, Laria	17 Nov 1898	*55*
HUNT, Joseph H /div	LOWE, Marguerite V /div	7 May 1932	*137*
HUNT, Joseph W	BRADY, Sarah S	16 Jul 1893	*46*
HUNT, Lewis B	THOMPSON, Eliza H	29 Jan 1873	*16*
HUNT, Lewis J	KIDWELL, Emma	9 Jul 1884	*33*
HUNT, Lockwood	HUME, Margaret	22 Jun 1926	*115*
HUNT, Russell F	MARSHBURN, Lilly V	19 Jan 1918	*93*
HUNTT, Wade H	HUNTT, Lottie Lee	7 Apr 1909	*76*
HUNTER, Albert B	LOREN, Lois M	7 Jun 1911	*81*
HUNTER, Charles H /c	ROBINSON, Carrie E /c	27 Oct 1903	*66*
HUNTER, George /c	HONESTY, Mattie /c	17 Nov 1897	*53*
HUNTER, James B	JOHNSON, Annie E	17 May 1882	*30*
HUNTER, James H /c wid	TEBBS, Cecelia /c	6 Dec 1903	*65*
HUNTER, James Jr	TROTH, Rebecca	30 Mar 1881	*28*
HUNTER, James T /c	WHALEY, Sarah J /c wid	7 Jan 1874	*17*
HUNTER, James T /c	HORTON, Gertrude L /c	21 Jun 1903	*64*
HUNTER, John C /wid	JOHNSON, Emma J	7 Dec 1881	*29*

HUNTER, John C	TERRETT, Lucy S	27 Mar 1891	*43*
HUNTER, Nathaniel Chapman	NEWLON, Eliza J Florence	1 Oct 1884	*33*
HUNTER, Robert */c*	TURLEY, Maggie */c*	10 Feb 1880	*24*
HUNTER, W A	BLOXTON, Georgia Belle	2 Jul 1923	*105*
HUNTER, W H	ROUSER, Ola B	10 Aug 1904	*67*
HUNTER, Washington */c wid*	PORTER, Margaret */c wid*	10 Dec 1884	*34*
HUNTER, William Jr	MASON, Mary W	25 Dec 1877	*23*
HUNTER, William S	MANKIN, Minnie Lee	20 Jun 1895	*49*
HUNTINGTON, R L */wid*	DEAVERS, Annie	28 Oct 1909	*77*
HUNTT, Thomas E	FORTNEY, Nora	28 May 1890	*41*
HURD, W L	GRAY, M L	11 Mar 1916	*90*
HURLANDER, Harold W	ROSE, Sarah Lewis	17 Feb 1923	*104*
HURLEY, Alonzo */c*	WILLIAMS, Rose */c*	11 Sep 1898	*55*
HURLEY, Alonzo A */c*	PERRY, Clara E */c*	5 Sep 1921	*101*
HURLEY, Ray	EASTERDAY, Clara E	14 May 1932	*137*
HURST, Eugene G	HORSEMAN, Myrtle I	9 Jul 1929	*125*
HURST, J E	REID, Virginia A	1 Mar 1860	*5*
HURST, John R	BIRCH, Cora E	14 Jan 1903	*64*
HUTCHINSON, Amandly A	COCKERILLE, Nannie	18 Jan 1871	*13*
HUTCHINSON, E G	MURPHY, Ellenora	16 Feb 1887	*37*
HUTCHINSON, William A */wid*	WHALEY, Martha A */wid*	25 Apr 1872	*14*
HUTCHISON, Cook F	HUTCHISON, Gabriel A */wid*	6 Jan 1881	*28*
HUTCHISON, E Barbour	AUD, Mary Anna	24 Feb 1915	*88*
HUTCHISON, Elijah P	KIDWELL, Sarah	4 Dec 1875	*19*
HUTCHISON, Frank A	ADAMS, Bertha K	15 Jan 1914	*86*
HUTCHISON, Fred H	GUNNELL, Martha E	6 Dec 1919	*97*
HUTCHISON, Herod H	BERRY, Martha Ann */wid*	26 Dec 1878	*24*
HUTCHISON, James E	WRENN, Gabriel Anna	14 Dec 1869	*11*
HUTCHISON, John C	HOLLIDAY, Addie L	20 May 1908	*75*
HUTCHISON, John G	HUTTON, Elizabeth	19 Jan 1860	*5*
HUTCHISON, Joseph H	JAMES, Cora L	3 Dec 1884	*34*
HUTCHISON, L	TOWNSHEND, Jennie	6 Feb 1884	*32*
HUTCHISON, Philip A */wid*	FLEMING, Aminta	12 Jun 1895	*49*
HUTCHISON, Philip A */wid*	ADRIAN, Clara A. Fleming */div*	26 Feb 1920	*97*
HUTCHISON, Robert A */wid*	HOLDEN, Bettie	21 May 1903	*64*
HUTCHISON, Samuel W	HUTCHISON, Mary A	15 Feb 1882	*30*
HUTCHISON, Sanford M	FITZHUGH, Elizabeth M	6 Jan 1881	*28*
HUTTON, Thomas	HUTCHISON, Sarah E	3 Nov 1859	*4*
HYMAN, Reginald V	SOPER, Gertrude	14 Apr 1921	*100*
HYNSON, John E	PINKARD, Jessie	3 Oct 1931	*134*
HYSON, Charles V */c*	JOHNSON, Florence */c wid*	19 Oct 1916	*91*
HYSON, Thornton W */c*	FERGUSON, Sarah F */c*	18 Jun 1885	*35*

IDEN, B B	OLIVER, Elizabeth P	20 Feb 1907	*72*
IDEN, George R	SHAFER, Ida B	23 Jun 1892	*45*
IDEN, Jacob J	PEACOCK, Mary A	3 Mar 1857	*3*
IDEN, James	FOLLIN, Bessie Irene	6 Nov 1907	*73*
IDEN, John N	SMITH, Mary V	6 Apr 1870	*12*
IDEN, Mandly T */div*	WINDSOR, Eva E	28 Aug 1907	*73*
INGLING, Geo W	SISSON, Marie B	8 Oct 1923	*106*
INNIS, Alexander	LEMOINE, Virginia	7 Apr 1858	*3*
IRBY, Samuel J	WEISEL, Dorothy V	27 Aug 1930	*129*
IRISH, Ralph S	SHACKLETTE, Warwich A	16 Apr 1927	*117*
IRWIN, Elum A	SCOTT, Hyacinth	2 Sep 1922	*103*
IRWIN, John Clyde Jr	TRUMAN, Ellen	30 May 1932	*137*
ISOM, Philip */c*	CARTER, Bertha M E */c*	28 Mar 1932	*136*
IVES, Albert H	JENKINS, T Jane	19 Nov 1867	*8*
IVES, Claude J	PEARSON, Annie E	26 Jan 1898	*54*
IVES, Reuben */wid*	HOTCHKISS, Mary */wid*	1 Sep 1869	*11*
IVES, Sheldon S	NEAL, Jennie L	24 Dec 1872	*15*
IVES, Willis C	GRIFFITH, Alice V	15 Sep 1882	*30*
JACKSON, A W */c wid*	GARRETT, Louise */c*	19 Sep 1895	*50*
JACKSON, Albert	LEE, Anna M	14 Nov 1867	*8*
JACKSON, Barney */c*	HENDERSON, Lea */c*	16 Feb 1890	*41*
JACKSON, Boyd F	WILSON, Blanche V */wid*	30 Aug 1920	*98*
JACKSON, Charles */c*	WRIGHT, Nellie */c*	12 Feb 1893	*46*
JACKSON, Charles */c*	JACKSON, Luvenia */c*	26 Oct 1904	*67*
JACKSON, Charles */c div*	TERRELL, Rebecca */c*	7 Oct 1912	*83*
JACKSON, Charles H S */c*	SMITH, Chainey M */c*	22 Oct 1890	*42*
JACKSON, Charlie */c*	SMITH, Mabel */c*	2 Oct 1909	*77*
JACKSON, Clarence */c*	LUCAS, Virginia */c*	13 Sep 1917	*93*
JACKSON, Clarence T */c*	BELFIELD, Frances */c*	5 May 1932	*137*
JACKSON, Dallas */c*	MOULTON, Rachael */c*	13 Jan 1870	*12*
JACKSON, Edgar M	OLIVER, Eugenia	22 May 1877	*22*
JACKSON, Edward */c*	STOTTS, Carrie */c*	25 May 1902	*62*
JACKSON, Edward */c wid*	GANTT, Alberta */c wid*	22 Nov 1910	*79*
JACKSON, Edward */c*	GASKINS, Bertha */c wid*	15 May 1927	*118*
JACKSON, Eugene E */c*	BOOTH, Inez C */c*	7 Jul 1915	*88*
JACKSON, George P	READSHAW, Alice F	16 Sep 1903	*65*
JACKSON, Harrison	ELLIS, Lizzie */c*	23 Jan 1908	*74*
JACKSON, Jacob	JACKSON, Frances	31 Jan 1872	*15*
JACKSON, James */c wid*	KING, Sarah */c wid*	1 Aug 1918	*94*
JACKSON, James	THOMAS, Lillie May */c*	6 Aug 1923	*105*
JACKSON, James */c*	ELLIS, Nora */c wid*	6 Aug 1928	*122*
JACKSON, James */c*	HARRIS, Beatrice */c*	13 Aug 1930	*129*

JACKSON, James A /c	JACKSON, Martha /c	18 Jun 1891	43
JACKSON, James M /c	DESKIN, Mary F /c	20 Apr 1895	49
JACKSON, James T	GUNNELL, Margaretta	17 Nov 1868	10
JACKSON, John	JOHNSON, Ariana /c	26 Dec 1873	16
JACKSON, John /c	LEWIS, Ginnie /c	15 Jan 1883	32
JACKSON, John	SELVY, Lucy /wid	11 Mar 1894	47
JACKSON, John E /c	CARROLL, Annie J /c	29 Oct 1922	103
JACKSON, John T J	PEACOCK, Elizabeth	26 Feb 1873	16
JACKSON, John T J /wid	MACKEY, Catherine /wid	14 Feb 1911	80
JACKSON, John W /c	TEBBS, Martha /c	19 Aug 1877	22
JACKSON, Josias /c	JORDAN, Eliza /c	28 Dec 1876	21
JACKSON, Leonard /c	TERRELL, Geneva /c	21 Feb 1924	108
JACKSON, Lewis E /c	LOMAX, Melvina /c	7 Apr 1877	22
JACKSON, Lifus /c wid	WEST, Susan /c wid	10 Dec 1885	35
JACKSON, Lifus /c wid	SINKFIELD, Mary /c wid	3 Jul 1898	54
JACKSON, Lifus /c wid	HAMILTON, Martha /c wid	1 Sep 1907	73
JACKSON, Mandeville /c	JONES, Maggie /c	25 Agu 1883	31
JACKSON, Raymond /c	KIOH, Hattie /c	16 Sep 1902	63
JACKSON, Richard T	SHARPER, Virginia /c	8 Feb 1887	37
JACKSON, Robert S /c	GADDIS, Elizabeth /c	25 Sep 1929	126
JACKSON, Solomon	JACKSON, Lavinia /c	23 Jul 1903	65
JACKSON, Theodore H /c	CLEMENS, Almira F /c	30 Aug 1899	57
JACKSON, Thomas	COOK, Ann Maria /c	18 Apr 1879	25
JACKSON, Thomas H	COSBY, Annie /c	6 Jan 1885	34
JACKSON, W H /c	JONES, Blanche /c	18 Apr 1889	40
JACKSON, Walter /c	COOPER, Elizabeth /c	20 Sep 1920	99
JACKSON, William A /c	SHIRLEY, Amanda M /c	19 Sep 1889	40
JACKSON, William H /c	WARNER, Charlotte /c	22 Oct 1917	93
JACKSON, William Henry /c	HOPKINS, Lillian B /c	27 Dec 1900	59
JACKSON, Wyatt N /wid	TURNER, Annie M /wid	31 May 1899	56
JACOBS, A R /wid	ALLDER, Emma J	18 May 1898	54
JACOBS, Alfred	O'BRIEN, Mary L	29 Nov 1870	13
JACOBS, John	WHITE, Florence A	29 Nov 1866	7
JACOBS, Johnie W	HARRELL, Carrie E	11 Sep 1926	116
JACOBS, W F M	GREEN, Sarah V	6 Jul 1858	3
JACOBS, William M	SIMMS, Pearl	28 Jun 1921	100
JACOBSON, Michael /div	BUSSE, Dorothy M	6 Jun 1921	100
JAGER, Raymond F	SPEAKE, Lavinia B	29 Sep 1930	129
JAMERSON, Elias /c wid	FAIRFAX, Ann /c	25 Mar 1890	41
JAMES, Henry /c	HALL, Catherine /c	20 Nov 1884	34
JAMES, Philip /c	BOWMAN, Ida /c	20 Nov 1884	34
JAMES, Spencer	DOWNS, Lizzie O	7 Dec 1915	89

JERMAN, Arthur	MILLENAX, Claris	11 Feb 1931	*131*
JERMAN, Calvin M	DOVE, Ida	6 Sep 1900	*59*
JERMAN, Charles M	WYSONG, Mary J	17 Mar 1887	*37*
JERMAN, Edward	LANHAM, Elizabeth /wid	18 Oct 1893	*47*
JERMAN, Edward	NASH, Madeline	17 Jul 1926	*115*
JERMAN, Edward T /wid	COCKERILLE, Rosa A	30 Sep 1896	*51*
JERMAN, Elmer	TAYLOR, Mary V	8 Apr 1923	*105*
JERMAN, John F	SMITH, Josephine M	21 Feb 1884	*33*
JERMAN, Joseph	TRUMBLE, Annie	3 Jun 1925	*111*
JERMAN, Joseph W	HALEY, Sarah E	5 Apr 1866	*9*
JERMAN, Joseph W /wid	SIMPSON, Mattie E /wid	1 Jun 1904	*66*
JERMAN, Thomas J /wid	MULHOLLAND, Margaret	5 Nov 1890	*42*
JESTER, James Graham	ENGLAND, Elizabeth	16 Nov 1887	*38*
JETER, Robert /c	DIXON, Lyddie /c	14 Oct 1897	*53*
JEWELL, Edward C	HAVENER, Laura V	23 Dec 1895	*50*
JEWELL, John	FERTNEY, Maud	15 Jul 1891	*43*
JOHNS, Kensey	STUART, Laura	7 Oct 1858	*4*
JOHNSON, Benjamin /c	GASKINS, Virginia /c	31 Jan 1869	*10*
JOHNSON, Brook /c	GIBSON, Ida /c	9 Jul 1908	*75*
JOHNSON, Charles B	ROBEY, Effie Ada	3 Mar 1923	*104*
JOHNSON, Cliff /c	BLACKWELL, Susan /c	20 Jan 1876	*20*
JOHNSON, Cornelius W Jr	SCHOFIELD, Mamie A	31 Jan 1900	*58*
JOHNSON, Delvin J /c	NAILOR, Susan Emeline /c	12 Feb 1880	*26*
JOHNSON, Dennis /c	DESKINS, Julia /c	10 Dec 1896	*52*
JOHNSON, Douglas L /c	SCOTT, Ruth L /c	18 Nov 1915	*89*
JOHNSON, Edward /c	TATE, Charlotte /c	10 Jan 1901	*60*
JOHNSON, Emmett L	SPITTLE, Rosa V	11 May 1914	*86*
JOHNSON, Ernest C	PIERCE, Sarah Frances	25 Jan 1932	*136*
JOHNSON, Fletcher /c	CARTER, Mary Ellen /c	20 Aug 1891	*43*
JOHNSON, Fred S	SHAW, Florence S	10 Mar 1922	*102*
JOHNSON, Gaylord H	SISSON, Annie M	12 Apr 1876	*20*
JOHNSON, George W	PRATT, Mary M	29 May 1895	*49*
JOHNSON, Glascoe /c	PARKER, Sarah /c	25 Mar 1891	*43*
JOHNSON, Harry B /wid	HOWARD, Margaret F	2 Aug 1919	*96*
JOHNSON, Harry V	BICKSLER, Bertie B	15 May 1918	*94*
JOHNSON, Henry H /c	ALEXANDER, Jennie E /c	21 Oct 1920	*99*
JOHNSON, Henry M	EASTWOOD, Mary A	16 Sep 1930	*129*
JOHNSON, Howard M	LANAHAN, Catherine L	14 Oct 1929	*126*
JOHNSON, Irvin J	WEAVER, Mary Almetta	28 Jun 1933	*142*
JOHNSON, J L H /c	SHARPER, Annie M /c	6 Apr 1903	*64*
JOHNSON, James /c wid	STROTHER, Priscilla /c	7 Aug 1890	*41*
JOHNSON, James W /c	MORARITY, Sinah /c	14 Jan 1883	*31*

JOHNSON, John /c	HALL, Mary /c	29 Nov 1877	22
JOHNSON, John /c	TAYLOR, Betsey /c wid	5 Apr 1893	46
JOHNSON, John /c	JACKSON, Nora /c	10 Jul 1898	54
JOHNSON, John F /wid	BROOKE, Beulah	17 Apr 1900	58
JOHNSON, John H /wid	BROMLEY, Catharine E /wid	14 Aug 1905	69
JOHNSON, Joseph	HALEY, Louise	7 Aug 1928	122
JOHNSON, Lorenzo N	KINCHELOE, Namie T	26 Nov 1912	83
JOHNSON, Manly	WHEELER, Jannie	10 Aug 1870	13
JOHNSON, Nathaniel	WILEY, Alberta	3 Feb 1881	28
JOHNSON, Noble	WOOD, Malinda	18 Sep 1906	71
JOHNSON, Oscar /c	WELLS, Martha /c	18 Sep 1882	30
JOHNSON, Oscar M /c	DAVENPORT, Mary J /c	11 Oct 1883	32
JOHNSON, Perry M	MEALY, Blanch	30 Sep 1924	109
JOHNSON, Philip A	GODWIN, Bettie	3 Jul 1855	1
JOHNSON, R D /c	SAUNDERS, Carrie /c div	3 Nov 1916	91
JOHNSON, Rice /c wid	JACKSON, Sarah /c wid	16 Feb 1928	121
JOHNSON, Roy	SUTPHIN, Mabel	10 Mar 1913	84
JOHNSON, Tobe /c	BURKE, Mary J /c	5 May 1888	38
JOHNSON, Wade /c	ROBERSON, Mary /c wid	5 Oct 1912	83
JOHNSON, William /c wid	BECTON, Annie /c	10 Oct 1897	53
JOHNSON, William /c	MARSHALL, Bertha /c	10 Feb 1916	90
JOHNSON, William B	WILLIAMS, Ethel W /c	16 Apr 1908	74
JOHNSON, William E	DORSEY, Susan /c	11 Jan 1881	28
JOHNSON, William Henry	WAINE), Sarah Jane	25 Feb 1872	15
JOHNSON, Willis	BOWER, Mary	29 Jul 1923	105
JOHNSON, Wilson /c	NEWMAN, Luvenia /c	4 Jul 1901	60
JOHNSON, Wright C	ROUFNER, Irene /wid	28 Aug 1926	115
JOHNSON, Zach	THOMAS, Bertie /c	3 Aug 1899	57
JOHNSTON, Sam R	EGE, Mary G	21 Jun 1859	4
JOHNSTON, Vivian Kirk	RILEY, Nora Agnes	18 Jun 1921	100
JOHNSTON, W F	HUNTER, Sarah E	14 Jan 1868	9
JONES, A Carroll	KAHRL, Marie	16 Jul 1930	128
JONES, Albert	DIMSEY, Bertha	27 Oct 1909	77
JONES, Aubrey	BILLER, Orpha	20 Sep 1928	122
JONES, Bollie B	CREAMER, Ella L	24 Nov 1926	116
JONES, Charles	MOORE, Mary /c	28 Dec 1927	120
JONES, Charles Bayne	SULLIVAN, Esie R	30 Jul 1910	79
JONES, Charles W /wid	HALLEY, Mary E	27 Dec 1905	70
JONES, Claude C	GRAYSON, Anna Beatrice	29 Jun 1910	78
JONES, Clement	JENKINS, Nellie	12 Feb 1880	26
JONES, Curvin F	DE FREHM, Ina M	5 Apr 1930	127
JONES, Dewey /c	SIMMONS, Laurie E /c	18 May 1918	94

JONES, Douglass /c	JACKSON, Mary /c	15 Jul 1916	90
JONES, Edward T	CLATTERBUCK, Grace E	18 Aug 1930	129
JONES, Emanuel H	BROOKS, Sarah E	1 Feb 1877	21
JONES, Everett A	MATHIS, Elizabeth L	21 Dec 1925	113
JONES, George /c	DODSON, Anner /c	21 Aug 1915	89
JONES, George	PORTCH, Alice M	29 Nov 1930	130
JONES, George W /c	ALEXANDER, Maggie L /c	11 Oct 1881	29
JONES, George W	HULLINGS, Lillian F	24 Feb 1892	44
JONES, H L	DREW, Irene C /wid	20 Oct 1913	85
JONES, Henry /c wid	JONES, Agnes /c	13 May 1916	90
JONES, Henry B	BAYLISS, Jessie A	5 Nov 1902	63
JONES, Herbert H /c	TINSLEY, Geneva R /c	15 Aug 1922	103
JONES, Isam	THOMPSON, Alice /c	23 Dec 1883	32
JONES, J B	FOLLIN, Ann America	9 Sep 1869	11
JONES, J R	BEAVERS, Eva L	23 Apr 1902	62
JONES, James F	SIMS, Virginia	16 Jun 1930	128
JONES, James M	SHARVEN, Nina F	27 Aug 1913	85
JONES, James W	KIDWELL, Mary Ellen	19 Dec 1872	15
JONES, James Walter	NEWCOMB, Mary Gertrude	10 Oct 1917	93
JONES, John /c	WASHINGTON, Kate /c	26 Sep 1885	35
JONES, John /c wid	JACKSON, Sallie /c	16 Dec 1899	57
JONES, John T	REID, Lenora V	6 Apr 1915	88
JONES, Joseph /c	ADAMS, Felcia /c wid	15 Dec 1898	55
JONES, Layman	YONGE, Gwendolene V	30 Aug 1913	85
JONES, Notlie B /c	TILMAN, Martha /c	20 Mar 1901	60
JONES, Rhesa H	TYERS, Annie E	17 Jun 1908	75
JONES, Richard /c	ANDERSON, Mary /c	29 Jun 1905	69
JONES, Robert /c	BUSH, Jane /c	14 Jun 1896	51
JONES, Roland M	SMOOT, Julia W	18 Jul 1867	7
JONES, Trueman S	SUMMERS, Mary E	5 Feb 1867	7
JONES, W B	GREENWOOD, Kate J	12 Feb 1927	117
JONES, Waldo H	MERRILL, Edna G	15 Dec 1929	127
JONES, William	WILLIAMS, Ellen /c wid	14 Feb 1868	9
JONES, William	GREEN, Leanna	8 Feb 1872	15
JONES, William E /c	TAYLOR, Pearl G /c	3 Jul 1919	96
JONES, William McKinley /c	WALKER, Jennie /c	5 Feb 1924	108
JONES, William W	SHERWOOD, Annie R	3 Apr 1884	33
JONES, Wilton V	LEPLEY, Pauline G	23 Aug 1932	139
JOPLING, Henry	PULMAN, Nannie M	7 Jan 1891	43
JORDAN, Edward C	FISHER, Mary Elizabeth	12 Sep 1928	122
JORDAN, Harry /c	NAPPER, Anna R /c	4 Dec 1912	83
JORDAN, John Henry /c	JOHNSON, Sallie /c	29 Nov 1893	47

JORDAN, Solomon	JACKSON, Eliza	5 Jul 1868	9
JORDAN, Solomon /c wid	WILLIAMS, Maria /c wid	19 Dec 1875	19
JORDAN, William Wells	VROOM, Elizabeth Riddle	30 Jun 1885	35
JOSEY, John C	BERNDGEN, Marcella	28 Feb 1931	131
JUBB, W Joseph	CATON, Loretta M	24 Oct 1920	99
JUDKINS, William E	BALL, Mary G	15 Nov 1855	1
JULIAN, Fred N	PARHAM, Jessie R	18 Jun 1916	90
JULIUS, Peter /c wid	PARKER, Mary /c	13 Apr 1876	20
KAGAY, B F Jr	HARRISON, Elizabeth R T	21 Jul 1886	36
KANE, J J	SANGER, Lula Florence	25 Dec 1905	70
KANE, Jerry	WATSON, Mary	11 Jun 1870	12
KASAL, Frederick	HECK, Elsie	21 Aug 1929	125
KATES, James W	POE, Grace E	31 Jul 1931	133
KEAN, Alfred H	HARPER, Flora Scott	7 Oct 1916	91
KEANE, Thomas Jos.	SMART, Elizabeth Blanche	6 Jun 1921	100
KEARNES, Edris	MILLS, Martha E	28 Dec 1880	27
KEARNES, John R	BEACH, Sarah E	28 May 1870	12
KEARNS, Andrew	DAVIS, Pearl Virginia	14 Jan 1928	121
KEARNS, Charles C	MARKS, Ina I	8 Feb 1888	38
KEARNS, David E	KIDWELL, Virginia A	25 Apr 1882	30
KEARNS, William H	SIMPKINS, Maude B	27 Aug 1920	98
KEARNEY, John B	BAKER, Sara	2 Jun 1915	88
KEARNEY, William A	RYDER, Abbie	19 Mar 1911	80
KEATING, Leo	CULLEN, Marie	29 Jan 1924	108
KEDDY, Clyde A	PERRY, Stevena	7 Jan 1922	102
KEEGAN, Charles R	HINKLE, Florence D	12 May 1917	92
KEENE, Benjamin B	JENKINS, Anna	24 Oct 1872	15
KEENE, James O	DODSON, Elizabeth Virginia	31 Dec 1874	18
KEENER, Clarence	KIDWELL, May	18 Apr 1923	105
KEEZER, Dexter M	MILLETT, Annie C	22 Jun 1927	118
KEFFORD, John W /c	GIBSON, Emma /c	15 Mar 1888	38
KEISENDOFFER, Henry	GARNER, Laura E	11 Jun 1884	33
KEITH, Henny /c	PARKS, Emma /c	28 Sep 1876	20
KEITH, Thomas Randolph	MOORE, Edith M	16 Nov 1899	57
KELLEY, Delbert E	SAYRE, Ollie Eileen	22 Jun 1929	125
KELLEY, Delmus L	AUTRY, Sarah Eliz /div	16 Nov 1933	144
KELLEY, M Wesley	ARMSTRONG, Mamie J /wid	15 Nov 1908	75
KELLY, Charles /c	TURNER, Ada E /c	19 Mar 1891	43
KELLY, Henry Wise	SWETNAM, Julia K	3 Nov 1920	99
KELLY, James	BAIRD, Gertrude	5 Jul 1910	79
KELLY, Michael A	JOHNSTON, Emma D	8 Oct 1910	79
KELLER, Louis P	HEAD, Elizabeth M	12 Dec 1900	59

KELSEY, Robert /c	KNIGHT, Florence /c	6 Jan 1896	50
KEMPEL, Philip C	CODER, Gertrude M	28 Jul 1905	69
KEMPER, Joseph R	DOAK, Hazel H	27 Jun 1931	132
KENNEY, Rufus T /c	SHARPER, Mary E /c	25 Jul 1912	83
KENNY, Daniel /wid	MOROCKER, Marie J	19 Nov 1922	104
KENNY, William H /c	GASKINS, Sarah /c	2 Mar 1900	58
KENNARD, Charles W Jr	LONG, Catharine A	9 Dec 1913	85
KENNEDY, Andrew J /wid	MAHONEY, Sarah E /div	21 Sep 1912	83
KENNEDY, Elwood W	HILEMAN, Mary Frances	24 Jun 1933	142
KENNEDY, John T	ARNOT, Ethel Clephane	26 Apr 1921	100
KENNEDY, Steele M	SIMS, Betty B	19 Aug 1933	143
KENNER, Aaron /c	HARROD, Lillie /c	16 Dec 1903	65
KENT, Paul	LEA, Irene	3 Jan 1933	141
KENYON, Byron Jacob	VIOLLAND, Adrienne Gray	6 Feb 1895	49
KENYON, Eugene B	REYNOLDS, Carrie S	4 Sep 1890	41
KENYON, George L	SMITH, Lottie M	1 Sep 1867	8
KENYON, Howland	GUNNELL, Lena	15 Feb 1913	84
KENYON, Paul S	SNYDER, Ada Elnora	1 Nov 1901	61
KEPHART, Luther	THOMPSON, Rosie	24 Jan 1907	72
KEPHART, Luther H /wid	GRIFFITH, Sarah F	14 Dec 1921	101
KEPHART, Maurice W	JOHNSON, Jennie J	13 Feb 1884	32
KEPHART, William H /wid	TIPPETT, Mary E	12 Jun 1906	71
KERANS, Jackson H	SEARS, Ethel M	11 Jul 1924	108
KERBY, Bernard /wid	COLLARD, Mary C	6 Jun 1876	20
KERBY, F A /wid	DAY, Annie	29 Dec 1874	18
KERBY, James E	SEWELL, Sarah Alice	24 Feb 1857	3
KERCHEVALL, Benjamin B	VEALE, Nannie E	24 Feb 1869	10
KERNS, John N	KENDRICK, Martha	18 Feb 1874	17
KERNS, John W	BELL, Jessie P	4 Oct 1905	69
KERNS, Joseph	SUTHERLAND, Emma	19 Jan 1887	37
KERNS, William S	TILLETT, Alice J	18 Jan 1877	21
KERNOLL, Alansin J	MOORE, Elmira	9 Nov 1854	1
KERR, Virgil E /wid	LEEDS, Dora	23 Feb 1886	36
KERRICK, Milton F	HOWDERSHELL, Maude A	8 Oct 1919	96
KERSEY, Harry C	IONS, Estelle	10 Jan 1899	56
KESSLER, Calvin E	BOVEE, Helen E	10 Jun 1925	111
KESSLER, Gordon A	MARCERON, Lillian	30 Apr 1929	124
KESTERSON, William	KIDWELL, Susie	17 Aug 1897	53
KETTLER, Clifford T	POLING, Chloe E	15 Sep 1931	133
KEUCHHAM, Lorenz	ESSIG, Anna	23 Oct 1927	119
KEW, Victor Piercy	HENRY, Mildred K	6 Mar 1920	97
KEYES, John L	BELL, Florence F	10 Sep 1930	129

KEYES, Jerome W	DURRER, Helen A	21 Jan 1933	*141*
KEYES, Shirley	JOHNSON, America	9 Mar 1864	*5*
KEYS, David /wid	STEEL, Jennie	23 Aug 1875	*18*
KEYS, Edward W	KIDWELL, Susie C	10 Sep 1908	*75*
KEYS, George L	DUTTON, Belva V	26 Sep 1906	*71*
KEYS, Philip Jr	KIDWELL, Hattie M	15 Jan 1913	*84*
KEYS, George Washington	SIMPSON, L Victoria	18 Jan 1881	*28*
KIDWELL, Addison /wid	KIDWELL, Ann Eliza /wid	18 Nov 1868	*10*
KIDWELL, Albert	ELLIS, Martha E	12 Feb 1868	*9*
KIDWELL, Alfred Leigh	POOLE, Ruth V	27 Oct 1926	*116*
KIDWELL, Andrew	KIDWELL, Mary E	19 Feb 1884	*33*
KIDWELL, Andrew /wid	WREN, Aurelia	21 Jun 1905	*69*
KIDWELL, Andrew J	DODSON, Sarah F	26 Dec 1882	*31*
KIDWELL, Archie	BOWLING, Christine	14 Nov 1931	*134*
KIDWELL, Bert E	JERMAN, Elizabeth	14 May 1923	*105*
KIDWELL, C H	HOPKINS, Lucretia	26 Aug 1862	*5*
KIDWELL, Charles A	KIDWELL, Caroline V	10 Feb 1859	*4*
KIDWELL, Charles C	HORNBECK, Phebe Ann	23 Jun 1870	*12*
KIDWELL, Charles F	LOVELESS, Mary C	1 Jan 1896	*50*
KIDWELL, Charles W /div	KEYS, Elsie M	30 Jan 1926	*113*
KIDWELL, Clarence	WISE, Alice /wid	22 Sep 1927	*119*
KIDWELL, Edgar B	THOMPSON, Ella	11 Mar 1889	*39*
KIDWELL, Edward	ROBEY, Clara	28 Apr 1881	*28*
KIDWELL, Eli T	MILLS, Jane M	30 Jan 1868	*9*
KIDWELL, Ernest	JENKINS, Mabel	24 Nov 1927	*120*
KIDWELL, Ernest /wid	COSTELLO, Dolly	3 Jun 1929	*124*
KIDWELL, Ernest A	HART, Kate	14 Feb 1893	*46*
KIDWELL, Frank	KIDWELL, Mabel	5 Jan 1929	*124*
KIDWELL, Franklin	CONSTABLE, Fannie	14 Jan 1902	*62*
KIDWELL, Fred H	STAATS, Thelma	10 Jun 1925	*111*
KIDWELL, Frederick A	SEXTON, Ida M	4 Jan 1893	*46*
KIDWELL, George E	HEFFNER, Clara Louise	7 Nov 1906	*71*
KIDWELL, George H	MONEY, Rosa L	6 Jun 1883	*31*
KIDWELL, George M	JONES, Louisa J	25 Oct 1882	*30*
KIDWELL, George W	WELLS, Mattie A	24 Sep 1885	*35*
KIDWELL, Howard	COCKERILLE, Mae Bell	28 Jun 1930	*128*
KIDWELL, James L	COCKERILLE, Elizabeth	24 Jan 1876	*20*
KIDWELL, James R	SHAW, Lydia /div	13 Aug 1901	*60*
KIDWELL, Jeremiah	THOMPSON, Rosa B	11 Mar 1889	*39*
KIDWELL, Joe	LOVELACE, Beula Margrett	27 Apr 1916	*90*
KIDWELL, John	SMITH, Mary /wid	23 Nov 1892	*45*
KIDWELL, John H	CROSON, Eliza A	15 Jun 1865	*6*

KIDWELL, John H	CROSON, Laura F	1 Mar 1870	12
KIDWELL, John Robert Jr	REYNOLDS, Marie S	28 Apr 1932	137
KIDWELL, John T	KEARNS, Maria E	23 Dec 1865	6
KIDWELL, John T	GRIFFIN, Mary I	20 Aug 1871	14
KIDWELL, Joseph A	PORTER, Della E	27 Mar 1888	38
KIDWELL, Levi B	KIDWELL, Laura A	16 Sep 1877	22
KIDWELL, Lewis N	KIDWELL, Mary J	24 Sep 1884	33
KIDWELL, Melvin L	HARRISON, Catherine P	18 Apr 1871	13
KIDWELL, Morris S	HUNTT, Daisy A	20 May 1890	41
KIDWELL, Palmer	THOMPSON, Carrie	27 Dec 1899	57
KIDWELL, Richard T	KIDWELL, Ann E	12 Oct 1854	1
KIDWELL, Samuel C	LOVELESS, Annie E	20 Feb 1890	41
KIDWELL, Silas B	HORSTMAN, Birtie	18 Jun 1902	62
KIDWELL, Thomas	LIGHTFO OT, Rose E	21 Sep 1899	57
KIDWELL, Vernon L	THOMPSON, Florence D	8 Nov 1916	91
KIDWELL, W R	THOMPSON, Mary A /wid	29 Nov 1870	13
KIDWELL, W R /wid	TRUMBLE, Maggie F	4 Apr 1897	52
KIDWELL, Walter	ANDRES, Martha C	12 Apr 1905	68
KIDWELL, William A	MORROW, Lizzie	25 Jul 1897	53
KIDWELL, William B	STEEL, Allice /wid	3 Aug 1857	3
KIDWELL, William C	KIDWELL, Eveline	18 Jun 1872	15
KIDWELL, William W	KIDWELL, Sarah E	4 Apr 1914	86
KIDWELL, Winthrop	FRANCE, Josephine	13 Apr 1882	30
KILMER, Lester L	LEWIS, Alma R	25 Sep 1928	122
KIMBALL, Wilford H	COUNSELMAN, Elsie May /div	22 Dec 1928	123
KIMBRO, Paul R	BLANK, Hedwig	7 Mar 1931	131
KINCHELOE, Daniel F	BYRNE, Gertrude B	15 Sep 1908	75
KINCHELOE, Samuel C	BROWN, Lou B	10 Dec 1884	34
KING, Adolphus /wid	HAVENER, Sarah E	9 Jun 1897	52
KING, Albert Hovey	PENISTON, Nelle Graves	1 Oct 1908	75
KING, Ashel	LLOYD, Lydia M	6 Mar 1900	58
KING, Benjamin F	BRUFFY, Virginia	19 Jul 1897	53
KING, Charles A	DAVIS, Etta L	25 Dec 1890	42
KING, Charlton R	WALSTENHOLME, Margaret E	15 Oct 1918	94
KING, Daniel /c	STOKES, Mildred /c	20 Jun 1929	125
KING, Emore	STONE, Margaret M	11 Sep 1910	79
KING, George Raymond	FINCH, Helen	28 May 1921	100
KING, Gilbert L	COURTNEY, Elsie M	9 Nov 1929	126
KING, Howard G	HIGHAM, Emma K	15 Jul 1931	132
KING, James E	WATKINS, Lula G	6 Feb 1906	72
KING, John A /wid	SIPES, Florence B	30 May 1925	111
KING, John D	CURTIS, Bessie /div	26 Mar 1917	91

KING, John T	RUPPERT, Margaret B K	3 Mar 1926	*114*
KING, John W	UPPERMAN, Irene C	5 May 1909	*76*
KING, Richard	LEEDS, Bertha Virginia /wid	1 Jul 1933	*143*
KING, Willford Isbell /wid	PATTERSON, Jane E	6 Sep 1919	*96*
KINGMAN, F V	WESTON, Marietta	3 Jan 1860	*4*
KINNEY, Thomas /wid	DAY, Elizabeth J /wid	29 Aug 1900	*59*
KIRBY, E F	REID, Florence E	20 Nov 1889	*40*
KIRBY, Ernest C	LE HEW, Lavinia B	29 Mar 1930	*127*
KIRBY, Foster B	ROW, Dorothy M	29 Mar 1908	*74*
KIRBY, Francis A	SEWELL, Henrietta C	5 Jan 1868	*8*
KIRBY, George F	NELSON, Kate A	17 Sep 1868	*9*
KIRBY, James O	COLLARD, Rachel B	10 Jul 1860	*5*
KIRBY, Joshua	NELSON, Henrietta	2 Feb 1860	*5*
KIRBY, Walter E	KIRBY, Minnie M	30 Apr 1896	*50*
KIRBY, Ward T	HIRST, Ada Virginia	5 Dec 1900	*59*
KIRIVAN, Anthony	JOACHIMS, Helen	17 Feb 1932	*136*
KIRK, Francis Marion	BECKWITH, Videan Marion Legare	9 Jul 1933	*143*
KIRKMAN, Andrew	BRAMBLEE, Frances V	20 Jun 1877	*22*
KISER, Ralph	BROWN, Daisy	26 Jul 1918	*94*
KISNER, Ernest Chris.	POSEY, Mollie B	13 Sep 1933	*143*
KISTENMACHER, Howard Julius	MARTIN, Virginia Clara	2 Jan 1933	*141*
KITCHEN, Charles J	SORRELL, Catherine L	30 Jun 1915	*88*
KITCHEN, John H	ADAMS, Elsie G	2 Oct 1912	*83*
KITE, Gilbert D	FRENZEL, Edith	10 Feb 1921	*100*
KITSON, Marshall	LYLES, Hannah	6 Nov 1898	*55*
KITSON, Samuel	MONROE, Eliza	4 Jan 1872	*14*
KITSON, Samuel	SIMS, Stacy Eudora	22 Dec 1915	*89*
KITTLITZ, Rudolph F	PORTER, Ida M	8 May 1889	*40*
KLINE, Leonard M	CLARKE, Pansy L	18 Feb 1933	*141*
KLINE, Richard F	MULLINIX, Nellie N	6 Jun 1931	*132*
KLOCK, Benjamin Irving	RICHARDS, Mary F	22 Dec 1902	*63*
KLOCK, Jonathan	WALTERS, Sarah Jane	24 Aug 1871	*14*
KLOMPARENS, John H	BROWDER, Vera Marion	22 Apr 1933	*142*
KNIESCHE, Robert F	LOEFFLER, Katheryn	10 Sep 1932	*139*
KNIGHT, Harold	BAGGOTT, Effie	16 Feb 1903	*64*
KNIGHT, William M	WATKINS, Bessie H	12 Nov 1901	*61*
KNODE, Howard C	TAULELLE, Rose C /div	24 Jun 1911	*81*
KNOTT, Loyal	MILLER, Mary E	2 Sep 1924	*109*
KNOTT, William James	KIDWELL, Victoria	not legible 1857	*3*
KNUDSTRUP, Aksel J C	DAVIS, Florence E	29 Jul 1933	*143*
KOCI, Fred J	EDGERTON, Elizabeth	2 Feb 1932	*136*
KOEHNLEIN, John	DAY, Katherine	14 Jun 1930	*128*

KOENIG, Godfrey /wid	PRATT, Alice V /wid	6 Nov 1907	73
KOERNER, Elwood Stanley	LUDWIG, Louise M	18 Nov 1933	144
KOON, A L	FREEMAN, Jennie H	17 Apr 1884	33
KRAFT, George E Jr	MCLEAN, Marie H /wid	7 Oct 1925	112
KRAFT, Henry Andrew Jr	WOLF, Lillian Mae	6 Jun 1933	142
KRAFT, Paul Edward	FOWLER, Margaret Rae	18 Nov 1933	144
KRANTH, Ivan A	WHALIN, Dorothy M	27 Jun 1927	118
KRAUSE, Kurt W	HOBGOOD, Mary L	3 Oct 1923	106
KREITLER, Herman /wid	ROESER, Thusnelda C	20 Jun 1908	75
KREMER, Alvin W	FOY, Ann	1 Apr 1931	131
KRIGBAUM, James L	GROVES, Emma T	11 Jun 1932	137
KRUG, William A	HUGHES, Viola J	26 Jun 1912	82
KRUSE, Clarence H	CARROLL, Joanna T	1 Nov 1904	67
KRUSE, Clarence H /wid	GOETZE, Katherine	26 Dec 1920	99
KUEHLING, B C	COCKERILLE, C F	9 Feb 1875	18
KUEVER, Cecil Paul	BRYANT, Frances Eveline	18 Feb 1933	141
KYE, Charles /c div	BLACKBURN, Alcinda /c	19 Dec 1924	110
LA MOTHE, John D	WALKER, Margaret M	30 Aug 1894	48
LACEY, Beverly Jr	MUNDAY, Armata A	6 Apr 1897	52
LACEY, Earl R	HILL, Elaine D	11 Jun 1932	137
LACEY, George D	EDGARTON, Esther	12 Sep 1925	112
LACEY, Hunter	RUNYON, Monteray	1 May 1925	111
LACEY, John E	ANDERSON, Jennie	23 Jan 1926	113
LACEY, Lewis W /div	REEVES, Laura	12 Jan 1931	131
LACEY, Talbert	FAIRFAX, Mary E	27 Nov 1919	97
LACEY, W S	CRUMBAUGH, Lottie	1 Jan 1897	52
LACY, Amos Lee	EISLER, Anna P	16 Dec 1933	145
LACY, Harry	FAIRFAX, Rena	31 May 1911	80
LACY, James W	MITCHELL, Mary P	27 Jun 1910	78
LACY, John	DEAN, Bessie	6 Oct 1910	79
LACY, John T	MEIDEL, Marie A	22 May 1915	88
LACY, Richard A	GRIMSLEY, Mary E	18 Jan 1885	34
LACY, Robert John	WIMER, Mary Sue	11 Dec 1933	145
LACY, William B /wid	O'SHAUGHNESSY, Mary	10 Jan 1893	46
LADUE, George	SHEELS, Mae A	17 Apr 1911	80
LADUE, George W	MITCHELL, Virginia E	5 Nov 1888	39
LADUE, George W /wid	SHEETS, Mrs. N C /wid	10 Apr 1916	90
LADUE, Robert L	SHEETS, Nellie E	15 Dec 1915	89
LAGGEN, John T	MCCARTY, Katie	16 Oct 1895	50
LAING, James	MILLER, Addie V	21 Nov 1877	22
LAIRD, John L	DAY, Mary Wright	12 Jun 1907	73
LAIRD, Joseph Packard	PAGE, Matilda Coleman	15 Nov 1916	91

LAIRD, William Henry	PACKARD, Rosa Jane	28 Aug 1869	*11*
LAMB, Monroe /wid	KEYTON, Daisy F /wid	26 Jun 1931	*132*
LAMBERT, C H [Dr.]	HARRISON, Laura G	8 Dec 1870	*13*
LAMBERT, Francis L	LANHAM, Effie D	24 Dec 1912	*84*
LAMBERT, Herbert	COMPHER, Annie G	20 Nov 1912	*83*
LAMBERT, James /c	JACKSON, Mazie /c	1 Sep 1915	*89*
LAMBERT, John	LEACH, Elizabeth	18 Feb 1856	*2*
LAMBERT, John /c	SIMMS, Maggie /c	15 Sep 1912	*83*
LAMBERT, John /c wid	ELLIS, Nellie /c	18 Mar 1914	*86*
LANAGAN, William H	GILLETT, Helen H	22 Nov 1919	*97*
LANCASTER, Charles W /c	NELSON, Pearl E /c	4 Jun 1932	*137*
LANCASTER, James A /c wid	JOHNSON, Ophelia /c	20 Feb 1929	*124*
LANDS, George H	KALB, Marie C	25 Jan 1924	*108*
LANDSTREET, John	NEVITT, Mary E	18 Oct 1893	*47*
LANE, Harry /c	HARRIS, Lewetta /c	27 Mar 1928	*121*
LANE, Joseph F /c	BROWN, Belle /c	18 Nov 1913	*85*
LANE, Richard /c	BELL, Lizzie /c	11 Jun 1879	*25*
LANE, Thomas Alphonsus	GEE, Jean Margaret	3 Jun 1933	*142*
LANE, William F	KEPHART, Gracie E	11 Jun 1902	*62*
LANE, William G	DEAN, Nora M /wid	24 Dec 1914	*88*
LANG, Donald R	HOLMES, L Elizabeth	15 Jun 1929	*125*
LANG, Welby Carter	HURST, Mary Virginia	28 Dec 1898	*56*
LANGER, Joseph T /wid	CARMEAU, Kate G /div	11 Aug 1919	*96*
LANGFORD, Sidney W /wid	BOHEIM, Marie	8 Oct 1926	*116*
LANGLEY, George	MASON, Mary E	2 Nov 1920	*99*
LANGLEY, Milton	MONCH, Adelaide	5 Jul 1927	*118*
LANHAM, Edward C	FOLLIN, B	26 Jan 1871	*13*
LANHAM, Horatio P /wid	MARKS, Elise	16 Nov 1879	*25*
LANHAM, J C	FOLLIN, Anna L	9 Oct 1866	*7*
LANHAM, Robert B	FOLLIN, Minnie O	17 Feb 1876	*20*
LANIER, John D	COCKERILLE, Mabel	7 Jun 1920	*98*
LANKFORD, William R /wid	CRAWFORD, Bertha Irene	15 Mar 1919	*95*
LANNAN, Andrew J	LUNSFORD, Ella M	7 Aug 1901	*60*
LAONHARDT, J P	RAUB, Mary A	13 Mar 1884	*33*
LARCOUMBE, John William	THOMPSON, Mabel C	30 Jul 1919	*96*
LARRICK, Leonard L	KIRBY, Viola May	22 Mar 1929	*124*
LARSEN, Oluf /wid	MCDANIEL, Maude V	14 Dec 1922	*104*
LARTRAM, Claude B	SAMPSON, Nettie F /wid	20 Mar 1918	*94*
LASSITER, William R	MORAN, Charlotte	20 Feb 1932	*136*
LATCH, Edward G	VANDER VIES, Marie	1 Mar 1926	*114*
LATCHER, John	FREY, Lillian	11 Aug 1919	*96*
LATHAM, Francis J	HARLOW, Alice M	17 Sep 1923	*106*

LAWLER, Norman F	BLUNT, Mabel J	26 Nov 1928	*123*
LAWRENCE, Cassius M	SHEAR, Addie M	7 Jun 1893	*46*
LAWRENCE, Rev. J P /wid	NEVITT, Margaret L	26 Jan 1876	*20*
LAWSON, George /c wid	BOYD, Mary E /c	26 Dec 1907	*74*
LAWSON, Josephus	DAINTY, Elizabeth	8 Jun 1871	*15*
LAWSON, Sterling L	WALLER, Martha L	18 Apr 1927	*118*
LAWSON, William /c	PETERS, Hattie	1 Dec 1917	*93*
LAY, Theodore A Jr	MCKINLEY, Isabel E /div	3 Mar 1910	*78*
LEACHMAN, John B	COFFIN, Mary Frank	1 Aug 1923	*105*
LEAMAN, Melvin G	GARNETT, Anna E	10 Dec 1902	*63*
LEARNED, George Frederick	CHAPMAN, Mary L	24 Nov 1874	*17*
LEARY, John	DAVIS, E Rowena	5 Jun 1907	*73*
LEBERKNIGHT, Max H	MACBETH, Alice	12 Oct 1932	*139*
LEDMAN, John F /wid	KIDWELL, Lavinia	8 Jan 1856	*2*
LEDMAN, L A	DAVIS, Lue Emma	7 Jun 1883	*31*
LEDMAN, Lycurgus	MAYHUGH, Lavinia C	31 Mar 1868	*9*
LEE, A C /c	JACKSON, Frances /c	19 Oct 1893	*47*
LEE, Arthur /c	PARKER, Rebecca /c	8 Nov 1887	*38*
LEE, Bunnie /c	PARKER, Sarah /c	28 Jul 1887	*42*
LEE, Charles /c	JOHNSON, Lucy /c	20 Oct 1887	*42*
LEE, Charles /c wid	GILLAM, Sarah /c wid	15 Nov 1905	*69*
LEE, Charles Wagner	DONALDSON, Saidee Smithson	26 Jul 1905	*69*
LEE, Charleton /c	FARR, Annie /c	10 Jan 1878	*23*
LEE, Edgar Washington	HAISLIP, Susan	16 Feb 1871	*13*
LEE, Ernest /c	SUTTON, Ella /c	23 Nov 1882	*31*
LEE, Ernest /c	JACKSON, Bernice /c	7 Apr 1924	*108*
LEE, Frank J	HARRISON, Minnie E	19 Jan 1913	*84*
LEE, George /c	JORDAN, Indi /c	16 Jan 1886	*36*
LEE, George /c	FOLEY, Ida /c	21 Feb 1907	*72*
LEE, George B	WAPLE, Annie A	10 Mar 1896	*50*
LEE, George E	HOSKINS, Olive V	25 Aug 1920	*98*
LEE, George Jr /c	MCDANIEL, Elenor F /c	20 Apr 1921	*100*
LEE, Harry L /c	BYRD, Willie /c	4 Feb 1926	*114*
LEE, Henry /c wid	THORNTON, Dulsey /c	28 Dec 1882	*31*
LEE, Henry /c	TAYLOR, Rachel Ann /c	16 Feb 1893	*46*
LEE, Isaac /c	PAYNE, Benidene B /c	22 Jul 1926	*115*
LEE, James /c	CARTER, Lillie /c	23 Dec 1886	*42*
LEE, James Edward	WILLIAMS, Mary	26 Jun 1870	*12*
LEE, James Jackson /c wid	JOHNSON, Mary A /c wid	16 Dec 1880	*27*
LEE, James Thomas	ARRINGTON, Sarah J	8 Jul 1880	*26*
LEE, Jarvey /c	PROCTOR, Maria /c	3 Nov 1890	*42*
LEE, John McKenney /c	HARPER, Hattie L /c	9 Apr 1919	*95*

LEE, Joseph Benjamin Franklin	ROBERTSON, Ella Blanche	8 Apr 1933	*141*
LEE, Joshua /c wid	WILLIAMS, Julia /c wid	30 Sep 1880	*27*
LEE, Lewis L /c	PAYNE, Zelma /c	11 Feb 1933	*141*
LEE, Louis H	BATCHELLER, Betty	14 Nov 1932	*140*
LEE, Ludwell	CARTER, Mary H	7 Oct 1885	*35*
LEE, M R	SPINDLE, Martha A	9 Oct 1892	*44*
LEE, Matthew /c	WASHINGTON, Frances /c	11 Sep 1926	*116*
LEE, Maurice /c	BELL, Esther L /c	26 Apr 1905	*68*
LEE, Norman Clifton	FOLLIN, Florence Elizabeth	4 Jan 1899	*56*
LEE, Philip D C /wid	BADEN, Zella R	17 Oct 1893	*47*
LEE, R J	LANE, Janine E	30 Jul 1919	*96*
LEE, Reuben M	KIDWELL, Ann E	15 Aug 1854	*1*
LEE, Reuben R	JONES, Martha L	29 Jan 1880	*24*
LEE, Robert	COCKERILLE, Mary	14 Apr 1915	*88*
LEE, Robert E	PATTON, Sarah E	12 Jun 1895	*49*
LEE, Robert E /c	BARNETT, Elnora /c	25 Jun 1896	*51*
LEE, Robert E	NICHOLS, Edna D	22 Nov 1919	*97*
LEE, Robert E	SHANNON, Harriet	20 Aug 1931	*133*
LEE, Russell T	WINFIELD, Eugenia B	21 Apr 1928	*121*
LEE, S L /c wid	ODERICK, Edna L /c	10 Jun 1914	*86*
LEE, Squire L /c wid	TINNER, Elmira /c	30 Apr 1917	*92*
LEE, Thomas /c	HUNTER, Sally /c	20 Aug 1895	*49*
LEE, Thomas Alexander	BURNS, Cornelia	21 Dec 1881	*29*
LEE, Thomas W	HAIGHT, Maggie	7 Oct 1874	*17*
LEE, Thomas William	SCHNEIDER, Louise Julia	11 May 1910	*78*
LEE, Wesley /c	MURRAY, Emma /c	3 Aug 1893	*46*
LEE, William /c	NEAL, Emma /c	9 Dec 1888	*39*
LEE, William /c	BUNDY, Mirtha /c	11 Aug 1908	*75*
LEE, William D	SAFFER, Emma E	11 Dec 1889	*40*
LEE, Wyndham R	DOWNING, Margaret F	19 Aug 1924	*109*
LEEDS, J W	DODSON, Hattie Pearl	13 Aug 1916	*90*
LEEDS, R H	FOLLIN, Ada V	14 Dec 1899	*57*
LEEDS, Walter S	KENYON, Fannie S	30 Jun 1896	*51*
LEEF, William H	HERNDON, Alice W	10 Oct 1924	*109*
LEESNITZER, Edward B	CRADDOCK, Stella M	26 May 1926	*114*
LEITH, William	SHEAR, Caddie May	10 Feb 1904	*66*
LEIZEAR, Melvin L	VAUGHAN, Gertrude E	22 Aug 1932	*139*
LEMMON, Frank H	RITZ, Edith	22 Jul 1920	*98*
LEMOINE, Adam	CADE, Mabel E	12 Mar 1932	*136*
LENARD, James E	WELLS, Bertie	21 Aug 1907	*73*
LENDERMAN, Hal Watson /div	FINIELS, Kathryn Jane /div	14 May 1927	*118*
LENT, Andrew /wid	MAYHUGH, Nancy /wid	13 Apr 1857	*3*

LENT, Benona S	BROUGHTON, E A	15 Jan 1856	2
LENT, Edgar	KIDWELL, Lula	1 Apr 1908	74
LENTZ, John	RHIEL, Catharine	12 Nov 1855	1
LEONARD, Charles J	PAULY, Marcella L	2 Jun 1927	118
LEONARD, Marion D	ALVEY, Mae F	9 Jul 1928	122
LEONARD, Nevellainer	MORGAN, Katie Marjorie	29 Mar 1933	141
LESNER, Paul A	GENTRY, Dora E	4 Feb 1930	127
LESNY, Karl /div	OTTO, Lena /wid	23 Jul 1929	125
LESTER, Albert H	MARSHALL, Helen M	8 Dec 1920	99
LESTER, Thomas	CROUCH, Daisey	28 Sep 1904	67
LESTER, William	MAKELY, Edith Elizabeth	25 Feb 1928	121
LEUCHTENBERGER, Robert C /wid	CARPENTER, Lola /wid	11 Sep 1927	119
LEVERING, Thomas H	CRONE, Isabel H	9 Jan 1926	113
LEWIS, Alfred Jr /c	FRY, Littie /c	28 Apr 1898	54
LEWIS, Daniel W	NEWCOMB, Margaret B	3 Nov 1855	1
LEWIS, Earl A R	MCCLANAHAN, Margaret L	29 Nov 1919	97
LEWIS, Fay F /div	HARTMAN, Erna	20 Jul 1917	92
LEWIS, H R /wid	ARMSTRONG, Cath Eliz. /wid	15 Sep 1925	112
LEWIS, Henry /c	STOTTS, Daisy M /c	26 Jul 1915	89
LEWIS, Henry R	DAVIS, Cordelia	25 Sep 1890	42
LEWIS, Hillard R /c div	HILL, Natalie S /c wid	16 Dec 1930	130
LEWIS, James /c	SMITH, Harriet /c	6 Sep 1896	51
LEWIS, James Jr /c	QUANDER, Eunice	7 May 1933	142
LEWIS, James N	DAVIS, Ethel	24 Nov 1912	83
LEWIS, John	CHAMBERS, Mary A	9 Apr 1870	12
LEWIS, John H /wid	MCCAULEY, Mary S	20 Jul 1891	43
LEWIS, Joseph D /c	CARY, Annie /c	2 Jul 1896	51
LEWIS, LaFayette F	DE PUTRON, Maria B	16 Aug 1903	65
LEWIS, Lawrence E	MCNULTY, Agnes T	5 Feb 1917	91
LEWIS, Robert L Jr /c	NEWMAN, Willie M /c	26 Mar 1930	130
LEWIS, Wesley /c	ROBINSON, Susie /c	3 Jul 1879	25
LEWIS, William /c	PEYTON, Maggie /c	20 Dec 1899	57
LEWIS, William H	BARNUM, Cora A	21 Nov 1871	22
LEWIS, William H /c	MINOR, Rosa /c	27 Sep 1908	75
LIBBY, Herbert F	MOORE, Amy A	25 Oct 1920	99
LIEB, Bernard W	ANDERSON, Edith	22 Sep 1923	106
LIGHTBOWN, B L	GRAMS, Florence I	5 Nov 1913	85
LIGHTBOWN, Millard J	LOOMIS, Clella P	26 Oct 1907	73
LIGHTFOOT, Joseph H	WARFORD, Lillie B	4 Sep 1889	40
LIGHTFOOT, Samuel N	CROUCH, Rosie	8 Feb 1911	80
LILLARD, William H	WAKEFIELD, Rita M	2 May 1915	88
LINDEN, Bernard A	HARLOW, Marie L /wid	28 Jul 1926	115

LINDSAY, Alan McKay	MCDANIEL, Edith Agnew	24 Aug 1923	106
LINDSAY, George E	SIMPSON, Mildred R	24 May 1930	128
LINEBURG, Hesler	STUBBS, Lutie Mae	22 Jan 1927	117
LINKINS, William /c	BROWN, Rachael /c	25 Dec 1877	23
LINTON, John /wid	STONESTREET, Sallie T	17 Jan 1889	39
LISTON, Eugene J /div	BELMONT, Celie A /wid	3 Aug 1933	143
LITTLE, Harold Rankin	PARKER, Josephine Ruth	20 Aug 1932	138
LITTLEHALES, George R	WARREN, Dorothy B	14 Jul 1923	105
LITTLES, William E /c	WAINES, Edith /c	31 Jan 1878	23
LIVERA, Celeste	WINSTON, Catharine /wid	8 Jun 1920	98
LIVINGSTON, Alexander D	WALKER, Mary A	6 Aug 1917	92
LLEWELLYN, John R	FOY, Mary Alice	16 Aug 1911	81
LLOYD, Charles E	ROGERS, Cora	14 Nov 1922	104
LLOYD, H W /wid	CARLIN, Jane E	23 Nov 1886	37
LLOYD, John H	HUNTINGTON, Mildred	13 Mar 1889	39
LLOYD, Lester L	SPALDING, Mary H	7 Jul 1910	79
LLOYD, R B /wid	PAXTON, Ella M	5 May 1891	43
LLOYD, William E	SIMMS, Florence M	24 Mar 1910	78
LOANG, Christopher L	TOWLES, Mildred A	17 Aug 1931	133
LOBER, John	WILLIAMS, Margaret	6 Aug 1924	109
LOCKHARDT, Alfred	PUGH, Bessie	21 Jun 1888	38
LOCKNANE, William N	AYRE, Ida R	15 Jul 1926	115
LOCKWOOD, Samuel /wid	BATES, Louisa J	19 Mar 1856	2
LOCKWOOD, William A	COCKERILLE, Nellie L	15 Aug 1928	122
LOGGINS, Edward /c	TAPLET, Bessie /c	28 May 1891	43
LOMAX, Inman /c	TUCKER, Mary /c	16 Feb 1875	18
LONDON, Joseph /wid	WILLIAMS, Eliza /wid	8 Oct 1857	3
LONG, Garland Lee	CRIPPEN, Hazel May	21 Jan 1933	141
LONG, Isaac T /wid	BALLARD, Lillie T	28 Apr 1909	76
LONG, Joseph /c	HENDERSON, Lizzie /c	27 Dec 1881	29
LONG, Leonard W	HUFFMAN, Myrtle E	14 Dec 1910	80
LOOR, Jesse	BARBOUR, May	8 Aug 1928	122
LOUK, Gordon	SAULS, Lenore	19 Oct 1921	101
LOVE, Jesse	BROWN, Anna	8 Jan 1914	86
LOVE, Thomas R /wid	TYLER, Sallie B	30 Nov 1869	11
LOVELACE, Arthur A	FORD, Julia M	28 Oct 1915	89
LOVELESS, Addison H	ROBERTS, Patricia B	6 Sep 1930	129
LOVELESS, Damon	TURNER, Edith V	14 Jan 1924	108
LOVELESS, Dewey Lee	HUNT, Goldie May	19 Dec 1923	107
LOVELESS, Everett L	WEEKS, Irene	17 Jun 1929	125
LOVELESS, George A	POWELL, Elsie S	27 Aug 1921	101
LOVELESS, Preston	TURNER, Charlotte L	2 Sep 1927	119

LOVING, Frank	FISHEL, Anna M	11 Jul 1927	*118*
LOVING, William Bernard	HOFF, Carolin Frances /div	20 May 1933	*142*
LOVING, William Harrison	FORD, Alice Louise	24 Dec 1933	*145*
LOWD, Howard G	MARDEN, Marion V	26 Oct 1933	*144*
LOWD, Jack I	HAYES, Claira E	11 Apr 1925	*111*
LOWE, Enoch M	POWELL, Martha E	25 Oct 1859	*4*
LOWE, George A /c	PAGE, Rose E /c	15 Jan 1890	*42*
LOWE, Henry F	BRINKERHOFF, Hattie E	19 May 1892	*44*
LOWE, Hilton C	REST, Eleanor L	21 Nov 1931	*134*
LOWE, Howard J	VIRTS, Esther L	18 Dec 1926	*117*
LOWE, J H	CHALMERS, G A	3 Apr 1914	*86*
LOWE, Samuel R	WOODYARD, Lucinda	3 Apr 1866	*6*
LOWERS, Robert P /c	HODGES, Maybelle /c	21 Feb 1933	*141*
LOWERY, Arthur Walton /wid	MCKEAND, Flora Christine /wid	10 Aug 1933	*143*
LOWRY, Leslie E	WATT, Annie Alice	21 Jun 1905	*69*
LOY, H W	KIRBY, Ethel O	30 Sep 1913	*86*
LUCAS, Henry /c wid	SHELTON, Delia /c	17 Jul 1902	*63*
LUCAS, Jesse /c	THOMAS, Mary /c	12 Dec 1894	*48*
LUCAS, Oscar J /c	TINNEY, Gladys E /c	27 Aug 1930	*129*
LUCAS, Samuel /c	CLARKE, Sarah J /c	28 Dec 1882	*31*
LUCAS, Stewart T /c	CLARK, Edith /c	7 Mar 1900	*58*
LUCAS, Thomas /c	DAY, Mary /c	30 Dec 1909	*78*
LUCAS, Thomas F	CARR, Esther Mae /div	6 Feb 1932	*136*
LUCKETT, Daniel G	MCCOY, Esta Belle	9 Mar 1916	*90*
LUCKETT, James N	MONEY, Ella L	15 Dec 1880	*27*
LUCKETT, Jerry /c	BROWN, Anna /c	4 Sep 1884	*33*
LUCKETT, Jerry /c wid	NELSON, Janie /c wid	16 Nov 1893	*47*
LUCKETT, Samuel /c	HOLLINS, Lizzie /c	5 Sep 1889	*40*
LUCKETT, William /c	GADDIS, Annie /c	23 Nov 1882	*32*
LUDLOW, Daniel	BEACH, Eliza J	22 Dec 1872	*15*
LUDLOW, Daniel /wid	HALL, Eliza	6 Oct 1896	*51*
LUDLOW, Luther L	DAVIS, Gladys	28 Sep 1922	*103*
LUEBBERS, William E K	HANKER, Lona E	1 Oct 1932	*139*
LUKENS, Ephraim C	BRISCOE, Anna	14 Apr 1870	*12*
LUKENS, Paul Francis	GIBSON, Helen Elizabeth	20 Oct 1920	*99*
LULL, Martin J	CROCKER, Aurelia R	10 Jul 1860	*5*
LUPTON, James Robert	ROBERTS, Margaret H	26 Oct 1917	*93*
LUSKEY, Ernest A	REAGAN, Lillian Louise	25 Jun 1921	*100*
LUTEMAN, Albert Ross	DOUGHERTY, Sarah Florence	13 Apr 1890	*41*
LYELL, Arthur M	WARD, Sara Rebecca	8 Jul 1908	*75*
LYLES, Charles W	KITSON, Ocie May	4 Dec 1898	*55*
LYLES, Ernest T	TERRETT, Jessie G	24 Dec 1911	*82*

LYLES, Halle C	JAVINS, Onedia V	11 May 1919	95
LYLES, James	LYLES, Mattie	7 Dec 1902	63
LYLES, John	DEWEY, Ann	6 Feb 1868	9
LYLES, John W /wid	MOORE, Susannah L /wid	12 Jun 1877	22
LYLES, Joseph	DEAVERS, Mary Jane /wid	20 Feb 1868	9
LYLES, Thomas H	BRAWNER, Lucy A	15 Jun 1892	45
LYLES, William E	WILLIAMS, Maggie M	1 Jun 1887	38
LYLES, William T /wid	SIMPSON, Mary	14 Dec 1899	57
LYMAN, Henry A /wid	GRESHAM, Fannie W	10 Oct 1900	59
LYNCH, John E	MATTINGLY, May H	3 Oct 1918	94
LYNCH, Martin	KEYHO, Margaret	23 Apr 1867	7
LYNCH, Thomas Francis	WOODS, Effie Turner /wid	27 Sep 1922	103
LYNCH, Vernon M	WILLIAMS, Minnie J	17 Aug 1909	77
LYNCH, W N	WALKER, Sarah E	13 Feb 1882	30
LYNN, John Thomas	RECTOR, Harriet C	3 Feb 1870	12
LYNN, John W	BOYCE, Edith A	9 Oct 1888	39
LYONS, E E	CATON, Carrie F	13 Nov 1918	95
LYONS, James E	OLIVER, Nora C	24 Jan 1899	56
LYONS, James T	FARR, Nannie E	18 Dec 1873	16
LYONS, W V	RECTOR, Hazel Thompson	23 Aug 1926	115
MACE, Joseph Ralph	TUBMAN, Ellen L	14 Apr 1930	127
MACHEN, James P	CHICHESTER, Georgie D	6 Sep 1866	6
MACK, Edward /c	HOLLINGS, Eliza	18 Sep 1879	25
MACK, Edward /c wid	GASKINS, Alice /c	11 Jan 1888	38
MACK, Robert	THOMPSON, Minnie	25 Oct 1900	59
MACK, William /c	MUNDLE, Bettie /c	27 Dec 1906	72
MACKAL, Henry C /wid	BALL, Caroline L	30 Apr 1912	82
MACKAL, William Whann Jr	HOXTON, Mary Earle	21 May 1929	124
MACKENZIE, Charles E	MCGROARTY, Kathleen	17 Jun 1914	86
MACRAE, G H T	JAMESSON, Maggie	24 Dec 1868	10
MADDOX, Charles W	HOUSTON, Helen F	8 Nov 1924	110
MADDOX, Everett B	WEIR, Olivia C	23 Oct 1911	81
MADDOX, William	RODGERS, Elizabeth	24 Dec 1900	59
MADDOX, William E	HARRISON, Bertha E	9 Sep 1902	63
MADISON, Clarence M	HARLOW, Ada /wid	26 Nov 1929	126
MADISON, Howard /c	LEWIS, Susie /c	22 Sep 1913	85
MADISON, Howard /c div	BRENT, Bessie /c	3 Jul 1918	94
MAFFETT, J L	MAFFETT, Maggie E	18 Dec 1901	61
MAFFETT, John D	KENYON, Alice	2 Apr 1902	62
MAFFETT, Peter F	DAVIS, Ellen V	4 Dec 1856	2
MAFFETT, Thomas J	PAXEN, Rachel A	29 Oct 1867	8
MAFFETT, Tyler F /wid	MAFFETT, Marion K /wid	12 Apr 1933	142

MAFFETT, William H	KENYON, Marion	2 Apr 1902	62
MAGARITY, Albert	HUNTER, Mamie	29 Sep 1880	27
MAGARITY, Henry T	WALCOTT, Sara H	20 Apr 1929	124
MAGARITY, James L	MCDANIEL, Laura	10 Apr 1872	14
MAGARITY, James W	BREWNER, Kate	14 Oct 1874	17
MAGARITY, John S	TORREYSON, Annie	20 Dec 1894	48
MAGARITY, Morrell	WREN, Irene Thelma	2 Feb 1921	100
MAGNER, Edward	CARLIN, Maggie M	27 Aug 1905	69
MAGNER, Michael	HORGAN, Catherine	6 Feb 1912	82
MAGNER, Patrick Henry	SNIDER, Evalina	17 Nov 1886	36
MAGNER, Peter	HASSETT, Bridget	30 Apr 1876	20
MAGNER, Peter	KEALY, Mary	28 Nov 1911	81
MAGNER, Peter Jr	SUTHERLAND, Lucy Ann	15 Jun 1892	45
MAGNER, Peter Jr /wid	BARKER, Katie	15 Sep 1920	99
MAGNER, Peter M /wid	HOGAN, Mary E	28 Oct 1914	87
MAGRUDER, Howard /c	BANKETT, Sophronia /c	10 Dec 1919	97
MAGRUDER, William /c	SHEPHERD, Nancy /c	25 Dec 1873	16
MAHAR, Thomas F	WELLS, Mary	17 Dec 1879	26
MAHONEY, D C	GILLETT, Edna M	21 Oct 1903	65
MAHONEY, Edward E	THOMPSON, Sarah E	24 Jul 1891	43
MAIN, Kemp	FOLLIN, Nellie I	2 Oct 1901	61
MAKELL, John Thomas /c	RUMMELS, Flora /c	5 Oct 1895	50
MAKELY, Albert	RICE, Frances	23 Jul 1872	15
MAKELY, Cassius E	WOODYARD, Delsie D	4 Jun 1913	84
MAKELY, Clarence W	WOODYARD, Susie M	3 Jun 1908	75
MAKELY, J Willard	AYRES, M Amanda	30 Dec 1902	65
MAKELY, Leander	AYRE, Jane M	20 Mar 1878	23
MAKELY, Metrah	DE BUSK, Lelia N	20 Feb 1932	136
MAKELY, Robert K	FAIRFAX, Rose E	25 Dec 1912	84
MALEY, John C	FAIRFAX, Margaret M	7 Dec 1914	87
MALEY, John E /wid	FAIRFAX, Margaret	24 Dec 1914	87
MALEY, Norman S	FAIRFAX, Rhoda M	28 May 1925	111
MALLE, Harry E	GUNNER, Catherine S	26 Sep 1931	133
MALONEY, John J /c wid	YOUNG, Carrie /c wid	12 Nov 1929	126
MALONEY, John T	AYRES, Annie W	6 Jun 1894	48
MALTBY, Clarence Walter	ZINK, Leoda May	5 Oct 1920	99
MALTBY, Philo	MARKS, Mary C	26 Sep 1880	27
MANNY, Theodore Bergen	SHERMAN, Elsie Besley	20 Aug 1923	105
MANY, W P	CARR, Nellie May	22 Dec 1923	107
MANCHESTER, Henry B	ASHFORD, Ella A	3 Jan 1889	39
MANCHLY, John W	WALZEL, Mary	30 Dec 1930	130
MANGUM, James Frank	CRANLEIGH, Evelyn A	16 Jun 1930	128

MANKER, William A	SNEEDON, Frances Ann	12 Oct 1865	6
MANKIN, Charles E	LYNCH, Valinda A	20 Dec 1881	29
MANKIN, George Tyree	DAVISON, Susie A	14 Dec 1911	81
MANKIN, R Moses /wid	MANKIN, Lillian G /wid	14 Sep 1933	143
MANLEY, Thomas /c	LEE, Etta /c	21 Nov 1878	24
MANLEY, William Grant	MCLEMORE, Dorothy	20 Jun 1931	132
MANN, Henry B	RUPPERT, Amelia	21 Nov 1918	95
MANN, Wilson K	HARAN, Margaret C	16 May 1931	132
MANSHA, Joseph	HALL, Louise	6 Dec 1930	130
MANVELL, Harry C	LEWIS, Janet H	18 Jun 1924	108
MANVELL, William	CREASEY, Hylda A	2 Oct 1924	109
MARCHER, James /wid	COLEMAN, Eliza	27 Sep 1866	7
MARINE, Frederick A /c	LEE, Annie M /c	23 Nov 1910	80
MARKER, Franklin	QUILTY, Frances A /wid	18 Sep 1906	71
MARKHAM, Carl William /div	HOLDEN, Esther /wid	9 Oct 1933	144
MARKS, Charles H	STEELE, Sarah E	17 Oct 1867	8
MARKS, Edd	JONES, Frances	28 Dec 1893	47
MARKS, John H	BROOKS, Margaret Ann	4 Apr 1856	2
MARKS, Richard C	CRANDALL, Emma E	17 Apr 1914	86
MARMION, Louis P /div	WALKER, Mary C	22 Aug 1932	139
MARR, Joseph H	PAYNE, Ethel M	14 Aug 1914	87
MARR, William J	PROCTOR, Louise V	26 Apr 1932	137
MARSHALL, Charles L	DAVIS, Salina	23 Dec 1875	19
MARSHALL, Edward A	DAVIS, Sarah S	5 Oct 1903	65
MARSHALL, Frank /c	JACKSON, Henrietta /c	19 Mar 1885	34
MARSHALL, Frank /c wid	BOWMAN, Betsy /c	14 Sep 1890	42
MARSHALL, Frank /c wid	SHELTON, Mora /c	23 Sep 1905	69
MARSHALL, French /c	CORBIN, Mary /c	10 Feb 1881	29
MARSHALL, George W	PAYNE, Emma M	2 Jan 1877	21
MARSHALL, James /c	PARKS, Mary /c	30 Dec 1883	32
MARSHALL, James R /div	HASLUP, Xenia McC	17 Jun 1909	77
MARSHALL, Lee R /c	WEST, Rosanna /c	3 Jul 1926	115
MARSHALL, Lewis W /c	FERGUSON, Ada B /c	3 Dec 1908	76
MARSHALL, Simpson F	BEACH, Mary Ellen	15 Jan 1856	2
MARSHALL, Solomon /c	PINKETT, Bessie /c	18 Sep 1906	71
MARSHALL, Solomon /c wid	KEMP, Irene /c wid	1 Jan 1933	141
MARSHALL, William B	ENGLISH, Lena	14 Oct 1924	109
MARSHALL, William D /c wid	FLETCHER, Lillie /c	27 Nov 1902	63
MARSHALL, William E /div	GILLIS, Clarice E	4 May 1925	111
MARSHALL, William P	FAIRFAX, Rebecca A	26 Dec 1906	72
MARSHALL, William Paul /wid	DENTY, Maude /wid	24 Nov 1920	99
MARSTELLER, E H	MASON, Marie	26 Nov 1873	16

MARSTELLER, James A	JONES, Lillian	30 May 1908	75
MARTIN, Albert H	BONHAM, Agnes Cecilia	14 Apr 1933	141
MARTIN, B F /wid	DUNCAN, Mary L /wid	30 Oct 1912	83
MARTIN, Eugene L	DANIEL, Amelia A	9 Apr 1900	58
MARTIN, George /c wid	BUTLER, Catherine /c	17 Apr 1924	108
MARTIN, J H	RICE, Mattie Louise	25 Jan 1905	68
MARTIN, James M	WHEELER, Naomi M	8 Aug 1931	133
MARTIN, John Henry /wid	WILBERN, Gertrude	28 May 1926	114
MARTIN, John S	WASHBURN, Sarah	26 Feb 1874	17
MARTIN, Joseph E	STUDDS, Virginia C	13 Feb 1882	30
MARTIN, Lawrence J	FRAZIER, Hazel	23 May 1922	102
MARTIN, N L	FOLLIN, Idella /wid	28 Sep 1904	67
MARTIN, Robert B	FRENZEL, Clara V	30 Apr 1925	111
MARTIN, Rosevelt /c	JONES, Helen /c	16 Oct 1926	116
MARTIN, Stephen F	SMITH, Mattie E /div	1 Jun 1912	82
MARTIN, Thomas B	ELLIS, A F	28 Jan 1885	34
MARTIN, W H	KIDWELL, Rose	15 Jan 1907	72
MARTIN, Walton J	BACHELDER, Hulda M /wid	19 Apr 1919	95
MARTIN, William A /wid	FERGUSON, Bettie T /wid	15 Nov 1910	79
MARTZ, J T	WILLIAMS, Flora J	22 Nov 1919	97
MASON, Benjamin H	WOODRUFF, Iva A	29 Jun 1887	38
MASON, Frank M /c	PERRY, Sally M	26 May 1881	28
MASON, George /c	POSEY, Josephine /c	18 Nov 1877	22
MASON, Howard O	CHESLEY, Dorothy A	19 Dec 1929	127
MASON, James M	CHICHESTER, Madge T	8 Oct 1884	33
MASON, John P H /wid	MILLAN, Bessie B	22 Jun 1899	56
MASON, landon R	AMBLER, Lucy	28 Oct 1875	19
MASON, Maynadier /wid	FITZHUGH, Mary A	10 Jan 1854	1
MASON, O M /c wid	HARRIS, Katherine /c div	6 Apr 1911	80
MASON, Oscar /c	DULANY, Adella /c	31 Oct 1881	29
MASON, Russell /c	HONESTY, Cora /c	7 Aug 1912	83
MASON, Thomas E	DAVID, Mary	4 Jun 1930	128
MASON, Thomas Henry /c	NORRIS, Ida /c	6 Jul 1876	20
MASON, Thompson	BOOKMAN, Marie	11 Dec 1913	85
MASON, William R /c	TERRELL, Beatrice /c	8 Jan 1912	82
MASON, William R /c wid	TAYLOR, Luella /c	13 Sep 1915	89
MASSEY, Alonzo /c	COOK, Jenny /c	30 Dec 1874	18
MASSEY, John W Jr	WHEELER, Florence L	9 Jun 1924	108
MASSIE, Charles Henry /c wid	BOTTS, Marie E /c	24 Oct 1929	126
MASSIE, Edward /c	TAYLOR, Margaret	26 Dec 1872	15
MASSIE, Henry /c	SCOTT, Charlotte /c	27 Dec 1879	26
MATHERS, Andrew J	NELSON, Laura V	9 Sep 1856	2

MATHERS, Andrew J /wid	PETTITT, Hester A	16 Dec 1874	18
MATHERS, D W	WELLS, Cecelia	30 Dec 1894	48
MATHERS, Leiton	WHITTEN, Robena E	1 Jun 1917	92
MATHERS, Tilden	WILT, Ione	22 Mar 1899	56
MATTHEWS, Armistead /wid	PETTITT, Mary Jane	9 Oct 1865	6
MATEER, James T	FORTNEY, Olivia A	16 Dec 1880	27
MATEER, Robert H	JOHNSON, Emeline Frances	21 Feb 1855	1
MATEER, Rufus E	CRIPPEN, Janie T	27 Sep 1899	57
MATEER, S J	CARROLL, Ann E	31 Dec 1867	8
MATERS, Hugo	DOVA, Iva	3 Sep 1921	101
MATHERS, Willie F	DAVIS, Hazel G	13 Nov 1920	99
MATHERSON, William /wid	MCCULLOCK, Grace Randolph /div	18 Jun 1925	111
MATTERN, Fred C	VAN VREAN, Lillian E	8 Jun 1907	73
MATTINGLY, Bernard J	FLAHERTY, Mary M	19 Feb 1928	121
MATTINGLY, Frank Holt	ELLIS, Maud Ernestine	6 Dec 1905	70
MATTINGLY, James I	VON BRIESEN, Carolyn W	27 Nov 1931	134
MATTISON, George	EICHELBERGER, Kitty /wid	19 Apr 1923	105
MATTOCKS, Robert W	TRAMMELL, Iola B	20 Feb 1889	39
MAUCK, Lloyd O	MATHIAS, Bertha S	27 Jun 1931	132
MAURICE, George Holbrook	EGLIN, Ethel	12 Dec 1898	55
MAUST, George C /div	SMALL, Ruth I	6 Jun 1916	90
MAXON, John C	PHILLIPS, Edna E	20 Jun 1917	92
MAY, Douglass C	COOPERING, Margaret Virginia	20 Jun 1918	95
MAY, Edmond /wid	HUYCK, Rebecca	29 Aug 1867	8
MAY, Henry R	BRASSE, Erna C	25 Oct 1918	95
MAYER, William H	URON, Linda	29 Jan 1902	62
MAYHUGH, Edgar M	MCMULLEN, Alma M	15 Jun 1917	92
MAYHUGH, F G	DAVIS, Georgeanna	31 Oct 1867	8
MAYHUGH, George L	LEWIS, Harriet A	9 Feb 1893	46
MAYHUGH, John F	RAY, Lizzie	28 Jun 1896	51
MAYHUGH, McClelland L	JAEGER, Henrietta A	31 Dec 1927	120
MAYNARD, Everett P	WALTHER, Catherine C	5 Jan 1929	124
MAYNARD, James Leslie	BLACKENEY, Drusilla Josephine	19 Apr 1926	114
MAYO, Merrill Frank	PAYNE, Lucy Priscilla	6 Mar 1933	141
MAZZULLO, Archie A	SMITH, Carrie E /div	23 Jul 1912	82
MCASHAN, J E Jr /div	CUMMINGS, Marjoria P	10 Apr 1925	111
MCCABE, William J /div	MCCORMICK, Lydia	2 Sep 1916	90
MCCAFFREY, John	SOULE, Mary C	3 Jun 1885	35
MCCANDLISH, Fairfax Shield	DONOHOE, Mary LeGrand	9 Nov 1911	81
MCCANN, Francis T	RAGAN, Ella M	5 Jul 1885	35
MCCANN, George P	TYLER, Myrtle E	24 Oct 1924	109
MCCARD, Richard W /c wid	ARNOLD, Amanda /c wid	20 Nov 1905	69

MCCARDELL, W S	ROWELL, Annabel	17 Sep 1904	67
MCCARTHY, John Calvin	BLADEN, Aline Phillis	24 Nov 1926	116
MCCARTY, A W	GRIMES, Anna L	7 Jul 1917	92
MCCARTY, Charles	HUNTT, Debbie	24 May 1891	43
MCCARTY, Dennis	CARLIN, Maggie P	25 Apr 1908	74
MCCARTY, John	NELSON, Barbara	8 Jan 1902	62
MCCARTY, John E	LLOYD, Irene M	10 Jan 1882	29
MCCARTY, John E /wid	THOMPSON, Beatrice E	15 May 1893	46
MCCATHRAN, Francis F	SHOOK, Mildred	13 Mar 1923	104
MCCAULEY, Daniel H	MAYHUGH, Rosa J	25 Dec 1912	84
MCCAULEY, Elmer L /wid	THOMPSON, Helen E	28 Feb 1930	127
MCCAULEY, John /wid	KIDWELL, Lavinia /wid	21 Dec 1883	32
MCCAULEY, John	THOMPSON, Mattie	5 Dec 1899	57
MCCAULEY, John Henry	HERBERT, Alice G	3 Jun 1891	43
MCCAULEY, Willard L	ADAMS, Agnes M	27 Nov 1913	85
MCCLAIN, Baxter D	CONROY, Katharine	7 Jul 1898	54
MCCLARY, William A	DOVE, Ruby V	22 Oct 1930	130
MCCLAYLAND, Albert	WILLS, Coritta A	28 Sep 1932	139
MCCLELLAND, Louis T	HUNTERMARK, Theresa Catherine	25 Feb 1933	141
MCCOFFREY, William O /div	GOLDEN, Helen Cecelia	24 Jul 1926	115
MCCOLLUM, Blaine	LOWRY, Elizabeth M	19 Oct 1925	112
MCCORKELL, Abraham /wid	GRAY, Amy Ann	16 Jan 1872	15
MCCORT, Michael	STONE, Loretta M	3 Jan 1906	70
MCCOWAN, William J /c	NUNBY, Avis /c	7 Sep 1931	133
MCCOY, A C	BLAUVELT, Janie R /wid	14 Jan 1914	86
MCCOY, John R	STEELE, Lawrence A	10 Jun 1930	128
MCCRARY, Samuel E	HILTON, Lucille R	8 May 1932	137
MCCREERY, Lester	BASTOW, Minnie	5 Feb 1896	50
MCCREERY, Lester /wid	SPEER, Almira F	7 Dec 1904	67
MCCUEN, Henry I	DRAPER, Beulah	2 Feb 1922	102
MCCULLOUGH, George Washington	MASON, Anna N	16 Oct 1873	16
MCDANEL, Frank Leslie	BAYLISS, Jennie	21 Apr 1919	95
MCDANIEL, Arthur Raymond	BURROWS, Mary Gertrude	16 Apr 1920	98
MCDANIEL, Everd K	MCGUIRE, Evangeline	10 Nov 1921	101
MCDANIEL, Samuel B	ADAMS, Rosa	19 May 1886	36
MCDERMOTT, Thomas F	POWER, Veronica T	17 Apr 1895	49
MCDONALD, Andrew D /wid	BRITTON, Ella H /wid	22 Oct 1932	139
MCDONALD, Charles L	LINEBURG, Anna R	16 Apr 1927	117
MCDONALD, Malcolm O	GARDES, Marie L	15 Mar 1926	114
MCDONALD, William /wid	PENFORD, Isabella /div	14 Jan 1932	136
MCDONALD, William L	LOHMAN, Dorothy Jane	19 Aug 1920	98
MCDONOUGH, William	RECTOR, Rosabelle	26 May 1855	1

MCDOWELL, Wilson /c	PROCTOR, Fannie /c	27 Oct 1909	77
MCELWEE, William J	BRAWNER, Leona M /wid	29 Oct 1927	119
MCFARLAND, John T	GRAVES, Eleanor G	14 Oct 1927	119
MCFARLAND, W D	MOHLER, Rita	15 Aug 1922	103
MCFARLAND, William F	MITCHELL, Maggie	28 Oct 1885	36
MCGAHEY, Charles N /wid	WEEKS, Carrie B	11 Feb 1930	127
MCGAHEY, James J	FANNON, Catherine	24 Jun 1897	53
MCGARRY, Wallace A	SLYE, Mildred	19 Feb 1932	136
MCGARVEY, William M	CARLIN, Marjorie T	5 Jun 1929	124
MCGLINCY, Willis W /wid	BRADWAY, Jennie M /div	29 May 1929	124
MCGLUE, James H	CHAMBERS, Helen May	16 Nov 1927	119
MCGRATH, Murel G	PIERCE, Montana F	19 Aug 1932	138
MCGRIM, John F	GROSS, Mary E	27 Apr 1928	121
MCGUIN, B F /wid	HOLDEN, Katie	12 Sep 1922	103
MCGUIN, Harry	KITSON, Elsie V	10 Apr 1912	82
MCGUIN, Robert	BAYLISS, Pearl E	21 Sep 1921	101
MCGUIRE, George /c	DAVIS, Josephine /c	26 Jul 1898	55
MCGUIRE, J P Jr	MASON, Clara	10 Jul 1860	5
MCGUIRE, John W	HACKETT, Hazel H	30 Jun 1933	142
MCHUGH, James M	CARTER, Imogene P	18 Jul 1930	128
MCINTOSH, Bayard Livingston	GOODMAN, Roberta Caroline	5 Jan 1907	72
MCINTOSH, Carl	HILL, Jessie A	7 Oct 1926	116
MCINTOSH, John C	WHITE, Mildred I	24 Oct 1931	134
MCINTOSH, Luther L	PEYTON, Catharine M	22 Jul 1890	41
MCINTOSH, Luther L /wid	ROGERS, Alice Ann	20 Apr 1898	54
MCINTOSH, Thomas	HAVENER, Mary E	16 Jun 1902	62
MCKAY, Charles H	CHAMBERS, Reba	9 Sep 1920	99
MCKEAN, Rev. John /wid	BARKER, Ruth	10 Sep 1884	33
MCKENNA, Harry P	SARTIVELL, Grace A	14 Sep 1922	103
MCKENNEY, Raymond	MCVERRY, Irene	21 May 1918	94
MCKENZIE, Adolphus	VAN KANNER, Effie A /div	8 Jul 1924	108
MCKEOWN, Thomas H	KIRBY, Elsie M	28 Dec 1892	45
MCKIE, George McFarland	MANKIN, Ethel O	2 Jun 1902	62
MCKITRICK, Frank R	BABBITT, Nellie A	9 Jun 1928	121
MCLANE, Raymond	TIPPETT, Marion E	8 Apr 1922	102
MCLEAREN, George M	GREEN, Violett E	25 Jun 1927	118
MCMASTER, David	LEEDS, Bertie E	18 Jan 1906	70
MCMILLEN, Zenus	MOXLEY, Esther	27 Sep 1899	57
MCMINEMY, Clare F	PHIPPS, Marguerite	26 Jun 1926	115
MCMULLEN, Caleb	GODFREY, Eva	18 Dec 1899	57
MCMULLEN, Jacob	ROBEY, Bessie	7 Oct 1901	61
MCMULLEN, Marion	BOYER, Mary	2 Sep 1883	32

MCMULLEN, Paul J	BUCKLEY, Ollie M	5 Jan 1897	*52*
MCMULLEN, Robert T	CROSON, Annie J	27 Apr 1898	*54*
MCNAIR, W D	NICKELL, Virginia	11 Sep 1919	*96*
MCNAIR, William /wid	HUNTER, Laura Virginia	25 Jul 1857	*3*
MCNEAL, David	GUNNELL, Gertrude W /div	4 Dec 1873	*16*
MCNEY, Ernest E	TERRY, Lillian R	29 Dec 1926	*117*
MCNISH, Alvin G	HARIG, Lillian	27 May 1923	*105*
MCPHERSON, Carroll J	BROWN, Fern	1 Sep 1923	*106*
MCPHERSON, John	MULLINIX, Ruth	1 Jul 1933	*142*
MCVEAN, Albert H	SMITH, Jennie E	12 Dec 1878	*24*
MCWHORTER, James Kyle	MILLAN, Virginia Lee	16 Jun 1869	*11*
MCWHORTER, William David	MILLAN, Mary Jones	27 Nov 1866	*7*
MCWRIGHT, Harold R	MOWBRAY, Katherine I	23 Sep 1929	*126*
MEADE, Joseph F /c	WILLIAMS, Mary F /c	7 Dec 1884	*34*
MEDLEY, Isaac	CARTER, Martha	28 Dec 1871	*14*
MEEK, Roy C	RISTON, Ruth	1 Jul 1896	*51*
MEHOVES, John /wid	TALBOT, Harriett /wid	13 Jul 1926	*115*
MELTON, James E	KIDWELL, Marjorie E	29 Oct 1927	*119*
MELTON, William	BARRE, Rena B	28 Oct 1907	*73*
MELVILLE, Andrew /wid	SHREVE, Barbara Ann	13 Sep 1875	*19*
MELVIN, Lewis	HARRIS, Mary C	31 Dec 1868	*10*
MENCHEY, F LeRoy	WILSON, Mary C	11 Jan 1932	*136*
MENDELL, Harry F	LAFFERTY, Rose	1 Jun 1925	*111*
MENTZEL, John	HALLEY, Laura	6 Feb 1894	*47*
MERCER, G S	BICKSLER, Kate	2 Jun 1896	*51*
MERCER, Walter S	COCK, Ida V	29 Oct 1885	*35*
MERCHANT, Henry D	HARLOW, Vera S	19 Jun 1921	*100*
MERCHANT, Malcolm B	DYER, Mamie V	5 Jun 1900	*58*
MERCHANT, R B	BURNSIDE, Hattie A	29 May 1895	*49*
MERCHANT, William S	SKINNER, Laura V /wid	15 May 1902	*62*
MEREDITH, James L /c	SMITH, Julia Mae /c	4 Jun 1931	*132*
MERIADETH, Floyd E	GHEEN, Mary Pearl	9 Jan 1926	*113*
MERO, J William	TALBOTT, Ada E	2 Aug 1893	*46*
MERRICK, Stephen E /wid	SLITZ, Frances	2 Aug 1921	*101*
MERRIFIELD, George Alpheus	Lyon /wid		
	*DICKENSO*N, Margaret Gray /div	16 Jan 1908	*74*
MERRILL, F J	STOBERT, May	20 Feb 1889	*39*
MERRY, Eliphalet R	CENTER, Lizzie	6 May 1879	*25*
MERRY, Eliphalet R Sr /wid	SWIMLEY, May B	21 Nov 1931	*134*
MERRYMAN, Emerson A	JOHNSON, Frances E	23 Dec 1872	*15*
MERRYMAN, Francis	KITSON, Sarah A	12 Oct 1882	*30*
MERRYMAN, Ralph L	O'NEILL, Blanch V /wid	29 Dec 1933	*145*

MERRYMAN, Sanford	DOTSON, Mary M	22 Oct 1882	30
MERRYMAN, William F	SHIPLEY, Carrie	25 Aug 1920	98
MERSON, Kermit L	GOODWIN, Lois V	11 Dec 1929	126
MERSON, Richard A	COOK, Lydia A	19 Dec 1894	48
MESSERSMITH, Paul B	LOUTHER, May	31 Jul 1926	115
MEYER, Baldemaro /c	NORMAN, Anna /c	17 Feb 1923	104
MEYERHOFFER, William J	FOLLIN, Eliza	11 May 1926	114
MICKELSON, Alfred	WILEY, Mary Susan	8 May 1923	105
MIDDLETON, A W	MAHORNEY, Lulie D	24 Jun 1885	35
MIDDLETON, B W	BRADLEY, Mary E	29 Dec 1897	54
MIDDLETON, Ben	DETWILER, Ann R	25 Dec 1889	40
MIDDLETON, Dr. A L /wid	BERRY, Alzine S	19 May 1897	52
MIDDLETON, Edward H	THOMPSON, Clara L	30 Sep 1914	87
MIDDLETON, W F	JARRETT, Bertha C	23 Sep 1904	67
MILBURN, Harold R	HARKINS, A Jane /div	9 Jul 1932	138
MILES, E Paul	REYNOLDS, Frances N	23 Feb 1932	136
MILES, Henry /c	WASHINGTON, Rebecca /c	30 Dec 1870	13
MILLAN, Benjamin C	ROBINSON, Hilda A	25 Jun 1927	118
MILLAN, J Leroy	COLLINS, Emaretta K	20 Mar 1890	41
MILLAN, John A	HAIGHT, Mary Emma	18 Jun 1916	90
MILLAN, William Walter Jr	JONES, Bernice Hines	27 Jun 1921	100
MILLANTREE, Martin /c wid	SEALS, Fanny /c wid	30 Dec 1886	37
MILLARD, E E	REID, Edna J	5 Apr 1892	44
MILLARD, Everett E	TRACEY, Annie L	14 Apr 1892	44
MILLARD, Samuel	DYER, Olive L	8 Aug 1900	58
MILLER, Albert C	CHAMPION, Mary	30 May 1931	132
MILLER, Carl	BIRCH, Edith	23 Jun 1926	115
MILLER, Clyde /c	GIRL, Lillie /c wid	26 Sep 1926	116
MILLER, Elmer E	TURNER, Jane B	28 Oct 1933	144
MILLER, Enoch D	BOWMAN, Sallie M	27 Dec 1908	82
MILLER, George E	LYLES, Belle F	30 May 1883	31
MILLER, George William	JACOBS, Bessie Ann	4 Jun 1911	80
MILLER, George William Jr	AYRES, Edna Mae	16 Dec 1933	145
MILLER, Herbert	SINKALINE, Vera Violet	8 Sep 1924	109
MILLER, Ira B	SHIFFLETT, Mary C	10 Jun 1913	84
MILLER, James R	CECIL, Mary A	14 Aug 1930	129
MILLER, John /c	GADDESS, Jennie /c	28 Sep 1876	20
MILLER, John	PULMAN, Sarah B	12 Dec 1877	22
MILLER, John A /c	PERKINS, Lavinia /c	11 May 1875	18
MILLER, Joseph W	MORAN, Mary A	8 Oct 1932	139
MILLER, Landon R	SHRINER, Eva A	14 Nov 1917	93
MILLER, Levi B	YATES, Nina M	10 Jan 1931	131

MILLER, Richard /c wid	ODRICK, Milly /c	6 Apr 1876	20
MILLER, Russell	DRIVER, Cleo K	30 Jun 1932	138
MILLER, Samuel P	BEARD, Mary M	9 Mar 1917	91
MILLER, William F	KERR, Mabel A	25 Feb 1902	62
MILLER, William J	HEIDENREICH, Rosalie M	10 Jul 1927	118
MILLISON, Harry A	HARRYMAN, Audrey	3 May 1932	137
MILLNER, Percy M /wid	RILEY, Jessie G /div	19 Jun 1925	111
MILLS, Chalmers E	MOLBY, Grace M	27 Nov 1931	134
MILLS, Clinton	SNYDER, Daisy	8 May 1905	68
MILLS, Daniel	SHEA, Annie M	3 May 1905	68
MILLS, Edward	HARRISON, Rosa Lee	27 Feb 1902	62
MILLS, Eugene	ARNOLD, Lena	7 Aug 1904	67
MILLS, George McCarty	ADAMS, Ann E	14 Mar 1868	9
MILLS, J J	MONEY, B V	12 May 1909	74
MILLS, John /c	GOINGS, Martha /c	18 Jul 1876	20
MILLS, John E /c	CARTER, Sarah Jane /c	11 Nov 1874	17
MILLS, Kenneth N	CHURCH, Maybelle A	6 Sep 1923	106
MILLS, Leon E /div	MOHLER, Etta	26 Nov 1923	106
MILLS, Nathan	FAIRFAX, Lillian	11 Jun 1911	81
MILLS, Raymond E	MARTIN, Juanita	4 May 1929	124
MILLS, Robert Burr	PAXEN, Sarah E	29 Oct 1867	8
MILLS, S J	DAVIS, Minnie L	25 Dec 1892	45
MILLS, Thomas R	ROGERS, Annie E	21 Apr 1917	92
MILLS, Whiting A	DE GRANGE, Ella A	15 Nov 1893	47
MILLS, William Lee	DAY, Lillian L	4 Jun 1917	92
MILSTEAD, James E	BALLENGER, Margaret M	18 Oct 1858	4
MILSTEAD, Thomas G	BALLENGER, Ida M	28 Jul 1891	43
MILTON, Brinton R	SIMMS, Sarah A	12 Sep 1876	20
MILTON, John	PETTIT, Annie Cleone	29 Dec 1906	72
MINER, Andrew /c	CLARK, Emma /c	2 Apr 1879	25
MINER, Layton H	STOUT, Mary L	28 Jul 1920	98
MINNICK, Daniel B	CLARK, Elsie M	19 Jul 1924	108
MINOR, Albert G	CARLIN, Lucelia /wid	11 Jun 1895	49
MINOR, Dock /c	SAMUEL, Mary /c	24 Sep 1928	122
MINOR, Forney	LACY, Maggie	2 Sep 1902	63
MINOR, Walter E	BIGGERS, Elizabeth C	23 Nov 1929	126
MISKELL, Thomas	JENKINS, Lydia Ann	16 Jan 1855	1
MITCHELL, Anthony /c	COLLINS, Martha /c	15 Oct 1903	65
MITCHELL, Austin /wid	BURNSIDE, Bertha	14 Feb 1931	131
MITCHELL, Francis L	WORSTER, Anna	27 Feb 1855	1
MITCHELL, J E /wid	FAIRFAX, Martha	9 Aug 1860	5
MITCHELL, James /c	MOX, Evelyn /c wid	5 Sep 1875	18

MITCHELL, John E	PETTITT, Madge	2 Jul 1875	*18*
MITCHELL, L M	PULTZ, Nellie Lee	7 Jul 1924	*108*
MITCHELL, Matthew /c	HARVEY, Roberta S /c	26 Apr 1930	*127*
MOCK, Dempsie	GARNER, Martha Alice	1 Dec 1908	*76*
MOCK, Dewey	ROBEY, Hattie	11 Sep 1924	*109*
MOCK, John William	HOLLIDAY, Virgie	14 Sep 1905	*69*
MOCK, Minor C	JONES, Ethel E	8 Feb 1923	*104*
MOELLER, Talbott D	HOPKINS, Edna Virginia	16 Dec 1933	*145*
MOFFETT, Carl G	JEWELL, Lizzie	26 Apr 1894	*48*
MOHLER, C J	ROBINSON, Sally	21 Dec 1876	*21*
MOHLER, C J /wid	KING, Ettie Lee /wid	20 Jul 1898	*55*
MOHLER, Frank S	PATTON, Mollie R	16 Jul 1903	*65*
MOHLER, John F	EATON, Mildred May	15 Jun 1927	*118*
MOLAIR, John	WOODYARD, Frances	26 Feb 1857	*3*
MOLLISON, Robert W	RICE, Katherine P	26 Aug 1925	*112*
MONCH, Albert R	SUTPHIN, Lola E	8 Oct 1929	*126*
MONCH, William B	MILLS, Annie M	25 Nov 1924	*110*
MONEY, A C	YOUNG, Julia A	6 Feb 1889	*39*
MONEY, Albert	PEACOCK, Nannie	27 Jan 1876	*20*
MONEY, Cornelius	WALKER, Joanna	3 Feb 1876	*20*
MONEY, Gray	PHILLIPS, Mattie	20 Oct 1915	*89*
MONEY, H H /wid	MOONEY, Laura	11 Mar 1922	*102*
MONEY, Harry T	BROOKE, Daisy	30 Jan 1913	*84*
MONEY, Henry H	CARLIN, Mary A	24 Sep 1878	*24*
MONEY, John C	JOHNSON, Sarah E	15 Jan 1859	*4*
MONEY, John T /wid	FOLLIN, Frances A	31 Jan 1883	*31*
MONEY, Joseph L	SLACK, Ida C	1 Sep 1897	*53*
MONEY, Lawson /wid	WILLIAMS, Ann M	22 May 1865	*6*
MONROE, E P	PLASKETT, Marie K	12 Nov 1919	*96*
MONROE, Edward /wid	LYLES, Nancy	6 Mar 1898	*54*
MONROE, John L	TRIPLETT, Effie W	4 Dec 1873	*16*
MONROE, John L	STEELE, Mary E	20 Sep 1905	*69*
MONROE, Larmar	JENKINS, Maud M	8 Jun 1904	*66*
MONROE, Robert /c	WEST, Sarah /c	15 Nov 1888	*39*
MONROE, William /c	PARKER, Celia /c	19 Feb 1882	*30*
MONROE, Wilson H /c	STEWART, Lillian G /c	18 Jul 1909	*77*
MONTAGUE, James /c	HALL, Bertha Ann /c	28 Mar 1908	*74*
MONTAGUE, Nelson /c	PAGE, Rosemond /c	30 Aug 1928	*122*
MONTGOMERY, George D	MILLER, Blanche E	5 Mar 1921	*100*
MOODY, John M	BROWN, Dollie	1 Jan 1885	*34*
MOON, John	BALLENGER, Caroline	14 Dec 1888	*39*
MOONY, George K	IVES, Elmira B	16 May 1856	*2*

MOORE, Alfred	HUNTER, Helen	7 Nov 1867	8
MOORE, Claude Hughlett /div	THOMPSON, Katherine	1 Jan 1919	95
MOORE, Donald M	THOMSON, Grace	7 Oct 1929	126
MOORE, James /c	JOHNSON, Ruby /c	12 Feb 1903	64
MOORE, James D Jr	SIMMS, Mary Emma	7 Dec 1926	116
MOORE, John H	PICKETT, Mattie L	23 Jun 1897	53
MOORE, Joseph /c wid	DAVIS, Annie /c wid	2 Nov 1903	65
MOORE, Luther S	LAKE, Ruth Virginia	31 Oct 1931	134
MOORE, M D	GRAY, Olif Saphronia	29 Dec 1927	120
MOORE, Oscar	POWELL, Susan E	20 Apr 1859	4
MOORE, Randolph /c	HOLLAND, Marian L /c	3 Jun 1914	86
MOORE, Samuel Henry /wid	DEVINE, Evelyn A	7 Sep 1904	67
MOORE, Walter D	BROWN, Lillian A	27 May 1898	54
MOORE, William E	WILLIAMS, Sally E	27 Feb 1868	9
MOORE, William G	BROADAS, Rebecca A	1 Jun 1869	11
MOORE, William L	PETTITT, Susannah	18 Sep 1866	6
MORAN, George W /wid	CROSON, Ella G	18 Dec 1901	62
MORAN, Harvey	SNIDER, Zadie	24 Mar 1897	52
MORAN, J J	ROYSTON, Lena B	11 Mar 1918	93
MORAN, R E	HAVENER, Alice /wid	3 Feb 1909	76
MORAN, R E /wid	COOK, Effie M	13 May 1913	84
MORARITY, George /c	MELVIN, Alice /c	5 Oct 1884	33
MORARITY, John R /c	MELVIN, Martha /c	3 Jan 1892	44
MORARITY, Joseph /c	TURNER, Della /c	1 Nov 1885	35
MORARITY, Thomas /c	GIBSON, Venie /c	14 Nov 1896	51
MORARITY, Victor /c	PERRY, Elizabeth /c	7 Dec 1928	123
MOREHEAD, Lewis /wid	MURPHY, Emma E	16 Feb 1897	52
MORELAND, Harry H	JOLLY, Florence V	18 Jun 1910	78
MORGAN, David	CUMBERLAND, Eva	6 May 1912	82
MORGAN, Nelson /c	WHEELER, Alice /c	2 Apr 1885	34
MORGAN, Philip	THORTON, Ethel	4 Sep 1916	90
MORRIS, Frank A	MAHONEY, Jessie J	17 May 1916	90
MORRIS, Jesse	MASON, Annie	6 Apr 1924	108
MORRIS, John W	MASON, Nellie Stella	27 May 1929	124
MORRIS, Robert H /c	LEWIS, Julia /c	2 May 1878	23
MORTIMORE, John F	CLEVELAND, Hannah L	not legible 1857	3
MORTON, Charles Wm	STALCUP, Dorothy D	20 Aug 1932	138
MORTON, Jesse	PARKER, Jennie	28 Dec 1869	11
MORTON, Stephen /c	LUCAS, Annie /c	15 May 1879	25
MORTON, William M /wid	HUNTER, Alice W	5 Sep 1867	8
MOSBY, John /c	BROWN, Maria /c	7 Dec 1877	22
MOSS, Madison D /wid	BREADY, Ella W	15 Feb 1896	46

MOSSBURG, George W /wid	THOMPSON, Hazel	17 Jun 1920	98
MOUNTJOY, William /wid	BUTLER, Virginia	10 Oct 1866	7
MOXLEY, David Anderson /wid	TYSON, Anna Maria	2 Aug 1892	45
MOXLEY, David N	STAATS, Nellie	10 Jun 1903	64
MOYERS, Waldo B	CORRELL, Elinor C	5 Dec 1932	140
MUD, Frederick	DANIELS, Louisa A	21 May 1903	64
MUDD, Thomas	BILLER, Sarah E	9 Mar 1925	110
MUDD, William	DOVE, Mollie	8 Nov 1899	57
MUDDEMAN, Henry	SCOTT, Hannah	28 Dec 1869	11
MUELLER, Carl J	PULMAN, Agnes M	1 Dec 1909	77
MUELLER, Robert C	MALIN, Anne M	20 Feb 1932	136
MULCAHY, Daniel J	BALL, Dorothy	27 Nov 1926	116
MULHOLLAND, A P	BUCKLEY, Theresa	4 Nov 1914	87
MULHOLLAND, Patrick	WESTON, Susan	22 May 1873	16
MULLEN, Samuel R	BOYCE, Florence M	25 Jun 1903	64
MUNDAY, L Walton	THOMPSON, Alice D	26 Dec 1897	54
MUNDAY, O S /wid	HITE, Lena	5 May 1923	105
MUNDLE, John /c	MACK, Ida /c	31 Dec 1904	68
MUNFORD, George T	HOFFMAN, Grace	5 Mar 1926	114
MUNOZ, Raymond Anibal Jr	BROCK, Margaret L	31 May 1932	137
MUNSCATTA, Chin	JACKSON, Mary /wid	27 Nov 1910	80
MUNTZING, Meredict J	YATES, Helen A	19 Aug 1933	143
MURFEE, James T	SHACKLEFORD, Evelyn P	4 Oct 1930	129
MURNANE, James	MCMAHON, Lizzie A	3 Jul 1883	31
MURPH, Iane Lewis	RIGG, Susannah	28 Nov 1929	126
MURPHY, Henry Stafford	WALKER, Sarah deSanssun	30 Apr 1901	60
MURPHY, James F	SEAL, Elizabeth L	25 Jun 1932	138
MURPHY, James T	LINCOLN, Lucille K	17 Nov 1920	99
MURPHY, Joseph W	WITHERS, Alice A	26 Oct 1908	75
MURRAY, Albert G /c	WELCH, Mary /c	12 Jun 1890	41
MURRAY, Curtis /c	HONESTY, Golda /c	28 Dec 1813	85
MURRAY, Harry	JONES, Katie Nancy	22 May 1928	121
MURRAY, Jesse	HUNTER, Catherine Ann	17 Sep 1867	8
MURRAY, Josh Ray	BROOKS, Eveline	28 Apr 1870	12
MURRAY, Marshall /c	ROBINSON, Mamie /c	12 Apr 1905	68
MURRAY, Richard /c	MATTHEWS, Dora /c	3 Jun 1908	75
MURRAY, Samuel /c	SUMMERS, Luvenia /c	15 Jul 1909	77
MURRAY, Samuel K /c div	TINNER, Edith M /c	19 Feb 1918	93
MURRAY, Thomas J /wid	NEWMAN, Fannie A	2 Mar 1859	4
MURRAY, Vernon /c	SMITH, Mary /c	13 Nov 1924	110
MURRAY, William	ELGIN, Catherine L /wid	27 Feb 1855	1
MURRELL, James W	BESLEY, Naomi	14 Oct 1908	75

MURRILL, William Alphonso	LUTTRELL, Edna L	1 Sep 1897	*53*
MURTAUGH, William	LYNN, Elizabeth	3 Dec 1903	*65*
MUSACCHIA, D L /div	PROVENZA, Rose J	13 Mar 1930	*127*
MUSGRAY, James D Jr /c wid	WEST, Carlette /c wid	1 May 1925	*111*
MUTERSBAUGH, Earle T	HALL, Jean A	17 Oct 1924	*109*
MUTERSBAUGH, John W	CROSSMAN, Mary E	14 Dec 1898	*55*
MYERS, Eustace	WARD, Helen	19 Dec 1925	*113*
MYERS, Harry B	THOMAS, Marjorie G	8 Nov 1905	*69*
MYERS, Howard F	NEFF, Mary E	26 Apr 1909	*76*
MYERS, James	ELLISON, Elizabeth	1 Aug 1913	*84*
MYERS, John T	NEFF, Zella M	24 Jul 1919	*96*
MYERS, Jonathan W	THOMPSON, Margaret M	16 Oct 1907	*73*
MYERS, Thomas J /wid	TURNER, Mary E	23 Oct 1892	*45*
MYERS, William H /wid	MATHIAS, Myrtle A /wid	24 Apr 1921	*100*
MYERS, William H	FINCH, Dixie	29 Nov 1922	*104*
NAILOR, George	JACKSON, Mary /wid	7 Sep 1873	*16*
NAILOR, Jarett /c	CHAMBERS, Lucy /c	7 Dec 1912	*83*
NAILOR, Lawrence /c	HARRIS, Lela /c	21 May 1905	*68*
NAILOR, Phililp	SMITH, Amanda	20 Dec 1866	*7*
NALLS, C Leonard	RAGAN, Ellen	28 May 1913	*84*
NALLS, Carroll	ROGERS, Mattie	29 Jan 1921	*100*
NALLS, James N	WINSTON, Louisa E	9 Mar 1904	*66*
NALLS, Welby M	MIDDLETON, Elena J	29 Oct 1930	*130*
NAPFEL, Charles J	GOODRICK, Julia M	3 Oct 1928	*122*
NAPPER, Alfred /c	QUANDER, Susannah /c	12 Oct 1883	*32*
NAPPER, Frank /c	WILLIAMS, Susan /c	29 Dec 1864	*5*
NASH, Charles H	STRUDER, Emma L	16 Nov 1904	*67*
NASH, Harold K	PRICE, Fay D	30 Dec 1930	*130*
NASH, James B	FLEMING, Katharine A	18 Jun 1927	*118*
NASH, William A	CLEVELAND, Mabel T	27 Aug 1917	*93*
NAYLOR, Arthur W /c	HARRIS, Sylvia /c	20 Oct 1912	*83*
NAYLOR, Lawrence L /c	ROBERSON, Susannah /c	22 Dec 1875	*19*
NAYLOR, Phil	SMITH, Amanda	20 Dec 1866	*9*
NEAL, Albert B	GIBBS, Janette	14 Nov 1928	*123*
NEAL, Edward /c	DADE, Jennie /c	22 Nov 1882	*31*
NEAL, James H /c	EWING, Ollie Lee /c wid	20 Sep 1930	*129*
NEAL, John /c	WILLIAMS, Hattie /c	7 Sep 1904	*67*
NEAL, Thomas /c	LEE, Mary /c	25 May 1882	*30*
NEALE, William H /c	BARNES, Millie /c wid	17 Sep 1902	*63*
NEFF, Edward Joseph	BRUCHIE, Alice Virginia	6 Oct 1923	*106*
NEFF, Edwin E	MYERS, S Bessie	9 Oct 1917	*93*
NEFF, Joseph C	HAISLIP, Anna M Patton /wid	7 Jun 1927	*118*

NEILD, Stanley C	HINES, A Jeanette	21 Aug 1932	*138*
NEITZEY, Joseph E	STOUT, Catharine A	6 Sep 1885	*35*
NEITZEY, Wilfred H	ROUSE, Marguerite A	10 Oct 1927	*119*
NEITZEY, William M	STOUT, Mary E	30 Oct 1887	*38*
NELSON, John /c	HOLLAND, France Rebecca /c	1 Dec 1904	*67*
NELSON, Joseph F	CARLIN, Alice A	30 Nov 1903	*65*
NELSON, Justus C	DEWEY, Elsie M /wid	13 Jun 1918	*94*
NELSON, Kermit A	JOHANNES, Ruth	6 Jul 1927	*118*
NELSON, Napoleon	SHEPHERD, Bessie	30 May 1900	*58*
NELSON, William W	KEECH, Helen H	5 Jul 1913	*84*
NELSON, Winfree E	BEALE, Mary G	4 May 1929	*124*
NEVITT, Hugh Cox	NEVITT, Emily R	20 Dec 1876	*21*
NEVITT, Robert G	LEE, Mary G	14 Dec 1871	*14*
NEVITT, Samuel E	MARDERS, Mary J	1 May 1855	*2*
NEVITT, William Marders	ARNOLD, Cassie	2 Aug 1893	*46*
NEWCOMB, Edward	MAGNER, Mary	19 Apr 1893	*46*
NEWLON, John M	BERRY, Emma	20 Apr 1887	*37*
NEWLON, Nathan G	BENNETT, Laura	12 Jan 1917	*91*
NEWLON, Richard L /div	MOBLEY, Rowe W /div	20 Jul 1932	*138*
NEWLON, Samuel Richard	HOGELAND, Lena B	16 Dec 1885	*35*
NEWMAN, Benjamin F	GOODING, Sarah E	13 Feb 1867	*6*
NEWMAN, Charles /c wid	DAWSON, Hattie Lee /c wid	3 Feb 1914	*86*
NEWMAN, Charles Franklin	FORBES, Emma J	25 Apr 1882	*30*
NEWMAN, Charles H	SUDDEN, Julia	30 Dec 1871	*14*
NEWMAN, Conrad /c	WAYNES, Emma /c	17 Dec 1879	*26*
NEWMAN, George C /c	WILLIAMS, Catharine /c	10 Oct 1905	*69*
NEWMAN, Harry M /c	PEARSON, Sadie L /c	30 Mar 1904	*66*
NEWMAN, Hiram	BARLOW, Mary E	22 Feb 1876	*20*
NEWMAN, Isham /c	MORGAN, Georgie /c	31 Oct 1877	*22*
NEWMAN, James /c	SCOTT, Mome /c	26 Dec 1928	*123*
NEWMAN, John	DENNEY, Fanny	4 Oct 1868	*10*
NEWMAN, John S /c	COATES, Belle /c	26 Jan 1929	*124*
NEWMAN, Peter O	BAYLISS, Esther A	30 Dec 1869	*11*
NEWMAN, Raymond /c	BROOKS, Willie /c	23 Dec 1908	*76*
NEWMAN, Robert /c	HARRIS, Lucy /c	26 Nov 1905	*70*
NEWMAN, Robert C	BERKLEY, H S	6 Dec 1859	*4*
NEWMAN, Samuel /c	RATCLIFFE, Jennie /c	19 May 1873	*16*
NEWMAN, William H /c	THOMPSON, Martha E /c	11 Apr 1877	*21*
NEWMAN, William H /c	HORTON, Rose /c	20 Sep 1899	*57*
NEWTON, Alfred /c	LAWSON, Malinda /c	19 May 1879	*25*
NEWTON, Grant R	MEHRLING, Mary E	4 Oct 1916	*91*
NEWTON, Robert L /c	GIBSON, Louisa /c	8 Feb 1891	*43*

NEWTON, Walter	PETTITT, Nora V	7 Oct 1886	36
NEYMAN, Benjamin Lombard	LUSTIG, Ilona H	28 Jul 1928	122
NICE, Henry /wid	ARNOLD, Drusilla	22 Jun 1875	18
NICHOLAS, Moses /c wid	HONESTY, Cora /c	6 Aug 1902	63
NICHOLS, Harvey L	WILLIAMS, Allie	20 Dec 1910	80
NICHOLSON, William T	JACKSON, Mary Alice	20 Jun 1877	22
NICKENS, James W /c	EWELL, Alice /c	5 Jun 1890	42
NICKENS, R L /c wid	BROOKS, Mary F /c	30 Dec 1903	66
NICKOLSON, W F	PORTER, Helen	26 Sep 1923	106
NICOLL, Henry H /wid	SAUERWEIN, Mildred A /div	27 Mar 1933	141
NIELSEN, Neils M /wid	CHRISTIANSEN, Ruth E	14 Jan 1930	127
NIGH, Omar I /div	HEIMSLEY, Marie Killinger /wid	30 Nov 1922	104
NOAKES, Albert /c wid	JOHNSON, Ida /c	14 Aug 1910	79
NOBLE, James Jr	BUTLER, Mabel V	30 Dec 1930	130
NOLAND, Edward	HAUBENS, Lucille	16 Mar 1933	141
NORMAN, Charles W	LONG, Inez E	28 Jul 1915	89
NORMAN, Stanton R /div	PARKER, Kathryn R /wid	31 Jul 1928	122
NORRIS, Ambrose /c	BLACKWELL, Emily /c	19 Feb 1874	17
NORRIS, Ambrose /c	JAMES, Stella J /c	3 Apr 1903	64
NORRIS, Charles /c	JACKSON, Courtney /c	3 Feb 1876	20
NORRIS, Elmer L	PERRY, Kathryn Lucy	14 Jan 1933	141
NORRIS, Fred Douglass /c	SIMPSON, Sarah /c	12 Aug 1918	94
NORRIS, Richard /c	HARRIS, Effie /c	18 Aug 1917	92
NORRIS, Robert /c	WOODEN, Rebecca /c	24 Dec 1916	91
NORRIS, Sandy /c	PAYNE, Lethy /c	30 Dec 1880	27
NORTHROP, Clarence G	SEAVER, May V	16 Oct 1889	40
NORTON, George /c	JACKSON, Sarah /c	18 Jul 1925	112
NORTON, James H M	WILEY, Frances E /div	7 Jul 1917	92
NORTON, Patrick J	BALLARD, Mary Gladys	1 Jul 1933	143
NOURSE, Philip B	GRAHAM, Harriet F	17 Oct 1906	71
NUSSEAR, Lewis E	CORNWELL, L Myrtle	1 Dec 1916	91
NYE, Clair B	GARBER, Annie E	3 Oct 1921	101
O'BANNION, Henry J	HUTCHISON, Martha	10 Feb 1884	32
O'BANNON, Corbin /wid	SIMPSON, Mary E	23 Jun 1917	92
O'BANYON, Strother /c	DUNCAN, Fanny /c	20 Dec 1879	26
O'BRIEN, Edward J	MONROE, Ada M	13 Aug 1915	89
O'BRIEN, George N	WOLFERT, Ruby Ada	17 Nov 1923	106
O'BRIEN, John Richard	PUMPHREY, Ruth Monona	9 Oct 1933	144
O'CONNOR, G V	BARNARD, Virginia	8 Mar 1930	127
O'CONNOR, Thomas L	BASYE, Lillie	28 Aug 1895	49
O'CONNOR, Frederick	BENNETT, Louise	23 Feb 1929	124
O'CONNORS, Patrick	LEE, Martha M /wid	4 Apr 1898	54

O'MEARA, J T	FRENZELL, Nellie	30 Oct 1895	50
O'MEARA, Valenchia	LYNCH, Ida J	8 Mar 1877	21
O'MERA, Earl T	ROBEY, Luvine May	15 May 1928	121
O'ROARK, G W	DALZELL, Elizabeth B	5 Mar 1914	86
O'ROARK, Vernon	FISHER, Mary E	5 Mar 1932	136
O'SHAUGHNESSY, Charles B	HURST, Frances V	27 Dec 1932	140
O'TOOLE, William P	SEWARD, Elanora	15 Jan 1925	110
ODOR, Frank	WRENN, Onie	21 Nov 1900	59
ODRICK, Frank /c	WILLIAMS, Martha E /c wid	24 Nov 1903	65
ODRICK, Richard /c	SEALS, Eliza J /c	7 Dec 1882	32
OFFUTT, Edward T	DIEDERICK, Anna E	25 Sep 1901	60
OFFUTT, William A	LEIGH, Mary	16 Apr 1878	23
OGDEN, Herbert L	FITZGERALD, Flossie Lea	2 Feb 1933	141
OLIVER, Calvin	TRICKETT, Catherine	4 Jan 1888	38
OLIVER, Cornelius Jr	CORNWELL, Mary A	22 Sep 1885	35
OLIVER, E E	REID, M R	24 Mar 1885	34
OLIVER, George G	HIRST, Mary M	26 May 1909	77
OLIVER, J R	CABANIS, Blanch J	30 Apr 1924	108
OLIVER, Lewis Benton Brumback	WATKINS, Daisy Madelyne	2 Jun 1915	88
OLIVER, William S /wid	SAFFLE, Mary /wid	25 Nov 1888	39
OLLIVER, James /wid	ROBEY, Sarah E	26 Aug 1865	6
OLLIVER, James	WILEY, Carrie L	21 Apr 1896	50
OLLIVER, John F	THOMPSON, Mary	23 Sep 1874	17
OLLIVER, William H	CORNELL, Elizabeth	1 Mar 1866	6
OLIVE, John R /wid	YOUNG, Cora Alice	10 Mar 1926	114
ONTEN, Joshua /c wid	TINNER, Emma B /c	27 Dec 1921	102
ORCUTT, Albert /wid	BASTOW, Isabella M	11 Feb 1869	10
ORMSBEE, Orrin	FRANKS, Mary F /wid	4 Jan 1883	31
ORMSBEE, Solomon	ALFRED, Ellen	26 Sep 1877	21
ORNDORFF, Weldon	MILLER, Margaret	10 Sep 1925	112
ORR, Joseph G	BRAGG, Sadie E	12 May 1926	114
ORRISON, Lloyd F	GRESHAM, Annie w	27 Jun 1906	71
ORRISON, Robert H	HUTCHISON, Fanny	11 Mar 1869	10
OSBORN, Earl L	LEONARD, Cora	3 Apr 1922	102
OSGOOD, Harry D	BROOKS, Leonora	21 Dec 1897	54
OSTERMAN, Joseph V	MILLER, Margaret E	23 Apr 1927	118
OTIS, William H	HALL, Clara M	26 Aug 1901	60
OTTO, Domar Samuel /div	SANFORD, Nettie Lee /wid	29 Nov 1928	123
OWEN, Thomas A	TYERS, Sarah	26 Apr 1882	30
OWENS, Richard /c	BROOKS, Diana /c wid	27 Aug 1878	23
PADGETT, William B	WILLIAMSON, Alice C	20 May 1886	36
PADMORE, Thorald F /c	ROGERS, Ella E /c	6 Jun 1918	94

PAGE, Henry /c	HORTON, Aurelia /c	28 May 1901	60
PAGE, James F	JENKINS, Rebecca J	14 Jun 1886	36
PAGE, Rev. Frederick	HARVEY, Caroline	10 Jun 1885	35
PAGE, William M /c	DENNEY, Ruth L /c	14 Feb 1933	141
PAIGE, Richard Frank	BLOUNT, Evelyn /div	11 Jul 1933	143
PALADIN, Francis L	TRAVIS, Anna Frank	25 Oct 1911	81
PALMER, Dr. R Vernon	WALTERS, Ella V	8 Dec 1897	53
PALMER, Harry	CASSERLY, Catherine	16 Jun 1930	128
PALMER, John Thomas /wid	POOLE, Mary C	29 Apr 1896	50
PALMER, Waterman	REYNOLDS, Kate E	7 Dec 1887	38
PALMER, William H	BARNES, Lillie	1 Feb 1877	21
PALMORE, Garland W	WILLIAMS, Willa Ruth	12 Jun 1920	98
PARKER, Burnett /c	HARRIS, Lucy /c	12 May 1880	26
PARKER, Charles Jr /c	BECKWITH, Albertina /c	29 Nov 1899	57
PARKER, Charles W	ENGLAND, Jessie B	7 May 1900	58
PARKER, Foxhall Alexander	ELLSWICK, Anna E	3 Apr 1919	95
PARKER, Henry	FAIRFAX, Harriet	9 Jun 1867	7
PARKER, Howard /c div	PRATHER, Lucy /c	15 Jan 1932	136
PARKER, Jacob /c wid	WILLIAMS, Priscilla /c	24 Oct 1869	11
PARKER, John /c	ROBINSON, Sally /c wid	24 Oct 1867	8
PARKER, Joseph B	SEWELL, Marie A	10 May 1915	88
PARKER, Layfayette	JAVINS, Mary E	5 Apr 1875	18
PARKER, Moses /c	HILL, Sarah /c	29 Dec 1881	29
PARKER, Solomon M /c	WASHINGTON, Mary M /c	14 May 1891	43
PARKER, Vincent /c	MILLS, Ann /c wid	1 May 1880	26
PARKER, Walter /c	MELVIN, Ruth /c	11 Feb 1897	52
PARKINSON, C J	CARTER, Lillian E	10 Feb 1916	90
PARKS, John A /c	JACKSON, Mary E /c	1 Sep 1921	101
PARRIGAN, Welford	ROPER, Marie E /wid	10 Sep 1930	129
PARRISH, J W	BRUIN, F Carinne	27 Dec 1883	32
PARROTT, Rev. Benjamin Lee	LANHAM, Dora	22 Feb 1899	56
PARROTT, W T	CLARK, Lillian M	30 Nov 1921	101
PASSALACQUA, Louis A	CHRISTIAN, Jacqueline B	22 Jan 1926	113
PATRICK, James /wid	TRAMMELL, Ann	19 Nov 1860	5
PATTEN, Vito	WARRINGTON, Mabel	25 Jun 1932	138
PATTERSON, Jacob D	LOOMIS, Celestia	9 Dec 1855	2
PATTERSON, O E	SPEER, Cecilia B	16 Feb 1907	72
PATTERSON, T Frank	BROOKS, Oda E /div	24 Feb 1931	131
PATTON, A J	COX, Lena A	14 Apr 1920	97
PATTON, C B	SMITH, Nettie V	7 Jun 1899	56
PATTON, Edward M	TESTERMAN, Goldie P	14 Mar 1932	136
PAULSEN, Waldmar	WATTS, Blanche	2 Aug 1930	129

PAXSON, Earl F	PORT, Edith T	3 Oct 1921	*101*
PAXTON, John Hall	HEALEY, Ann	22 Sep 1925	*112*
PAYNE, Amos P	BRUNNER, Mary E /wid	7 Dec 1869	*11*
PAYNE, Charles Robert	CARICO, Alwilda	18 Apr 1894	*47*
PAYNE, Claude /c	WATSON, Ella /c	5 Oct 1912	*83*
PAYNE, Claude T	PUTNAM, Ann E	1 Mar 1897	*52*
PAYNE, Fred /c	HANEY, Fannie /c	21 Feb 1906	*70*
PAYNE, George	ATHEY, Beatrice	25 Feb 1931	*131*
PAYNE, Giles /c wid	PINKETT, Ann M /c wid	27 Apr 1883	*32*
PAYNE, Harry E	HABERKORN, Helen	9 Aug 1932	*138*
PAYNE, Irvin	GORHAM, Amanda /c	20 Dec 1916	*91*
PAYNE, Isaac /c	SMITH, Emma F /c	8 Nov 1894	*48*
PAYNE, J Luther	PAYNE, Janie M	13 Nov 1889	*40*
PAYNE, John N	ARNOLD, Elsie	28 May 1927	*118*
PAYNE, Marshall	BRUMBACK, Edith	9 Jun 1931	*132*
PAYNE, Melvin M /wid	CROSS, Lucy M	2 May 1888	*38*
PAYNE, Peter	BROWN, Rosa	30 Nov 1871	*14*
PAYNE, Richard E /c	BORGUS, Blanche E /c	18 Oct 1910	*79*
PAYNE, Richard T /div	KELLY, Anne C	6 Feb 1932	*136*
PAYNE, Robert	JACKSON, Amanda	15 Sep 1867	*8*
PAYNE, Robert /c	CARTER, Georgianna /c	11 Nov 1876	*21*
PAYNE, Robert L	TILLETT, Lizzie	26 Apr 1906	*70*
PAYNE, Robert T	ELLIS, Lucretia	19 Jan 1870	*12*
PAYNE, Robert T /wid	MARSHALL, Ruth R	2 Mar 1909	*76*
PAYNE, S A	PAYNE, Augusta S	28 May 1879	*25*
PAYNE, Taten /c	DODSON, Quincy /c	2 Jul 1910	*79*
PAYNE, Taten /c wid	HORTON, Bessie /c	18 Dec 1912	*83*
PAYNE, Theodore W /wid	NEWLON, Edmonia	25 Jan 1893	*46*
PAYNE, Virgil T /c	PAGE, Maude L /c	10 Jun 1919	*95*
PAYNE, William /c	LEWIS, Laura /c	23 Sep 1880	*27*
PAYNE, William N	LYNCH, Ella E	25 Jan 1893	*46*
PAYNE, William S	FAIRFAX, Cora M	14 Jun 1893	*46*
PEABODY, John	VOSBURG, Esther	12 Aug 1871	*14*
PEARL, John J	HARDIN, Dorothy M	17 Feb 1930	*127*
PEARSON, C W	DAVIS, Ruby J	25 Dec 1915	*89*
PEARSON, Chancellor	JAVINS, Sallie /wid	11 Apr 1922	*102*
PEARSON, Charles	FITZHUGH, Sarah T	8 Apr 1866	*6*
PEARSON, Charles C /c	BROOKS, Mary /c	16 May 1914	*86*
PEARSON, Egbert /c	CARTER, Lena /c	23 Jan 1912	*82*
PEARSON, Francis P	SMALL, Mabel	30 Aug 1927	*119*
PEARSON, Francis W	PEARSON, Cora A	31 Oct 1872	*15*
PEARSON, Harvey /c	SHELTON, Rose /c	20 Mar 1898	*54*

PEARSON, Henry A	BAKER, Mary S	6 Dec 1877	22
PEARSON, James	NELSON, Jane	13 Mar 1870	12
PEARSON, James /c	RANSELL, Lizzie /c	20 Dec 1883	32
PEARSON, John	PARKER, Elizabeth	27 Apr 1871	15
PEARSON, John /c	REID, Fanny /c	28 Dec 1877	23
PEARSON, John /c	HORTON, Lucy V /c	12 Jun 1901	60
PEARSON, John S	SAUNDERS, Catherine V	27 Feb 1866	6
PEARSON, Joshua /c	BANKS, Caroline /c	1 Nov 1885	35
PEARSON, Joshua /c	LEWIS, Alice Brewer /c wid	27 Sep 1906	71
PEARSON, Maurice L	HUNTT, Nellie I	29 Jun 1910	78
PEARSON, Otis Edward	BEATTY, Annie Mae	15 Aug 1931	133
PEARSON, Richard /c wid	HANEY, Mary /c wid	27 Nov 1889	40
PEARSON, Robert	HUMMER, Mattie	27 Sep 1883	32
PEARSON, Robert A	CORNWELL, Martha V	20 Mar 1894	47
PEARSON, Sandy	FORD, Winnie	4 Jul 1867	7
PEARSON, Thomas /c	POSEY, Martha /c wid	7 Oct 1877	22
PEARSON, Thomas E	PEACOCK, Ann E	24 Nov 1904	67
PEARSON, Thomas J	HOLLENBACK, Nettie L	7 Feb 1893	46
PEARSON, William	REID, Florence	3 Mar 1909	76
PECK, Frank E	MIDDLETON, Helen Brooke	25 Jun 1913	84
PECK, James H	REAGAN, Margaret	21 Dec 1905	68
PECK, Julius J /wid	BENNETT, Mary J	17 May 1877	22
PEEL, George C	WILDMAN, Mary	4 Apr 1931	131
PEGELOW, Carlton W	WOOD, Ive E	5 Nov 1932	139
PEGELOW, Paul F	SHEPHERD, Mary Elizabeth	4 Jun 1927	118
PELHAM, Burril /c	ROBINSON, May /c	3 May 1888	42
PELLANT, George	LEE, Minnie	5 Jan 1889	39
PENDLETON, Charles A	REID, Grace B	15 Oct 1919	96
PENDLETON, William G	DAWSON, Maria Mason	7 Oct 1908	75
PENN, Frederick M	HOWDERSHELL, Mary Ellen	2 Dec 1908	76
PENN, Stephen	ROGERS, Edith	28 Jan 1924	108
PENN, Walter L /wid	FAIRFAX, Ann M /wid	4 May 1882	30
PENN, William T	THOMPSON, Ruth Lee	1 Dec 1897	53
PERKINS, Carl Reah /wid	BURKHART, Viola Emelia	23 Jun 1933	142
PERKINS, Francis Olin	BRUNNER, Mary Elizabeth	6 Sep 1922	103
PERKINS, Samuel F Jr	DAVIS, Loretta E	23 Dec 1931	135
PERRY, Charles /c	LEWIS, Mabel /c	10 Nov 1915	89
PERRY, George L	SISSON, Lillie M	21 Sep 1892	45
PERRY, Harry H	BROSIUS, Mary K /wid	8 Dec 1867	8
PERRY, James /c	GASKINS, Margaret /c	29 Dec 1870	13
PERRY, James I /c	MUSE, Fannie E /c	30 Dec 1931	135
PERRY, James M	TYLER, Emma J	20 Jun 1871	15

PERRY, John Henry /c	TURNER, Pinkie	22 May 1887	37
PERRY, Wade /c	ASHTON, Lula /c	31 Aug 1893	46
PERRY, Wade /c wid	JOHNSON, Susan /c wid	26 Oct 1919	96
PETERKIN, George William	LEE, Constance G	29 Oct 1868	10
PETERS, Robert /c	SMITH, Ida /c	27 Nov 1897	53
PETERS, W O	CLARKE, Mary A	17 Sep 1923	106
PETERSON, Charles A /wid	MILLS, Madeline /wid	12 May 1925	111
PETERSON, William L /c	THOMAS, Bessie M /c	10 Nov 1932	139
PETTITT, A Jackson	FRANCE, Matilda	14 Dec 1882	31
PETTITT, Albert	LLOYD, Sadie	20 May 1914	86
PETTITT, Benjamin F	PHILLIPS, Florence	15 Sep 1928	122
PETTITT, Edward /wid	CAIN, Amelia	11 Feb 1897	52
PETTITT, Edward /wid	TILLETT, Daisey	18 Jun 1904	66
PETTITT, Edward W	DULANY, Eliza	26 Nov 1873	16
PETTITT, G H	WASHBURN, May E	26 Apr 1922	102
PETTITT, George C	GRIMSLEY, Sallie	4 Nov 1924	110
PETTITT, George Gillingham	TYLER, Mary E	1 Oct 1899	57
PETTITT, George M	DODSON, Linda A	18 Jun 1894	48
PETTITT, George W /wid	CROSON, Mary V	13 Oct 1865	6
PETTITT, George W	HILL, Elizabeth E	2 Oct 1873	16
PETTITT, H H	HARRISON, S E /wid	27 May 1858	3
PETTITT, Henry E	PEPPERS, Cora E	4 Dec 1890	42
PETTITT, Hiram H /wid	COOK, Olive O	21 Aug 1909	77
PETTITT, John McGill	HARRISON, Sallie V	8 Nov 1899	57
PETTITT, Joseph Edward	CARSON, Sara Catherine	1 Nov 1916	91
PETTITT, Lewis	LLOYD, Maggie	16 Jul 1913	84
PETTITT, Paul C	PETTITT, F Ethel	16 Oct 1906	71
PETTITT, Samuel /wid	GHEENS, Eliza C /wid	25 Dec 1865	6
PETTITT, T J /wid	THOMPSON, Bertie M /wid	27 Jul 1912	83
PETTITT, Thomas Hayward	DOVE, Sarah Eliza	12 Feb 1905	68
PETTITT, William M	PEARSON, Nellie E	4 Mar 1920	97
PETTY, George F /wid	ANDERSON, Clara A /wid	6 Jul 1929	125
PEVERILL, Edward	LYLES, Eva	11 Nov 1918	95
PEVERILL, George W	LYLES, Fannie L	28 Dec 1892	45
PEYTON, Armstead	GIBSON, Adaline	24 Oct 1872	15
PEYTON, Harrie L	PULMAN, Jennie M	16 Jul 1903	65
PEYTON, Martin T	CRIMMIN, Alice A	4 Nov 1896	51
PEYTON, Philip B /wid	BALLENGER, Nannie H	27 Dec 1905	70
PEYTON, Sandy /c	PEARSON, Ada /c	19 Nov 1898	55
PHELPS, E Victor	WILLIAMS, Salina R	10 Oct 1905	69
PHELPS, J L	PETTITT, Viola	27 Jul 1921	101
PHELPS, Robert W	GILBERT, Mary	13 Oct 1928	123

PHILIPS, Charles W	KIRBY, Rowenna	7 Feb 1870	*12*
PHILLIPS, Archie	SCHNEIDER, Katie	17 Nov 1910	*79*
PHILLIPS, Aubrey A	CRICKENBERGER, Geraldine R	29 Jun 1929	*125*
PHILLIPS, Donald B	GUNNELL, Mary N R	11 Aug 1928	*122*
PHILLIPS, Ernest /c	STOCKETT, Emma /c	12 Jun 1920	*98*
PHILLIPS, Eugene Kirby	WRENN, Annie S	9 Nov 1898	*55*
PHILLIPS, George W	DODSON, Hilda A	5 Apr 1926	*114*
PHILLIPS, Harold /c	GIBSON, Cora /c	23 Mar 1915	*88*
PHILLIPS, James A	MCFURLONG, Lona	28 Jun 1922	*103*
PHILLIPS, James Nelson	ROWE, Bernie Helen /div	17 Jan 1923	*104*
PHILLIPS, John	HEFFNER, Lillie S	24 Sep 1891	*43*
PHILLIPS, Joseph T	TARBERT, Edith G	24 Jun 1909	*77*
PHILLIPS, Lewis	MAGEE, Jane	30 Mar 1858	*3*
PHILLIPS, Merrill F /div	COX, Verna L	1 Sep 1929	*125*
PHILLIPS, Walter L	BETHUNE, C Jean	1 Nov 1930	*130*
PHILLIPS, William W	SPRINGMAN, Ruth W	23 Jan 1915	*88*
PHIPPS, Steve P Jr	PUGH, Nannie E	10 Sep 1932	*139*
PICKEREL, John Edward /c wid	GASKINS, Henrietta /c wid	13 Oct 1920	*99*
PICKETT, E Watts	WEBSTER, Elizabeth Z	23 Dec 1933	*145*
PIER, William H /wid	POSTON, Maude E	17 Feb 1917	*91*
PIERPOINT, C C	LOWE, Frances A	18 Apr 1907	*72*
PIERPOINT, James A	WRENN, Anna V	3 Jul 1926	*115*
PIERPOINT, Oscar B	JOHNSON, Maria E	18 Jun 1890	*41*
PIERSON, David	STEELE, Jane C	5 Mar 1874	*17*
PIERSON, J E /c	TURNER, Hannah E /c	20 May 1897	*52*
PIERSON, Raymond V	WOODRUFF, Iva C	5 Nov 1921	*101*
PIGGOTT, A B	LYNCH, Cora E	4 Sep 1907	*73*
PIGGOTT, Eugene H	LONG, Adah M	12 Jun 1926	*114*
PIKE, Carl A	MCBRYDE, Margaret V	12 Aug 1921	*101*
PINDER, Edward E	ELSEROAD, Annie J	27 Jul 1931	*133*
PINKETT, Edward /c	FORD, Katie R /c	27 Dec 1898	*56*
PINKETT, Edward /c div	SELVIN, Mary /c wid	14 Nov 1900	*59*
PINKETT, James William /c	WASHINGTON, Cora /c	19 Mar 1896	*50*
PINKETT, Wesley /c	BANKS, Eliza /c	1 mar 1887	*37*
PINN, William /c	JACKSON, Alice G /c	24 Sep 1896	*51*
PIPER, Harrison /c	GENERALS, Elizabeth /c	3 Nov 1874	*17*
PITTS, James H	CROUCH, Susie H	26 Sep 1894	*48*
PITTS, Robert	ELGIN, Ethel	30 Nov 1910	*80*
PITZER, David	KAUFFMAN, Valda L	2 Aug 1930	*129*
PLANK, Howard J	KING, Mamie R /wid	23 Dec 1909	*78*
PLASKETT, Christopher W	RAYNOR, Emma J	1 Mar 1881	*28*
PLEASANT, Samuel /c wid	JACKSON, Ada B /c wid	25 Oct 1932	*139*

POBST, Rufus M	RINKER, Verna R	5 Feb 1927	*117*
POGUE, Billingsley Garner	PALMER, Lillia Dent	13 Feb 1933	*141*
POGUE, William D	ZAUGG, Jeraldine	2 Aug 1930	*129*
POHL, H H	POWER, Mary	27 Apr 1898	*54*
POINDEXTER, Charles W	BALLARD, Ella T	11 Jun 1878	*23*
POLAND, Darius	CLAYBORNE, Ora	20 Nov 1930	*130*
POLAND, Guy	KORZENDORFER, Helen	27 Mar 1922	*102*
POLAND, Luther L	MORGAN, Mary /wid	17 Nov 1874	*17*
POLEN, Wickliff	KIDWELL, Edith A	29 Sep 1926	*116*
POLITO, Frank A	WHITE, Alice V	11 Dec 1925	*113*
POLLARD, William Thompson	RUSSELL, Lyda Grimes	7 Jun 1904	*66*
PONTIER, Eugene D	JULIEN, Paula Lualia	20 Sep 1910	*79*
POOL, James H	NICHOLS, Laura A	30 Jan 1873	*16*
POOL, Louis Reed /wid	ROCK, Ida Mary	21 Sep 1904	*67*
POOL, Thomas E	WILLIAMS, Annie G	30 May 1872	*15*
POOL, Thomas J	WILLIAMS, Harriet Louisa	2 Mar 1871	*13*
POOLE, Benjamin E	CADARR, Julia L	29 Apr 1896	*50*
POOLE, Ernest H	FOLLIN, Drusilla A	27 Oct 1903	*65*
POOLE, James A	THORNE, Mary H	14 Oct 1896	*51*
POOLE, Jesse R	HUTCHISON, Mary A	16 Oct 1913	*85*
POOLE Joseph R	KEYS, Josie	11 May 1913	*84*
POOLE, Louis A	FINNELL, Iola K	25 Aug 1926	*115*
POOLE, Marvin A	DAILY, La Veta May	27 Dec 1924	*110*
POOLE, R H	TRAMMELL, Effie	18 Feb 1906	*70*
POOLE, Ross J	BRILL, C Virginia /wid	28 Apr 1917	*92*
POOLE, Thomas E /wid	BARKER, Mary C /wid	16 Oct 1888	*39*
POPE, Theodore /c	JOHNSON, Isabella /c	16 Apr 1931	*131*
POPEL, Samuel H	REYNOLDS, Dora L	10 Jan 1931	*131*
PORTER, George V /c	WHYTE, Thelma /c	10 Sep 1924	*109*
PORTER, Ira E	SEEF, Cora C	31 Aug 1911	*81*
PORTER, John Payne	BATES, Lucy Lee	17 Nov 1933	*144*
PORTER, Robert S /wid	GROVE, Nannie B	11 Sep 1889	*40*
PORTER, Russell /c	BALL, Louise /c	30 Oct 1926	*116*
PORTS, Noah	STEELE, Mary E	6 Mar 1870	*12*
POSEY, Magruder	KINCHELOE, Hollis	29 Apr 1930	*127*
POSEY, Stephen	CROUCH, Mattie	29 Oct 1902	*63*
POSS, John P	YOUNG, Esther E	19 Nov 1867	*11*
POST, William M	STUART, Mary C	19 Oct 1854	*1*
POSTON, James W	KIDWELL, Annie	28 Aug 1892	*45*
POSTON, Otis William	KING, Clara K /wid	10 Sep 1931	*133*
POSTON, Raymond L	BROOKS, Sallie B	2 Sep 1914	*87*
POTTER, Charles	TRICE, Elizabeth Ann	12 Apr 1859	*4*

POTTER, Charles /wid	SNIDER, Sarah Elizabeth	18 Dec 1884	34
POTTER, Edward W /wid	DEAVERS, Eliza V	25 Nov 1885	35
POTTER, Edward W	DOVE, Clara A	4 Jul 1917	92
POTTER, James	SIMMS, Mary L	22 Nov 1923	106
POTTER, Joseph	LYLES, Jane	27 Apr 1854	1
POTTER, Joseph	WESTON, Emma J	16 Mar 1875	18
POTTER, Joseph /wid	PEARSON, Grace	18 Oct 1924	109
POTTER, Joseph M	DOVE, Gracie E	18 Apr 1917	92
POTTER, Nelson /wid	SNIDER, Laura E	5 Apr 1885	34
POTTER, William	COLE, Fannie E	27 Nov 1878	24
POWELL, David /c	COLLINS, Dorothy /c	22 Feb 1927	117
POWELL, G Harvey /wid	COOKE, Nora Blair	12 Jun 1923	105
POWELL, Henry E	BIRCH, Kate V	16 Apr 1890	41
POWELL, Herbert M	WILLIAMS, Esther	10 Oct 1918	94
POWELL, James H	BYRNE, May	16 Jan 1920	97
POWELL, John D /c	MORTON, Mary /c	15 Jul 1903	65
POWELL, Joseph H	MONCURE, Mary A	1 Sep 1891	43
POWELL, R W	CROWELL, Grace T	24 Jan 1912	82
POWELL, Robert /c	WILLIAMS, Louisa /c	28 Dec 1897	54
POWELL, Sherwood Bell	THOMPSON, Alice	23 Aug 1921	101
POWELL, Thomas L /wid	ADAMS, America	8 Mar 1877	22
POWELL, Walter	HITOFFER, Daisy	9 Nov 1893	47
POWELL, Walter /c	RANDOLPH, Hattie /c	1 Aug 1901	60
POWELL, Warren /wid	OLIVER, Isabelle	22 Dec 1908	76
POWELL, William E	KERNOLL, Eliza Jane	1 Jun 1854	1
POWELL, William F	BEACH, Jane A Jr	5 Apr 1900	58
POWER, Charles A	MURTAUGH, Mary E	3 Oct 1907	73
POYCHER, Jonathon David	CHAPMAN, Elizabeth V	24 May 1931	132
PRESGRAVES, Charles J	HENDERSON, Laura L	23 Dec 1884	34
PRESGRAVES, G W	THOMPSON, Annie /wid	26 May 1897	52
PRESGRAVES, Henry D	CROSS, Genevieve	9 Apr 1902	62
PRESGRAVES, Stanley M	LYNCH, Limmie F	27 Oct 1921	101
PRESTON, Desansner Garden	GREEN, Alice Bouldin	8 Jan 1916	90
PRICE, Alonzo /c wid	GILMORE, Elizabeth F /c	27 Sep 1932	139
PRICE, Frank N	LEWIS, Tinny K	17 Jan 1878	23
PRICE, Lawrence Hilton	BURDETTE, Deborah Jane	20 May 1916	91
PRICE, M Myron Jr	PRICE, Ida S	6 Mar 1926	114
PRIESTLEY, Stanley V	BAUMAN, Edith M /div	6 Apr 1925	111
PRIMM, George A /c	MARTIN, Alice G /c	14 Nov 1921	101
PRINCE, Samuel	CLEARY, Gertrude	8 Jun 1929	125
PRINTZ, Garland L	WILEY, Elizabeth L	13 Jun 1929	125
PROCTOR, Arthur /c	HARRISON, Hester /c	1 Sep 1897	53

PROCTOR, George E	ELLIS, Minnie	16 Oct 1906	71
PROCTOR, George Henry	WILLIAMS, Louisa V	30 Nov 1880	27
PROCTOR, Henry /c	DOUGLASS, Corenne /c	26 Aug 1919	96
PROCTOR, Samuel /c	WASHINGTON, Florence M C /c	25 Nov 1914	87
PROFFIT, George H /c	MORTON, Belle /c	29 Jan 1915	88
PROVINCE, Clarence J /wid	COPE, Laura Y /wid	7 Feb 1923	104
PRUDY, Alvin	FULLERTON, Dorothy	16 Sep 1926	116
PRUETT, Horace W	BEISTEL, Susie /div	7 Jan 1928	121
PRUITT, William R /div	KAHL, Emma	5 Nov 1930	130
PRULITSKY, Joseph	BROOKE, Maude	22 Sep 1928	122
PUCHETT, George H /wid	KITSON, Eleanor V	16 Sep 1932	139
PUGH, J Ray	RICHMOND, Nancy C	24 Sep 1928	122
PUGH, Job D	HARRIS, Daisy	6 Sep 1922	103
PUGH, John	GURNS, Ella N	1 Jun 1896	51
PUGH, William W	PUGH, Laura V	8 Dec 1886	37
PULLMAN, David	STUDDS, Annie A	18 Oct 1866	7
PULMAN, Charles O	MARTIN, Lucy V	16 Mar 1882	30
PULMAN, Peter R	ROSE, Lillie A	26 Jan 1881	28
PULLIN, Wilmer Earl	JENNINGS, Amy	23 Jan 1926	113
PUMPHREY, Asa C	GARRETT, Melva G	30 Dec 1933	145
PURDHEW, William S	MURPHY, Katie L	3 Jul 1918	94
PUTMAN, Edgar C	RALSTON, Edith May /div	13 Nov 1926	116
PYLES, J Chester	HAMILTON, Josephine B	16 Jun 1909	77
QUAIL, William	LIPSCOMB, Phebe D	27 May 1856	2
QUANDER, George W	PENN, Mary /c	27 Feb 1900	58
QUANDER, James A /c	SHIPPEN, Mabel S /c	31 Oct 1931	134
QUANDER, James E /c	WILLIAMS, Laura /c	4 Apr 1878	23
QUANDER, Joseph /c	BLACKBURN, Ruth A /c	30 Dec 1908	76
QUANDER, Osman /c	CARTER, Letty /c	24 Apr 1870	12
QUICK, Armstead T	MAGARITY, Eliza J	4 Sep 1879	25
QUICK, Dr. Tunis C	THORNE, Virginia	21 Apr 1897	52
QUICK, Otis	MCDANIEL, Lucy	22 Jun 1904	66
QUICK, Ralph Andre	GARNER, Ruth Martha	1 Jun 1910	78
QUIGG, Lewis	CLARK, Annie V	18 Apr 1885	34
QUIGG, Lewis	DETWILER, Mary E /wid	5 Jun 1893	46
QUINN, Nicholas /c	WORMLY, Fanny /c	25 Jan 1895	49
RADKE, William A /wid	PAYNE, Alberta /div	9 Jul 1932	138
RAEBURN, Arthur E	CARSON, Elizabeth A	22 Aug 1925	112
RAFFERTY, John T	BLOXOM, Matilda J /wid	18 Oct 1892	45
RAFFO, John	FRYE, Julia	1 Feb 1926	113
RAINEY, Robert L	HILL, Thelma B	30 Sep 1931	134
RALEY, Elmer C Jr	MILLER, Lenore A	25 Nov 1933	144

RAMIREZ, Manuel	NORTON, Daisy M	4 Sep 1918	94
RAMSAUR, Kenneth Aubrey /div	SHEPHERD, Arlynne M	12 Dec 1932	140
RAMSAY, D McCarty /wid	ORRISON, Lillian N	19 Jun 1901	60
RANDALL, George H /c	BERKLEY, Florence B /c	12 Jul 1917	92
RANDALL, Henry /c	HENSHAW, Mary R /c	26 Apr 1877	22
RANDALL, William Henry /c	BROWN, Annie /c	25 Oct 1905	69
RANDOLPH, Julius C /c	SANFORD, Alberta W /c	30 May 1928	121
RANDOLPH, Oscar DeWolf	CRAWFORD, Alice Laurie	19 Jun 1911	81
RANKIN, William M /wid	HORGAN, Mary C	14 Nov 1910	79
RANSELL, Jacob /wid	SMITH, Celia	14 Mar 1872	14
RANSELL, William /c	COLLINS, Jennie /c wid	2 Jun 1906	71
RANSOM, A H /c	JOHNSON, Clara /c	12 Mar 1914	86
RAPPAPORT, Julius L /wid	JONES, Hattie M /wid	19 Aug 1932	138
RASMUSSEN, Parley B	PARKER, Irene M	2 May 1921	100
RATCLIFFE, Edward R	COCKERILLE, M Edith	27 Oct 1926	116
RATCLIFFE, Richard H /c	HORTON, Mary E /c	20 Jan 1876	20
RATCLIFFE, Richard H /c wid	PEARSON, Virginia /c	27 Mar 1907	72
RAULERSON, James A /wid	SHELTON, Mabel E	19 Jun 1909	77
RAWLINGS, Joseph E	HAYDEN, Ellen L	21 Apr 1920	98
RAYMER, John G A	PARSONS, Katherine S	7 Jun 1930	128
RAYMOND, Arthur K	NEWLON, Nina B	8 Nov 1894	48
RAYMOND, Charles W	TYERS, Annie	12 Jul 1881	28
RAYMOND, Harry Sam	DAPPISH, Violet Dolores	25 Aug 1931	133
REA, George H	STONE, Jennie L	10 Jun 1902	62
READY, James	WALSH, Alice	29 Oct 1868	10
REAGAN, Timothy J	BENNETT, Irene Alice	20 Dec 1916	91
RECKER, William	SCHLICHTING, Amalia	7 Oct 1873	16
RECTOR, Alfred /c	BALTIMORE, Eliza /c	5 Dec 1886	37
RECTOR, Clyde W	PHILLIPS, Annie W	15 Jan 1895	49
RECTOR, Dudley H	HALL, Frances E	23 Jun 1931	132
RECTOR, Jefferson Franklin	KING, Flora Temple	3 Nov 1881	29
RECTOR, John S	LYNN, Frances A /wid	8 Dec 1865	6
RECTOR, John Sinclair	NIELSON, Esther Cecelia	10 Apr 1923	105
RECTOR, Lewis E	DODD, Catharine O	19 Nov 1902	63
RECTOR, Marion Vernon	CLEVELAND, Constance B	30 Apr 1902	62
RECTOR, William H /c	JONES, Annie M /c	10 Jan 1927	117
RECTOR, Willie /c	GASKINS, Harriet A /c	1 Mar 1900	58
REDMAN, Dennis /c	SCOTT, Sarah E /c	23 Mar 1892	44
REED, Fred C	JOHNSON, Gladys W	27 Sep 1926	116
REED, George J	POOLE, Gracie	18 Dec 1900	59
REED, Lemuel F	BORDEN, Charlotte A	16 Nov 1898	55
REED, Ranzel Raymond	BOWMAN, Emma /wid	1 Jun 1922	102

REED, T Edgar	SHIPLEY, Miriam L	19 May 1927	118
REEDER, Theodore F /wid	CONSIDINE, Mary F	12 Feb 1920	97
REEDY, Charlie	SCOTT, Ethel /div	16 Dec 1922	104
REEVES, Robert E	STORM, Mariam C	22 Jun 1929	125
REID, Benjamin E	FUNSTEN, Mary E	10 Oct 1868	10
REID, Charles J	DAWSON, Mary F	7 May 1868	9
REID, Edward /wid	SIMPSON, Huldah V	24 Mar 1892	44
REID, Edwin C	NELSON, Mary V	19 Dec 1866	7
REID, Edwin C /wid	SKINNER, Priscilla T	26 Dec 1876	21
REID, Eston L	THOMPSON, Eva A	9 Jan 1898	56
REID, Franklin P	BARTON, Lillie C	7 Nov 1877	22
REID, James H	HEATH, V C	4 Feb 1857	3
REID, James S	VEAL, Florence J	23 Jan 1875	18
REID, Jesse W	WOODYARD, Mary L	12 Mar 1932	136
REID, John H /c wid	WALTERS, Marian I /c	13 Oct 1924	109
REID, Joseph H	HUBART, Elizabeth Winona	15 Jan 1924	108
REID, L G	LYNN, Mary F	29 Apr 1908	74
REID, Richard L	MCMILLEN, Lillie C	31 Jan 1905	68
REID, Robert /c	TAYLOR, Laura H /c	27 Dec 1883	32
REID, Robert L	REID, Margaret Ellen	15 Mar 1888	38
REID, Robert Lee /wid	DENHAM, Josephine	8 Aug 1894	48
REID, Thomas J	LEE, Lizzie	6 Oct 1886	36
REID, W F P	PICKETT, Sallie K	28 Mar 1912	82
REID, Walter H	STALLING, Helen C	4 May 1916	90
REID, Wellington D	BEACH, Jane Elizabeth	2 Jan 1855	1
REID, William E	FOLLIN, Martha J	26 Sep 1871	14
REISS, Lewis G	CLINE, Ellen	16 Apr 1932	137
REMSBURG, Allen E	TAYLOR, Virginia /div	27 Jun 1931	132
RENNER, Benjamin	PEARSON, Jane /wid	4 Oct 1871	14
REYNOLDS, Francis H	GARDNER, Mary L	30 Jan 1879	24
RHODES, J C	BUCKLEY, Alta V	2 Dec 1908	76
RHODES, Samuel T /wid	WAPLE, Sarah E	18 Jul 1923	105
RHODES, W Irving /div	BOYLE, Evelyn M	3 Jul 1929	125
RICHEY, Robert C	SHERMAN, Grace W	13 Mar 1931	131
RITCHEY, Wylie L	TINKHAM, Nevada H	29 Aug 1931	133
RICE, C W /wid	DAVIS, Alice Marshall /wid	14 Sep 1904	67
RICE, Charles Erwin	CHAMBERS, Gertrude	30 Aug 1920	98
RICE, Charles W	DONALDSON, Carrie J	3 Mar 1880	26
RICE, Charlie	JOHNSON, Dorothy	23 Sep 1919	96
RICE, Frank W	CARSON, Edith Lee	29 Oct 1924	110
RICE, Grafton H	DAUGHERTY, Rosa D	9 Jul 1902	62
RICE, James R	DANIEL, Stella I	30 Jul 1910	79

RICE, Robert H	HASTAND, Florence J	19 Oct 1910	*79*
RICHARDS, Archie H	BURKHOLDER, Mattie E	23 Jan 1895	*49*
RICHARDS, Berkley D	JACOBS, Sallie A	6 Feb 1894	*47*
RICHARDS, Emory	DYER, Frances J	16 Feb 1929	*124*
RICHARDS, Harry T	AYRES, Mary Ellen	29 Sep 1927	*119*
RICHARDS, James	BAYLISS, Mazie	24 Jul 1914	*86*
RICHARDS, Lewis /c wid	SUMMERALL, Fannie /c wid	20 Oct 1920	*99*
RICHARDS, Paul F E	REID, Frances E	1 Dec 1932	*140*
RICHARDSON, Charles	MASON, Clara	16 Jul 1890	*41*
RICHARDSON, Charles E Jr	WAINWRIGHT, Frances N	15 Apr 1926	*114*
RICHARDSON, Charles H	MAGARITY, Hilda F	29 Aug 1932	*139*
RICHARDSON, Charles R	PULMAN, Irene F	29 Sep 1927	*120*
RICHARDSON, Clarence	KENNER, Gertrude /c	26 Dec 1900	*62*
RICHARDSON, George H	HOAG, Elizabeth S	30 Dec 1856	*2*
RICHARDSON, Henry /wid	HARRIS, Susan	26 Dec 1902	*62*
RICHARDSON, Simeon W	BOOY, Boukje	1 Jun 1921	*100*
RICHARDSON, Thurman L	WHITE, Dorothy E	13 Feb 1932	*136*
RICHMOND, Adolph T	CUMMINS, Cynthia V	26 Dec 1917	*93*
RICHMOND, D A	MARTIN, Jennie V	21 Oct 1880	*27*
RICHMOND, Loren /wid	GARRISON, Rosalie	6 Oct 1885	*35*
RICKETTS, Walter M /div	CORNELIUS, Nell	7 Jan 1933	*141*
RICKS, William W	SCHALTZ, Anna	5 Jul 1930	*128*
RIDDLE, Charles A	MUNOZ, Harriet J	4 Sep 1926	*115*
RIDENOUR, William S	ASKEY, Esther S	3 Jun 1929	*124*
RIDER, Charles W	GRESHAM, Maria L	20 Dec 1913	*85*
RIDER, Harry A	BRAUN, Edna M	27 Jun 1933	*142*
RIDGELEY, Melvin Lee	SULLIVAN, Mabel Virginia	31 Jul 1923	*105*
RIDGWAY, John	LEWIS, Judith	1 Sep 1876	*20*
RIDGWAY, John R /wid	SNIDER, Alinda	30 Jun 1886	*36*
RIELEY, Amos B	BOWMAN, Cora E	12 Jun 1920	*98*
RIELLY, James J	MCGROW, Elizabeth	26 Jan 1926	*113*
RIFENBARK, Frank	POOLE, Margaret W	30 Jul 1928	*122*
RIGG, John H	HARRISON, Irene	25 Nov 1886	*37*
RIGGLES, Claud E	TAYLOR, Annie E	23 Sep 1903	*65*
RIGGLES, Walter B	STEELE, Sadie	1 Feb 1905	*68*
RIGGLES, William L	BUTT, Catherine L	23 Dec 1879	*26*
RIKER, George A	KEYS, Theresa V	3 Jan 1884	*32*
RILEY, Bird E	TROUGHTON, Martha V	24 Jun 1933	*142*
RILEY, George /c	WOODEN, Lula /c	4 Oct 1924	*109*
RILEY, George William /c	JOHNSON, Maria /c	14 Jun 1890	*41*
RILEY, George William /c wid	HONESTY, Laura /c	20 Oct 1897	*53*
RILEY, Harold V	NELSON, Daisy M	11 Jan 1930	*127*

RILEY, Raymond	MONCH, Florence V	4 Aug 1912	83
RILEY, Thomas D	CLEVELAND, Rosie /wid	17 Jul 1915	88
RILEY, William M	WRENN, Rosa	20 Dec 1877	22
RINCK, Henry T /div	WANZER, Muriel B /div	4 Oct 1921	101
RINKER, Jacob L	RICKETTS, Helen /wid	1 Nov 1927	119
RINKER, Lee Preston	MURRAY, Stella M	1 Sep 1931	133
RIPPEY, Donald McKay	NEHRMAN, Lydia Anna	2 Jun 1923	105
RISTON, George Washington	HARRISON, Laura B /wid	27 Aug 1873	16
RITCHIE, Abner Cloud	FORD, Maria Virginia	1 Aug 1907	73
RITTER, Charles G	HARTSHONE, Mary C	28 Feb 1930	127
RITTER, Clarence E	NICHOLSON, Lucile	23 Feb 1928	121
RITTER, Theodore	MELCHER, Louise	22 Apr 1929	124
RIVIERE, Thomas Albert	MEHLER, Dorothy L	26 Jul 1933	143
ROACH, Charles P Jr	COAKLEY, M E	18 Mar 1913	84
ROANE, Daniel Carter /c	HENDERSON, Juphenia R /c	16 Sep 1933	143
ROAT, William F	BAYLISS, Lena V	11 Nov 1903	65
ROBEY, Ananias	SPINDLE, Agnes	11 Sep 1901	60
ROBEY, Benjamin	SANDERS, Mary I	20 Feb 1925	110
ROBEY, Carl E	WILLETT, Hettie E	13 Dec 1899	57
ROBEY, Charlie	WISE, Carrie	21 Mar 1931	131
ROBEY, Chester	SANDERS, Virgie	6 Mar 1931	131
ROBEY, Early L	MCCARTY, Beattrice /wid	18 Apr 1900	58
ROBEY, Edgar W	ROBY, Ella A	31 Oct 1877	22
ROBEY, Elida	CROSON, Mary R	8 Aug 1900	58
ROBEY, Ernest L	BREADY, Edith M	6 May 1896	51
ROBEY, George B	DONOHOE, Susie M	15 Sep 1914	87
ROBEY, George E	KIDWELL, Emily M	25 Jan 1871	13
ROBEY, Harry G	BLEVINS, Zellah C	11 Oct 1930	130
ROBEY, Herman	BERGER, Minnie A	10 Jul 1898	54
ROBEY, J Frank	ROBEY, Appalonia E	21 Feb 1906	70
ROBEY, James T /wid	BARLOW, Priscilla T	19 Mar 1868	9
ROBEY, James T /wid	BEAVERS, Margaret A	8 Mar 1864	5
ROBEY, James T /wid	COOKE, Annie V	26 Sep 1894	48
ROBEY, James W	KIDWELL, Margaret A	11 Jan 1871	13
ROBEY, Jasper M	LEDMAN, Dearing	19 Feb 1908	74
ROBEY, John Henry	POTTER, Carrie E	9 Jun 1903	64
ROBEY, Lewis Irving	THOMPSON, Edith	31 Dec 1901	61
ROBEY, Louis Early	KIRK, Helen Leona	18 Nov 1923	106
ROBEY, M G	SUTPHIN, Ludie	6 Dec 1905	70
ROBEY, William	ROBEY, Frances	27 Dec 1883	32
ROBEY, William /wid	JONES, Jennie	14 Jul 1895	49
ROBEY, William G	WOODYARD, Gladys C	13 Jul 1925	112

ROBY, Eli G	CATON, Willa	1 May 1856	2
ROBY, John T	THOMPSON, Susannah	19 Dec 1876	21
ROBY, Lewis H	HUNTT, Charlotte E	1 Jan 1867	7
ROBY, William P /wid	ROBY, Artesha	2 Oct 1855	1
ROBERSON, Charles	WATTS, Jösephine	26 Dec 1869	11
ROBERSON, Joseph	RIGG, Maud	18 Nov 1891	44
ROBERSON, Pendleton	ROBERSON, Virginia	12 May 1870	12
ROBERTS, Charles G	SPEER, E Ophelia	23 Feb 1864	5
ROBERTS, Courtland L	HAWES, Mollie E	15 Aug 1927	119
ROBERTS, Ervin M	DAVIS, Maud G	31 Dec 1917	93
ROBERTS, Fred S	KILLINGER, Clara F	14 Aug 1926	115
ROBERTS, Richard	RILEY, Ellen /wid	20 May 1866	6
ROBERTS, Richard B	SHEPHERD, Gladys B	3 Aug 1920	99
ROBERTS, Robert	KELBAUGH, Grace	15 Jun 1931	132
ROBERTS, Thomas L	EDWARDS, Kate L	26 Dec 1932	140
ROBERTS, William	SKILES, Margie	26 Jul 1928	122
ROBERTSON, B Norman	PAYNE, Zola B	23 Aug 1930	129
ROBERTSON, Charles E	SINE, Minnie E /div	5 Dec 1927	120
ROBERTSON, Delbert M	DUNBAR, Murriell E	10 Nov 1925	113
ROBERTSON, Edward Henry	LEE, Louise M	18 Mar 1933	141
ROBERTSON, John W	HOBSON, Ruby Lee	17 Dec 1926	117
ROBERTSON, Percy J	SPENCER, Dorothy N	16 Apr 1925	111
ROBERTSON, Reynolds	STALCUP, Hazel G /div	23 Jun 1928	121
ROBINSON, A W	STAPLES, Emma J	12 Dec 1877	23
ROBINSON, Allen /c	JOHNSON, Lucy /c	6 Nov 1879	25
ROBINSON, Arthur G	DORSEY, Kathleen M	16 Jan 1907	72
ROBINSON, Asberry /c	ROBINSON, Susan /c	14 Sep 1893	46
ROBINSON, Charles /c	ROBINSON, Julia /c	26 Dec 1881	29
ROBINSON, Charles /c	LEE, Virginia /c	4 Aug 1887	42
ROBINSON, Elmer M	KIDWELL, Roda May	22 May 1902	62
ROBINSON, Ernest /c	WATERS, Beatrice /c	19 Apr 1925	111
ROBINSON, Fielding	HUNTER, Isabella	9 Jun 1870	12
ROBINSON, George /c	GREEN, Mildred /c	2 Jun 1895	49
ROBINSON, Ira	CRONK, Annie D	18 Sep 1895	50
ROBINSON, Jacob /c	GIBSON, Ruth /c	28 Feb 1920	97
ROBINSON, James /c	BANKS, Emma /c	20 Jan 1904	66
ROBINSON, Jo Albert /c	SCOTT, Laures /c	26 Aug 1909	77
ROBINSON, John E /c	MURRAY, Carrie E /c	3 Dec 1910	80
ROBINSON, Lorenzo /c	HARRIS, Elmira /c	2 Nov 1907	73
ROBINSON, Manadear /c	HARRIS, Beatrice /c	3 Nov 1917	93
ROBINSON, Milton	SCOTT, Julia /c	12 Mar 1906	70
ROBINSON, Nelson /c	WYATT, Mattie /c	3 Nov 1904	67

ROBINSON, Raymond /c	ROBINSON, Marcia /c	10 Mar 1926	*114*
ROBINSON, Robert /c	LEE, Lillian /c	28 Feb 1920	*97*
ROBINSON, Sidney /c	ROBINSON, Almira /c	24 Jul 1930	*129*
ROBINSON, Tascoe D /c	HARRIS, Julia Ann /c	27 Dec 1893	*47*
ROBINSON, Thomas /c	JONES, Salina /c	25 Aug 1883	*31*
ROBINSON, Thomas /wid	RILEY, Jennie	16 Dec 1900	*59*
ROBINSON, Thomas E	GOOD, Luella M	14 Apr 1925	*111*
ROBINSON, Thomas H	KIDWELL, Jemima W /wid	19 Jun 1870	*12*
ROBINSON, W O	SHERMAN, Mary C	15 Jun 1918	*94*
ROBINSON, Walter L	BRADY, Maggie	5 Oct 1907	*73*
ROBINSON, Willard P /c	ROBINSON, Lillian M /c	11 May 1929	*124*
ROBINSON, William /c	HARRIS, Susanna /c	31 Jan 1878	*23*
ROBINSON, William /c wid	JOHNSON, Sarah /c	25 Oct 1888	*39*
ROBINSON, William /c	PARKER, Sadie /c	28 Jan 1911	*80*
ROBINSON, William /c	MURRAY, Marie /c	28 Oct 1933	*144*
ROBINSON, William C /c	WILLIAMS, Mary /c	16 Sep 1903	*65*
ROBSON, Lewis /c	SMITH, Virginia /c	16 Aug 1903	*65*
ROCKWELL, Samuel Hollister	NEAL, Ella M	28 Dec 1880	*27*
RODEN, Andrew	SCHILLER, Ophelia Harding /div	18 Mar 1908	*74*
RODGERS, Frank	LLOYD, Effie	20 Feb 1901	*60*
RODGERS, James N	SHIPMAN, Mary E	18 Jan 1882	*29*
RODGERS, John M	OGDEN, Sallie	2 Nov 1898	*55*
RODGERS, John R	SHEAR, Gertrude	15 Jun 1922	*102*
RODGERS, William	DODSON, Ida May	11 Oct 1894	*48*
RODIER, Louis	ROLLER, Annie	13 Aug 1919	*96*
ROEMMELE, William F	MEDINA, Helen	16 Jul 1932	*138*
ROESER, R E	HARDESTER, Della V	18 Feb 1924	*108*
ROGERS, Albert	KING, Lydia	18 Feb 1909	*76*
ROGERS, Boyce	SCHURTZ, Virginia	28 Nov 1912	*83*
ROGERS, Edward	GILLINGHAM, Anna L	12 Feb 1896	*50*
ROGERS, Eugene A	LANTZ, Clara E	8 Jan 1923	*104*
ROGERS, Gardner M	STRUDER, Maggie	23 Feb 1924	*108*
ROGERS, George E /wid	SHIPMAN, Annie V	26 Mar 1890	*41*
ROGERS, Guy T	ROW, Edith W	16 Jun 1914	*86*
ROGERS, Harrison H	LLOYD, Annie	14 Aug 1901	*60*
ROGERS, Henry P	BEACH, Emily Jane	15 Jan 1884	*32*
ROGERS, Leonard L	PETTITT, Nellie R	21 Oct 1918	*94*
ROGERS, Malcolm	TAYLOR, Blanche	21 Jun 1926	*115*
ROGERS, Owen E	LLOYD, Grace	10 Dec 1912	*83*
ROGERS, Richard T /wid	BAGGOTT, Osie R	15 Sep 1901	*60*
ROGERS, William E	CLEVELAND, Lucy K	8 Sep 1928	*122*
ROGERS, William G	TEMPLEMAN, Nellie M	2 Aug 1922	*103*

ROLLINGS, Harry West Jr /wid	YEAKLE, Lillian Lee	7 Jan 1926	*113*
ROLLINS, Douglas H /div	LEE, Lucie K	8 Nov 1933	*144*
ROLLINS, Herbert /c	ROY, Estelle /c	28 Nov 1931	*135*
ROLLINS, Vivian S /wid	MARSHALL, Esther	24 Jul 1927	*118*
ROLSTON, Franklin I	SUTPHIN, Olive	6 Feb 1913	*84*
ROME, Victor J	DE BUTTS, Frances D	24 Dec 1932	*140*
ROONEY, John C	KEPHART, Daisy M	26 Jul 1922	*103*
ROOT, Shirley Brown	CRIPPEN, Dora Virginia	16 Sep 1933	*143*
ROSE, Earl F	SIMMONS, Eva E	5 Jul 1932	*138*
ROSE, Roy	HAWES, Carrie V	2 Feb 1926	*113*
ROSE, Russell E	PUTT, Vera Jane	27 Sep 1929	*126*
ROSEN, Kirby F	COYNER, Cora St C	29 May 1917	*92*
ROSEN, Morton H	LEVINE, Sophia K	24 Jul 1918	*94*
ROSENCRANS, Carl William	REARICK, Helen Marjorie	16 Sep 1933	*143*
ROSS, Clyde Pothems	COBB, Ruth	6 Apr 9122	*102*
ROSS, Colvin	CLINE, Lena	18 Dec 1920	*99*
ROSS, John Thomas	COOK, Susan B	7 Sep 1887	*38*
ROTCHFORD, Ralph W	TAYLOR, Blanche E	26 Dec 1900	*59*
ROTHGEB, Ralph Russell	HARNAGE, Dorothy A	22 Dec 1931	*135*
ROURKE, Patrick	CORRIGAN, Mary	26 Jan 1868	*9*
ROUSE, James B	NEITZEY, Margaret E	25 Mar 1915	*88*
ROUTH, Oswald R	SANBORN, Myrtle A	2 Jun 1888	*38*
ROUZEE, George Albert	NELSON, Annie L	19 Jan 1870	*12*
ROUZEE, John E	JOHNSON, Mary E	16 Feb 1870	*12*
ROW, Thomas	TERRETT, Eva E	18 Feb 1903	*64*
ROW, Thomas H	O'SHAUGHNESSY, Edna F	25 Oct 1933	*144*
ROW, Wilson	GORHAM, Alice M	5 Apr 1911	*80*
ROWE, William H	CRAMPTON, Mary Virginia	29 Dec 1916	*91*
ROWELL, Elias B	HORSTMAN, Emily	24 Dec 1885	*35*
ROWLAND, Maitland McG	CORNELL, Nellie V	3 Jul 1926	*115*
ROWLES, Robert P	FRISTOE, Robert Lee	12 Oct 1911	*82*
ROY, Enoch /c	GREEN, Jennie /c	17 Nov 1903	*65*
ROY, Lee /c	STILES, Mary /c	28 Apr 1910	*78*
ROY, Marshall	LEE, Carrie	27 Jun 1872	*15*
ROY, Richard /c	BURLEY, Jane C /c	15 Dec 1874	*18*
ROY, Smith /c	WATERS, Catherine /c	12 May 1874	*17*
ROYALL, Richard J	HARLOW, Agnes N	7 Nov 1920	*99*
ROYS, Lawrence P	PAYNE, Susan V	24 Mar 1913	*84*
RUCK, Sidney Thomas	BAKER, Alice	25 Nov 1914	*87*
RUCKER, William W	QUICK, Hazel N	19 Jun 1915	*88*
RUFF, Valentine /wid	GROTEVANT, Lee A	16 Aug 1909	*77*
RUMMELS, Alfred /c	BENSON, Alice /c	30 Jan 1890	*41*

RUMMELS, George /c	TERRELL, Bessie /c	7 Sep 1908	75
RUMSEY, Murray E /div	OSGOOD, Rosa C	20 Oct 1928	123
RUNNER, Winfield /c	MURRAY, Sarah /c	17 Apr 1879	25
RUPPERT, Bernard P /wid	FISHER, Katherine	5 Aug 1897	53
RUSH, Philip L /wid	CATTS, Grace B /wid	3 Nov 1913	85
RUSHE, Noble Franklin	LEEBRICK, Nannie M	16 Apr 1916	90
RUSK, David Franklin	GROVES, Nellie A	14 Apr 1928	121
RUSSELL, Clem Donald	MALTERN, Lucille E	5 May 1933	142
RUSSELL, Julien W	CAMPBELL, Eleanor	27 Oct 1898	55
RUSSELL, Mercur L	BRADFORD, Bernice M	15 Jun 1933	142
RUSSELL, Robert /c	HARRIS, Gertrude /c	20 Aug 1928	122
RUSSELL, William McMillan	HEISS, Martha M	29 Mar 1910	78
RUSSELL, Willis	DIXON, Harriet	24 Mar 1866	6
RUST, Albert B	TULLASS, Wilhelmina H	21 Jan 1921	100
RUST, John Warwick	HOOE, Anne Emily	27 Sep 1911	81
RUTH, Harry	KADES, Dora	28 Nov 1931	135
RUTLEDGE, St Charles /c	MITCHELL, Marie	21 Mar 1922	102
RYAN, C Dale	KLEIN, Mildred S	22 Feb 1923	104
RYDER, Cecil A	BROOKBANK, Mary E	12 Mar 1909	76
RYER, Henry Scott	BROWN, Mary Eleanor	1 Jun 1906	71
RYON, Oliver	SASSCER, Helen	26 Jan 1904	66
SABINE, Walter L	POND, Florence G	12 Mar 1925	110
SADLER, James E /c	BROOKS, Mattie E /c	30 Dec 1902	63
SAFFELL, Frank H	GILLINGHAM, Sallie A	12 Nov 1894	48
SAFFER, John F	KERNS, Eleanor	4 Oct 1930	129
SAFFER, John S	CUNNINGHAM, Rosa M	20 Aug 1901	60
SAGE, Benjamin A	PAYNE, Gladys O /wid	2 Jul 1931	132
SALMON, William A /wid	RICHARDSON, Florence M	17 Jul 1923	105
SALSBURY, Burt F	SHREVE, Bertha Lillian	1 Dec 1914	87
SALSBURY, H L /wid	MINNIX, Lucie /wid	2 Jun 1909	77
SAMPSELLE, Franklin C	OLIVER, Mollie B	30 Nov 1898	55
SANDERS, Alvin M	WILLINGHAM, Margaret L	14 Jun 1927	118
SANDERS, Arthur /c	STEWART, Helen /c	1 Sep 1920	98
SANDERS, Charles S	FOLLIN, Rosa L	22 Mar 1892	44
SANDERS, Daniel /wid	TOWNSHEND, Angelina S	23 Oct 1860	5
SANDERS, Earl D	VAN SICKLER, Bessie E	8 Apr 1914	86
SANDERS, Henderson	FOLLIN, Laurena	19 Sep 1872	15
SANDERS, James R	FOSTER, Blanche	24 Oct 1922	103
SANDERSON, Levi F /wid	HOGAN, Hattie P	18 Oct 1869	11
SANGER, John S	BREEDEN, Sadie V	24 Apr 1912	82
SANGSTAD, Olaf	GRAHAM, Elizabeth B	20 Jun 1899	56
SAUER, Herman A	FOUCHE, Nellie E	7 Nov 1931	134

SAULS, Hugh G	FERGUSON, Clara M	15 Jan 1898	*54*
SAUMENIG, Harry Shields	RIDGELEY, Rachael J	31 Dec 1917	*93*
SAUNDERS, C N */wid*	JOHANSON, Mrs. A E */wid*	17 Jun 1909	*77*
SAUNDERS, D Lee	CROSS, Martha E	26 Dec 1889	*40*
SAUNDERS, Daniel	MONROE, Hellen M	13 Apr 1854	*1*
SAUNDERS, Harrison	FOLLIN, Mary C	25 Jan 1866	*6*
SAUNDERS, John T */wid*	KITCHEN, Georgianna	16 Dec 1879	*26*
SAUNDERS, John W */c*	BICKFORD, Catherine A */c*	16 Sep 1931	*133*
SAUNDERS, William B	REID, Rose E	1 Dec 1891	*44*
SAUTER, Norman W	TWOGOOD, Kathleen M	19 Sep 1918	*94*
SAUVEUR, Clarence	BRYANT, Minnie	13 Oct 1928	*123*
SAWYER, J G */wid*	HAUGH, Georgia M */div*	3 Jul 1924	*108*
SAWYERS, James G	HARDING, Olive R	23 May 1909	*76*
SAYLES, Herbert C */c*	SHULL, Edna */c*	7 Jan 1929	*124*
SCHAAFF, James L	SHREVE, Ella M	26 May 1880	*26*
SCHAAFF, John T	SHAFFER, Alberta	1 Oct 1932	*139*
SCHAEFER, Charles A	COLE, Ella V	30 Oct 1889	*40*
SCHAEFER, Henry	HOPKINS, Elizabeth T	27 Feb 1887	*37*
SCHAEFER, Howard C	WRIGHT, Virginia B	29 Jan 1927	*117*
SCHAEFER, Philip G	WADDELL, Docia V	30 Dec 1902	*63*
SCHAEFFER, Raymond S	WEATHERHOLTZ, Lena May	13 Sep 1923	*106*
SCHAEFFER, Walter C	SCHAFER, Ruth	24 Mar 1927	*117*
SCHAENHERR, Karl E */wid*	HORTON, May A	22 Feb 1930	*127*
SCHAFLURT, Dr. William G */wid*	CROCKER, Mary L */wid*	27 Nov 1929	*126*
SCHAUB, Richard A	HEWITT, Alice M	12 Aug 1926	*115*
SCHEFFEL, Paul E	LAMBERT, Lucy L	5 Aug 1914	*86*
SCHEID, Arthur H	MILLS, Mary Blanche	29 Oct 1906	*71*
SCHENCK, George L	BUEHLER, Daisy E */div*	24 May 1930	*128*
SCHINDEL, Lee Burton */div*	GARRISON, Rosie Louise */div*	29 Jul 1933	*143*
SCHMARONIAN, Arsene B	MERRIFIELD, Edith O	17 Apr 1900	*58*
SCHMIDT, Charles E	SCHLEY, Naomi R	10 Jun 1931	*132*
SCHMIDT, Charles William Jr	MOSCA, Victoria Mary	2 Oct 1931	*134*
SCHMIDT, Fred William	LLOYD, Norvell Owen	7 Jun 1933	*142*
SCHNAITH, Bernhard */wid*	REAGAN, Mary Elizabeth	18 Jul 1904	*68*
SCHNAPPINGER, Harris E	PRIOR, Emma M	16 Jun 1932	*138*
SCHNEIDER, Frank C	BLUNDON, Lillian M	11 Apr 1916	*90*
SCHNEIDER, J G	WILLIAMS, Ethel Mae	4 Jul 1910	*79*
SCHNEIDER, Jacob T	HAWES, Emma G	17 May 1911	*80*
SCHNEIDER, John L	FOX, Eva	20 Aug 1906	*71*
SCHOLZ, Robert O	LUNNEY, Frances V	27 Jan 1921	*100*
SCHON, Harry J	BOWERS, Marguerite C	21 Sep 1925	*112*
SCHONDAU, Frederick F	KIDWELL, Ethel Mae	2 Oct 1911	*81*

SCHOOLEY, Elmer E	MACNEIL, Maggie J /div	1 Jan 1907	72
SCHOOLEY, Heber V	SCHOOLEY, Annie V	18 Oct 1905	69
SCHOOLEY, Horace P	HARRISON, Elva	17 Sep 1901	60
SCHUBERT, James A	YOUNG, Julia Sager /div	11 Apr 1929	124
SCHUERMAN, A M	HERING, Emma S	26 Nov 1914	87
SCHULPE, Charles	SAUVEUR, Victoria Louise	3 Jun 1924	108
SCHULTE, J I	COLBATH, Mary F	2 Jun 1910	78
SCHULTZ, Harry E	BINDLEY, Elmira M	14 Mar 1911	80
SCHULTZ, William McK /wid	TALBERT, Margaret R	23 Oct 1930	130
SCHURTZ, Clarence	ROGERS, Dora	19 Dec 1912	83
SCHWAB, Ernest	DEAN, Bessie /wid	23 Jul 1927	118
SCHWEITZER, William T Jr	BUSH, Virginia C	19 Sep 1924	109
SCIPIO, Lewis /wid	HANY, Eliza /wid	1 Dec 1864	5
SCOTT, Abraham	ROANE, Mary F	10 Feb 1870	12
SCOTT, Abram /c wid	CLARK, Ella /c	10 Jul 1881	28
SCOTT, Abram /c wid	BOTTS, Willie Ann /c	5 Oct 1890	42
SCOTT, Benjamin L /wid	JORDAN, Dollie A /wid	30 Jul 1902	63
SCOTT, Cecil	KIDWELL, Viola	18 Dec 1928	123
SCOTT, Charles	SILLEX, Maggie	16 Aug 1902	63
SCOTT, Charles /c	HARRIS, Edith /c	14 Sep 1905	69
SCOTT, Cyrus	HARRIS, Amanda /wid	21 Nov 1868	10
SCOTT, Edgar	THOMPSON, Catherine	21 May 1868	9
SCOTT, Frederick	CAUDLE, Elsie	1 Nov 1923	106
SCOTT, Frederick	TAYLOR, Blanche Inez	6 Mar 1928	121
SCOTT, Fulton	KINCHELOE, Elizabeth	11 Dec 1928	123
SCOTT, George W /div	SHELDON, Alice P /wid	23 Jun 1917	92
SCOTT, James A Jr /c	SMITH, Emma V /c	12 Nov 1885	35
SCOTT, Lindsay	SMITH, Annamae /div	5 Oct 1928	122
SCOTT, Luther /c	HARRIS, Reaner /c	4 Sep 1902	63
SCOTT, Nathan /c	HARRIS, Geneva /c	26 Sep 1909	77
SCOTT, Robert A	WALTERS, Martha H	21 Sep 1882	30
SCOTT, Ulysses /c	THOMPSON, Elva /c	21 Sep 1929	126
SCOTT, William R	MARTIN, Caroline G /wid	5 May 1930	128
SEAL, Harvey D	HORN, Mary Elizabeth	18 Jun 1925	111
SEALS, Ferdinand Jr /c	NELSON, Hannah /c	9 Aug 1885	35
SEALS, Moses M /c	BOSTON, Ida /c	9 Aug 1885	35
SEAMANS, Gilbert T	HUMMER, Sina M	19 Dec 1904	67
SEATON, George W	KERBY, Anna L	19 Dec 1876	21
SEATON, George W /wid	CATON, Francis E	7 May 1890	41
SEATON, George W /wid	DOVE, Sarah /wid	4 Aug 1910	79
SEATON, William S	NASH, Margaret L	26 May 1922	102
SEAY, J W Jr	FORBES, Minnie E	7 Nov 1906	71

SEBASTIAN, L L	FRENZEL, Louise	7 Sep 1927	*119*
SEE, Charlie	STEELE, Viola	9 Dec 1932	*140*
SEEK, Gilbert	SCHMICK, Edith */wid*	2 Nov 1909	*77*
SEELEY, C H	LEE, Mary C	23 Nov 1904	*67*
SEERY, Spencer W Jr	DAWSON, Elizabeth C	10 Oct 1931	*134*
SEGAL, David */wid*	BELL, Edith	11 Jun 1912	*82*
SEIBERTH, William E	WAINWRIGHT, Mary Louise	1 Sep 1920	*98*
SEIFERT, Charles W */wid*	CONLIN, Frances L	23 May 1932	*137*
SELBY, William T	BEAHM, May Frances	6 May 1931	*132*
SELECMAN, Redmon */wid*	BURKE, Letitia	11 Dec 1866	*7*
SELECMAN, Redmon */wid*	WILLCOXEN, Mary E */wid*	9 Apr 1873	*16*
SELECMAN, Thomas H	SKINNER, Georgie L	17 Oct 1867	*8*
SELECMAN, Thomas R	BURKE, Virginia F */wid*	14 Dec 1865	*6*
SELECMAN; William R	ARUNDLE, Hellen Eugenia	27 Jan 1871	*13*
SELKE, Clarence B	HULTS, Willetta Van Tassell	6 Feb 1933	*141*
SELVIE, John */c*	PAYNE, Mary L */c*	10 Oct 1878	*24*
SELVIN, Frank */c*	RUCKER, Lee */c*	21 Dec 1902	*63*
SELZO, George A	CORALLO, Mary R	4 May 1932	*137*
SENGER, Daniel C	LEESE, Helen A	20 Aug 1928	*122*
SENNE, Ernest B	HALL, Annie L	16 Nov 1898	*55*
SENNE, Henry H	HALL, Maggie E	30 Aug 1893	*46*
SENSENEY, Leonard M	LEE, Linnie B	19 Jun 1919	*96*
SESSA, Peter G	VAIN, May	30 May 1932	*137*
SETTLE, Joseph A	WELLS, Bessie G	17 Jan 1877	*21*
SEWALL, Joseph P	MCCAULEY, Mary E	22 Nov 1886	*36*
SEWALL, Wilbur J	LEIGH, Cora E	28 Feb 1916	*90*
SEWALL, William H	HUNTER, Jannett D	28 Nov 1866	*7*
SEXTON, John R	LANE, Rosie	10 Jan 1906	*70*
SEYMOUR, Harrison	SISSON, Myrtle	5 Oct 1929	*126*
SEYMOUR, John	DODSON, Nellie (Mollie)	24 Dec 1896	*52*
SEYMOUR, Worth G	HADEN, Mary F	9 Dec 1930	*130*
SHA, Roy H	PARKINSON, Doreen	4 Sep 1920	*98*
SHACKLEFORD, H H	LEITH, Kathleen V	25 Sep 1915	*89*
SHACKLEFORD, Henry	FORTNEY, Nettie	20 Jan 1931	*131*
SHALKOP, Paul E	LINN, Verna E	16 Jun 1928	*121*
SHARP, Harold C	BAKER, Selba Brown	25 Oct 1933	*144*
SHARPE, Howard W	ROBERTSHAW, Helen H	22 Aug 1933	*143*
SHARPER, L H */c*	HENDERSON, Millie E */c*	3 Sep 1885	*35*
SHARPER, William S */c*	HENDERSON, Mary F */c*	30 May 1855	*35*
SHARVEN, Samuel M	PHIFER, Lena B	1 Oct 1908	*75*
SHAW, A B	GREEN, Mary O */wid*	5 Apr 1868	*9*
SHAW, Benjamin Allan	BLOOM, Ella Parkhurst	19 Jul 1924	*109*

SHAW, Edward M	KITTENGER, Annie L	11 Nov 1932	*140*
SHAW, Gilbert Henry	WOOD, Edith May	4 Mar 1925	*110*
SHAW, J T */wid*	MARTIN, Ida R	31 Aug 1881	*29*
SHAW, James P	BASTOW, Lillie A	21 Dec 1887	*37*
SHAW, Robert Amos	BRAYDON, Annie O */wid*	8 Feb 1926	*114*
SHAW, Samuel B	MCGLASSEL, Jennie T	24 Dec 1868	*10*
SHAW, William H */c*	WILLIAMS, Henrietta */c*	2 Jun 1890	*42*
SHAW, William P	WELLS, Emma J	28 Oct 1908	*75*
SHAY, E H */wid*	CORNWELL, Mildred	30 Aug 1930	*129*
SHEA, John T	STEPHEN, Jean A	7 Jul 1932	*138*
SHEAD, Abram C	DOOLEY, Maggie V	17 May 1917	*92*
SHEAR, Deming	SHERMAN, Elizabeth	22 Jun 1921	*100*
SHEAR, Fred	BRADLEY, Annie	16 Nov 1904	*67*
SHEAR, Sydney	SHERMAN, Fannie M	31 May 1874	*17*
SHEARER, John A */wid*	MURRAY, Janie A	11 Feb 1907	*72*
SHEEHAN, John	RECTOR, Vivian	30 May 1930	*128*
SHEEHAN, John J	CUMBERLAND, Margaret A	18 Aug 1925	*112*
SHEETS, George	KIDWELL, Ruth E	20 Jan 1915	*88*
SHEFFIELD, Albert J	HEDRICK, Mildred F	10 Dec 1932	*140*
SHELLY, G W	SMITH, Sallie T	17 Apr 1877	*22*
SHELTON, Benjamin */c*	FOLKS, Lizzie */c*	3 Dec 1902	*63*
SHELTON, Thornton */c wid*	BAKER, Mary */c wid*	21 Aug 1890	*41*
SHEPHERD, Edward */c*	NEWMAN, Annie */c*	12 Sep 1906	*71*
SHEPHERD, Marvin E	BAYLISS, Shirley A	14 Nov 1931	*134*
SHEPHERD, Milton */c*	BELL, Julia */c*	8 May 1930	*128*
SHEPHERD, William */c*	WILLIAMS, Alice */c*	21 Apr 1891	*43*
SHEPHERD, William	FERGUSON, Nellie Lee	9 May 1899	*56*
SHEPHERD, William */div*	MADDOX, Elizabeth */wid*	23 Jul 1925	*112*
SHERIER, James T	CARLIN, Mary E	21 Sep 1876	*20*
SHERIER, Michael	CARLIN, Margery	29 Sep 1879	*25*
SHERMAN, Franklin Jr	BERRY, Grace	12 May 1903	*64*
SHERMAN, Wells Alvord	BESLEY, Elsie May	23 May 1895	*49*
SHERRIN, Michael	MURTAUGH, Elizabeth	25 Oct 1874	*17*
SHERWOOD, D C	MURNANE, Honora A	28 Nov 1912	*83*
SHERWOOD, George F	WAPLE, Minnie B	21 Mar 1900	*58*
SHERWOOD, John W	WILLIAMS, Mary A	14 Dec 1869	*11*
SHERWOOD, John W	DONALDSON, Hattie	19 Nov 1884	*34*
SHERWOOD, Robert J	MILLS, Mary V	29 Dec 1869	*11*
SHICKLEY, Herbert G	BERKERHISER, Dorothy C	3 Dec 1931	*135*
SHIFFLET, David C	KANE, Iva	25 Dec 1905	*70*
SHIFLET, Walter T	LYNCH, Mabel	8 Aug 1928	*122*
SHILLING, Fred E */wid*	CROWE, Martha L	27 Jun 1931	*132*

SHILLINGER, C B	KELLOGG, Esther B	15 Feb 1930	*127*
SHIPMAN, Stephen P	HUTTON, Iris E	24 Sep 1919	*96*
SHIPMAN, William E	TWOMEY, Katherine	19 Oct 1927	*119*
SHIRLEY, A T */c*	WILLIAMS, Martha */c*	22 Dec 1885	*35*
SHIRLEY, James	WELLS, Cendarilla	15 Dec 1898	*55*
SHIRLEY, Jessie	LOVELESS, Ida	1 Dec 1924	*110*
SHIRLEY, Tilden	WILLS, Sarah	15 Apr 1924	*108*
SHIRLEY, Twyman A */c*	RIDDLES, Minnie E */c*	8 Aug 1889	*40*
SHOCKEY, Ralph N	BRASHEARS, Jennie May	14 Oct 1925	*112*
SHOEMAKER, Levi T	GILLINGHAM, Susan E	18 Aug 1897	*53*
SHORT, John J	CORKERY, Johanna A	24 Apr 1889	*40*
SHORTS, Burr */c wid*	MCKNIGHT, Harriet */c wid*	6 Jul 1882	*30*
SHORTS, Lewis */c wid*	MOORE, Maggie */c*	10 Jun 1891	*43*
SHOULDER, Page O	TROSTLE, Cora B	4 Sep 1926	*115*
SHOWALTER, Glen E	ALLEN, Grace A	27 Dec 1932	*140*
SHREVE, B B */wid*	CRANFORD, Eliza A	15 Jun 1898	*54*
SHREVE, Carroll V	ELLISON, Fannie May	30 Oct 1906	*71*
SHREVE, J F	FEBREY, Annie E	10 Feb 1881	*28*
SHREVE, R S	PORTER, Mary R	22 Dec 1896	*52*
SHREVE, R Eugene T	PATTERSON, Sarah M	23 May 1888	*38*
SHREVE, W H	FEBREY, Lillie	31 Jan 1883	*31*
SHREVE, William J	BERRY, Mary A	5 Jul 1881	*28*
SHROY, Charles William	PURDUM, Blanche M	2 Feb 1932	*136*
SHRYOCK, George W	SKINNER, Virginia M	28 Feb 1872	*14*
SHUMATE, Reuben R	ATKINS, Susie M	26 Nov 1924	*110*
SIDES, Jesse L	COOPER, Minetta	3 Jun 1919	*95*
SILL, Andrew C	BARBER, Emma M	3 Jan 1893	*46*
SILLERY, James F	OESTREICHER, Frieda D	17 Mar 1918	*93*
SILVER, Edwin H */div*	PHELPS, Ida	26 Oct 1931	*134*
SIMMONS, Kenneth	FOX, Mary	12 Nov 1927	*119*
SIMMONS, Oliver P	JARRELL, Mary A	27 Aug 1917	*93*
SIMMS, Albert */c*	SIMMS, Rosa */c*	1 Oct 1908	*75*
SIMMS, Albert	TALBERT, Carrie V	15 May 1915	*88*
SIMMS, Albert */c wid*	WILKERSON, Bessie */c*	27 Feb 1927	*117*
SIMMS, Bartlette	SINCLAIR, Frances E	4 Nov 1926	*116*
SIMMS, Charles */c*	ROBINSON, Ada M */c wid*	10 Dec 1932	*140*
SIMMS, Clarence	LYLES, Lilly	11 Nov 1911	*81*
SIMMS, Custis C	TYLER, Mary E	27 Jun 1900	*58*
SIMMS, Dan */c wid*	ELLIS, Mary */c wid*	17 Sep 1933	*143*
SIMMS, Daniel */c*	SIMMS, Bertie */c*	14 Jun 1905	*68*
SIMMS, Daniel G */c*	WANDSOR, Alice */c*	13 Jan 1898	*54*
SIMMS, Ernest	HALL, Bettie	23 Jun 1897	*52*

SIMMS, Everett	PEVERILL, Katherine	15 Dec 1915	89
SIMMS, George /wid	DEAVERS, Hariet /wid	12 Jan 1860	4
SIMMS, George J /wid	PETTITT, Lizzie	18 Feb 1908	74
SIMMS, George J /wid	DUVALL, Albertine K /wid	11 Jan 1921	100
SIMMS, Henry	MORTON, Ann M	31 Jan 1867	7
SIMMS, James H /c	LEE, Mattie /c	10 Jan 1907	72
SIMMS, James H /c wid	BROOKS, Irene /c wid	2 Sep 1911	81
SIMMS, Joseph /c	DESKIN, Julia /c	15 Feb 1896	50
SIMMS, Walter Steward	HORTON, Elethea Rebecca	5 Jul 1911	81
SIMMS, William A	NEITZEY, Anna May	31 Mar 1928	121
SIMONDS, Walter	DAVIS, Nellie	10 Mar 1924	108
SIMONS, A J	BEACH, Sarah J	11 May 1893	46
SIMONS, Homer M	HOLTZCLAW, Mary M	3 Sep 1932	139
SIMPKINS, Albert E	LEWIS, Cora D L	4 Aug 1930	129
SIMPSON, Charles E	SHAFER, Margaret E	1 May 1889	40
SIMPSON, E T	WEATHERHOLTZ, Elva M	5 Jul 1928	121
SIMPSON, G C	MITCHELL, M M	7 Mar 1879	25
SIMPSON, H M /wid	MILLAN, Eliza M /wid	1 Dec 1859	4
SIMPSON, Henry Clay	PAYNE, Anna V	10 Jan 1883	31
SIMPSON, Henry Clay /wid	RECTOR, Sallie /wid	10 Aug 1897	53
SIMPSON, Henry R /wid	IDEN, Minnie Lee	26 Feb 1917	91
SIMPSON, James	ALLCOCK, Mary Ann	26 Dec 1855	1
SIMPSON, James E	DENHAM, Mamie E	8 Jul 1900	58
SIMPSON, James W F	COLLINS, Emma	21 Feb 1883	31
SIMPSON, John F	STEWART, Frances A	27 Nov 1860	5
SIMPSON, Joseph	NEALE, Ella	4 Sep 1870	13
SIMPSON, L Thomas	CLATTERBUCK, Ida	24 Sep 1893	46
SIMPSON, Reuben	TAYLOR, Mary E	25 Jan 1858	3
SIMPSON, Robert I	HAPPOLDT, Zelah	13 Sep 1900	59
SIMPSON, Robert J	FORD, Mary R	9 Oct 1860	5
SIMPSON, William J	RICE, Nellie D	18 Nov 1908	75
SINCLAIR, C A S	SWANN, Louisa J	12 Apr 1910	78
SINKFIELD, Samuel Ed /c	SMITH, Keziah /c	25 Jun 1874	17
SIPPERLY, Charles	TYSON, Susan M	4 Mar 1889	39
SIPPERLY, Frank /div	HINE, Bessie	17 Feb 1930	127
SISSON, C M	BEAVERS, Ida /wid	1 May 1911	80
SISSON, Carlton W	SPEER, Madeleine M	29 Jul 1922	103
SISSON, Edward L	TOBIN, Della L	26 Sep 1916	90
SISSON, Lewis T	JOHNSON, Jesse F	24 Feb 1876	20
SISSON, Robert T /wid	NEWMAN, Nancy E	27 Feb 1855	1
SISSON, Samuel	CROSON, Lucy	31 Mar 1923	104
SKIDMORE, Lewis F	TUCKER, Ann E	5 Dec 1854	1

SKILLMAN, Bernard A /wid	BAILEY, Winifred	10 May 1922	*102*
SKILLMAN, Bernard L	BEACH, Lillie	15 Jan 1919	*95*
SKILLMAN, J C /wid	CROSON, Florence /wid	28 Oct 1926	*116*
SKILLMAN, Roy E	CLARKE, Myrtle Irene	29 Apr 1925	*111*
SKILLMAN, Wiliard	CORNELL, Nellie	8 Sep 1922	*103*
SKINNER, Andrew J	LEE, Helen S	29 May 1883	*31*
SKINNER, James P	WILLIAMS, Elizabeth E	13 Feb 1866	*6*
SKINNER, Joshua	MARDERS, Betty A	23 Sep 1879	*25*
SKINNER, Samuel G	SMITH, Fannie	11 Sep 1907	*73*
SKINNER, Upton Herbert	KIDWELL, Sarah L	19 Jul 1882	*30*
SKINNER, W W	GRAHAM, Gertrude	11 Oct 1860	*5*
SLACK, Howard H	MILLARD, Mabel I	15 Aug 1914	*87*
SLACK, Joseph W	COCKERILLE, Agnes V	12 Sep 1923	*106*
SLADE, Cook F	FITZHUGH, Sarah E	2 Jun 1887	*38*
SLADE, Cook Fitzhugh Jr	AUTRY, Cora Belle	30 Dec 1933	*145*
SLAUGHTER, Richard /c	HOLMES, Minnie /c	20 Apr 1908	*74*
SLAYTON, William	JOHNSON, Julia	26 Mar 1880	*26*
SMALL, Earl Franklin	BROSNAHAN, Nora Louise	10 Nov 1928	*123*
SMALL, John A /wid	FUNK, Sophie T	30 Sep 1909	*77*
SMALLWOOD, Carroll William	LYLES, Anna Louise	12 Apr 1933	*142*
SMALLWOOD, Curtis A	CATON, Dolores	20 Apr 1932	*137*
SMALLWOOD, Dr. John P /wid	BROWN, Penelope	29 Oct 1927	*119*
SMALLWOOD, Millard /c	DUNCAN, Mildred /c	17 Mar 1931	*131*
SMARR, Charles E	MCCLINTOCK, Orie V	21 Dec 1886	*37*
SMARR, James	CRANDALL, Mabel Greer /div	6 Jul 1925	*112*
SMARR, Mack C	BENNETT, Ethel D	24 Aug 1912	*83*
SMEAK, Carroll D	HURLEY, Marion /div	2 Aug 1924	*109*
SMILLIE, Joseph	DAVIS, Ada A	14 Nov 1906	*71*
SMITH, Addison /c wid	HARRIS, Frances /c wid	2 Dec 1907	*74*
SMITH, Adrian	GESS, Courtney	15 Dec 1930	*130*
SMITH, Albert W Jr	CLAGGETT, Leila Bell	21 Mar 1906	*70*
SMITH, Alfred /c	JOHNSON, Ella /c	10 May 1893	*46*
SMITH, Alonzo T	KINGMAN, Hannah M	30 Sep 1857	*3*
SMITH, Arthur J	ZEIGLER, Violet L	30 Jul 1932	*138*
SMITH, Benjamin /c	BURNETT, Annie /c	5 Sep 1889	*40*
SMITH, Benjamin /c wid	KNOX, Estella /c	18 Mar 1896	*50*
SMITH, Charles /c	DEAN, Mima /c	24 Jun 1883	*31*
SMITH, David	HALL, Mary C	5 Aug 1883	*31*
SMITH, Donald L	CLINE, Betsy M	20 Nov 1929	*126*
SMITH, Dudley D	SPARROW, Susan J	21 Jun 1859	*4*
SMITH, Eddie	KIDWELL, Mary	23 Jun 1919	*96*
SMITH, Edward S	VORHEES, Mary	29 Mar 1875	*18*

SMITH, Edward S /wid	TAYLOR, Laura A /wid	6 Jun 1917	92
SMITH, Edward W	ROY, Louisa	8 Mar 1868	9
SMITH, Elmer O	DUVALL, Eva	18 Apr 1917	92
SMITH, Eugene /c	POWELL, Louise /c	5 Jun 1922	102
SMITH, Fenton /c	RUSSELL, Ella /c	13 Jan 1882	29
SMITH, Fitzhugh Lee	CARTER, Kassie	29 Sep 1923	106
SMITH, Frank /c	BURKE, Lizzie /c	29 Aug 1909	77
SMITH, Frederick F /c	QUANDER, Irene /c	24 Jun 1915	88
SMITH, George Fred	BOWER, Evelyn Goldie	28 Jun 1933	142
SMITH, George Mason /div	EARNSHAW, Helen R	31 Jul 1915	89
SMITH, Harrison /c	FISHER, Matilda A /c	21 Sep 1879	25
SMITH, Henry G	ADAMS, Belle	27 Oct 1881	29
SMITH, Henry W /wid	SHREVE, Julia M	25 Feb 1879	25
SMITH, Ira R T	SEAMAN, Emma H	3 Aug 1909	77
SMITH, Isaac P	TRAMMELL, J R /wid	11 Sep 1860	5
SMITH, James /c	MURRAY, Hattie /c	19 Dec 1900	59
SMITH, James Allen	SYLCURK, Helen Mae	18 Sep 1929	126
SMITH, James Moore /wid	BONHAM, Mary Lillian	4 Jan 1911	80
SMITH, James N	REID, Mary C	7 Dec 1898	55
SMITH, James W /c	DEAN, Edith M /c	22 Feb 1921	100
SMITH, Jeremiah /wid	REID, Kitty /wid	6 Jun 1868	9
SMITH, John /c	FOLKS, Mary /c	6 Feb 1926	114
SMITH, John Hober	HUNTT, Elizabeth L	16 Mar 1887	37
SMITH, John J	MARANVILLE, Nancy Jane	4 Dec 1855	2
SMITH, John T	MUNDY, Kate S	6 Feb 1890	41
SMITH, John W	THOMPSON, Mary M	15 Dec 1903	65
SMITH, Joseph N /wid	GUNNELL, Isadora	1 Nov 1911	81
SMITH, Lewis R	REYNOLDS, Florence M	6 Aug 1927	118
SMITH, Linton	LAPHAM, Mildred M B	20 Dec 1911	82
SMITH, Louis M /wid	FREEMAN, Elizabeth	27 Sep 1890	42
SMITH, Merriweather L	DEARDORFF, Mildred	15 Jun 1927	118
SMITH, Oscar	HALL, Caroline	16 Jul 1868	9
SMITH, Ralph I	BALLARD, Margaret L	31 Dec 1913	85
SMITH, Robert T	KRAUS, Alice L	21 Apr 1932	137
SMITH, S J	MCGARITY, Kate	24 Jun 1908	75
SMITH, S Ernest	VAN HORN, Ellen Janet	21 Dec 1880	27
SMITH, Sherwood /c	LEWIS, Mary Elizabeth /c	26 Dec 1928	123
SMITH, Sidney B	SUTTON, Mariana	3 Sep 1866	6
SMITH, Theus /wid	JOHNSON, Alberta	30 Aug 1923	105
SMITH, Thomas W	SULLIVAN, Grace P	28 Nov 1911	81
SMITH, Turner Ashby	BEACH, Sarah J	6 Feb 1884	32
SMITH, Wallace B	HILLMAN, Eleanor	6 Apr 1911	80

SMITH, Willard W	THOMAS, M Lois	30 Aug 1905	69
SMITH, William /c	JONES, Lillie May /c	9 Mar 1920	97
SMITH, William /c	JENNINGS, Pauline /c	18 Sep 1924	109
SMITH, William H /c	SHEPHERD, Katie R /c	27 Apr 1903	64
SMITHSON, George F	YOST, Mary S	14 Oct 1916	91
SMITHWICK, Beaden	TRAMMELL, Hattie R	26 Jun 1910	78
SMOOT, Samuel C /wid	NEVITT, Lillie H	24 Jun 1908	75
SMOOT, William H	O'BRIEN, Hannah	8 Nov 1871	14
SMOOT, William M	COCKERILLE, Susie B	5 May 1897	52
SNELL, J E	GIBBS, Grace M	12 Mar 1903	64
SNIDER, Henry	KIDWELL, Lizzie	5 Jun 1915	88
SNIDER, M A	CORNELL, Claude	1 Sep 1912	83
SNIDER, Robert S	GROVE, Minnie B	22 Nov 1919	97
SNIDER, William P	CAYLOR, Lavinia G	6 Feb 1879	24
SNOOK, Charles W	HOAGLAND, Mollie C	9 May 1878	23
SNOW, Clarence L	DROWN, Florence C	1 Nov 1930	130
SNOWDEN, John	PAYNE, Emily /c	14 Apr 1885	34
SNUGGS, John L	TROUTMAN, Ethel Mary	11 Nov 1933	144
SNYDER, Turner	COCKERILLE, Elida	2 Oct 1914	87
SNYDER, Turner /wid	MOCK, Audrey	19 Oct 1919	96
SOMMERS, Lewis /c	WILLIAMS, Irene /c	6 Feb 1913	84
SONNEMAN, Warren E	JOHANSEN, Caroline S	25 Nov 1931	134
SONQUIST, David E	BROKARD, Dorothy C	6 Aug 1927	119
SORREL, Joseph F	MONEY, Laura C	31 Jul 1889	40
SORREL, Richard /wid	CORNELL, Mary A	5 Oct 1868	10
SORRELL, J Frank Sr /wid	BORDEN, Ella	22 Jun 1918	94
SOUDER, Alpheus D	HORSEMAN, Grace	15 Dec 1908	76
SOULES, William C	PETRI, Elsie Belle	15 Jan 1932	136
SOUTHALL, George	HERL, Evelyn S	19 Nov 1930	130
SPAGNIER, Hillier /c wid	ANDERSON, Lizzie /c	31 Jan 1878	23
SPANGLER, Paul C	ADAMS, Ruth B	19 Nov 1921	101
SPARKS, Willie D	BRUMBACK, Mabel Ruth	15 Dec 1921	101
SPAULDING, Albert	THOMPSON, Mary	1 Jun 1905	68
SPAULDING, Clinton C /wid	INGALLS, Eva /div	12 Aug 1933	143
SPAULDING, R C	THOMPSON, Nannie	1 Sep 1915	89
SPAULDING, Russell C	CUMMINGS, Sarah A	27 Apr 1863	5
SPAYTLE, George W	SALSBURY, Annis	20 Jun 1918	94
SPEAKMAN, W A /wid	DE PUTRON, Edith S	12 Nov 1907	74
SPEAKS, Everett	GHEEN, Martha J	28 Feb 1867	7
SPEAKS, Forest Douglas /c	PELHAM, Sarah Louise /c	1 Dec 1926	116
SPEAKS, Joseph /c wid	MURRAY, Caroline /c wid	20 Sep 1900	59
SPEARMAN, John	LLOYD, Pauline	25 Aug 1919	96

STEARN, Charles E	HALL, Violett	10 Mar 1930	*127*
STEARN, Charles M	CRUMBAUGH, Ruth	3 Jul 1909	*77*
STEEL, John W /wid	MAYHUGH, Eliza	19 Jun 1870	*12*
STEELE, Anthony	KAUPP, Theresia /wid	9 Jun 1864	*5*
STEELE, Carson /wid	HAMILL, Mary C	16 Nov 1886	*36*
STEELE, David	WASHBURN, Ada R	19 Nov 1872	*15*
STEELE, David /wid	HENRY, Flora Jane /wid	11 Dec 1913	*85*
STEELE, David A /wid	BRYANT, Adowa /div	28 Feb 1894	*47*
STEELE, Edgar	WOOSTER, R C	24 Jul 1879	*26*
STEELE, Harry J	KENDRICK, Annie E	25 Dec 1906	*72*
STEELE, James C	LEWIS, Catharine	14 Oct 1858	*4*
STEELE, James W Jr	RIGGLES, Mary A	27 Dec 1911	*82*
STEELE, John C	MARKHAM, Bridget	22 Jun 1884	*33*
STEELE, John C /c	ENGLISH, Oneida	11 May 1931	*132*
STEELE, John W /wid	DAVIS, Mary	28 Sep 1880	*27*
STEELE, Lee /c	DIXON, Hattie /c	1 Oct 1903	*65*
STEELE, W H	GOODING, Ann V	18 Dec 1869	*11*
STEERS, Edward Sr /wid	STILES, Sarah C /wid	26 Dec 1878	*24*
STEERS, James	GARWOOD, Mary R	18 Dec 1856	*2*
STEERS, Lemuel	VIOLETT, Mary A	28 Feb 1867	*7*
STEFANOWICZ, Walter	STRUZIK, Lillian	28 Feb 1931	*131*
STEIN, John N C	SMEHA, Louise A	19 Sep 1931	*133*
STEINER, Scott N	BASKETTE, Myrtle L	24 Oct 1931	*134*
STELLA, R Clifton	LEMP, Anna M	3 Jun 1924	*108*
STELY, L Newton	KEPHART, Florence M	26 Dec 1898	*56*
STENHOUSE, Walter A	WALKER, Edna M	24 Sep 1930	*129*
STERLING, Earl /wid	HOFFMAN, Paulyne	24 Sep 1924	*109*
STERLING, Thomas	HILL, Elizabeth	15 Oct 1926	*116*
STERN, David L	LUCAS, Marie E	21 Feb 1925	*110*
STEVENS, Clarence	GEORGE, Olive	6 Dec 1906	*72*
STEVENS, Richard R	NEWTON, Nellie	9 Jan 1925	*110*
STEVES, Oliver Ruben	HILL, Maggie E	15 Oct 1884	*33*
STEWARD, Charles W	WYNKOOP, Florence M	12 Aug 1896	*51*
STEWART, Charles D N	STROMAN, Emma K	27 Nov 1878	*24*
STEWART, Charles L /wid	HOWARD, Henrietta V	13 Mar 1872	*14*
STEWART, Edward F	STOKES, Sarah	2 Jan 1896	*50*
STEWART, Frank /c	MOORE, Carrie /c	21 Mar 1886	*36*
STEWART, James /c	JACKSON, Lottie /c	23 Mar 1921	*100*
STEWART, John Henry Jr /c	HUGHES, Mary Elsie /c	31 Dec 1901	*61*
STEWART, John R	CARPER, Elizabeth	23 Dec 1884	*34*
STEWART, Maurice W /c	LEE, Irene /c	21 Oct 1900	*59*
STEWART, Robert	HUNT, Selina J /wid	17 Mar 1898	*54*

STEWART, Thomas	SMITH, Mima /wid	8 Dec 1867	9
STEWART, Walter /c	HORTON, Clara /c	19 Dec 1900	59
STICKLEY, Wade A	HARPER, Ellen R	12 Nov 1932	140
STIEFF, M J	KULICK, Katherine M	1 Sep 1927	119
STIFLER, Robert C	TUNIS, Margaret	2 Apr 1931	131
STILES, Jerry /c	JACKSON, Irene /c	16 Feb 1915	88
STILES, Joseph	PRIDMORE, Sarah C	29 Nov 1855	2
STOCKHAUSEN, Charles L /wid	HAWTHORNE, Frances	18 May 1933	142
STONE, Albert C	TIFFANY, Mary E	12 Jan 1911	80
STONE, George E	CROUCH, Janie	28 Dec 1898	56
STONE, James E	DAVIS, Sarah C	16 Jan 1866	6
STONE, John C /wid	DAVIS, Mary C /wid	17 Oct 1924	109
STONE, John W F	ELGIN, Sarah A	25 Oct 1860	5
STONE, Ormond /wid	BRENNAN, Mary F	9 Jun 1915	88
STONE, Robert Lee	WOODYARD, Margaret V /wid	24 Nov 1890	42
STONE, Thomas K	CURTIN, Mary	20 Dec 1877	22
STONEBURNER, T R	CREED, Bettie V	23 Feb 1891	43
STONNELL, Sherwood B	COCKERILLE, Nettie	19 Dec 1877	21
STORM, Henry A	MYERS, Catharine L	12 Apr 1905	68
STORM, John A	MAGARITY, Sarah A	6 Nov 1877	22
STORTZ, John G /wid	DYER, Laura V /wid	4 Jun 1895	49
STORY, Mark R	MOULTON, Harriet	11 Sep 1860	5
STOTLER, Charles M	MATTHEWS, Ida May	19 Nov 1901	61
STOTT, Robert	GOULD, Elmira S	15 May 1856	2
STOTTS, J W /c	RILEY, Mary J /c	4 Nov 1914	87
STOY, E Dutton	LOVEDAY, Alice Lee	17 May 1930	128
STOY, Elmer C	CAYLOR, Maria M	28 Apr 1903	64
STRANGE, Archie /c	RUSSELL, Annie /c wid	1 May 1884	33
STRANGE, Archie /c wid	WANZER, Irene /c	24 Oct 1906	71
STRANGE, George /c	WILSON, Ida /c	29 Aug 1892	45
STRATTON, Clarence E	DERRICK, Madge L /wid	13 Sep 1930	129
STRATTON, Phil M	WOOD, Dorothy E	3 Aug 1929	125
STRAUSS, John	WITT, Laura L	31 Mar 1931	131
STRAYER, Urd Lee	FLOHR, Hilda Irene	17 Aug 1918	94
STRICKLIN, William F /wid	WRAY, Susan B	28 May 1926	114
STROESSNER, Christian	BOUTELLER, Amelia	2 May 1864	5
STROMAN, Henry Clay	CARPER, Gracie M	26 Dec 1889	40
STRONG, Conrad M /div	JOHNSON, Edna E	28 Sep 1929	126
STRONG, Edgar Ellis Jr	FEATHERSTONE, Cora Mae	19 Dec 1933	145
STROTHER, Alfred /c	CRAIG, Delia /c	20 Oct 1914	87
STROTHER, George /c	MARSHALL, Fannie /c	28 Sep 1897	53
STROTHER, Jackson /c wid	LEE, Betsy Ann /c wid	26 Jul 1868	9

STROTHER, Wilbur /c	BRADLEY, Cora /c	14 May 1902	62
STROTHER, William /c	FRENCH, Sarah /c	10 Aug 1876	20
STRUDER, Gilbert L	PETTITT, Minnie W	6 Feb 1915	88
STRUDER, Thomas	DEILER, Arline	25 Feb 1928	121
STUARD, Samuel /c	STRICKLAND, Pauline	1 Nov 1926	116
STUART, George C	HOXTON, Ann R	18 Apr 1907	72
STUART, Henry J	BURLEIGH, Famie M	24 Dec 1891	44
STUART, Robert /c	WESTON, Missouri /c	17 Jun 1888	38
STUDDS, David A	PATTON, Sarah E	16 Jan 1883	31
STUDDS, John	WARRING, Amanda	15 Jan 1880	24
STUDDS, William R	JOHNSON, Ellen B	23 Oct 1878	24
STULTZ, Albert R	KEENE, Augusta H	12 Jul 1933	143
STULZ, Erdmann T	SAUM, Julia C	20 Jul 1908	75
STUMP, Adam	YOUNT, Emma O	13 Oct 1881	29
STURDIVANT, Junius /c	MEADOWS, Mary /c	25 Jun 1932	138
STYLES, Francis H	LANE, Eleanor	7 Mar 1924	108
STYLES, Henry /c	JACKSON, Melvina /c	26 Mar 1914	86
STYLES, Samuel H	RILEY, Mary E	8 Jun 1892	44
SUDDATH, Frank	MORGAL, Ruby E	28 Apr 1923	105
SUDDATH, Stanley	ENNIS, Glenna	4 Sep 1920	98
SUDLER, Emory B /c	THOMAS, Cora B /c div	20 Jul 1929	125
SUGGS, Roland /c	FERGUSON, Cordelia /c	14 Jan 1933	141
SUGHRUE, Daniel	COWLEY, Margaret	27 Sep 1869	11
SUIT, Samuel S	DEAL, Daisy E	3 Jul 1913	84
SUKEY, Grover C	FAY, Ann E	12 Sep 1923	106
SULLIVAN, Charles J	BROWN, Katie F	8 Jun 1893	46
SULLIVAN, Daniel	LYONS, Vernice Espey	21 Jul 1920	98
SULLIVAN, William J	LOWE, Margaret M	14 Mar 1912	82
SUMMERALL, Louis C /c	STRIBLING, Fannie E /c	19 Jun 1913	84
SUMMERS, Chester M /div	CASSEY, Mary /wid	25 Oct 1924	110
SUMMERS, Clarence R F /c	BELL, Clara /c	27 Oct 1903	65
SUMMERS, Dorsey /c	SHEPHERD, Alice /c	30 Dec 1879	26
SUMMERS, Edward /c	SHEPHERD, Amelia /c	17 May 1891	43
SUMMERS, Emory L	HOKE, Elizabeth V	14 Dec 1929	127
SUMMERS, John W	WATKINS, Amanda L	25 Jan 1872	15
SUMMERS, R P H	DUTTON, Susanna B	19 Jun 1906	71
SUMMERS, William	DAVIS, Hester /c	15 Nov 1892	45
SUMMERS, William /c	FULLER, Mary /c	27 May 1903	64
SUMMERS, William W	PALMER, Jennie	12 Dec 1872	15
SUMMEY, Daniel Fritchey	JENKINS, Helen F	17 Aug 1893	46
SUPINGER, McKinley	EVANS, Wildia V	7 Dec 1925	113
SURATO, Lawrence	COCKERILLE, Louise	13 Jan 1928	121

SUSCOE, Everett LeRoy	POOLE, Vivian R /div	20 Jul 1931	132
SUTHERLAND, Arthur L	CHAPMAN, Helen M	6 Jun 1900	58
SUTHERLAND, James	ALFRED, Elsie	9 Jan 1929	124
SUTHERLAND, William Thomas	CURREN, Mamie	20 Sep 1906	71
SUTHERLIN, Howard A	DAVIDSON, Myrtle	29 Jun 1932	138
SUTPHIN, Derwood	KIDWELL, Leish	14 Mar 1924	108
SUTPHIN, E J	ANDERSON, Jobie /wid	29 May 1911	80
SUTPHIN, Ned	BEANS, Florence Z	19 Aug 1933	143
SUTPHIN, Willie	ROBEY, Eva	16 Dec 1912	83
SUTTON, J M /c	FAIRFAX, Minnie /c	30 May 1910	78
SUTTON, John W	WILLETT, Cora L	14 Dec 1886	37
SUTTON, John Walter	NEVITT, Roberta L	22 Apr 1884	33
SWAILES, Robert /c	BANKS, Sarah /c	21 Oct 1886	42
SWAIN, Julius G /wid	REID, Catharine Ann /wid	31 Jan 1856	2
SWAN, Daniel N /div	SIMS, Sue	6 Aug 1932	138
SWAN, John C	BRODT, Gertrude V	21 Aug 1903	65
SWANSON, A Gilmer /div	GRAY, Catherine I /div	26 Mar 1913	84
SWARINGEN, W F /div	KEWLEY, Alice	7 Jul 1921	100
SWART, Bernard J	FOX, Helen Edith	14 May 1927	118
SWART, Stacy S	FUNKHAUSER, Hattie I	24 May 1916	90
SWART, Wesley W	GOODING, Lula May	29 Jan 1896	50
SWARTZ, Harry L	SINGHAS, Florence H	22 Aug 1931	133
SWEENEY, Albert A	HOSE, Eleanor /wid	15 Feb 1922	102
SWEENEY, J H	COCK, Ellen	31 Jan 1860	5
SWEY, Hussien A	JOHNSON, Maude E	30 Jan 1932	136
SWIFT, Wilmer E	STEWART, Viola Pearl	3 Jul 1919	96
SWINDELLS, William N	BURY, Anna Belle	15 Oct 1898	55
SWINDLEHURST, Carl	GERNS, Margaret E	14 Oct 1930	130
SWINK, E F	MAGARITY, Carrie	9 Feb 1881	28
SWINK, John F /wid	FOLLIN, Henrietta M	9 Sep 1869	11
SWINK, John F /wid	OLIVER, Octavia	2 Jan 1879	24
SWINK, Zachary Taylor	WALKER, Julia A	1 Nov 1875	19
SWOPE, Daniel Paul	RUST, Maggie Estelle	3 Nov 1902	63
SYDNOR, Charles William	MOORE, Elizabeth B	1 Sep 1910	79
SYDNOR, Robert W	DAVIS, Huldah L	11 Sep 1926	116
SYKES, Sydney D	REED, Annie H /div	24 Nov 1927	120
SYLVANDER, Roy C	BLANCKE, Olga	12 Dec 1923	107
SYPHAS, Wesley /c	DAVIS, Alma R /c	25 Aug 1927	119
TABLER, William E	ETTA, Dolores G	17 Nov 1928	123
TALBERT, James W	GORHAM, Emma V	12 Oct 1915	89
TALBERT, John T	TALBERT, Sarah J	16 Apr 1868	9
TALBERT, Silas	DEAVERS, Lizzie	22 Apr 1880	26

TALBOT, Frank	NEITZEY, Janie Rebecca	11 Aug 1907	73
TALBOTT, Thomas Melville	FEBREY, Ella B	28 Sep 1876	21
TALBOTT, Thomas Melville /wid	NOURSE, Annie Kathleen	1 Jun 1892	44
TALIAFERRO, Alexander A /c wid	SMYTH, Clara H /c div	2 May 1917	92
TALIAFERRO, Gawin C	GODWIN, Emma	27 Dec 1855	2
TANNER, Fred M	GAINES, Jennie	28 Nov 1887	38
TASKER, W Alvin	SWIFT, Margaret L	4 Jun 1928	121
TATE, Alvyn A	MOTEN, Laurinda /c	17 Aug 1929	125
TATE, Arthur /c	DAVIS, Etta /c	14 Jan 1914	86
TATE, George Smith	MARKS, Edna L	20 Oct 1917	93
TATE, Robert /c	MACK, Sarah /c	18 Jan 1877	21
TAUS, Joseph Howard	GANTZ, Mary Elizabeth	20 Jun 1932	138
TAVENER, Thomas F	POOLE, Daisy D	15 Aug 1899	57
TAVENNER, Jonah	WAFFOTT, Laura A	23 Aug 1910	79
TAVENNER, Thomas E /wid	SANFORD, Marcella	29 Sep 1931	134
TAWES, F B Jr	KLOTSCH, Helen	15 Nov 1924	110
TAYLOR, Alfred E	BEAVER, Frances C	27 Feb 1932	136
TAYLOR, Alfred Holmead	MOORE, Gertrude	17 Jun 1886	36
TAYLOR, Arthur	VANDYCK, Roberta	3 Nov 1881	29
TAYLOR, Benjamin D	COGAN, Martha E	1 Feb 1874	17
TAYLOR, Berkely H	GORHAM, Narcissa R /wid	7 Oct 1933	144
TAYLOR, C E	MURPHY, Etta	26 Dec 1905	70
TAYLOR, Charles /div	HARROVER, Laura M /div	27 Jul 1914	86
TAYLOR, Charles /wid	HOLLISTER, Rosa	26 May 1928	121
TAYLOR, Charles H /c	PEARSON, Susie /c	23 Apr 1890	41
TAYLOR, Charles H /c wid	SHEPHERD, Georgia A /c	5 Dec 1931	135
TAYLOR, Daniel	FORSYTH, Jane Elizabeth	22 Dec 1868	10
TAYLOR, Ernest E	RIGGLES, Naomi V	30 Jun 1915	88
TAYLOR, F R	CROSSMAN, Florence C	30 Nov 1923	106
TAYLOR, Fred /c	WILLIAMS, Mamie /c	20 Sep 1899	57
TAYLOR, George	HUNT, Ettie	24 Mar 1897	52
TAYLOR, George H	JAVINS, Sarah Olive	28 Mar 1905	68
TAYLOR, George P	JOHNSON, Georgeana	5 Jan 1882	29
TAYLOR, George R	THARP, Alice	17 Apr 1917	91
TAYLOR, Harvey	DODSON, Nora M	6 Jul 1922	103
TAYLOR, Harvey	TAYLOR, Pansy	28 May 1929	124
TAYLOR, Henry /c wid	ROY, Harriet /c wid	10 Dec 1908	76
TAYLOR, Henry /c	NASH, Victoria /c	27 Dec 1930	130
TAYLOR, Henry /c wid	BROOKS, Mary /c	13 Apr 1931	131
TAYLOR, James /c wid	THOMPSON, Julia /c	20 May 1886	36
TAYLOR, James /c wid	BROOKS, Emma Jane /c wid	1 Jan 1898	56
TAYLOR, James E	SUTHERLAND, Mary	5 Nov 1874	17

TAYLOR, James R	KEYS, Mary I	27 Jun 1906	71
TAYLOR, John /c wid	SCOTT, Margaret /c wid	4 Jan 1894	47
TAYLOR, John H /wid	FOX, Mary E	4 Sep 1881	29
TAYLOR, Joseph /c	SEALS, Lavenia /c	27 Sep 1877	22
TAYLOR, Joseph L	BAYLISS, Daisy /div	15 Jan 1920	97
TAYLOR, Mahlon R	MOCK, Mary H	7 Aug 1884	33
TAYLOR, Norman G	BURTON, Laura A	11 Nov 1881	29
TAYLOR, Richard	TURNER, Mary /wid	16 Mar 1867	7
TAYLOR, Robert /c	HUNTER, Cora /c wid	30 May 1895	49
TAYLOR, Robert Lee	HALL, Melvia	24 Dec 1930	130
TAYLOR, S T	BOUCHER, Alice M	24 Sep 1902	63
TAYLOR, Samuel C	TAYLOR, Alice J	2 Aug 1877	22
TAYLOR, Thomas Jr	FOX, Susanna	21 Apr 1857	3
TAYLOR, W A	MENTZER, Hattie V	20 May 1912	82
TAYLOR, W W	SPINDLE, Panola P	1 Nov 1891	44
TAYLOR, Walter /c	DADE, Julia E /c	15 Apr 1909	76
TAYLOR, Walter L	ROTCHFORD, Katie E	17 Sep 1889	40
TAYLOR, Wiliiam L	CUNNINGHAM, Alice	14 Aug 1919	96
TAYLOR, William /wid	BEACH, Mildred /wid	18 Sep 1855	1
TAYLOR, William A /c	WEBB, Lucy A /c	19 Jan 1898	54
TAYLOR, William D	COOMBS, Grace L	12 Dec 1911	81
TAYLOR, William D	COOK, Lillian D	22 Nov 1921	101
TAYLOR, William W	HYATT, Florence P	15 Jan 1908	74
TEBBS, George Dewey	WARVIN, Grace Weir	8 May 1926	114
TEBBS, Jacob /c	BRIGGS, Susie /c	20 Mar 1900	58
TEBBS, Sandy	CAMPBELL, Caroline	19 Oct 1871	14
TEBBS, Thomas	GLASSCOCK, Anna	15 Aug 1866	6
TEBBS, Thomas F	THORNTON, Caroline Maria	25 Jul 1855	1
TENNISON, A S	ALLEN, Sarah	5 May 1859	4
TENNISON, Theo	CAMP, Mary	24 Mar 1857	3
TERRELL, Benjamin /c wid	KELLY, Etta /c	11 Sep 1931	133
TERRELL, Daniel /c	GASKINS, Lena /c	31 Dec 1921	102
TERRELL, Jacob B /c	JOHNSON, Parthenia T /c	1 Aug 1928	122
TERRELL, Richard /c	TURNER, Sally /c	23 Jan 1908	74
TERRELL, William /c	MCKNIGHT, Burney /c	8 Mar 1875	18
TERRETT, Henry B	BAILEY, Dora Amelia	7 Jan 1903	64
TERRETT, S T	HUNTER, Agnes	4 May 1894	48
TERRETT, William W	RICHARDS, Priscilla G	25 Feb 1869	10
TERRY, Everett /c	COLLINS, Edith A B /c	15 Dec 1919	97
TERRY, Jesse L /c wid	HUNTER, Lillian E /c	10 Sep 1895	49
TERRY, William H	THOMPSON, Geneva	12 Aug 1933	143
THADA, Herbert	RICHMOND, Alice S	14 Oct 1919	96

THARP, J L /wid	CRITZER, Mattie /wid	25 Jun 1926	115
THAYER, Henry	BOERNSTEIN, Aida G	30 Apr 1899	56
THAYER, Herbert J	SIDBURY, Maude Alex	16 Jun 1933	142
THAYER, P J	JENKINS, Emma E	18 Oct 1899	57
THIGPEN, William /c	TAYLOR, Abbie /c	23 Feb 1908	76
THOMAS, Arthur /c	RANDALL, Sarah /c	25 Apr 1906	70
THOMAS, Arthur J	HOWELL, Blanche B	5 Sep 1931	133
THOMAS, Beverly /c	TINNER, Caroline /c	9 Jul 1896	51
THOMAS, Clinton /c wid	LUCAS, Miranda /c wid	28 Oct 1899	57
THOMAS, D S /c	SIMMS, Clara /c	14 Sep 1898	55
THOMAS, Daniel S /c wid	CURTIS, Adelle /c	6 Dec 1923	107
THOMAS, Edward /c wid	WINKFIELD, Ann E /c wid	9 Apr 1868	9
THOMAS, Eulah J /c wid	WEBB, Clarice H /c	12 Jun 1933	142
THOMAS, Frederick /c	NEWMAN, Lillie /c wid	17 Dec 1902	63
THOMAS, George /wid	GREEN, Catherine /c	7 Jun 1905	68
THOMAS, George /c	FRENCH, Margaret /c	4 Jun 1913	84
THOMAS, George /c	HARRIS, Anginina /c	26 Dec 1922	104
THOMAS, George W /c	PARKER, Mary /c	5 Feb 1875	18
THOMAS, George W /c wid	JONES, Kate A /c	1 Sep 1881	29
THOMAS, George W /c wid	WALLER, Fanny /c wid	28 Dec 1893	47
THOMAS, Glen C	GARTON, Lora Lee /wid	20 Aug 1918	94
THOMAS, Henry /c	FOLKS, Carrie /c	18 May 1902	62
THOMAS, Jesse A	BOUTON, Clarissa C P	11 Dec 1908	76
THOMAS, John /c	BURKE, Lula /c	29 Dec 1907	74
THOMAS, John E	LEE, Ida B /c	14 Oct 1908	75
THOMAS, Lawrence /c	HILL, Della /c	26 Dec 1931	135
THOMAS, Luther W /c wid	CLIVES, Annie B /c	18 Dec 1911	81
THOMAS, Milton E	DAVIS, Minnie M	14 Nov 1894	48
THOMAS, Newton /c	BOWMAN, Mattie /c	25 Feb 1897	52
THOMAS, Odie Augustus /c	DESKIN, Rhodie Virginia /c	20 Mar 1919	95
THOMAS, Picton P	AYRES, Bettie R	22 Jan 1868	9
THOMAS, Robert F	PEARSON, Mary E	21 Feb 1866	6
THOMAS, Silas A	MITCHELL, Mary F	19 Apr 1860	5
THOMAS, Thomas /c	BLACKWELL, Martha /c	30 Mar 1876	20
THOMAS, William	SMITH, Alice	7 Feb 1900	58
THOMPSON, Alfred H	BUCKLEY, Annie L	16 Jan 1884	32
THOMPSON, Alpheus G	BEAVERS, Laura V	5 Jul 1894	48
THOMPSON, Archibald M	LANE, Lucy	12 Mar 1890	41
THOMPSON, Arthur	FERRIS, Laura L	10 May 1868	9
THOMPSON, Arthur J	THOMPSON, Cordelia M	15 Feb 1893	46
THOMPSON, B F	LAWS, Laura C /wid	26 Feb 1895	49
THOMPSON, B M	SHIMMEL, Ella	13 Jan 1904	66

THOMPSON, Benjamin F	HURST, Florence L	27 Jul 1929	*125*
THOMPSON, Carl A	BURLEIGH, Gaynell O	17 Feb 1904	*66*
THOMPSON, Charlie B	BURLEIGH, Katherine H	6 Aug 1915	*89*
THOMPSON, Clifton H	THOMPSON, Clara	5 Apr 1917	*91*
THOMPSON, Clyde Elton	KITCHEN, Annie Ward	20 Jan 1904	*66*
THOMPSON, Daniel	FERRIS, Alice V	11 Apr 1878	*23*
THOMPSON, Daniel D	SNOWDEN, Elizabeth E	24 Apr 1885	*35*
THOMPSON, David	STROTHER, Mary */c wid*	23 Jul 1914	*86*
THOMPSON, Dewey C	MASSIE, Ruth V	13 Aug 1923	*105*
THOMPSON, Eddie */c*	RANSEL, Jemima */c*	17 Dec 1896	*52*
THOMPSON, Edward E	PETTITT, Ida Mabel	13 Jan 1887	*37*
THOMPSON, Egbert A */wid*	MONROE, Virginia E	12 Jun 1900	*58*
THOMPSON, Elisha H	HUNTT, Mary V	21 Dec 1871	*15*
THOMPSON, Emet L	MCFARLAND, Bertie M	7 Jul 1903	*65*
THOMPSON, F A	MONEY, E C	21 Jun 1888	*38*
THOMPSON, Frank	MOHLER, Edna E	4 Jul 1904	*66*
THOMPSON, Frederick M	WELLS, Sarah J	25 Jan 1855	*1*
THOMPSON, G L	MCGUIN, Sallie P	10 May 1916	*90*
THOMPSON, George	MOSBY, Martha */c*	19 Nov 1896	*51*
THOMPSON, George H	BLADEN, Florence E	29 Jul 1869	*11*
THOMPSON, George H	PEYTON, Matilda R	26 Oct 1879	*25*
THOMPSON, George M	RYER, Emma J	4 Jun 1867	*7*
THOMPSON, Guy	THOMPSON, Julia May	5 Jan 1906	*70*
THOMPSON, Harold	FONES, Louise G	6 Apr 1931	*131*
THOMPSON, Harry T	GRIGSBY, Mary E	6 Dec 1930	*130*
THOMPSON, Harvey W	BAUGHM, Emma A	26 Apr 1905	*68*
THOMPSON, Henry */c*	WILLIS, Mollie */c*	2 Oct 1875	*19*
THOMPSON, Isaiah */wid*	FORTNEY, Mary C	30 Jul 1884	*33*
THOMPSON, J W	MURTAUGH, Winifred M	27 Jan 1904	*66*
THOMPSON, James */c*	TUCKER, Agnes */c*	12 Jan 1897	*52*
THOMPSON, James */c*	DAVIS, Edith */c wid*	23 Aug 1924	*109*
THOMPSON, James S	VOLTAIRE, Mildred T */wid*	26 Jun 1926	*115*
THOMPSON, Jeremiah	HART, Amelia E	31 Aug 1869	*11*
THOMPSON, Jeremiah */wid*	DAVIS, Susie L	27 Mar 1889	*39*
THOMPSON, John */c*	FIFER, Estelle M */c*	16 Mar 1931	*131*
THOMPSON, John R	ANDERSON, Ethel V	10 Jan 1926	*113*
THOMPSON, John S	MATEER, Jennie E	4 Dec 1884	*34*
THOMPSON, Julian D	WELLS, Esther M	30 Apr 1901	*60*
THOMPSON, Leith W	MCMILLEN, Bessie Lee	27 Jun 1905	*69*
THOMPSON, Lewis */c*	TEBBS, Harriet A */c*	27 Jun 1874	*17*
THOMPSON, Lewis */c div*	MELONTREE, Mary J */c*	17 Dec 1889	*40*
THOMPSON, Lewis E	PETTITT, Emsey	21 Dec 1875	*19*

THOMPSON, Malcolm E	BUCKLEY, Adalaide	2 Jun 1870	*12*
THOMPSON, Morris /c	DAY, Carrie /c	27 Feb 1896	*50*
THOMPSON, Mortimore	CAMPBELL, Florence A	4 Jan 1877	*21*
THOMPSON, Ralph E /div	BALL, Mary Elizabeth	12 Jun 1929	*125*
THOMPSON, Robert T /wid	RATCLIFFE, Marian	5 Sep 1854	*1*
THOMPSON, Russell	ARNOLD, Julia	3 Feb 1919	*95*
THOMPSON, Stacy L	JENKINS, Lillie E	30 Aug 1915	*89*
THOMPSON, W S	THOMPSON, Ida B	3 Oct 1888	*39*
THOMPSON, Walter E	FRITTER, Emma J	7 Feb 1912	*82*
THOMPSON, William /c wid	LEE, Betty /c wid	19 Apr 1879	*25*
THOMPSON, William	FASTNAUGHT, Jennie	8 Mar 1880	*26*
THOMPSON, William /c	VASS, Rachel /c	1 Oct 1888	*39*
THOMPSON, William A	VANGENDER, Bessie May	1 May 1913	*84*
THOMPSON, William A Jr	PECK, Florence M	5 Mar 1919	*95*
THOMPSON, William H	BAUGHMAN, Edith E	17 Sep 1924	*109*
THOMPSON, William R	MARSHALL, Helen R	26 Jan 1915	*88*
THOMPSON, William T	THOMPSON, Louisa	3 Feb 1886	*37*
THOMPSON, William W	WILLIAMS, Annie	22 May 1888	*38*
THOMPSON, Willis	CAMPBELL, Lulie B	29 Dec 1886	*37*
THOMPSON, Wilson	MATEER, Mary A	29 Dec 1881	*29*
THOMPSON, Wilson H	THOMPSON, Frank A	14 Jan 1874	*17*
THOMPSON, Yancy /c	CONOWAY, Grace /c	2 Dec 1874	*18*
THOMPSON, Yates	MILLARD, Lulie	9 Apr 1891	*43*
THORNBURG, Edward J	WILLIAMS, Helen E	22 Nov 1930	*130*
THORNE, Jacob S	DONALDSON, Beulah G	18 Dec 1900	*59*
THORNETT, Bertram F /wid	WHETZEL, Tracy V	6 Feb 1930	*127*
THORNTON, Charles /c	WILLIAMS, Harriet /c	19 Dec 1876	*21*
THORNTON, Charles H /c wid	WILLIAMS, Emma /c	19 Aug 1894	*48*
THORNTON, Clarence C Jr	BISHOP, Mary Louise	11 Aug 1928	*122*
THORNTON, Washington /c	FLETCHER, Frances /c	22 Aug 1882	*30*
THORNTON, William H	DAY, Mary E	10 Feb 1857	*3*
THORP, Columbus	LLOYD, Lillie	28 Jun 1921	*100*
THORPE, Frank B	BRADY, Maude B	30 Apr 1907	*72*
THROCKMORTON, H W	UPTON, Rebecca E	1 Jan 1858	*3*
THURMAN, Clarence U	BARNARD, Lois E	15 Aug 1918	*94*
THURSTON, John B	SCHLEIB, Barbara	7 Sep 1931	*133*
TIBBS, Frank /c	GREEN, Sarah /c	6 Jul 1904	*68*
TILLETT, G W	FORD, Anna	2 Jan 1883	*31*
TILLETT, Leon Lewis	RANDALL, Mary Etta /wid	6 Nov 1933	*144*
TILLETT, Robert W	CLEVELAND, Mary M	27 Feb 1912	*82*
TILLMAN, Alexander /wid	JAMES, Alice	18 Jul 1872	*15*
TINDER, Milton	KIDWELL, Bertie	26 May 1908	*75*

TINDER, William C	DODSON, Irene L	7 May 1932	*137*
TINNER, Alfred L /c	WILLIAMS, Annie /c	3 Jun 1886	*36*
TINNER, Charles H /c	TAYLOR, Louisa /c	7 Mar 1889	*39*
TINNER, Frank J /c	COATES, Marjorie Virginia /c	24 Aug 1929	*125*
TINNER, Melvin /c div	DIXON, Rose /c div	15 Jan 1925	*110*
TINNER, Rudolph M /c	JOHNSON, Bertha /c div	19 Dec 1932	*140*
TIPPETT, Edgar S	ANDERSON, Katherine Agnes	6 Aug 1924	*109*
TOBIN, Franklin M	SUTLER, Juanita V	23 Jul 1933	*143*
TOBIN, Mathew C	SEELER, Margaret	3 Aug 1910	*79*
TODD, John T /wid	HILL, Margaret M	5 Feb 1884	*32*
TOLLIVER, William H /c	BALL, Elizabeth J /c wid	31 Oct 1923	*106*
TOMPKINS, Charles V	BIRD, Margaret R	16 May 1924	*108*
TOMPKINS, Richard W /c	SIMMONS, Katherine A /c	19 Sep 1918	*94*
TOMPKINS, Russell K	ROYER, Blanche A	11 Dec 1915	*89*
TOOMER, Horace N /c	BECKWITH, Clara E /c	26 Dec 1912	*83*
TORREYSON, Benjamin	THOMPSON, Alma W	10 Jun 1897	*52*
TORREYSON, Clarence G	LEWIS, Mamie E	25 Nov 1891	*44*
TORREYSON, Henry A	JONES, Emily J	18 Sep 1879	*25*
TORREYSON, L E	BATES, Ella V	30 Jul 1912	*83*
TORREYSON, Samuel Nelson	WELLS, Lillie O	4 Jan 1898	*54*
TORREYSON, William /wid	SIMPSON, Mary	17 Mar 1857	*3*
TOURTELOT, John H	DORSEY, Rita Brooke	9 Oct 1913	*85*
TRABAND, John H	HARRISON, Lettice C	20 Jun 1904	*66*
TRACEY, George /c	MCGEE, Mamie /c	6 Nov 1886	*37*
TRACY, Wilmer L	BRESLIN, Merry C	18 Oct 1930	*130*
TRAMMELL, Charles A	CORNELL, Maggie M	1 Jul 1885	*35*
TRAMMELL, J Y	LEEMAN, Mary E	30 Dec 1920	*99*
TRAMMELL, John A	COCKERILLE, Norma	28 Feb 1878	*23*
TRAMMELL, Laurence R	MOCK, Edna	23 Dec 1932	*140*
TRAMMELL, Lewis B	SANDERS, Minnie E	30 May 1914	*86*
TRAMMELL, Samuel J	TRAMMELL, Zella C	10 Jan 1882	*29*
TRAUBERGER, Ferdinand G /wid	GIBSON, Grace P	29 Sep 1923	*106*
TRAUTMAN, George F	MILLER, Mary M	20 Sep 1930	*129*
TRAVERS, George H	BEACH, Virginia Lee	4 Jul 1911	*81*
TRAVIS, William Livingston	WARD, Elsie	28 Dec 1933	*145*
TRAYLOR, Beverley A	BRUNNER, Matilda L	14 Dec 1880	*27*
TRAYLOR, Edward M Jr	WILDER, Fannie E	13 Nov 1933	*144*
TRAYNOR, Richard	WALLER, Ann	7 Dec 1928	*123*
TRICE, F M	HAISLIP, Jane C	23 Dec 1858	*4*
TRICE, Ltither R	STEERS, Mary Agnes	6 Nov 1873	*16*
TRICE, Marion /div	ARRINGTON, Hazel V .	9 Jul 1933	*143*
TRICE, Marion L	SISSON, Helen Elizabeth	21 May 1929	*124*

TRICE, Richard P /wid	HUGHS, Mary Jane /wid	18 Dec 1856	2
TRICE, Richard P /wid	DAWSON, Matilda A	21 Jul 1870	13
TRICKETT, George	BEEDLE, Mary	26 Aug 1856	2
TRICKETT, George W	TORRISON, Mary V	15 Oct 1915	89
TRICKETT, Grant L	ROBEY, Laura Caletta	5 Aug 1922	103
TRICKETT, William	COCKERILLE, America	8 Jan 1880	24
TRICKETT, William H	SLACK, Helena H	22 Aug 1906	71
TRIGGER, James A	VENNEBUSH, Cecelia	4 Mar 1930	127
TRIPLETT, Fred O	SMITH, Kate L /wid	26 Jan 1887	37
TRIPLETT, George W	TRIPLETT, Katharine L	29 Nov 1892	45
TRIPLETT, Harry E /wid	KENNEY, Mary J /wid	22 Jul 1926	115
TRIPLETT, Hayward F	RICHARDSON, H Virginia	3 Jan 1872	14
TRIPLETT, Walter Jones	CROSS, Mary Ellen	26 Dec 1871	15
TRISTANI, King	LINK, Lillas G	9 Nov 1933	144
TROMBLY, Stephen B	BEACH, Mary E	3 Nov 1870	13
TROTH, Frank W	HUNTER, Martha W	9 Mar 1881	28
TROTH, George H	AYRES, Emma V	11 Jun 1884	33
TROTH, Jacob H	CANFIELD, Mary E	15 Feb 1882	30
TROTH, Jacob Munson	WALTON, Ann	20 Sep 1860	5
TROTH, P H /wid	AUGUSTINE, Elizabeth B	27 Sep 1882	30
TROUGHT, Charles E	REID, Elsie May	5 Jul 1921	100
TROYMAN, Wesley C /c	JOHNSON, Lillie /c	22 Dec 1923	107
TRUAX, John B	DAINTY, Anna R	21 Dec 1869	11
TRUE, Rupert C	BEYMER, Regina	7 Aug 1922	103
TRUITT, Raymond A	GRIM, Rose Virginia	20 Aug 1931	133
TRUMBLE, Doc	CULLINANE, Hannah	16 Sep 1897	53
TRUMBLE, Edwin	LANE, Hattie	28 Dec 1898	56
TRUMBLE, Harrie F	DOVE, Cora C	6 Sep 1896	51
TRUMBLE, Johnson	CRIPPEN, Mary	21 Oct 1855	1
TRUMBLE, Martin	POSTON, Sarah M	6 Mar 1859	4
TRUMBLE, Robert Lee	DOVE, Nora	3 Jan 1889	39
TRUMBLE, Samuel H	BEACH, Mary E	27 Apr 1882	30
TRUMBLE, Vance S	BEACH, Ann E	2 Feb 1860	5
TRUMBLY, Joseph W	BROOKS, Gertrude	29 Feb 1924	108
TRUMPOWER, Leonard	COOK, Julia F	16 Feb 1928	121
TRUSSELL, H W	UNDERWOOD, E J	23 Feb 1904	66
TUCKER, Clarence L Jr	WOOD, Josephine A	22 Jul 1928	122
TUCKER, Francis Bland	LAIRD, Mary Goldsborough	5 Jun 1920	98
TUCKER, George	ROUZEE, Mary F	13 Apr 1870	12
TUCKER, James E Jr	TAYLOR, Belle Haven	29 Jun 1896	51
TUCKER, James Lewis	FOLLIN, Georgianna A	9 Sep 1869	11
TUCKER, John Frederick	STODDARD, Mildred Kinsell	14 Jan 1919	95

TUCKER, John P	FOLLIN, Frances M	31 Oct 1878	24
TUCKER, William /c wid	BROWN, Louisa /c wid	11 Dec 1884	34
TURBERVILLE, George R Lee	THORNTON, Ada S	19 Feb 1879	25
TURLEY, Charles Jr /c	GREEN, Ruth /c	28 Feb 1912	82
TURLEY, Charles W /wid	JONES, Ella M	11 Aug 1858	3
TURLEY, George E /c	MERDOCK, Kattie /c	7 Nov 1898	55
TURLEY, R A	HATTON, Mary J	24 Dec 1920	99
TURLEY, William	BRYCE, Amy	6 Jun 1870	12
TURLEY, William Thomas /c wid	EDMONDS, Molly /c	29 Oct 1875	19
TURNER, Benjamin /c	BRANHAM, Irene /c	1 Apr 1909	76
TURNER, Edward J /c	PERRY, Marie /c	6 Oct 1924	109
TURNER, Francis V /c	JONES, Martha A /c	22 Jun 1925	111
TURNER, Frederick J	WALTERS, Maryon Olive	26 Nov 1908	75
TURNER, Harry /c	BRUCE, Ethel M A /c	27 Jun 1931	132
TURNER, Herbert Richard	RUCKET, Cora H	27 Dec 1924	110
TURNER, Howard /c	STEWART, Mary A /c	21 Dec 1886	42
TURNER, James L	VANDYCK, Lizzie	14 Jan 1875	18
TURNER, James L	MYERS, Mary J	24 Feb 1892	44
TURNER, James U /c	HONESTY, Bertie /c	7 Dec 1898	55
TURNER, Lewis /c	BALL, Rachel /c	21 Sep 1898	55
TURNER, Olsworth /c	COLLINS, Bernice /c	22 Feb 1927	117
TURNER, Otis Lee	DAVIS, Edith Moran /wid	26 Mar 1932	136
TURNER, Robert L	DAILEY, Martha L	25 Jun 1919	96
TURNER, Roy E	HERMAN, Geneva	30 Jul 1924	109
TURNER, Ward	COURTNEY, Mary	24 Dec 1924	110
TURNER, William	DAVIS, Bessie F	14 Oct 1893	46
TURNER, William W /wid	GOLDING, Sarah C	21 May 1859	4
TURPIN, Harry L	RALEY, Amanda F	27 Oct 1933	144
TWINING, W H Jre	DAVY, Lucille J	28 Jun 1923	105
TWITCHELL, Frank Adams	PAYNE, Annie Irene	27 Jun 1907	73
TWOMBLY, George P	BALL, Bessie A	5 Jun 1901	60
TWOMBLY, John A	ABBOTT, Georgia M	22 Mar 1933	141
TWYMAN, Howard /c	TERRELL, Nettie /c	5 Apr 1916	90
TYERS, George	MARSHALL, Maggie	10 Jan 1882	29
TYERS, M E	TRICE, Sadie V	11 Sep 1912	83
TYLER, Charles W	FAIRFAX, Clara J	5 Nov 1896	51
TYLER, Claude	HARTBOWER, Rosie	21 Sep 1905	69
TYLER, Daniel Webster	FAIRFAX, Ann Elizabeth	18 Oct 1892	45
TYLER, Frank	FAIRFAX, Mary E	9 May 1894	48
TYLER, George W	DEAVERS, Catharine	10 Mar 1857	3
TYLER, James W	DEAVERS, Caroline	3 Jan 1860	4
TYLER, R T /c	STROTHER, Catherine /c	7 Dec 1876	21

TYLER, William /c	TURNER, Sallie /c	8 Jan 1888	38
TYRRELL, Eugene	JAGETTS, Mary E	6 Jan 1882	29
TYRRELL, Wilson /c	MORTON, Fannie /c	17 Dec 1878	24
TYSON, Andrew H	BUXTON, Clara F	9 Apr 1890	41
TYSON, Horace A	HOFFMAN, Rose A	4 Apr 1932	137
TYSSOWSKI, Thaddeus M	GREEN, Alice W	23 Feb 1881	28
UHTROFF, Edward J	SCHEVING, Myrtle K	1 Aug 1925	112
UNDERWOOD, Edwin M	ALLEN, Enid S /wid	16 Oct 1916	91
UNGER, Carl H	TRACEY, Frances E	24 Jan 1925	110
UNVERZAGT, Jonas Theodore	HIETT, Katie Lee	14 Jun 1899	56
UPDEGROVE, Frank E	SENNE, Hazel E	8 May 1915	88
UPMAN, Frank Jr	CLARK, Louise	5 Jan 1926	113
URAL, Johnnie /c	DAVIS, Marthenia /c	4 Dec 1904	67
URICHS, Robert	MEYER, Bessie	17 Nov 1919	97
URON, William Seltzer	BAKER, Ida M G	2 Sep 1916	90
USILTON, Norman D	DUVALL, Annie L	15 Apr 1908	74
UTTERBACK, B D	WRENN, Ellen E	3 Jun 1869	11
UTTERBACK, Benjamin D Jr /wid	GAINES, Susie V	1 Apr 1884	33
UTTERBACK, Enos M	NICHOL, Ethel May	27 Oct 1918	95
UTTERBACK, Ralph M	COMPTON, Merle L	2 Apr 1926	114
VALENTINE, Charles E	GONDOR, Sarah M	24 Jun 1925	111
VALENTINE, John R /c	HENDERSON, Eva /c	8 Sep 1904	67
VALENTINE, Joseph /c wid	COATES, Martha /c wid	14 Sep 1922	103
VALK, Nicholas Snowden	TALIAFERRO, Roberta	29 Aug 1894	48
VAN DE GRIFT, William B	BLACKMAN, Dorothy E	21 Jan 1933	141
VAN DEN AREND, Frederick	DRAIN, Gertrude V	27 Nov 1923	106
VAN METER, Solomon L Jr	CHAPIN, Lois	31 May 1924	108
VAN NOTE, Charles	LANGER, Edna E	8 Kim 1027	114
VAN PATTEN, Frank L	BROWN, Nina O	9 Aug 1900	59
VAN PATTEN, Herbert W	COCKERILLE, Sarah Margaret	22 Nov 1930	130
VAN SICKLER, Elisha Holmes	JAMES, Margaret Virginia	24 Oct 1893	47
VAN SICKLER, Scott	HESS, Mary E	24 May 1899	56
VANARDELL, James William	CANFIELD, Mary Caroline	7 Nov 1922	103
VANDERSLICE, William T	GHEEN, Sarah Q	15 Oct 1868	10
VANDERSLOOT, F E /wid	HANNA, Mary Ann	27 Jun 1877	22
VANDEVENTER, Henry S	WHINEREY, Adelia M	29 Oct 1908	75
VANDEVENTER, Maurice G	WILLCOXEN, Bessie	26 May 1879	25
VANDYCK, Frank R	HUNTER, Nellie D	7 Apr 1880	26
VANDYCK, Rob H	RICE, Mary I	9 Aug 1924	109
VANSKIVER, Charles	TRAMMELL, Rosie L	11 Jul 1899	56
VASS, Henry /c	LEWIS, Mary E /c	10 Aug 1886	36
VAUGHAN, James W	DAVIS, Gertrude	12 Jun 1912	82

VAUGHAN, Samuel B /wid	PLITT, Sabina F M	11 Mar 1908	74
VAUGHN, John E	LADUE, Alice E	8 Oct 1887	38
VEACH, C C	LEWIS, Ava	23 Dec 1896	52
VEALE, Thomas	DE BELL, Mary E	24 Feb 1859	4
VEIL, Fred William	STILES, Viola Grace	30 Jan 1933	141
VEITCH, William H /wid	CAMP, Olive J /wid	10 Aug 1898	55
VENEY, Noble /c wid	BUSH, Nannie /c	1 Oct 1887	38
VENEY, Richard /c wid	WOODEN, Rebecca /c	17 Jan 1894	47
VETTER, John H	PHILLIPS, Lois E	8 Sep 1926	116
VIANDS, F M	BAUCKMAN, Erie Hudson	6 Jun 1906	71
VIDETTO, John N	TERRY, Emma C	9 May 1918	94
VIGMAN, James	LINDSAY, Mary W	30 Aug 1932	139
VIOLETT, Thompson D	LEE, Minnie	26 Jun 1907	73
VIOLETT, Thompson W	STONE, Josephine	9 Jun 1859	4
VIOLETT, Willie J	GODFREY, Effie S /wid	11 Sep 1929	126
VIRTS, Jacob Edward Lee	HUNT, Hattie M	25 Oct 1893	47
VOEGLER, Lewis C /wid	SHREVE, Ruth L	17 Apr 1920	98
VOGT, F H	KERNS, Bertha	4 Feb 1920	97
VOIGT, William E	BEARD, Mildred C	30 Jun 1932	138
VON DACHENHAUSEN, Alexander	STEELE, Bessie L	14 Sep 1897	53
VORHEES, Alfred	WALKER, Maggie L	24 Feb 1881	28
WADE, Otis /c	LEE, Bertha /c	14 Jun 1923	105
WADE, Otis R /c wid	TAYLOR, Martha J /c	9 Dec 1903	66
WADLINGTON, David H /c	DRURY, Gladys L /c	8 Jun 1926	115
WAILES, William M Jr	KERR, Ruth D	20 Apr 1925	111
WAITE, George T /div	DAVIS, Mildred M	31 Dec 1914	87
WAKEFIELD, Andrew H	HUNSBERGER, Hannah M	15 Mar 1899	56
WAKEFIELD, E H	MUCH, Mamie G	2 May 1915	88
WAKEFIELD, Elhanan Winchester	TENNISON, Rebecca M	5 Sep 1865	6
WAKEMAN, B O	DRIVER, Crystal	14 Jun 1930	128
WALES, Charles A /c	BRENT, Catharine A /c	30 Sep 1891	43
WALKER, Albert Rhett /wid	HUNTER, Susan	25 Sep 1902	63
WALKER, Archie H	CUMMINS, Sadie V	19 Sep 1925	112
WALKER, Charles /c wid	STEWART, Rosetta /c	23 Jun 1910	78
WALKER, Charlie /c	PARKER, Maria /c	6 Aug 1901	60
WALKER, Clarence M	ROBEY, Annie M	27 Feb 1900	58
WALKER, Delbert A	WAKEFIELD, Bessie T	5 Nov 1917	93
WALKER, E Minor	AVERY, Dorothy	7 Jun 1930	128
WALKER, Edwin /c	NORMAN, Evangeline /c	19 Jun 1920	98
WALKER, Frank H /wid	JARVIS, Edith B	5 Jun 1901	60
WALKER, Gabriel /c	GASKINS, Maria /c	15 Apr 1880	26
WALKER, Harry J	FAULKNER, Helen W	27 Nov 1907	74

WALKER, Herbert W /wid	GIBBS, Frances T /wid	31 Oct 1925	113
WALKER, James	CRUMP, Lettie E	3 Sep 1895	49
WALKER, James H	SHREVE, Jennie	6 Nov 1884	34
WALKER, James P /c	NICKENS, Fanny /c	7 Nov 1901	61
WALKER, James T /c div	LOTT, Lillian T /c	1 Apr 1915	88
WALKER, John /c	JOHNSON, Annie /c	7 Aug 1890	41
WALKER, John	PATTON, Mollie V /wid	26 Jan 1905	68
WALKER, John S	CUMMINGS, Martha A	10 Jun 1858	3
WALKER, John W	ROBEY, Ada	12 Feb 1884	32
WALKER, Newton /wid	CHRISTIAN, Catharine /wid	16 Sep 1866	6
WALKER, Paul A	THORNTON, Mary E	12 Dec 1931	135
WALKER, R W /c	MONROE, Chloe /c	29 Apr 1915	88
WALKER, Richard F	OLIVER, Ann M	27 May 1875	18
WALKER, Thomas H /wid	CATON, Sarah J /wid	14 Feb 1883	31
WALKER, Wilbur S	BOWMAN, Bertha C	15 Aug 1914	87
WALKER, William /c wid	DAVIS, Alcinda /c	16 Nov 1886	36
WALKER, William C	NIXON, Bertha J	7 Jan 1903	64
WALKER, William T	KIDWELL, Margaret T	12 Apr 1880	26
WALLACE, Frank /c	PITCHER, Emma /c	24 Feb 1882	30
WALLACE, Starling L	BLETH, Margaret M /div	3 Oct 1931	134
WALLER, George W /c	GOFNEY, Fannie /c	26 Dec 1889	40
WALLER, Silas /c wid	SMITH, Emily /c wid	30 Nov 1899	57
WALSH, John P	O'HARA, Margaret Mary	24 Aug 1931	133
WALTER, Amos N	JENNINGS, Thelma Irene	8 Jul 1932	138
WALTER, Charles Samuel	WICKHAM, Helen Joan	24 Jan 1933	141
WALTER, J W	RITENOUR, Annie	15 Dec 1897	53
WALTERS, Alexander B	STORM, Anna W	8 Nov 1877	22
WALTERS, Christopher C	PATTERSON, Annie L	27 Feb 1881	28
WALTERS, J W	TYSON, L H	18 Apr 1867	9
WALTERS, James W	VANDYCK, Fannie	30 Nov 1876	21
WALTERS, Julian M	KIRBY, Martha S	20 Dec 1870	13
WALTERS, Lucien N	DUVALL, Leonora J	13 Jun 1878	23
WALTERS, Norman J /c	TURNER, Martha /c	4 Jun 1896	51
WALTERS, Walter C	COOK, Louise M	20 Sep 1930	129
WALTERS, William /wid	MONEY, Rachel L /wid	5 Jan 1890	41
WALTON, James N	MAGARITY, V A	13 Jan 1875	18
WALTON, Kirby F	REID, Lula M	10 Jul 1907	73
WALTON, Walter	WRIGHT, Anna S	16 Feb 1864	5
WANDLING, Homer L	WALTERS, Pearl F	29 Sep 1920	99
WANE, Benjamin /c	NERO, Rachel /c	29 Jan 1885	34
WAPLE, George H	CLARK, Nannie B	4 Dec 1901	61
WAPLE, John H	KIDWELL, Isabella	30 Dec 1873	16

WAPLE, John H /wid	MCDONALD, Martha J /wid	30 Dec 1916	91
WAPLE, Rufus C	MURRAY, Virginia D /wid	16 Jul 1932	138
WARD, Amasa J /div	DICK, Agatha E	17 Jun 1931	132
WARD, Charles N	DUFFY, Mary T	30 Apr 1932	137
WARD, Claude M /wid	KRETEN, Sophie E	2 Apr 1932	137
WARD, Elzie William /c	HOLT, Vashti /c	4 Nov 1933	144
WARD, George /c	TAYLOR, Elton /c	2 Feb 1882	29
WARD, John M /wid	EDDEN, Clara E	4 Jun 1931	132
WARD, William E	LEWIS, Gertrude A	6 Sep 1930	129
WARD, William H /c wid	GREEN, Georgia /c wid	7 Jul 1919	96
WARD, William R	MARDERS, Susie	25 Jan 1881	28
WARDER, Daniel E	RIKER, Lottie E	29 Jun 1903	65
WARE, John B	BRIGGS, Marguerite	16 Dec 1924	110
WARE, Macon	BYRNE, Kathryn M	29 May 1918	94
WARE, Sigmund S	WALKER, Elizabeth M	31 Dec 1878	24
WARFIELD, Richard D /wid	GUNNELL, Martha	27 Sep 1859	4
WARFORD, William Henry	THOMPSON, Elizabeth Baker	7 Apr 1864	5
WARNER, Frederick E	REYNOLDS, Lelia	26 Oct 1910	79
WARNER, Haywood /c	JAMES, Evelyn /c	1 Dec 1928	123
WARNER, Lewis C	DEWEY, Emma A	1 Jan 1871	13
WARNER, Ocicolo	FULK, Effie T	21 Apr 1920	98
WARNIG, Paul E	PARKER, Eva F	5 Sep 1925	112
WASHBURN, Isaac	ALLISTON, Mary E	31 Dec 1856	2
WASHBURN, M R	ALLISON, Jane F	18 Mar 1858	3
WASHINGTON, Ashby /c	HENDERSON, Nora /c	23 Jul 1924	109
WASHINGTON, Charles /c	LEWIS, Clara	1 Dec 1909	78
WASHINGTON, Daniel /c	LUCAS, Gusta /c	22 Nov 1910	79
WASHINGTON, George /c	WELCOME, Celia	27 Jul 1871	14
WASHINGTON, George W /c wid	NELSON, Caroline /c	20 Nov 1904	67
WASHINGTON, James	TURNER, Mary Elizabeth	8 Aug 1869	11
WASHINGTON, James /c	ADAMS, Edith /c	24 Mar 1913	84
WASHINGTON, Leonard C /c	HAILSTROCHS, Alice M /c	15 Aug 1931	133
WASHINGTON, Roscoe /c	BAILEY, Evelyn Eva /c	2 Sep 1931	133
WASHINGTON, Simon /c	SHELTON, Queen /c	7 Aug 1884	33
WATERS, Zack J /div	HELMS, Minnie K	18 Oct 1933	144
WATHEN, George C Jr	SISSON, Madeleine /div	18 Aug 1928	122
WATKINS, Charles T	HAUXHURST, Anna M	12 Dec 1867	8
WATKINS, David T	STRETCH, Edith M	5 Sep 1925	112
WATKINS, Edgar W	ENGLAND, Matie E	21 Oct 1880	27
WATKINS, George L	GHEEN, Hannah M	11 Sep 1867	8
WATKINS, Harry M	JONES, Clara Ethel	3 Oct 1906	71
WATKINS, Howard R /c	DAVIS, Lucy M /c	23 Jun 1932	138

WATKINS, Joseph Francis	GRILLBORTZER, Mary Catharine	2 Jun 1902	62
WATKINS, Warfield	THOMAS, Virginia	31 Jan 1894	47
WATKINS, William F	MILLS, Laura	10 Sep 1884	33
WATSON, Charles /c	TURNER, Martha /c	31 Jan 1878	23
WATSON, Edward	WELLS, Frances G	8 May 1931	132
WATSON, Garfield c /c	WAYNES, Ruthanna /c	28 Nov 1906	72
WATSON, James F	CAUSER, Ruth M	21 Apr 1926	114
WATSON, James H	MATHEWS, Emma J	29 Dec 1890	42
WATSON, O W	BARNES, Bessie J	2 Oct 1923	106
WATSON, Robert /c	COOPER, Jeanie /c	25 Dec 1898	56
WATSON, Robert /c	BAILEY, Gertrude /c	14 Dec 1913	85
WATSON, William	BREEDEN, Edith	30 Jan 1911	80
WATT, Egbert T	FRENZEL, Grace E	30 Jun 1917	92
WATTS, Peter	MUNDY, Hannah /wid	15 Feb 1868	9
WATTS, Robert /c	CLAY, Maggie /c	15 Sep 1891	43
WAUGH, Reubin Eugene /c	MARLOW, Irene Gladys /c	8 Mar 1933	141
WAY, N S	TROTH, Mary H	1 Jan 1873	16
WAYLAND, C O /wid	SPIVEY, Ruby Lee	25 Jul 1911	81
WAYNES, Ernest /c	WILLIAMS, Hettie /c	11 Feb 1906	70
WAYNES, Seth /c	WILLIAMS, Edna /c	16 Sep 1909	77
WEADON, Eugene F	DENTY, Mary E /div	17 Dec 1929	127
WEAKLEY, Harry M	SEAL, Della	14 May 1927	118
WEAST, James H /wid	BUTLER, Frances	19 Aug 1870	13
WEAST, John E	CAMPBELL, Henrietta	6 Apr 1880	26
WEAVER, Allen G	BUCKLEY, Anna	1 May 1926	114
WEAVER, Allen M	HALL, Carrie C	10 Jul 1917	92
WEAVER, David M	LOCKRIE, Florence M	9 Nov 1931	134
WEAVER, George W /c wid	SUMMERS, Sophia /c	1 Jul 1925	112
WEAVER, Robert /c wid	COATS, Carrie /c	27 Aug 1918	94
WEAVER, Walter /c	BALL, Harriett E /c	6 Oct 1896	51
WEAVER, Walter /c wid	CHEW, Betsey A /c wid	18 Dec 1919	97
WEAVER, Wash	BAYLOR, Lavinia	1 Jun 1871	13
WEBB, Allen E /c	SIMMS, Catherine E /c	27 Apr 1931	132
WEBB, George W /c	GLASCOE, Isabelle W /c	12 Mar 1930	127
WEBB, James E	ARNOLD, Eugenia N	17 Aug 1892	45
WEBB, Levi /c	GRAY, Sarah /c	9 Sep 1920	99
WEBB, Thomas /c	NICKENS, Jennie /c	20 Apr 1892	42
WEBSTER, Francis B	ANSLEY, Abigail F	3 Jul 1859	4
WEBSTER, Frederick A	JONES, Mary L	1 Mar 1910	78
WEBSTER, Haney /c	FERRIS, Martha /c	11 Apr 1901	60
WEBSTER, John R	SPEER, Eva Helen	1 Apr 1918	94
WEBSTER, Wilson /c wid	EDWARDS, Martha /c wid	3 May 1894	48

WEDDING, Ashton C	SMITH, Lillian F /div	1 May 1929	124
WEHRLY, Max S	COX, Maxine F	21 Sep 1932	139
WEILER, Joseph G	WHITE, Blanche R	21 Nov 1928	123
WEIR, Edgar W /wid	HOLDEN, Phebe	9 Apr 1902	62
WEIR, Tasker M	BIRCH, Eva S	18 Jun 1914	86
WEISENFLUCH, Irwin	WEIBEL, Louise E	9 Sep 1926	116
WELCH, Eugene	DONALDSON, Marion	27 Sep 1887	38
WELCH, Henry A	WILKINS, Lucy V	24 Nov 1927	120
WELDING, John F	WILLIAMS, Myrtle C	23 Apr 1914	86
WELLER, Galen Mark	SUTPHIN, Gertrude P	5 Oct 1931	134
WELLER, M C	MCFARLAND, Lillian G	10 Feb 1906	70
WELLINGTON, Malcolm	LOWE, Laura Jeane	6 Jul 1920	98
WELLS, Alfred A	DAVIS, Alice E	29 Jun 1910	79
WELLS, Charlie	VIOLETT, Nellie C	5 Nov 1914	87
WELLS, Claiborne	CUNNINGHAM, Mimie V	23 Jun 1904	66
WELLS, Edward	KIDWELL, Mary E	23 Jan 1890	41
WELLS, Fenton G	HOPKINS, Anny V	2 Jan 1868	8
WELLS, Henry H	TAYLOR, Mary L	13 Nov 1916	91
WELLS, Homer S	POWERS, Doris M	23 Dec 1933	145
WELLS, Ira C	BALL, Florence	29 Dec 1903	66
WELLS, J R	BYRNES, Daisy M	28 Nov 1900	59
WELLS, James H /wid	CORRISON, Martha /wid	22 Jun 1903	64
WELLS, James Henry /wid	MULLEN, Susan /wid	8 Mar 1891	43
WELLS, James I	ADAMS, Mary S	24 Aug 1879	25
WELLS, John H	THOMPSON, Estella M	20 Feb 1884	33
WELLS, John H	CURTIS, May	26 Dec 1922	104
WELLS, John L	HAMMOND, Lula J	21 Nov 1931	134
WELLS, John R	MULHOLLAND, Katie	11 Sep 1912	83
WELLS, John T	LEE, Frances M T	22 Dec 1891	44
WELLS, McKim Holliday	FORD, Pattie B	25 Feb 1874	17
WELLS, R S	SMITH, Celia	14 Oct 1903	65
WELLS, Robert /c wid	MOSELY, Cornelia /c wid	1 Sep 1878	24
WELLS, Robert	MULHOLLAND, Nannie	7 Jul 1898	54
WELLS, Walter F	BURKE, Mary Frances	25 Nov 1924	110
WELSH, John L	KLINE, Rose /div	30 Aug 1930	129
WENDEL, John H	HARTY, Georgia E	10 Oct 1931	134
WENZEL, George L	BORDEN, Maggie M	8 May 1907	73
WEST, Charles J /c	MARSHALL, Hilda /c	25 Jun 1930	128
WEST, Charles T /c	HILL, Mary /c	6 Feb 1887	37
WEST, Clarence	DAVIS, Susan M	3 Jul 1901	60
WEST, Daniel /c	ALEXANDER, Fannie /c	29 Dec 1872	15
WEST, Edward /c	SPAIN, Amanda /c wid	8 Aug 1914	87

WEST, George C	BROWN, Mabel V	26 Sep 1906	*71*
WEST, J S	KIRBY, Nellie M	14 Jul 1897	*53*
WEST, William A /c	HENDERSON, Idella /c	23 Sep 1897	*53*
WEST, William L	BERRY, Mary M	8 Oct 1923	*106*
WESTBROOK, Harvey A	CARLIN, Louise M	22 Sep 1928	*122*
WESTCOTT, Walter T	GALPIN, Ida G	19 Feb 1892	*44*
WESTGATE, George /wid	CROWELL, Nora	17 Apr 1907	*72*
WHALEN, John W	BUTT, Mary R	24 Nov 1886	*37*
WHALEN, John William	PETTITT, Mary L	3 Jan 1895	*49*
WHALEN, Milton	BEACH, Roxey	7 Jan 1876	*20*
WHALEN, Paul	SIMONDS, Zodie	9 Jul 1929	*125*
WHALES, James /c wid	CARTER, Millie /c	15 Jun 1905	*68*
WHALEY, Carl	MANKIN, Cecil	20 Nov 1901	*61*
WHALEY, Charles W /c	HENDERSON, Pauline A /c	15 May 1873	*16*
WHALEY, Everett B	CROSS, Fannie C	1 Jan 1890	*41*
WHALEY, Frank M	HUTCHISON, Elenora	1 Jan 1884	*32*
WHALEY, George W	WORSTER, Margaret E	8 Oct 1854	*1*
WHALEY, James W	ORRISON, Mary J	5 Mar 1867	*7*
WHALEY, John R	NEALE, Sarah Jane	17 Sep 1870	*13*
WHALEY, John W	HUTCHISON, Olive M	28 Feb 1912	*82*
WHALEY, Walter S	UTTERBACK, Jennie V	24 Feb 1867	*7*
WHARTON, Dabney M	LOVING, Helen S	4 Dec 1903	*65*
WHEELER, Clarence W	HODGES, Mary Alice L	27 Apr 1929	*124*
WHEELER, Earl August	SUTHERLAND, George Ann	14 Nov 1917	*93*
WHEELER, James A	WYNKOOP, Martina	1 Sep 1897	*53*
WHEELER, Leslie A	WEBSTER, Louise Price /wid	17 Nov 1927	*119*
WHEELER, Philip E	COULTER, Lou Emma	23 Feb 1892	*44*
WHEELER, Ray P	NISWANDER, Edna C	17 Jun 1914	*86*
WHEELER, Temple G	CALJOUW, Helen	1 May 1928	*121*
WHEELER, Victor B	ISHKANIAN, Grace M	22 Jul 1923	*105*
WHEELER, Walter /c	LEE, Lucy /c	28 Oct 1922	*103*
WHELAN, Augustus	WIET, Candace M	11 Jan 1894	*47*
WHITBECK, Isaiah /wid	CORNELL, Martha /wid	8 Jan 1873	*16*
WHITCOMB, Jack	VAN HOESEN, Dorothy M	20 Mar 1920	*97*
WHITE, Edward F	MILLS, Agnes /wid	11 Jun 1921	*100*
WHITE, Frederick H	RIXEY, Lillian P	15 Oct 1913	*85*
WHITE, George	JAMES, Mary N	18 Dec 1901	*62*
WHITE, George H /c wid	WILLIAMS, Matilda /c wid	12 Apr 1922	*102*
WHITE, Henry R /c	STEWART, Leebertha Ann /c	10 Aug 1892	*45*
WHITE, J M /wid	YOUNG, Ada E	5 Oct 1907	*73*
WHITE, Roscoe T	RIELY, Mary V	16 Aug 1918	*94*
WHITE, Silas /c	SHIRLEY, Mary J /c	24 Dec 1891	*44*

WHITE, Thomas H	HEAD, Mary A	11 Oct 1893	46
WHITE, Woodson /c wid	EDWARDS, Georgie /c wid	29 Dec 1891	44
WHITEHEAD, Joseph W	WILLIAMS, Salina	1863	16
WHITESELL, Clee	DAVIDSON, Virginia	17 Jan 1925	110
WHITESELL, Seber K	SPEER, Eunice D	13 Jun 1916	90
WHITING, Albert /c wid	GLASS, Maria F /c wid	5 Sep 1891	43
WHITING, Edward S Jr	JERMAN, Emma S	21 Jun 1917	92
WHITING, James /c	JOHNSON, Flora /c wid	19 Oct 1876	21
WHITING, Neville H	HYDE, Meta Herbert	25 Oct 1881	29
WHITING, Thomas	PEARSON, Virginia	6 Sep 1870	13
WHITMER, Grettan B	HOLSINGER, Mary V	5 Sep 1932	139
WHITMER, Martin L	RUFFNER, Mary E	25 Jun 1930	128
WHITMORE, Warren M	CHAMBERS, Elizabeth L	5 Apr 1926	114
WHITNEY, Clinton R	ELLS, Blanche L	24 Aug 1907	73
WHITNEY, William /c	MARSHALL, Elenora /c wid	20 Sep 1926	116
WHITTAKER, Benjamin	BICKSLER, Mary C	28 Jan 1868	9
WHITTHORNE, Brown Ridley	ARTHUR, Virginia Fincklen	1 Jan 1933	141
WIBERT, Isaac /wid	DAVIS, Hannah C /wid	11 Dec 1856	2
WIEHLE, J Robert	SHERWOOD, Marianna	4 Jan 1893	46
WIGGATON, Fred /wid	SPROUSE, Mary E /wid	29 Mar 1925	111
WIGHT, Henry T	DICKENS, Harriet W	6 Dec 1866	7
WIILETT, John W	WRENN, Alice V	20 Jun 1900	58
WIILETT, Norman A	BESECKER, Janet C	27 May 1932	137
WILLSON, Peter C	TERRETT, Hannah B	20 Nov 1882	30
WILSON, Clarence Lee	POOL, Blanche V	11 Apr 1916	90
WILSON, Columbus V	HARRISON, Ida S	11 Jan 1887	37
WILSON, Edward Homer	BREEN, Annie Mary	21 Oct 1931	134
WILSON, Folger P	TYSON, Frances J	5 Dec 1871	14
WILSON, James	BALLENGER, Lillie	9 Sep 1896	51
WILSON, John C	CATTS, Annie S	27 feb 1877	21
WILSON, Powell /c	JOHNSON, Jane /c	27 Dec 1874	18
WILSON, Richard /c wid	JONES, Maggie A /c wid	23 Jan 1908	74
WILSON, Thornton /c	JOHNSON, Anna /c	25 Dec 1877	23
WILSON, William /c	MOORE, Alcinda /c	20 Jun 1886	36
WILCOX, Jesse M	MILLER, Flora E	17 Oct 1914	87
WILCOX, Thomas A	GREEN, Ida H	11 Jun 1926	115
WILDS, Robert F	TRUSLOW, Janie C /wid	19 Dec 1923	107
WILEY, C E	DENHAM, Marie T /div	16 Dec 1912	83
WILEY, Charles Leslie	SEYMOUR, Violet Elizabeth	21 Feb 1925	110
WILEY, D J	PEARSON, Mary M	8 Apr 1868	9
WILEY, Edgar McCarty	WEBSTER, Mary Lee /div	1 Jun 1916	90
WILEY, George	MITCHELL, Sarah E /wid	11 Feb 1897	52

WILEY, Harry C /wid	MONEY, Hattie H	4 Oct 1888	39
WILEY, James	DAWSON, Martha A	13 May 1869	11
WILEY, Jesse H	SPEER, Harriet C	29 Jan 1903	64
WILEY, John W	PEARSON, Simonetta	28 May 1857	3
WILEY, R S	JONES, Bettie Sue	3 Sep 1902	63
WILEY, Robert	LEE, Anna Elizabeth	27 Jun 1867	7
WILEY, Walter Groomes	WRENN, Mattie	20 May 1885	35
WILEY, William Henry	FOLLIN, Rachael E	12 Dec 1894	48
WILKERSON, Armstead /c	DUNCAN, Katie /c	26 Jun 1904	66
WILKINS, Arthur /div	DUDLEY, Genevieve C /div	6 Jan 1926	113
WILKINS, Burr /c	LUCKETT, Lizzie /c	20 Feb 1879	25
WILKINSON, Harry H	BONHAM, Helen E	25 Nov 1924	110
WILKINSON, Hense S /c	NOKES, Gertrude /c	25 Dec 1926	117
WILKINSON, William C	NICHOLSON, Eva T	25 Aug 1886	36
WILKS, Edward J	BYRNE, Virginia Louise	2 Feb 1921	100
WILLARD, George T	KIDWELL, Maud R	23 Feb 1912	82
WILLCOXON, Albert T	ESKRIDGE, Mary H	20 Apr 1858	3
WILLCOXON, William D	MANNING, Mary	7 Nov 1876	21
WILLETT, James H	THOMPSON, Grace A	8 Dec 1909	78
WILLETT, James Thomas	KIDWELL, Ann V	27 Jul 1869	11
WILLIAMS, Albert /c	JONES, Blanche A /c	28 Feb 1884	33
WILLIAMS, Albert K	WARFIELD, Bettie V	27 Feb 1910	78
WILLIAMS, Alfred /wid	WILLIAMS, Rose Ann	5 Dec 1867	8
WILLIAMS, Ashton /c	PARKER, Alice /c	22 Jul 1880	27
WILLIAMS, Barnett	LEWIS, Maggie A	7 Sep 1870	13
WILLIAMS, Benjamin F /c	NEAL, Perly /c	26 Dec 1909	78
WILLIAMS, Carl D	KIDWELL, Mary F	24 Jul 1907	73
WILLIAMS, Charles M /wid	LACY, Virginia E	18 Dec 1912	83
WILLIAMS, Charles S	WHITE, Ruth V	6 Oct 1928	122
WILLIAMS, Claude E	ALCOCK, Reva D	2 Nov 1932	139
WILLIAMS, Dade /c	HONESTY, Victoria /c	22 Nov 1911	81
WILLIAMS, Earl	RECTOR, Mary Berry	13 May 1925	111
WILLIAMS, Ernest	TAYLOR, Alice	28 Aug 1894	48
WILLIAMS, Frederick /c	HONESTY, Ollie /c	16 Jun 1910	78
WILLIAMS, George /wid	BAKER, Julia /wid	20 Jul 1873	16
WILLIAMS, George /c	TURNER, Matilda L	14 Jul 1898	54
WILLIAMS, George A	KIDWELL, Hattie C	9 Aug 1894	48
WILLIAMS, George A /c	WATERS, Mazie /c	11 Jun 1915	88
WILLIAMS, George H	COCK, Carrie M	28 May 1867	7
WILLIAMS, Henry /c	CARTER, Armenia /c	19 Feb 1881	28
WILLIAMS, Henry /c wid	BLACKBURN, Martha G	4 Nov 1881	29
WILLIAMS, Henry /c	CORBIN, Harriet /c wid	7 Mar 1885	34

WILLIAMS, Howard	PETTITT, Mabel E	26 Jul 1915	89
WILLIAMS, Howard /c	WOODLAND, Gertrude /c	28 Dec 1927	120
WILLIAMS, James J /c wid	HONESTY, Catherine /c	3 Nov 1886	36
WILLIAMS, James K /c	QUANDER, Elizabeth /c	23 Apr 1870	12
WILLIAMS, Jeltie /c	WOODEN, Drusilla /c	13 Oct 1927	119
WILLIAMS, Jesse Z /c	WOODEN, Nellie /c	27 Sep 1916	90
WILLIAMS, John	FISHER, Rebecca T	10 Jun 1866	6
WILLIAMS, John /c	FORD, Eliza /c	9 Dec 1875	19
WILLIAMS, John /c	BRADFORD, Elizabeth /c wid	8 Jan 1878	23
WILLIAMS, John /c	STYLES, Mary Eva /c	3 May 1906	70
WILLIAMS, John /c	BANKS, Carrie /c	5 Nov 1908	75
WILLIAMS, John B	CROWELL, Nettie	3 Feb 1897	52
WILLIAMS, John T /c wid	HALL, Georgianna /c	15 Sep 1891	43
WILLIAMS, Joseph W	BROWN, Cora B	22 Jun 1876	20
WILLIAMS, Loyd	DUSTIN, Frances	28 Sep 1931	133
WILLIAMS, Mark A	WYMAN, Amelia H	11 Dec 1926	117
WILLIAMS, Moses T	WELLS, Sarah E	19 Nov 1879	25
WILLIAMS, Philip A	HURLEY, Bettie L	25 Dec 1931	135
WILLIAMS, Randolph /c	BROOKS, Annie /c wid	24 Sep 1905	69
WILLIAMS, Rev. Marshall /c wid	EDMONDS, Katie /c	15 Sep 1885	35
WILLIAMS, Robert /c	ROBINSON, Lucy /c	21 Apr 1881	28
WILLIAMS, Sandford /c	TURNER, Mary /c	30 Apr 1890	41
WILLIAMS, Smith J	DYER, Ruth Omega	9 Sep 1914	87
WILLIAMS, Thomas /c	FORD, Matilda /c	23 Dec 1880	27
WILLIAMS, Thomas A	BYRNE, Annie Lula	7 Dec 1904	67
WILLIAMS, Victor F	SMITH, Lyne S	13 Oct 1928	123
WILLIAMS, W S	GRIMES, A M	18 Oct 1874	17
WILLIAMS, Williard /c	RICKS, Eleanor /c	23 Aug 1923	106
WILLIAMSON, Earl	WILLIAMSON, Daisy Belle	27 Jun 1931	132
WILLIGE, Augustus	MCCARDEL, Annabel /div	5 Aug 1918	94
WILLIS, Edward M	TROTH, Maria S	1 Jan 1873	16
WILLIS, Linwood I	CURTIS, Opal G	7 Jun 1928	121
WILLIS, Perry G	WITHERINGTON, Cora	3 Mar 1931	131
WILLIS, Vattell McKinley /c	LIGGINS, Rosa Ethel /c	22 Nov 1927	120
WILLMAN, John P	ROGERS, Ann C	24 Nov 1927	120
WINCHESTER, Theodore W /c	WHITE, Bernice I /c	13 Feb 1932	136
WINE, Hubert	CROWELL, Maggie	24 Apr 1907	72
WINES, Edward F	BLADEN, Fannie H	5 Jun 1911	81
WINES, L W	STAMP, Ruth H	17 Oct 1910	79
WINES, William A	TRICKETT, Lucinda	31 Oct 1900	59
WINEBRENNER, George T /div	FERTELIER, Romaine E .	12 Aug 1932	138
WINSLOW, Gilbert F Jr	WILLIE, Mary Beatrice	18 Jun 1919	96

WINSTON, A C /wid	ROBERSON, Belle	9 Oct 1892	45
WINSTON, John /c	BURK, Nellie /c	29 Nov 1888	39
WINSTON, Willie /c	WINSTON, Sadie /c wid	15 Aug 1933	143
WINTER, Alpheus	WIEHE, Louise E O	7 Oct 1908	75
WINTERS, George	THOMPSON, Ethel L	1 May 1933	142
WINTERWERP, John C	KERBY, Margaret Norfolk	26 Oct 1898	55
WINZEL, George	JENKINS, Carrie M	24 Dec 1875	18
WISE, George T	KIDWELL, Alice	16 Nov 1915	89
WISE, George W /wid	RASS, Mary	29 Dec 1897	54
WISEMAN, Herbert G	PHELPS, Elizabeth	2 Jan 1932	136
WITHERS, Henry	HALL, Ellen	28 Aug 1870	13
WITHERS, James E	JERMAN, Priscilla A	5 Aug 1869	11
WOJCIK, Stanley	WILDMAN, Audrey	18 Apr 1931	131
WOLF, George P	GRAHAM, Belle Edwin	15 Jun 1916	90
WOLF, William B	PACK, Ruth G	29 Jan 1926	113
WOLFE, Arthur V	COLLINS, Sadie V	21 Dec 1912	83
WOOD, Charles C	WALL, Delia G /wid	7 Dec 1878	24
WOOD, Clarence Cornelius	DOWNING, Hattie N	17 Jun 1884	33
WOOD, Edgar Norman	HEDDERMAN, Mary Gertrude	22 Apr 1919	95
WOOD, Elmer	GALT, Virginia P	20 Jun 1929	125
WOOD, James Bentley	PIERPOINT, Mary Josephine	6 Jul 1931	132
WOOD, James R /c	SPRIGG, Matteele E /c	25 Sep 1913	85
WOOD, John A	JEWELL, Ginnie	2 Jul 1890	46
WOOD, Mark	DOVE, Carrie	7 May 1894	48
WOOD, Robert W	BALL, Pauline E	29 Aug 1924	110
WOOD, Stephen C Jr	HUNT, Eulah	25 Jun 1919	96
WOOD, Thomas J Jr	NORTH, Marion H	23 Oct 1930	130
WOOD, William A	CLEM, Viola E	29 Dec 1920	98
WOOD, Wilmer O	COOK, Edna M	4 Oct 1930	129
WOODALL, James	MEEKIUS, Virginia	6 Feb 1929	124
WOODARD, George R	GAINES, Alice	24 Dec 1888	39
WOODEN, Baker /c	HENDERSON, Emma /c	7 Aug 1924	109
WOODEN, Delbert /c	GILES, Nellie /c	18 Sep 1932	139
WOODEN, Samuel /c	DIXON, Ella /c	23 Dec 1897	54
WOODEN, Samuel /c wid	DORSEY, Rachel /c	17 Jun 1910	78
WOODEN, Thomas /c	EDWARDS, Ellen /c	18 Dec 1890	42
WOODEN, Wesley /c	NORRIS, Elizabeth /c	23 May 1930	128
WOODFIELD, Joseph F	WEAVER, Mary E	24 Apr 1918	94
WOODLEY, Joseph /c	HONESTY, Ruth /c	12 Aug 1914	87
WOODLEY, Joseph /wid	HENSEN, Rosie	27 Sep 1923	106
WOODRING, James H /wid	GALT, Nancy	28 Apr 1927	118
WOODRUFF, William M	PETTITT, Lottie E	18 Mar 1901	60

WOODWARD, Thomas D	RYAN, Josephine F	7 Oct 1896	*51*
WOODY, Arthur */c*	LEE, Bessie */c*	25 Jul 1890	*42*
WOODYARD, James P	WOODYARD, Margaret V	19 Dec 1872	*15*
WOODYARD, John F	MARSHALL, Jane C	22 Jan 1895	*49*
WOODYARD, Robert A	DAVID, Alice */div*	31 Aug 1922	*103*
WOODYARD, Walter W */div*	KINCHELOE, Alice */wid*	16 May 1908	*74*
WOOLFE, Robert D	AYRE, Mary K	5 Feb 1874	*17*
WOOLSTON, William R	MILLER, Ruth C	10 May 1932	*137*
WORSTER, William B	FREZEE, Mary */div*	2 Apr 1879	*25*
WORTH, Harry Russell */div*	SYLVESTER, Ida W	24 Nov 1933	*144*
WREN, Wyatt A */wid*	HADAWAY, Margaret A */wid*	9 Sep 1926	*116*
WRENN, Albert */wid*	HARRISON, Hanna A	15 May 1883	*31*
WRENN, Gabriel H	FOX, Laura C	9 Mar 1875	*18*
WRENN, James H	HURST, Anna R	16 Dec 1884	*34*
WRENN, James H */wid*	HURST, Alice V	6 Apr 1899	*56*
WRENN, James O	WRENN, Lula	27 Aug 1872	*15*
WRENN, Jesse	MORGAN, Effie	31 Jul 1926	*115*
WRENN, Raymond N	HOLDEN, Winnie V	11 Oct 1915	*89*
WRENN, Robert	CROSS, Sarah Elizabeth	9 Oct 1872	*15*
WRENN, Robert */wid*	CROSS, Anna H F	8 Jun 1887	*38*
WRENN, Rufus W	PHILLIPS, Mary A	9 Nov 1898	*55*
WRENN, Washington C	UTTERBACK, Susan L	21 Dec 1881	*29*
WRENN, William H	CLARK, Ann E	10 Apr 1873	*16*
WRIGHT, Anderson */c*	GASKINS, Willy Ann */c*	13 Apr 1871	*15*
WRIGHT, George P	BUTLER, Fannie N	15 Oct 1856	*2*
WRIGHT, H F	LEEDS, Florence	29 Mar 1899	*56*
WRIGHT, Henry */c*	PEARSON, Marcie B */c*	24 Dec 1893	*47*
WRIGHT, Herschell Emmett	MILLER, Wavie A	26 Mar 1919	*95*
WRIGHT, Jessie */c*	ROBINSON, Bertha */c*	18 Apr 1906	*70*
WRIGHT, Joseph M P	CORBUSIER, Frances D	16 Jun 1928	*121*
WRIGHT, Kenneth T	ADDY, Hazel	12 Aug 1924	*109*
WRIGHT, Lloyd E	HAUXHURST, Ellen Louisa	23 Aug 1924	*109*
WRIGHT, T Shepherd	MASON, Emma M	23 Sep 1868	*9*
WRIGHT, WH */div*	GHEEN, Jennie E	1 Jul 1896	*51*
WUBBOLD, Joseph Henry	CATON, Jean Randall	21 Oct 1933	*144*
WUNDER, George O	COCKERILLE, Ann M	7 Oct 1858	*4*
WYCROFF, Royal */wid*	WOODALL, Bess	31 Oct 1924	*110*
WYEAST, James P	WILLIAMS, Laura E	12 Apr 1882	*30*
WYNKOOP, A E	WELLS, Virgie E	10 Dec 1901	*61*
WYNKOOP, Charles E	TRACEY, Minnie L	29 Dec 1898	*56*
WYNKOOP, Frank G */wid*	SEAY, Edna */wid*	15 Aug 1913	*84*
WYNKOOP, Joseph Thomas	DEAN, Fannie E	6 Aug 1867	*7*

WYNKOOP, L B	DAY, N V	21 Jan 1914	86
WYNNE, Lewis Bingley Jr	IDEN, Mary Ann /wid	30 Oct 1873	16
WYSONG, W H H	JONES, Sarah J	8 Jul 1868	9
YAFFEY, Robert J	KEREN, Doris	2 Apr 1925	111
YATES, James R	DARNE, Leithe Lee	2 Jan 1895	49
YATES, John C /div	SWINK, Margaret F	28 Nov 1914	87
YOUELL, Guy	HUFF, Ressie	14 Jul 1925	112
YOUNG, Archie	JAVINS, Clara	25 Sep 1901	60
YOUNG, Charles B /c wid	LOWE, Bettie /c wid	27 Dec 1933	145
YOUNG, Charles F	ADAMS, Beulah	11 Jan 1912	82
YOUNG, Eugene /c	JAMMERSON, Lavenia /c	7 Jul 1895	49
YOUNG, Henry /c	NEWMAN, Mary /c	1 Jan 1907	72
YOUNG, Herbert R	KAIN, Stella J	7 Apr 1921	100
YOUNG, Hoellman A	SUTTON, Faith Mae	2 Dec 1933	144
YOUNG, James P /wid	WILLIAMSON, Effie	18 Dec 1901	61
YOUNG, John Thomas	LEAMAN, Ruth Weir	21 Jul 1924	109
YOUNG, Mark	BRODERS, Virginia	21 Jan 1856	2
YOUNG, Marshall N	KIRBY, Vivienne N	29 Nov 1929	126
YOUNG, W Ralph /c	MINOR, Leah /c	14 Aug 1930	129
YOUNG, William H	DENTY, Emma J	21 Dec 1876	21
YOUNG, William Henry	DAVIS, Anna	13 Jun 1869	11
YOUNG, William L	WRIGHT, Pauline A	7 Aug 1933	143
YOUNT, Maurice A	JARRETT, Elma B	1 Jun 1918	94
YOWELL, Alexander A	FLETCHER, Elsie A	31 May 1930	128
ZIMMERMAN, Ernest	HARTBOWER, Catharine B	21 Jun 1905	69
ZIMMERMAN, George W	SIMPSON, Bertha	25 Aug 1923	106
ZIMMERMAN, Harry C	LAWRENCE, Julia E	3 Feb 1903	64
ZIMMERMAN, Levi	DEITZ, Annie	9 Jul 1901	60

AUGUSTINE
  Elizabeth, 141
AUSTIN
  Ragina, 20
AUTRY
  Cora, 127
  Sarah, 76
AVERY
  Dorothy, 144
AYRE
  Ida, 61, 86
  Inez, 37
  Jane, 89
  M, 40
  Mary, 154
AYRES
  Annie, 89
  Bettie, 137
  Edna, 96
  Emma, 141
  M Amanda, 89
  Mary, 115
  Mattie, 40

—B—

BABBITT
  Agnes, 55
  Nellie, 94
BACHELDER
  Ada, 33
  Hulda, 91
BADEN
  Zella, 84
BAGGERLY
  Minnie, 13
BAGGOTT
  Effie, 80
  Osie, 118
BAILEY
  Addie, 57
  Alice, 39

Dora, 136
Evelyn, 146
Gertrude, 147
Hattie, 66
Sallie, 3
Winifred, 127
BAIRD
  Gertrude, 76
BAKER
  Alice, 119
  Ida, 143
  Julia, 151
  Katharine, 72
  M Louise, 52
  Mary, 107, 124
  Sara, 76
  Selba, 123
BALDWIN
  Margaret, 55
BALL
  Bessie, 142
  Caroline, 88
  Dorothy, 26,
    100
  Edith, 34
  Elizabeth, 140
  Ella, 52
  Florence, 148
  Harriett, 147
  Ida, 12
  Lela, 46
  Lillian, 44
  Louise, 110
  Martha, 6
  Mary, 39, 76,
    139
  Pauline, 153
  Rachel, 142
BALLARD
  Ella, 110
  Lillie, 86
  Margaret, 128

Mary, 103
Varina, 20
BALLENGER
  Annie, 7
  Caroline, 98
  Ida, 97
  Janie, 23
  Lillie, 150
  Margaret, 97
  Nannie, 108
BALTIMORE
  Eliza, 113
BALTZER
  Fannie, 56
BANCROFT
  Albertine, 8
BANKETT
  Sophronia, 89
BANKS
  Beatrice, 50
  Caroline, 107
  Carrie, 152
  Eliza, 109
  Emma, 117
  Lizzie, 17
  Minta, 52
  Sarah, 134
BARBER
  Emma, 125
BARBOUR
  May, 86
BARCROFT
  Caroline, 17
  Rachael, 21

BARKER
  Elizabeth, 25
  Katie, 89
  Mary, 110
  Ruth, 94
  Virginia, 39
BARLOW

Mary, 102
Priscilla, 116
BARNARD
  Lois, 139
  Mary, 55
  Virginia, 103
BARNES
  Alma, 26
  Bessie, 147
  Helen, 54
  Iva, 46
  Juanita, 5
  Lillie, 105
  Lola, 66
  Millie, 101
  Nina, 4
BARNETT
  Elnora, 84
  Mollie, 2
BARNUM
  Cora, 85
  Emma, 5
BARRE
  Rena, 95
BARRS
  Bessie, 25
BARTLETT
  Eliza, 68
BARTON
  Fanny, 11
  Lillie, 114
BAS
  Gertrude, 3
BASKETTE
  Myrtle, 131
BASTOW
  Ann, 14
  Hattie, 10
  Isabella, 104
  Lillie, 124
  Minnie, 93
BASYE

Lillie, 103
BATCHELLER
Betty, 84
BATES
Ella, 140
Harriet, 26
Louisa, 86
Lucy, 110
BAUCKMAN
Erie, 144
BAUGHM
Emma, 138
BAUGHMAN
Edith, 139
BAUMAN
Edith, 111
Mildred, 21
BAXTER
Elvie, 57
BAYLISS
Daisy, 136
Esther, 102
Ethel, 20
Jennie, 93
Jessie, 75
Julia, 20
Lena, 116
Mazie, 115
Pearl, 94
Sarah, 35
Shirley, 124
Theo, 52
BAYLOR
Lavinia, 147
Susannah, 21
BEACH
Alice, 18
Ann, 141
Bessie, 67
Delila, 62
Eliza, 87
Emily, 118

Jane, 111, 114
Lillie, 127
Mary, 46, 50,
    58, 90, 141
Mildred, 8, 136
Nellie, 57
Priscilla, 3
Roxey, 149
Sarah, 9, 41,
    76, 126, 128
Susan, 34
Victoria, 55
Virginia, 140
Zarah, 43
BEAHM
Annie, 30
May, 123
BEAL
Mary, 19
BEALE
Mary, 102
BEANS
Florence, 134
BEARD
Hattie, 55
Mary, 97
Mildred, 144
BEASLEY
Helen, 58
BEATTIE
Pauline, 44

BEATTY
Annie, 107
BEAVER
Frances, 135
Olive, 40
BEAVERS
Anna, 60
Edith, 37
Eva, 75
Ida, 126

Laura, 137
Lorena, 32
Margaret, 116
Winnie, 45
BECKER
Mabel, 31
BECKWITH
Adalaide, 58
Albertina, 105
Clara, 140
Elnora, 58
Hattie, 1
Martha, 26
Minnie, 68
Videan Marion,
    80
BECROFT
Ruth, 20
BECTON
Annie, 74
Mag, 36
BEDAKER
Mary, 30
BEDORE
Joyce, 19
BEEDLE
Mary, 141
BEISTEL
Susie, 112
BELFIELD
Frances, 70
BELL
Clara, 133
Edith, 123
Esther, 84
Florence, 77
Jessie, 77
Julia, 124
Lizzie, 82
BELLER
Barbara, 41
BELMONT

Celie, 86
BENNETT
Angelina, 34
Ethel, 127
Irene, 113
Laura, 102
Louise, 103
Mary, 107
Rosa, 61
BENSON
Alice, 119
Elizabeth, 9
Ethel, 54
BERGER
Minnie, 116
BERKERHISER
Dorothy, 124
BERKLEY
Atalanta, 8
Florence, 113
H, 10, 102
BERKSHAW
Mary, 15
BERLO
Lillian, 39
BERNDGEN
Marcella, 76
BERNTSEN
Ruby, 61
BERRIEN
Mary, 59
BERRY
Alzine, 96
Emma, 102
Grace, 124
Martha, 69
Mary, 125, 149
BERRYHILL
Lorene, 45
BESECKER
Janet, 150
BESLEY

Elsie, 124
Naomi, 100
BEST
Dorothy, 19
BETHUNE
C Jean, 109
BEYER
Gehrta, 3
BEYMER
Regina, 141
BICKFORD
Catherine, 121
BICKSLER
Ann, 8
Bertie, 73
Emma, 30
Kate, 95
Laura, 56
Mary, 150
BIDDISON
Elva, 42
BIGGERS
Elizabeth, 97
BIGGS
Sadie, 41
BILLER
Orpha, 74
Sarah, 100
BILLSBOROUGH
Irene, 38
BINDLEY
Elmira, 122
BINNS
Blanche, 67
BIRCH
Agnes, 11
Carrie, 18
Cora, 69
Edith, 96
Eva, 148
Jennette, 52
Kate, 111

Maggie, 17
Mildred, 40
Ruth, 52
BIRD
Bessie, 62
Jane, 59
Margaret, 140
BISHOP
Mary, 139
BITZER
Ella, 24
BLACK
Frances, 46
Martha, 12
BLACKBURN
Alcinda, 81
Martha, 151
Ruth, 112
BLACKENEY
Drusilla, 92
BLACKMAN
Dorothy, 143
BLACKWELL
Emily, 103
Lois, 72
Martha, 137
Susan, 73
BLADEN
Aline, 93
Fannie, 152
Florence, 138
Olive, 3
BLAHA
Ruth, 22
BLAKE
Emily, 30
Mamie, 19
BLANCKE
Olga, 134
BLANK
Hedwig, 79
BLATCHLEY

Georgianna, 8
BLAUVELT
Janie, 93
BLETH
Margaret, 145
BLEVINS
Clyde, 22
Virgie, 17
Zellah, 116
BLINCOE
Eliza, 30
BLOOM
Ella, 123
BLOSS
Cora, 50
BLOUNT
Evelyn, 105
BLOXOM
Matilda, 112
BLOXTON
Georgia, 69
BLUNDON
Lillian, 121
BLUNT
Mabel, 83
Marion, 72
BOARMAN
Florence, 34
BODMER
Marjorie, 31
BOERNSTEIN
Aida, 137
BOHEIM
Marie, 82
BOHRER
Ruth, 37
BOND
Eleanor, 56
Norma, 53
BONDEY
Elizabeth, 6

BONHAM
Agnes, 91
Helen, 151
Mary, 128
BONTZ
Beauregard, 59
BOOKMAN
Marie, 91
BOOTH
Inez, 70
Minnie, 51
BOOY
Boukje, 115
BORDEN
Charlotte, 113
Ella, 129
Maggie, 148
Virginia, 29
BORGUS
Blanche, 106
BORTREE
Helen, 58
BOSTON
Ida, 122
BOSWELL
Sarah, 27
BOTELER
Mildred, 4
BOTTS
Barbara, 64
Julia, 40
Marie, 91
Narcissa, 67
Willie, 122
BOUCHER
Alice, 136
Alma, 40
Cora, 4
BOUTELLER
Amelia, 132
BOUTON

Emma, 135
Eva, 38
Eveline, 100
Gertrude, 141
Grace, 63
Hester, 67
Irene, 126
Leonora, 104
Lucinda, 67
Margaret, 90
Mary, 2, 68,
  103, 106,
  135
Mattie, 120
Nina, 60
Oda, 105
Sallie, 110
Sarah, 72, 75
Tillie, 7
Victoria, 53
Willie, 102
BROOME
Anne, 65
BROSIUS
Mary, 107
BROSNAHAN
Nora, 127
BROUGHTON
E, 85
BROWDER
Vera, 80
BROWN
Anna, 86, 87
Annie, 113
Belle, 5, 82
Charlotte, 67
Cora, 152
Daisy, 10, 80
Dollie, 98
Edloe, 3
Effie, 63
Eleanora, 50

Elsie, 30
Eva, 29
Fern, 95
Irene, 13
Ivy, 59
Jennie, 44
Katie, 133
Laura, 25
Lettie, 55
Lillian, 99
Lou, 17, 79,
  142
Louisa, 142
Mabel, 149
Margaret, 36
Maria, 99
Mary, 20, 24,
  26, 62, 120
Melva, 39
Nina, 143
Penelope, 127
Rachael, 86
Rosa, 106
BRUCE
Ethel, 142
Rosa, 67
BRUCHIE
Alice, 101
BRUFF
Mary, 29
BRUFFY
Virginia, 79
BRUIN
F Carinne, 105
BRUMBACK
Blanche, 30
Edith, 106
Mabel, 129
Mary, 2
BRUNNER
Emma, 10
Ida, 68

Mabel, 51
Mary, 106, 107
Matilda, 140
BRYANT
Adowa, 131
Elizabeth, 29
Frances, 81
Maggie, 4
Marietta, 18
Maude, 1
Minnie, 42, 121
Teine, 130
BRYCE
Amanda, 66
Amy, 142
BUCK
Grace, 59
BUCKLEY
Adalaide, 139
Alta, 114
Anna, 147
Annie, 137
Cora, 17
Elizabeth, 61
Emily, 32
Eugenia, 52
Gertrude, 15
Hattie, 45
Ida, 32
Julia, 19
Leota, 48
Marchie, 27
Martha, 66
Mary, 54
May, 19
Minnie, 50
Miriam, 130
Ollie, 95
Theresa, 100
BUEHLER
Daisy, 121
BUELL

Dorothy, 25
Mary, 27
Virginia, 53
BUNDY
Mirtha, 84
BURDETTE
Deborah, 111
BURDHAM
Elva, 28
BURGESS
Alice, 23
Blanche, 18, 41
Cora, 72
BURK
Nellie, 153
BURKE
Annie, 63
Elizabeth, 51
Frances, 29
Ida, 14
Letitia, 123
Lizzie, 128
Lula, 137
Mary, 74, 148
Mildred, 5
Virginia, 123
BURKETT
Edna, 47
BURKHART
Viola, 107
BURKHOLDER
Mattie, 115
BURLEIGH
Allie, 1
Famie, 133
Gaynell, 138
Katherine, 138
BURLEY
Jane, 119
BURNETT
Annie, 127

BURNHAM
  Katheryn, 64
BURNS
  Cornelia, 84
BURNSIDE
  Bertha, 97
  Hattie, 95
  Josie, 31
BURRISS
  Mamie, 2
BURRITT
  Mary, 2
BURROUGHS
  Emma, 42
  Mary, 6
  Nellie, 23
BURROWS
  Mary, 93
BURTON
  Anna, 56
  Laura, 136
  Mary, 15
BURY
  Anna, 134
BUSH
  Jane, 75
  Mary, 20
  Nannie, 144
  Virginia, 122
BUSHROD
  Mary, 17
BUSSE
  Dorothy, 71
BUTERHAUGH
  Rhoda, 58
BUTLER
  Carrie, 44
  Catherine, 91
  Dorothy, 27
  Elizabeth, 24
  Emma, 63
  Fannie, 154

  Frances, 10,
    147
  Gertrude, 58
  Isabella, 16
  Lilian, 62
  Mabel, 103
  Mamie, 130
  Margaret, 9
  Roberta, 61
  Virginia, 100

BUTT
  Catherine, 115
  Mary, 149
BUTTS
  Ruth, 43
BUXTON
  Clara, 143
BYRD
  Willie, 83
BYRNE
  Annie, 152
  Cordelia, 28
  Gertrude, 79
  Kathryn, 146
  May, 111
  Rena, 31
  Virginia, 151
BYRNES
  Daisy, 148

—C—

CABANIS
  Blanch, 104
CABBARD
  Hazel, 31
CADARR
  Julia, 110
CADE
  Mabel, 84

CAIN
  Amelia, 108
CALJOUW
  Helen, 149
CAMBRIDGE
  Henrietta, 60
CAMP
  Mary, 136
  Maud, 41
  Olive, 144

CAMPBELL
  Caroline, 136
  Eleanor, 120
  Florence, 139
  Henrietta, 147
  Jean, 54
  Julia, 32
  Laria, 68
  Louisa, 55
  Lulie, 139
  Maggie, 23
  Myrtle, 41
  Sarah, 9
CANFIELD
  Bella, 32
  Frances, 54
  Mary, 141, 143
  Sarah, 130
CANNON
  Frances, 11
CANS
  Mary, 61
CARICO
  Alwilda, 106
  Emily, 16
CARLIN
  Alice, 102
  Jane, 86
  Louise, 149
  Lucelia, 97
  Maggie, 89, 93

  Margery, 124
  Marjorie, 94
  Mary, 98, 124
CARLSON
  Hulda, 5
CARMEAU
  Kate, 82
CARNICK
  Alice, 49
CARPENTER
  Carrie, 13
  Lola, 85
CARPER
  Cora, 19
  Elizabeth, 131
  Gracie, 132
  Ida, 34
CARR
  Esther, 87
  N E Maude, 15
  Nellie, 89
CARRILL
  Elizabeth, 43
CARRINGTON
  Flora, 33
CARROLL
  Ann, 71, 92
  Annie, 71
  Ellen, 11
  Fannie, 13
  Gertrude, 50
  Joanna, 81
  Lucy, 22
  Margaret, 15,
    61
  Milly, 13
CARSON
  Edith, 9, 114
  Elizabeth, 112
  Sara, 108
CARTER
  Annie, 59

Armenia, 151
Bertha, 70
Dorothy, 56
Effie, 23
Emma, 54
Evelyn, 24
Georgianna, 106
Imogene, 94
Isabella, 15
Kassie, 128
Lena, 106
Letty, 112
Lillian, 105
Lillie, 83
Lizzie, 6
Louisa, 23
Margaret, 48
Martha, 95
Mary, 17, 73, 84
Millie, 149
Pauline, 22
Rose, 22
Sarah, 97
Susie, 7
CARTWRIGHT
Susan, 29
CARY
Annie, 85
Mary, 19
Rosalie, 4
CASH
Mary, 47
CASSELL
Mary, 3
Reba, 12
CASSERLY
Catherine, 105
CASSEY
Mary, 133
CASSIDY

Berta, 49
Lena, 67
Margaret, 23

CASTLEMAN
Frances, 31
CATES
Iola, 3
CATON
Artemesia, 14
Bettie, 10
Carrie, 88
Dolores, 127
Elizabeth, 50
Francis, 122
Jean, 154
Loretta, 76
Mary, 37
Pearl, 43
Sallie, 34
Sarah, 145
Willa, 117
CATTS
Annie, 150
Grace, 120
Lillian, 26
Mary, 58
CAUDLE
Elsie, 122
Versie, 5
CAUSER
Ruth, 147
CAWOOD
Amanda, 56
CAYLOR
E A, 20
Lavinia, 129
Maria, 132
CECIL
Gertrude, 41
Mary, 96
CENTER

Lizzie, 95
CHAKIR
Syida, 51

CHALMERS
G, 87
CHAMBERS
Elizabeth, 150
Gertrude, 114
Helen, 94
Lillian, 6
Lucy, 101
Mary, 85
Reba, 94
CHAMBLIN
Ruth, 14
CHAMP
Pearl, 50
CHAMPION
Mary, 96
CHAPIN
Lois, 143
CHAPMAN
Carrie, 67
Elizabeth, 111
Helen, 134
Mary, 83
CHASE
Frances, 16
Isabell, 46
CHAUNCEY
Nettie, 43
CHEEK
Margaret, 130
CHENOWETH
Elsie, 42
CHESLEY
Dorothy, 91
CHEW
Betsey, 147
CHICHESTER
Georgie, 88

Jenny, 63
Madge, 91
Martha, 14
Mary, 34
CHILDS
Rosie, 130
CHLOE
Magy, 27
CHOLSON
Anna, 12
CHRISTIAN
Catharine, 145
Jacqueline, 105
CHRISTIANSEN
Ruth, 103
CHRISTIE
Estelle, 22
CHURCH
Maybelle, 97
CLAGGETT
Leila, 127
CLAIR
Mamie, 37
CLAPDORE
Mary, 61
CLARK
Ann, 47, 112, 154
Annie, 112
Edith, 87
Ella, 122
Elsie, 97
Elvira, 47
Emma, 97
Evelyn, 15
Lillian, 105
Louise, 143
Nannie, 145
CLARKE
Alice, 2
Annie, 1
Bessie, 25

Eula, 8
Julia, 47
Mamie, 48
Mary, 108
Myrtle, 127
Pansy, 80
Sarah, 87
Susie, 13
CLASBY
Lillian, 59
CLATCHEY
Mary, 15
CLATTERBUCK
Grace, 75
Ida, 126
CLAY
Maggie, 147
CLAYBORNE
Ora, 110
CLAYTON
Rosalie, 63
CLEARY
Gertrude, 111
CLEM
Dora, 41
Marguerite, 40
Viola, 153
CLEMENS
Alice, 56
Almira, 71
CLEMENTS
Harriet, 33
Ivy, 4
CLEVELAND
Alice, 59
Carrie, 38
Constance, 113
Hannah, 99
Lucy, 118
Mabel, 101
Mary, 139
Rosie, 116

CLINE
Betsy, 127
Ellen, 114
Lena, 119
CLIVES
Annie, 137
CLOVER
Mary, 48
COAKLEY
M, 116
COATES
Belle, 102
Marjorie, 140
Martha, 143
Virginia, 32
COATS
Carrie, 147
Malinda, 41
COBB
Dorothy, 1
Ruth, 119
COCK
Carrie, 151
Ellen, 134
Ida, 95
Lillian, 130
Lora, 26
Nannie, 12
COCKERILLE
Ada, 36
Agnes, 127
America, 141
Ann, 48, 154
C, 26, 81
Edith, 23
Edna, 4
Elida, 129
Elizabeth, 78
Georgia, 62
Hattie, 49
Katie, 18
Louise, 133

M Edith, 113
Mabel, 82
Mae, 78
Mary, 32, 43,
    84
Nannie, 24, 69
Nellie, 86
Nettie, 132
Norma, 140
Pearl, 39
Rosa, 73
Ruby, 32
Sarah, 48, 143
Susie, 129
CODER
Gertrude, 77
COE
Madeline, 10
COFFER
Ella, 58
COFFIN
Mary, 83
COGAN
Martha, 135
COLBATH
Mary, 122
COLE
Ella, 121
Ellen, 41
Fannie, 111
Mahala, 60
Mary, 55
Sarah, 27
Sylvia, 6
COLEMAN
Annie, 27
Clara, 18
Eliza, 90
Julia, 23
COLES
Annie, 17
COLLARD

Mary, 77
Rachel, 80
COLLINS
Annie, 3
Bernice, 142
Dorothy, 111
Edith, 136
Emaretta, 96
Emma, 126
Jennie, 113
Martha, 97
Mary, 12, 59
Sadie, 153
COMMINS
Effie, 14
COMPHER
Annie, 82
COMPTON
Lucy, 35
Merle, 143
R, 17
Virginia, 35
CONARD
Pirl, 72
CONLIN
Frances, 123
CONNOR
Clara, 72
CONNORS
Margaret, 48
CONOWAY
Grace, 139
CONROW
Emma, 25
CONROY
Katharine, 93
Sarah, 28

CONSIDINE
Mary, 114
CONSTABLE
Fannie, 78

COOK
  Ann, 71
  Eassie, 42
  Edna, 153
  Effie, 99
  Emily, 30
  Emma, 13
  Jenny, 91
  Julia, 141
  Laura, 38
  Lillian, 136
  Louise, 145
  Lydia, 96
  Olive, 108
  Rosa, 9
  Susan, 119
COOKE
  Annie, 116
  Nora, 111
COOKSEY
  Cora, 6
  Fannie, 16
  Isabella, 48
COOLBAUGH
  Loretta, 56
COOMBS
  Grace, 136
COON
  Edna, 24
COOPER
  Amanda, 44
  Elizabeth, 71
  Fannie, 48
  Jeanie, 147
  Mildred, 45
  Minetta, 125
  Virginia, 36

COOPERING
  Margaret, 92
COPE
  Laura, 112

CORALLO
  Mary, 123
CORAM
  Fannie, 7
CORBIN
  Harriet, 47, 151
  Mary, 90
CORBUSIER
  Frances, 154
CORKERY
  Johanna, 125
CORNEAL
  Mary, 25
CORNELIUS
  Nell, 115
CORNELL
  Alice, 23
  Claude, 129
  Elizabeth, 104
  Maggie, 140
  Martha, 149
  Mary, 129
  Nellie, 119, 127
  Roberta, 13
CORNWELL
  Fern, 26
  L Myrtle, 103
  Martha, 107
  Mary, 104
  Mildred, 124
  Mrs. Richard,
    17
CORRELL
  Elinor, 100

CORRIGAN
  Mary, 119
CORRISON
  Martha, 148
CORSE
  Mary, 24
  R, 24

COSBY
  Annie, 71
COSTELLO
  Dolly, 78
COTTRELL
  Carrie, 55
COULTER
  Ida, 11
  Lou, 149
COUNSELMAN
  Elsie, 79
COURTNEY
  Elsie, 79
  Mary, 142
COWLEY
  Margaret, 133
COWLING
  Annie, 24
COX
  Christine, 19
  Lena, 105
  Maxine, 148
  Verna, 109
COYNER
  Cora, 119
CRADDOCK
  Stella, 84
CRAGG
  Lizzie, 37
  Sarah, 45
CRAGGS
  Sally, 39
CRAIG
  Delia, 132

CRAIGG
  Ruth, 4
CRAMPTON
  Mary, 119
CRANDALL
  Emma, 90
  Mabel, 127

CRANFORD
  Eliza, 125
CRANKUM
  Lucy, 5
  Maria, 26
  Martha, 16
  Nancy, 4
CRANLEIGH
  Evelyn, 89
CRAVEN
  Daisy, 53
  Janie, 30
CRAWFORD
  Alice, 113
  Bertha, 82
CREAMER
  Ella, 74
CREASEY
  Hylda, 90
CREED
  Bettie, 132
CREWS
  Mabel, 16
CRICKENBERGER
  Anna, 33
  Geraldine, 109
  Helen, 34
CRIMMIN
  Alice, 108
CRIMMINS
  Catherine, 34
  Marie, 67
  Mary, 21
CRIPPEN
  Arlie, 20
  Dora, 119
  Hazel, 86
  Helen, 59
  Janie, 92
  Mary, 141
CRITZER
  Doris, 43

DEILER
  Arline, 133
DEITZ
  Annie, 155
DELANY
  E, 14
DELLINGER
  Beulah, 59
DEMOSLAWSKA
  Lillian, 33
DENHAM
  Josephine, 114
  Mamie, 126
  Marie, 150
DENNEY
  Fanny, 102
  Ruth, 105
  Susan, 22
DENTY
  Annie, 35
  Emma, 155
  Frances, 7
  Mary, 8, 147
  Maude, 90
DERBYSHIRE
  Fay, 10
DERRICK
  Madge, 132
  Maggie, 4
DESKIN
  Julia, 126
  Mary, 71
  Rhodie, 137
DESKINS
  Julia, 73
  Pennie, 48
DESMOND
  Margaret, 31
DETWILER
  Ann, 96
  Bessie, 18
  Beula, 3

Blanche, 21
Elizabeth, 17
L, 18
Mary, 61, 112
Ruth, 24
DEVINE
  Evelyn, 99

DEWEY
  Ann, 88
  Elsie, 102
  Emma, 146
DEY
  Emma, 1
DICK
  Agatha, 146
DICKENS
  Harriet, 150
DICKENSON
  Margaret, 95
DICKEY
  Eliza, 56
  Mary, 13
  Rosa, 48
DICKINSON
  Ruth, 67
DICKSON
  Martha, 12
DIEDERICK
  Anna, 104
DIKES
  Elsie, 30
DILLON
  Julia, 66
DIMSEY
  Bertha, 74
  Julia, 27
DISNEY
  Juliet, 51
DIXON
  Edith, 23
  Ella, 153

Georgie, 43
Gertrude, 48
Harriet, 120
Hattie, 130, 131
Louisa, 66
Lucy, 37
Lyddie, 73
Mary, 22
Nettie, 15
Rose, 140
DOAK
  Hazel, 77
DOBSON
  Isabella, 50
DODD
  Catharine, 113
  Charlotte, 55
  Florence, 9
DODGE
  Nellie, 32
DODSON
  Agnes, 41
  Amanda, 57
  Anner, 75
  Annie, 65
  Elizabeth, 76
  Ella, 5
  Ellen, 34
  Hattie, 84
  Hilda, 109
  Ida, 118
  Irene, 140
  Leaster, 27
  Linda, 108
  Nellie, 123
  Nora, 135
  Quincy, 106
  Sarah, 78
DOHERTY
  Beatrice, 58
  Eileen, 40
DOHNER

Rosemary, 29
DOLL
  Dorothea, 59
DOLLY
  Martha, 4

DONALDSON
  Annie, 56
  Beulah, 139
  Carrie, 114
  Florence, 34
  Hattie, 124
  Marion, 148
  Saidee, 83
DONOHOE
  Mary, 92
  Susie, 116
DONOVAN
  Doris, 49
DOOLEY
  Ella, 39
  Maggie, 124
DORSEY
  Eliza, 3, 62
  Elizabeth, 62
  Helen, 43
  Kathleen, 117
  Laura, 66
  Mabel, 23
  Mary, 1, 49
  Rachel, 153
  Rita, 140
  Susan, 74
DOTSON
  Mary, 96
DOUGHERTY
  Mary, 68
  Sarah, 87
DOUGLASS
  Corenne, 112
DOVA
  Iva, 92

ELLISON
Elizabeth, 101
Fannie, 125
ELLMORE
Mae, 49
ELLS
Blanche, 150
ELLSWICK
Anna, 105
ELSEROAD
Annie, 109
ELTER
Mary, 1
ELY
Ottie, 16
EMBRY
Daisy, 60
ENGLAND
Elizabeth, 73
Jessie, 105
Matie, 146
ENGLISH
Lena, 90
Oneida, 131
ENNIS
Annie, 7
Glenna, 133
Lillian, 37
Rebecca, 9
ENSOR
Janice, 54
Violette, 23
ERASO
Cecile, 37
ERLMEIER
Frances, 5
ERWIN
Julia, 5
ESKRIDGE
Mary, 151

ESSIG

Anna, 77
ESTERLY
Dorothy, 29
E Alyce, 15
ETTA
Dolores, 134
EVANS
Alice, 55
Catherine, 64
Elephy, 2
Wildia, 133
EVERETT
Margaret, 63
EWELL
Alice, 103
Nannie, 42
EWING
Ollie, 101

—F—

FAGANS
Rosanna, 62
FAIRFAX
Ada, 35
Ann, 38, 71,
107, 142
Annie, 38
Bessie, 45
Clara, 142
Cora, 106
Eliza, 11
Eloise, 28
Essie, 63
Fannie, 4
Harriet, 105
Leah, 18
Lillian, 97
Lydia, 22
Margaret, 89
Martha, 97

Mary, 25, 35,
81, 142
Minnie, 134
Rebecca, 38, 90
Rena, 81
Rhoda, 89
Rosa, 22
Rose, 89
Sallie, 66
Susie, 58
Virginia, 42
FALCONER
Mary, 65
FANNON
Catherine, 94
FANT
Frances, 24
FARMER
Inez, 2
FARR
Annie, 83
Elsie, 57
Margaret, 49
Mary, 66
Nannie, 88
FASTNAUGHT
Jennie, 139
FAULKNER
Elizabeth, 62
Helen, 144
Margaret, 57
Mary, 36
FAVORITE
Grace, 28
FAY
Ann, 133
FEATHERSTONE
Cora, 132
FEBREY
Annie, 125
Ella, 135
Ida, 6

Lillie, 125
FEENEY
Louise, 52
FENSTERMAKER
Helen, 55
FERGUSON
Ada, 90
Anna, 7
Bettie, 91
Clara, 121
Cordelia, 133
Dorothy, 130
Esther, 25
Mary, 49, 52
Nellie, 124
Sarah, 5, 69
FERN
Loretta, 51
FERRIS
Alice, 138
Laura, 137
Martha, 147
FERTELIER
Romaine, 152
FERTNEY
Maud, 73
FETZER
Hester, 31
FIFER
Charlotte, 7
Estelle, 138
FILLINGAME
Josephine, 72
FINACOM
Mary, 45
FINCH
Dixie, 101
Helen, 79
Ivy, 66
FINIELS
Kathryn, 84
FINISECY

Eva, 47
FINKER
Ireatha, 21
FINKS
Frances, 19
FINN
Mary, 23
FINNELL
Iola, 110
Violett, 22
FISCHER
Martha, 33
FISHEL
Anna, 87
FISHER
Alice, 72
Catherine, 12
Elizabeth, 19
Hermorin, 29
Hilda, 17
Katherine, 120
Mary, 75, 104
Matilda, 128
Rebecca, 152
FISK
Eunice, 61
FISSELL
Rachel, 49
FITSPATRICK
C Louise, 30
FITZGERALD
Flossie, 104
Goldie, 50
FITZHUGH
Abigail, 17
Charles, 14
Elizabeth, 69
Ellen, 23
Mary, 91
Meek, 14
Sarah, 106, 127
FLAGG

Aveline, 43
FLAHERTY
Beatrice, 34
Mary, 92
Sylvia, 64
FLANIGAN
Mary, 3
FLANNAGAN
Margaret, 30
FLEMING
Aminta, 69
Clara, 1
Katharine, 101
Mary, 3
FLETCHER
Annie, 1
Elsie, 155
Elvira, 43
Frances, 139
Lillie, 90
Lucy, 11
Margaret, 22
Mary, 16
FLINN
Ann, 32
FLOHR
Hilda, 132
FLOWERS
Eva, 40
FLOYD
Margaret, 35
FOLEY
Ida, 83
FOLKS
Carrie, 137
Lizzie, 124
Lola, 13
Maggie, 10
Mary, 128
FOLLIN
Ada, 84
Ann, 42, 75, 82

Anna, 82
Annie, 6
Bessie, 70
Drusilla, 110
Eleanor, 53
Eliza, 96
Emma, 63
Florence, 84
Frances, 98,
  142
Georgianna,
  141
Henrietta, 134
Idella, 91
Kathryn, 55
Laurena, 120
Martha, 114
Mary, 121
Minnie, 82
Nellie, 89
Rachael, 151
Rosa, 120
FONDA
Mary, 1
FONES
Louise, 138
FORBES
Emma, 102
Mary, 9
Minnie, 122
FORCE
Edna, 35

FORD
Alice, 87
Amanda, 61
Anna, 139
Eliza, 152
Florence, 17
Gertrude, 17
Ida, 13
Julia, 86

Katie, 109
Mabel, 7, 53
Maria, 116
Martha, 22
Mary, 126
Matilda, 152
Nina, 53
Pattie, 148
Virginia, 4
Winnie, 107
FORESTER
Catherine, 38
FORREST
Elizabeth, 68
FORSYTH
Jane, 135
FORTNEY
Mary, 138
Nettie, 123
Nora, 69
Olivia, 92
FOSTER
Blanche, 120
Emma, 13
Juliet, 21
FOUCHE
Nellie, 120
FOWLER
Margaret, 81
Mary, 15
Ruth, 33
FOX
Alma, 49
Annie, 130
Bettie, 10
Eolene, 6
Eva, 121
Helen, 134
Laura, 154
Louise, 39
Mary, 125, 136
Susanna, 136

Marie, 18
GASTEN
Gladys, 61
GEATOR
Lula, 1
GEE
Jean, 82
GELINER
Grace, 53
GENERALS
Elizabeth, 109
GENTRY
Dora, 85
Eliza, 10
Wilma, 130
GEORGE
Olive, 131
GERARD
Agnes, 63
GERNS
Margaret, 134
GESS
Courtney, 127
GESSFORD
Lois, 25
GHEEN
Caroline, 38
Delina, 45
Hannah, 146
Jennie, 154
Martha, 31, 129
Mary, 26, 95
Sarah, 143
Virginia, 40
GHEENS
Eliza, 108
GIBBS
Frances, 145
Grace, 129
Janette, 101
GIBSON
Adaline, 108

Adeline, 36
Cora, 109
Emma, 76
Grace, 65, 140
Helen, 87
Ida, 73
Louisa, 102
Mamie, 42
Ruth, 117
Sarah, 16
Venie, 99
GILBERT
Blanche, 28
Katherine, 64
Mary, 108
GILES
Nellie, 153
GILL
Aurelia, 28
Rosie, 36
GILLAM
Sarah, 83

GILLEN
Mary, 11
GILLETT
Edna, 89
Helen, 82
GILLINGHAM
Adrienne, 68
Anna, 118
Mary, 46
Sallie, 120
Susan, 125
GILLIS
Clarice, 90
GILMORE
Elizabeth, 111
GINNELLEY
Ida, 32
Lizzie, 14
Mabel, 12

GIRL
Lillie, 96
GLADDEN
Lillie, 9
Victoria, 66
GLASCOE
Isabelle, 147
GLASS
Maria, 150
GLASSCOCK
Anna, 136
Eunice, 31
GLENN
Mary, 56
GODFREY
Effie, 144
Eva, 94
Sallie, 39
GODWIN
Bettie, 74
Emma, 135
G, 12
GOETZ
Rosa, 3
GOETZE
Katherine, 81
GOFNEY
Fannie, 145
GOINGS
Martha, 97
GOLDEN
Helen, 93
Sarah, 43
GOLDING
Sarah, 142
GONDOR
Sarah, 143
GOOD
Luella, 118
GOODALL
Ruth, 64
GOODE

Alice, 30
GOODING
Ann, 131
Lula, 134
Sarah, 102
GOODMAN
Roberta, 94
GOODRICK
Julia, 101
GOODSPEED
Catherine, 46
Grace, 28
Loretta, 41
GOODWIN
Lois, 96
Margaret, 6
GORDON
Eliza, 5, 47
Emma, 16
Mary, 5
Sylvia, 55

GORHAM
Alice, 119
Amanda, 106
Emma, 134
Narcissa, 135
Sallie, 64
GOSWELL
Margaret, 37
GOTT
Susette, 3
GOULD
Elmira, 132
GRAHAM
Belle, 153
Elizabeth, 120
Gertrude, 127
Harriet, 103
Kate, 67
GRAMS
Florence, 85

GRANIGAN
Ida, 4
GRANT
Maria, 4
GRAVES
Eleanor, 94
GRAY
Ada, 17
Amy, 93
Catherine, 134
Doris, 10
Edith, 27
Irene, 14
Louisa, 60
M, 69
Olif, 99
Sarah, 59, 147
Thelma, 19

GRAYSON
Anna, 74
GREELEY
Anna, 48
GREEN
Adaline, 16
Alice, 111, 143
Catherine, 137
Eddie, 48
Georgia, 146
Grace, 6
Ida, 150
Jane, 55
Jennie, 119
Leanna, 75
Lucretia, 16
Marion, 42
Mary, 27, 123
Mildred, 117
Ruth, 142
Sarah, 71, 139
Violett, 94
Virginia, 65

GREENLEASE
Beulah, 35
GREENWOOD
Kate, 75
Leahbell, 24
Sarah, 54
GREER
Urith, 3
GREHAN
Harriet, 10
GRESHAM
Annie, 104
Fannie, 88
Maria, 115

GRIFFIN
Mary, 79
Nancy, 32
GRIFFITH
Alice, 70
Janie, 31
Sarah, 77
GRIGSBY
Mary, 138
GRILLBORTZER
Mary, 147
GRIM
Rose, 141
GRIMES
A, 93, 152
Anna, 93
Mary, 46
Sarah, 39
GRIMPLES
Mary, 55
GRIMSLEY
Bessie, 12
Ella, 31
Katherine, 10
Mary, 81
Mattie, 52
Sallie, 108

GROH
Elizabeth, 1
GROOMES
Sophronia, 12
GROOMS
Mary, 31
Sarah, 16
GROSECLOSE
Elizabeth, 42
GROSS
Mary, 94
GROTEVANT
Lee, 119
GROVE
Minnie, 129
Nannie, 110
GROVES
Emma, 81
Nellie, 120
GUERTLER
Marie, 56
GULAGER
Clara, 46
GUNNELL
Alice, 53
Annie, 49
Catherine, 56
Emily, 12
Gertrude, 95
Isadora, 128
Julia, 30
Lena, 77
Linton, 26
Margaretta, 71
Martha, 69, 146
Mary, 10, 22,
56, 109
Matilda, 56
Virginia, 2
GUNNER
Catherine, 89
GURNS

Ella, 112

—H—

HAASE
Rosie, 18
HABERKORN
Helen, 106
HACKETT
Hazel, 94

HADAWAY
Margaret, 154
HADEN
Mary, 123
HADLEY
Dorothy, 8
HAIGHT
Eliza, 19, 58
Elizabeth, 58
Maggie, 84
Mary, 96
HAILSTROCHS
Alice, 146
HAINES
Dorothy, 12
HAISLIP
Anna, 101
Ella, 23
Jane, 140
Margaret, 36
Martha, 28
Minnie, 57
Susan, 83
HALE
Nellie, 46
HALEY
Louise, 74
Sarah, 73
HALGETT
Nellie, 68
HALL

Alma, 57
Annie, 21, 72, 123
Bertha, 98
Bettie, 125
Caroline, 128
Carrie, 147
Catherine, 71
Clara, 104
Dixie, 63
Eliza, 87
Ellen, 153
Emeline, 57
Eva, 40
Frances, 45, 113
Georgianna, 152
Jean, 101
Jennie, 36
Louise, 90
M Bernice, 67
Mabel, 16
Maggie, 123
Mary, 37, 74, 127
Melvia, 136
Melvina, 39
Nancy, 58
Naomi, 14
Nettie, 57
Rosa, 65
Violett, 131
HALLEY
Laura, 95
Mary, 74
HAMILL
Mary, 131
HAMILTON
Bridget, 13
Cornelia, 72
Josephine, 112

Kate, 36
M, 20, 71
Martha, 71
Mary, 6
HAMMOND
Lula, 148
Virginia, 53
HAMPTON
Maud, 45
Nellie, 36
Valeria, 8
HAMRICK
Irene, 47
HANEY
Fannie, 106
Mary, 107
HANKER
Lona, 87
HANNA
Mary, 143
HANTT
Hilda, 25
HANY
Eliza, 122
HAPPOLDT
Zelah, 126
HARAN
Margaret, 90
HARDESTER
Della, 118
HARDIN
Dorothy, 106
HARDING
Olive, 121
HARIG
Lillian, 95
HARKINS
A Jane, 96
HARLOW
Ada, 88
Agnes, 119
Alice, 82

Marie, 85
Vera, 95
HARMON
Elizabeth, 51
Maggie, 57
Ruby, 51
HARNAGE
Dorothy, 119
HARNDEN
Anner, 32
HARPER
Ellen, 132
Flora, 76
Gertie, 60
Hattie, 83
HARRELL
Carrie, 71
Julia, 59
HARRIS
Alice, 60
Amanda, 122
Anginina, 137
Anna, 2
Aurina, 16
Beatrice, 70, 117
Bertha, 20
Bettie, 11, 42
Catherine, 19
Costella, 8
Daisy, 38, 112
Edith, 122
Effie, 103
Elizabeth, 60
Elmira, 117
Florida, 17
Frances, 127
Geneva, 122
Gertrude, 60, 120
Ginnie, 130
Jannie, 60

Jeanette, 6
Julia, 118
Kate, 20
Katherine, 91
Lela, 101
Lewetta, 82
Lucretia, 60
Lucy, 102, 105
Margaret, 64
Maria, 19, 66
Martha, 26
Mary, 95
Nettie, 60
Ophelia, 16
Ora, 67
Reaner, 122
Sadie, 33
Sally, 10, 11
Sarah, 10
Susan, 115, 118
Susanna, 118
Susie, 2
Sylvia, 101
HARRISON
Annie, 45
Bertha, 88
Carrie, 24
Catherine, 79
Elizabeth, 76
Elva, 122
Gertrude, 23
Hanna, 154
Hattie, 56
Hester, 111
Ida, 150
Irene, 115
Isabella, 27
Jennie, 26
Laura, 82, 116
Lettice, 140
Lucy, 38
Lule, 20

Margaret, 52
Martha, 44
Mary, 58
Minnie, 83
Nellie, 60
Nina, 130
Rosa, 97
Rosanna, 57
S, 108
Sallie, 108
Virginia, 56
HARROD
Hazel, 22
Lillie, 77
HARROVER
Frances, 37
Laura, 135
Priscilla, 31
Sarah, 40
HARRYMAN
Audrey, 97
HART
Amelia, 138
Kate, 78
HARTBOWER
Catharine, 155
Mary, 5
Rosie, 142
HARTIG
Katherine, 43
HARTLE
Gertrude, 33
HARTMAN
Erna, 85
HARTSHONE
Mary, 116
HARTY
Georgia, 148
HARVEY
Caroline, 105
Roberta, 98
HASLUP

Xenia, 90
HASSETT
Bridget, 89
Margaret, 59
HASTAND
Florence, 115
HATHAWAY
Mary, 45
HATTON
Charlotte, 64
Ida, 57
Mary, 142
Sarah, 9
HAUBENS
Lucille, 103
HAUGH
Georgia, 121
HAUXHURST
Anna, 146
Ellen, 154
Nellie, 72
HAVENER
Alice, 99
Laura, 73
Mary, 94
Sarah, 79
HAVERTY
Beatrice, 4
HAWES
Carrie, 119
Emma, 121
Eugenia, 20
Mollie, 117
Rosa, 56
HAWKINS
Dortha, 40
HAWLEY
Ella, 55
HAWTHORNE
Frances, 132
HAYDEN
Ellen, 113

Lauretta, 21
HAYES
Claira, 87
HAYNES
Dianna, 18
HEAD
Bernedett, 64
Elizabeth, 76
Mary, 150
Rose, 39
HEALEY
Ann, 106
HEATH
Irene, 64
V, 114
HECK
Elsie, 76
HEDDERMAN
Mary, 153
HEDRICK
Mildred, 124
HEFFNER
Clara, 78
Lillie, 109
HEFFRON
Cassie, 19
HEIDENREICH
Elsie, 52
Rosalie, 97
HEIMSLEY
Marie, 103
HEISS
Martha, 120
HELLBACK
Phyllis, 29
HELMS
Minnie, 146
HENDERSON
Emma, 153
Eva, 143
Gracie, 29
Ida, 47

Idella, 149
Juphenia, 116
Laura, 111
Lea, 70
Lizzie, 86
Malinda, 60
Mary, 48, 123
Mattie, 20
Millie, 123
Nora, 146
Pauline, 149
Rita, 16
Vera, 34
HENEKE
Marie, 25
HENESSY
Blanche, 29
HENKE
Viva, 10
HENRY
Evelyn, 44
Flora, 131
Mildred, 77
HENSEN
Edna, 15
Rosie, 153
HENSHAW
Mary, 113
HERBERT
Alice, 93
Maria, 66
Nora, 66
HERING
Emma, 122
HERL
Evelyn, 129
HERMAN
Geneva, 142
HERNDON
Alice, 84
HERRELL
Naomi, 130

Ruth, 47

HESS
Mary, 143
HESTER
Frances, 2
HEWITT
Alice, 121
HICKOCK
Caroline, 25
HICKS
Grace, 11
HIETT
Katie, 143
HIGGINS
Louise, 18
HIGHAM
Emma, 79
HILEMAN
Mary, 77
HILL
Della, 137
Elaine, 81
Elizabeth, 108,
131
Jessie, 94
Lois, 9
Louise, 44
Maggie, 131
Margaret, 140
Mary, 148
Natalie, 85
Sarah, 105
Thelma, 112
HILLMAN
Eleanor, 128
HILTON
Ethel, 4
Lucille, 93
HINE
Bessie, 126
Katrina, 43

HINES
A Jeanette, 102
Julia, 59
HINKLE
Florence, 76
HINKLEMAN
Marie, 47
HIPKINS
Mary, 72
HIRST
Ada, 80
Mary, 104
HITCHCOCK
Rebecca, 40
HITE
Lena, 100
HITOFFER
Daisy, 111
HITT
Delia, 18
HIX
Georgie, 28
HOAG
Elizabeth, 115
Helen, 16
HOAGLAND
Mollie, 129
HOBGOOD
Mary, 81
HOBSON
Ruby, 117
HOCKMAN
Doris, 41
Ethel, 59
HODGES
Mary, 149
Maybelle, 87
HODGKIN
Alice, 34
Mary, 33

HOFF

Carolin, 87
HOFFMAN
Emily, 62
Gene, 8
Grace, 100
Paulyne, 131
Rose, 143
HOFFMASTER
Camille, 35
HOGAN
Betty, 26
Grace, 16
Hattie, 120
Mary, 89
HOGELAND
Lena, 102
HOKE
Elizabeth, 133
HOLDEN
Bettie, 69
C, 63
Esther, 90
Katie, 94
Mariana, 47
Nancy, 61
Phebe, 148
Phoebe, 47
Virginia, 29
Winnie, 154
HOLLAND
Cora, 40
Edlena, 72
France, 102
Maggie, 130
Marian, 99
Rhoda, 30
HOLLENBACK
Nettie, 107
HOLLIDAY
Addie, 69
Virgie, 98
HOLLIDGE

Lola, 17
HOLLINGS
Eliza, 88
HOLLINS
Lizzie, 87
HOLLIS
Sadie, 23
HOLLISTER
Mary, 38
Rosa, 135
HOLLY
Mary, 9
HOLMES
L Elizabeth, 82
Minnie, 127
HOLSINGER
Mary, 150
HOLT
Vashti, 146
HOLTZCLAW
Mary, 126
HONESTY
Bertie, 142
Catherine, 152
Cora, 91, 103
Golda, 100
Laura, 115
Lizzie, 1
Mary, 19, 40
Mattie, 68
Ollie, 151
Pearl, 11
Ruth, 153
Victoria, 151
Virginia, 39
HOOD
Myrtle, 36

HOOE
Anne, 120
HOOFF
Louise, 8

HOOVER
Doris, 14
HOPE
Ann, 3
HOPKINS
Anny, 148
Edna, 98
Elizabeth, 121
Gertrude, 49
Lillian, 71
Lucretia, 78
HORGAN
Catherine, 89
Mary, 113
HORN
Mary, 122
HORNBECK
Effie, 21
Phebe, 78
HORSEMAN
Grace, 129
Janie, 29
Myrtle, 69
Sadie, 8
HORSTMAN
Birtie, 79
Emily, 119
HORTON
Aurelia, 105
Bessie, 106
Blanche, 65
Clara, 132
Elethea, 126
Eliza, 16
Elizabeth, 16
Ella, 51
Gertrude, 68
Hattie, 52
Lucy, 66, 107
Lucyetta, 66
Mary, 113
May, 121

Rose, 102
Willie, 51
HOSE
Eleanor, 134
HOSKINS
Hulda, 22
Olive, 83
HOSTELLER
LaRue, 37
HOTCHKISS
Mary, 70
HOUGH
Sallie, 11
HOUSE
Leona, 59
HOUSTON
Helen, 88
HOUTZ
Edith, 64
HOWARD
Anna, 20
Henrietta, 131
Margaret, 73
Susan, 58
HOWDERSHELL
Lucille, 68
M, 25, 77, 107
Mary, 107
Maude, 77
HOWELL
Blanche, 137
Elizabeth, 12
HOXTON
Ann, 133
Mary, 88
HOYS
Catheryne, 6
HUBART
Elizabeth, 114
HUDDLESON
Elizabeth, 24
HUDNALL

Hattie, 28
HUEY
Margaret, 55
HUFF
Ressie, 155
HUFFMAN
Myrtle, 86
HUGHES
Cora, 52
Gertrude, 5
Kate, 55
Mary, 131
Viola, 81
HUGHS
Mary, 141
HULETT
Altie, 63
HULLINGS
Lillian, 75
HULTS
Willetta, 123
HUME
Margaret, 68
HUMMER
Dorothy, 28
Emma, 20
Ketturah, 9
Laura, 27
Martha, 1
Mary, 62
Mattie, 107
Sina, 122
HUNSBERGER
Annie, 39
Hannah, 144
HUNT
Alice, 29
Elizabeth, 49
Ettie, 135
Eulah, 153
Goldie, 86
Hattie, 144

Jessie, 1
Selina, 131
HUNTER
Agnes, 136
Alice, 99
Catherine, 100
Cecelia, 17
Cora, 136
Eugenia, 64
Grace, 24
Helen, 99
Isabella, 117
Jane, 7
Jannett, 123
Laura, 95
Lillian, 136
Mabel, 31
Madge, 38
Mamie, 89
Martha, 141
Mary, 25, 56
Mattie, 17
Nannie, 50
Nellie, 143
Nina, 45
Rachael, 47
Sally, 84
Sarah, 74
Susan, 144
Virginia, 51
HUNTERMARK
Theresa, 93

HUNTINGTON
Mildred, 86
HUNTT
Charlotte, 117
Daisy, 79
Debbie, 93
Elizabeth, 128
Emma, 25
Lottie, 68

Marcilla, 46
Martha, 25
Mary, 138
Nellie, 107
HURLEY
Bettie, 152
Katherine, 52
Marion, 127
HURSH
Georgia, 67
HURST
Alice, 154
Amy, 130
Anna, 154
Bessie, 53
Florence, 9, 138
Frances, 104
Jane, 9
Mary, 82
HUTCHINS
Elsie, 2
Emma, 19
HUTCHINSON
Bessie, 10
HUTCHISON
Effie, 12
Elenora, 149
Fanny, 104
Gabriel, 69
Julia, 49
Laura, 58
Lena, 20
Lillian, 12
Maggie, 38
Martha, 103
Mary, 27, 69,
110
Olive, 149
Sarah, 69
Susie, 62
HUTTON
Elizabeth, 69

Iris, 125
HUYCK
Rebecca, 92
HYATT
Florence, 136
HYDE
Meta, 150

—I—

IDEN
Mary, 155
Minnie, 126
INGALLS
Eva, 129
IONS
Estelle, 77
ISENHOUR
Ruby, 6
ISHKANIAN
Grace, 149
ISRAEL
Lillian, 29
IVES
Demis, 24
Elmira, 98

—J—

JACKSON
Ada, 109
Alice, 109
Amanda, 106
Augusta, 16
Bernice, 83
Carrie, 50
Courtney, 103
Eliza, 76
Fannie, 36

Frances, 70, 83
Georgiana, 72
Henrietta, 50,
90
Irene, 132
Laura, 43
Lavenia, 10
Lavinia, 71
Lillian, 21, 42,
55
Lottie, 131
Louisa, 4
Lucinda, 59
Luvenia, 70
Martha, 45, 56,
57, 66, 71
Mary, 75, 100,
101, 103,
105
Mazie, 82
Melvina, 133
Nora, 5, 74
Rebecca, 5
Sallie, 75
Sarah, 74, 103
Sophy, 24
Susan, 22, 46
JACOBS
Bessie, 96
Essie, 27
Mary, 28, 66
Sadie, 42
Sallie, 115
JAEGER
Henrietta, 92
JAGETTS
Mary, 143
JAMES
Alice, 139
Cora, 69
Evelyn, 146
Geneva, 22

Margaret, 143
Mary, 149
Stella, 103
Virginia, 35
JAMESSON
Jean, 34
Maggie, 88
JAMMERSON
Lavenia, 155
JARRELL
Mary, 125
JARRETT
Bertha, 96
Elizabeth, 38
Elma, 155
JARVIS
Edith, 144
JASPER
Frances, 55
JAVINS
Ada, 44
Bessie, 38
Clara, 155
Emma, 7
Hazel, 49
Marie, 4
Mary, 105
Onedia, 88
Rebecca, 37
Sallie, 106
Sarah, 135
JEFFREY
Creasey, 65
Ruth, 53
JEFFRIES
Lottie, 63
JENKINS
Alma, 32
Anna, 76
Annie, 9
Carrie, 153
Emma, 137

Harriet, 46
Helen, 133
Jessie, 27
Lillie, 34, 139
Louise, 59
Lydia, 97
Mabel, 78
Martha, 46
Mary, 14, 21,
  28, 43
Maud, 98
Nellie, 74
Rebecca, 105
T Jane, 70
JENNINGS
Amy, 112
Pauline, 129
Thelma, 145
JERMAN
Annie, 15, 34
Elizabeth, 78
Emma, 150
Mabel, 130
Mary, 44
Priscilla, 153
Rosa, 57
JEWELL
Ann, 66
Annie, 30
Ginnie, 153
Lizzie, 98
JOACHIMS
Helen, 80
JOHANNES
Ruth, 102
JOHANSEN
Caroline, 129
JOHANSON
Mrs. A, 121
Ruth, 57
JOHNSON
Alberta, 128

America, 78
Anna, 64, 150
Annie, 68, 145
Ariana, 71
Arminta, 10
Bertha, 51, 140
Bettie, 7
Catharine, 3
Clara, 113
Dorothy, 114
Edna, 132
Eliza, 10
Ella, 127
Ellen, 133
Emeline, 92
Emma, 68
Flora, 150
Florence, 69
Frances, 95
Georgeana, 135
Gladys, 113
Harriet, 46
Hattie, 40
Ida, 103
Isabella, 110
Jane, 27, 150
Jennie, 77
Jesse, 126
Julia, 127
Lillian, 48
Lillie, 141
Louisa, 1
Lucy, 83, 117
Lula, 66
Maria, 109, 115
Mary, 50, 63,
  83, 119
Maude, 134
Mildred, 53
Minnie, 30
Nellie, 56
Ophelia, 82

Parthenia, 136
Rachael, 4, 39
Roberta, 15
Ruby, 41, 99
Sallie, 20, 75
Sarah, 52, 66,
  98, 118
Susan, 20, 108
JOHNSTON
Emma, 76
Virginia, 37
JOINES
Jettie, 39
JOLLY
Florence, 99
JONES
Agnes, 75
Alice, 58
Allegra, 53
Annie, 113
Bernice, 96
Bettie, 151
Blanche, 71,
  151
Clara, 146
E Dora, 40
Edith, 14
Elizabeth, 21
Ella, 142
Emily, 140
Emma, 47
Ethel, 98
Frances, 21, 90
Hattie, 113
Helen, 91
Jane, 55
Jennie, 116
Julia, 46
Kate, 137
Katie, 100
Lillian, 91
Lillie, 129

Louisa, 78
Lucinda, 41
Maggie, 71,
  150
Margaret, 15
Martha, 84, 142
Mary, 17, 147
Salina, 118
Sallie, 28, 72
Sarah, 155
Vernita, 7
JORDAN
Dollie, 122
Eliza, 71
Georgianna, 59
Hannah, 47
Henrietta, 14
Indi, 83
Matilda, 60
JOYCE
Annie, 27
Dickie, 48
JULIEN
Paula, 110

—K—

KACHE
Virginia, 30
KADES
Dora, 120
KAHL
Emma, 112
KAHRL
Marie, 74
KAIN
Stella, 155
KALB
Marie, 82
KANE
Iva, 124
Laura, 18

KAUFFMAN
  Valda, 109
KAUPP
  Theresia, 131
KEALY
  Mary, 89
KEAN
  Rosa, 6
KEARNS
  Eva, 32
  Margaret, 9
  Maria, 79
  Martha, 9
KEECH
  Helen, 102
KEELER
  Beatrice, 50
KEENE
  Augusta, 133
  Clair, 63
  Lucy, 68
KEENER
  Eulah, 49
KEISTER
  Eveline, 66
KEITH
  Hannah, 67
  Mary, 15
KELBAUGH
  Grace, 117
KELLOGG
  Alice, 72
  Esther, 125
KELLY
  Anne, 106
  Etta, 136
  Helen, 37
  Mary, 23
KEMP
  Irene, 90
KENDRICK
  Annie, 131

Martha, 77
KENNEDY
  Agnes, 1
  Audress, 31
  Edna, 57
KENNER
  Gertrude, 115
KENNEY
  Mary, 141
KENYON
  Alice, 88
  Alma, 11
  Fannie, 84
  Ida, 14
  Marion, 89
KEPHART
  Daisy, 119
  Florence, 131
  Gracie, 82
KEPLER
  Kathryn, 12
KERBY
  Ann, 57, 122
  Anna, 122
  Margaret, 153
KEREN
  Doris, 155
KERFOOT
  Grace, 59
KERNOLL
  Eliza, 111
KERNS
  Bertha, 144
  Eleanor, 120
  Kate, 44
  Marjorie, 65
  Nellie, 40
KERR
  Edith, 9
  Mabel, 97
  Ruth, 144
KERSEY

Bessie, 3
KESTNER
  Margaret, 28
KEWLEY
  Alice, 134
KEYHO
  Margaret, 88
KEYS
  Elsie, 78
  F, 36
  Genevieve, 58
  Ida, 41
  Josie, 110
  Mary, 136
  Sarah, 28
  Theresa, 115
KEYTON
  Daisy, 82
KIATTA
  Marie, 32
KIDWELL
  Alice, 153
  Angelina, 21
  Ann, 27, 78,
    79, 84, 110,
    151
  Annie, 27, 110
  Bertie, 139
  Caroline, 61, 78
  Daisy, 3
  Edith, 110
  Emily, 116
  Emma, 68
  Ethel, 121
  Eveline, 79
  Fannie, 130
  Goldie, 42
  Harriet, 27
  Hattie, 78, 151
  Ida, 9
  Isabella, 145
  Jemima, 118

Jennie, 62
  Laura, 52, 79
  Lavinia, 83, 93
  Leish, 134
  Lillian, 6
  Lillie, 39
  Lizzie, 129
  Lula, 85
  Mabel, 78
  Margaret, 50,
    116, 145
  Marjorie, 95
  Martha, 21, 30
  Mary, 9, 21, 66,
    75, 78, 79,
    127, 148,
    151
  Maud, 151
  May, 76
  Nancy, 31
  Roberta, 66
  Roda, 117
  Rosa, 12
  Rose, 91
  Ruth, 124
  Sallie, 39, 63
  Sarah, 53, 66,
    69, 79, 127
  Susie, 77, 78
  Thelma, 18
  Victoria, 80
  Viola, 122
  Virginia, 76
  Waneta, 18
KILLAM
  Laura, 7
  Susan, 12
KILLIAN
  Grace, 50
KILLINGER
  Clara, 117
KINCHELOE

Alice, 154
Elizabeth, 122
Hollis, 110
Jannie, 32
Mabel, 55
Namie, 74
KINES
Bettie, 13
KING
Annie, 20
Clara, 110
Dorothy, 59
Ethel, 5
Ettie, 98
Flora, 113
Lydia, 118
Mamie, 109
Margaret, 55
Ruth, 39
Sarah, 70
KINGMAN
Hannah, 127
KINSLER
Willetta, 33
KINSMAN
Mary, 1
KIOH
Hattie, 71
KIRBY
Elsie, 94
Ethel, 87
Hazel, 130
Martha, 145
Minnie, 80
Nellie, 149
Nettie, 27
Rowenna, 109
Viola, 82
Virginia, 55
Vivienne, 155
KIRK
Grace, 58

Helen, 116
KITCHEN
Annie, 138
Georgianna, 121
Naomi, 8
KITSON
Eleanor, 112
Elsie, 94
Ocie, 87
Sarah, 95
KITTENGER
Annie, 124
KLEIN
Emma, 18
Mildred, 120
Violet, 26
KLINE
Rose, 148
Sallie, 26
KLINEFELTER
Harriett, 45
KLINGSBURY
Dorothy, 21
KLOCK
Loretta, 30
KLOTSCH
Helen, 135
KNAPP
Brenda, 41
KNIGHT
Florence, 77
Lavinia, 49
Maggie, 51
Maria, 31
KNISELY
Edna, 61
KNOX
Estella, 127
KOON
Jane, 49

KORZENDORFER
Helen, 110
Lena, 49
KRAEMER
Lillian, 33
KRAHNKE
Cleone, 59
KRAUS
Alice, 128
KRETEN
Sophie, 146
KREZELL
Marie, 6
KUHN
Harriett, 54
KUKE
Juanita, 53
KULICK
Katherine, 132

—L—

LA SALLE
Aldona, 50
LACEY
Alice, 54
Alma, 44
Mary, 44
LACKSEY
Lucretia, 33
LACY
Ella, 42
Lyda, 65
Maggie, 97
Nina, 2
Ramona, 28
Virginia, 151
LADUE
Alice, 144
Margaret, 29
LAFFERTY
Rose, 95

LAIRD
Mary, 141
LAKE
Ruth, 99
LAMBERT
Laura, 51
Lucy, 121
LAMP
Princess, 58
LANAHAN
Catherine, 73
LANDICK
Ruth, 44
LANDMAN
Lydia, 38
LANDRIAN
Palmyra, 8
LANE
Eleanor, 133
Hattie, 141
Janine, 84
Lucy, 137
Rosie, 123
LANGDEN
Ann, 45
LANGER
Edna, 143
LANGSTON
Eleanor, 37
LANHAM
Alpha, 50
Annie, 3
Dora, 105
Effie, 82
Elizabeth, 73
Hattie, 48
Idella, 48
Mary, 25
LANTERS
Mamie, 72
LANTZ
Clara, 118

LAPHAM
  Mildred, 128
LARGENT
  Mary, 14
LARKIN
  Lottie, 32
LATCHFORD
  Debbie, 39
LATHAM
  Etta, 65
LAVINUS
  Marguerite, 56
LAWRENCE
  Julia, 155
  Marie, 64
LAWS
  Laura, 137
LAWSON
  Eva, 66
  Malinda, 102
LAZENBERRY
  Alice, 51
LE HEW
  Lavinia, 80
LE MAT
  Eugenia, 43
LEA
  Irene, 77
LEACH
  Elizabeth, 82
LEAMAN
  Ruth, 155
LEAPLEY
  Bessie, 9
LEATHERMAN
  Vida, 67
LEDMAN
  Alcinda, 3
  Dearing, 116
LEE
  Alice, 36

Ann, 27, 70,
  90, 151
Anna, 70, 151
Annie, 90
Bertha, 144
Bessie, 154
Betsy, 132
Betty, 139
Birdie, 63
Carrie, 119
Constance, 108
Cora, 72
Delilah, 28
Eleanor, 130
Eliza, 13, 38
Elizabeth, 13
Etta, 90
Frances, 148
Hannah, 43
Harriette, 10
Helen, 2, 127
Ida, 137
Irene, 131
Lillian, 9, 56,
  118
Linnie, 123
Lizzie, 114
Louise, 117
Lucie, 119
Lucy, 60, 149
Malany, 22
Malinda, 20
Martha, 103
Mary, 4, 19,
  101, 102,
  123
Mattie, 126
Minnie, 107,
  144
Namie, 48
Pearl, 11
Virginia, 117

Winifred, 41
LEEBRICK
  Nannie, 120
LEEDS
  Bertha, 80
  Bertie, 94
  Dora, 77
  Florence, 154
  Lydia, 9
LEEMAN
  Mary, 140
LEESE
  Helen, 123
LEIGH
  Cora, 123
  Mary, 104
LEISTER
  Evelyn, 34
LEITH
  Kathleen, 123
LEMOINE
  Virginia, 70
LEMP
  Anna, 131
LENT
  Maggie, 40
LEONARD
  Cora, 104
  Winifred, 27
LEPLEY
  Pauline, 75
LESTER
  Ida, 14
  Melissa, 21
LEVINE
  Sophia, 119
LEVY
  Helen, 13
LEWIS
  Alcinda, 67
  Alice, 107
  Alma, 79

Amanda, 34, 38
Ava, 144
Catharine, 131
Clara, 146
Cora, 44, 126
Evangeline, 8
Gertrude, 146
Ginnie, 71
Harriet, 92
Jane, 8, 35, 90
Janet, 90
Jessie, 67
Judith, 115
Julia, 99
Kate, 35
Laura, 106
Mabel, 107
Maggie, 151
Mamie, 140
Martha, 61
Mary, 44, 128,
  143
Susie, 88
Tinny, 111
LIGGINS
  Rosa, 152
LIGHT
  Carrine, 22
LIGHTBOWN
  Maud, 2
LILLARD
  Rita, 6
LINCOLN
  Lucille, 100
LINDAWOOD
  Birtie, 45
  Margaret, 60
LINDSAY
  Evelyn, 30
  Mary, 144
LINEBURG
  Anna, 93

LINFOOT
  Laura, 13
LINK
  Lillas, 141
LINN
  Verna, 123
LIONS
  Mary, 11
LIPCOM
  Edith, 64
LIPSCOMB
  Phebe, 112
LLOYD
  Annie, 1, 118
  Effie, 118
  Elizabeth, 44
  Frances, 20
  Grace, 118
  Irene, 93
  Lavinia, 31
  Lillie, 139
  Lydia, 79
  Maggie, 108
  Norvell, 121
  Pauline, 129
  Rebecca, 34
  Sadie, 108
  Sarah, 3
LOCKRIE
  Florence, 147
LOCRAFT
  Lucile, 45
LOEB
  Marion, 49
LOEFFLER
  Katheryn, 80
LOGAN
  Dorothea, 21
LOHMAN
  Anna, 68
  Dorothy, 93

LOMACK
  Alice, 58
LOMAX
  May, 59
  Melvina, 71
  Susie, 45
LONG
  Adah, 109
  Catharine, 77
  Inez, 103
  Pearl, 60
LOOMIS
  Celestia, 105
  Clella, 85
LOREN
  Lois, 68
LORIA
  Ann, 38
LOTT
  Ida, 19
  Lillian, 145
LOUTHER
  May, 96
LOVE
  Isabella, 64
  Jessie, 49
  Mary, 3
LOVEDAY
  Alice, 132
LOVELACE
  Beula, 78
LOVELESS
  Annie, 79
  Ida, 125
  Mary, 78
LOVING
  Helen, 149
LOWE
  Betsy, 24
  Bettie, 155
  Edith, 62
  Eleanor, 51

  Frances, 109
  Laura, 148
  Lucretia, 22
  Margaret, 133
  Marguerite, 68
LOWELL
  Elizabeth, 67
LOWRY
  Elizabeth, 93
  Ella, 54
  Irvel, 13
LUCAS
  Amanda, 6
  Annie, 99
  Ellen, 55
  Ethel, 17
  Gusta, 146
  Marie, 131
  Mattie, 65
  Miranda, 137
  Virginia, 70
LUCKETT
  Lizzie, 151
LUDERS
  Bertie, 38
LUDLOW
  Phebe, 45
LUDWIG
  Louise, 81
LUNNEY
  Frances, 121
LUNSFORD
  Ella, 82
LUSKEY
  Annie, 50
LUSTIG
  Ilona, 103
LUTTRELL
  Edna, 101
LUTZ
  Ethel, 12

LYDECKER
  Lavinia, 44
LYLES
  Anna, 127
  Belle, 96
  Elizabeth, 37
  Eva, 108
  Fannie, 108
  Hannah, 80
  Jane, 111
  Jessie, 72
  Leon, 41
  Lilly, 125
  Mattie, 88
  Nancy, 98
  Nellie, 7
LYNCH
  Cora, 109
  Elizabeth, 47
  Ella, 106
  Ida, 104
  Limmie, 111
  Mabel, 124
  Mary, 24
  Valinda, 90
LYNN
  Ann, 32
  Elizabeth, 101
  Frances, 113
  Martha, 130
  Mary, 114
  Minerva, 48
LYONS
  Vernice, 133

—M—

MABEN
  Nelly, 2
MACBETH
  Alice, 83

MACK
Adelaide, 64
Edith, 51
Grace, 25
Ida, 100
Sarah, 135
MACKEY
Catherine, 71
MACNEIL
Maggie, 122
MADDEN
Geneva, 18
MADDOX
Elizabeth, 124
MAFFETT
Annie, 50
Lillian, 62
Maggie, 88
Marion, 88
MAGARITY
Carrie, 134
Eliza, 112
Hilda, 115
Sarah, 132
V, 145
MAGEE
Jane, 109
MAGNER
Mary, 102
MAGRUDER
Nancy, 47
MAHONEY
Jessie, 99
Sarah, 77
MAHONY
E, 62
MAHORNEY
Lulie, 96
MAILEY
J, 8
MAKELY
Edith, 85

Grace, 36
Jennie, 130
Martha, 48
Mary, 59
Virginia, 37
MALCOLM
Fannie, 67
MALEY
Nellie, 35
MALIN
Anne, 100
MALLETTE
Jennie, 61
MALONE
Mary, 14
MALONEY
Beulah, 21
MALORY
Harriet, 17
MALTERN
Lucille, 120
MANDLEY
Maggie, 13
MANKIN
Cecil, 149
Ethel, 94
Lillian, 90
Mattie, 51
Minnie, 69
MANN
Edith, 26
MANNING
Mary, 151
MANVELL
Dorothy, 43
MARANVILLE
Nancy, 128
MARCERON
Lillian, 77
MARCHANT
Elizabeth, 25

MARDEN
Marion, 87
MARDERS
Betty, 127
Mary, 102
Susie, 146
MARKHAM
Bridget, 131
MARKS
Edna, 135
Elise, 82
Eva, 50
Ina, 76
Mary, 89
Wenna, 52
MARLOW
Irene, 147
MARR
Sarah, 130
MARSHALL
Anna, 58
Bertha, 74
Elenora, 150
Esther, 119
Fannie, 132
Helen, 31, 85,
139
Hilda, 148
Jane, 154
Luana, 42
Maggie, 142
Margaret, 47
Mary, 35
May, 35
Minnie, 28
Nona, 35
Ruth, 106
Sarah, 45
MARSHBURN
Lilly, 68
MARSHER
Emma, 34

MARTIN
Alice, 111
Anna, 32
Caroline, 122
Clelia, 13
Elizabeth, 5
Frances, 28
Ida, 124
Jennie, 115
Juanita, 97
Louise, 13
Lucy, 112
Mary, 37
Mollie, 36
Nellie, 22
Velma, 9
Virginia, 59, 80
MASON
Anna, 93
Annie, 15, 99
Clara, 94, 115
Emma, 154
Hazel, 57
Josephine, 43
Kora, 24
Marie, 90
Mary, 69, 82
Nellie, 99
MASSIE
Ruth, 138
MATEER
Hattie, 1
Jennie, 138
Mary, 139
Mattie, 56
MATHERS
Catharine, 44
Cora, 72
MATHES
Mary, 2
MATHESON
Julia, 4

MELVIN
  Alice, 99
  Martha, 99
  Ruth, 105
MENTZER
  Hattie, 136
MERDOCK
  Kattie, 142
MERIGOLD
  Viola, 46
MERO
  Mary, 14
MERRIFIELD
  Edith, 121
MERRILL
  Edna, 75
MERRY
  Catherine, 33
METZGER
  Pearl, 57
MEYER
  Bessie, 143
MICON
  Margaret, 34
MIDDLETON
  Elena, 101
  Hannah, 15
  Helen, 107
  Minnie, 43
MILES
  Sarah, 60
MILLAN
  Bessie, 91
  Eliza, 126
  Mary, 51, 95
  Virginia, 95
MILLARD
  Goldie, 25
  Lillian, 11
  Lulie, 139
  Mabel, 127
  Sarah, 27

Vennie, 33
MILLENAX
  Claris, 73
MILLER
  Addie, 81
  Annie, 8, 51
  Blanche, 98
  Catherine, 3
  Charlotte, 12
  Claudia, 13
  Elizabeth, 57
  Ella, 38
  Etta, 33
  Evelyn, 30
  F, 54, 150
  Flora, 150
  Gladys, 43
  Helen, 49
  Julia, 11
  Lenna, 33
  Lenore, 112
  Margaret, 104
  Mary, 80, 140
  Ruth, 154
  Wavie, 154
MILLETT
  Annie, 76
MILLINER
  Clara, 5
MILLS
  Agnes, 149
  Alice, 53
  Amy, 56
  Ann, 8, 98, 105
  Annie, 98
  Blanche, 59
  Jane, 78
  Laura, 40, 147
  Madeline, 108
  Maggie, 130
  Marjoria, 46
  Martha, 76

Mary, 33, 121,
  124
  Sarah, 38
  Susan, 5
MILSTEAD
  Daniza, 51
  Emma, 63
  Ida, 33
  Lou, 19
  Susan, 3
MINNIX
  Lucie, 120
MINOR
  Leah, 155
  Rosa, 85
MITCHELL
  Cora, 4
  Effie, 21
  Emma, 42
  Florence, 65
  M, 81, 94, 98,
  120, 126,
  137
  Maggie, 94
  Marie, 120
  Mary, 81, 137
  Nora, 13
  Sarah, 38, 150
  Virginia, 81
MOBLEY
  Rowe, 102
MOCK
  Audrey, 129
  Edna, 140
  Joanna, 61
  Mabel, 38
  Mary, 136
MOFFETT
  Ethel, 72
  Pauline, 4
MOHLER
  Alma, 6

Edna, 138
  Etta, 97
  Fay, 47
  Rita, 94
  Sallie, 47
MOLBY
  Grace, 97
MOLINARD
  Nannie, 46
MONCH
  Adelaide, 82
  Ethel, 41
  Florence, 116
  Mary, 10
MONCURE
  Anna, 15
  Margaret, 13
  Mary, 30, 111
MONEY
  B, 97
  E, 87, 138
  Ella, 87
  Fannie, 68
  Hattie, 151
  Laura, 129
  Mary, 30, 33,
  48
  Narcissa, 54
  Rachel, 145
  Rosa, 78
  Sallie, 11
MONROE
  Ada, 103
  Chloe, 145
  Eliza, 80
  Hellen, 121
  Kate, 63
  Virginia, 138
MOON
  Cora, 65
  Jessie, 7

MOONEY
  Laura, 98
  Lucie, 42
MOORE
  Alcinda, 150
  Amy, 85
  Carrie, 131
  Edith, 76
  Elizabeth, 134
  Ella, 14
  Elmira, 77
  Eugenia, 18
  Florence, 26
  Geneva, 31
  Gertrude, 135
  Harriet, 60
  Irene, 43
  Kate, 27
  Maggie, 125
  Margaret, 38
  Mary, 74
  Mildred, 7
  Minnie, 14
  Oga, 38
  Rebecca, 41
  Susan, 40, 88
  Susannah, 88
  Zerita, 35
MORAN
  Charlotte, 82
  Mary, 96
MORARITY
  Alice, 60
  Sinah, 73
MORGAL
  Ruby, 133
MORGAN
  Anna, 19
  Effie, 154
  Estell, 56
  Georgie, 102
  Katie, 85

Mary, 110
MOROCKER
  Marie, 77
MORRIS
  Virginia, 4
MORRISON
  Lelure, 5
MORROW
  Lizzie, 79
MORTON
  Ann, 126
  Belle, 112
  Fannie, 143
  Mary, 111
MOSBY
  Martha, 138
  Victoria, 28
MOSCA
  Victoria, 121
MOSELY
  Cornelia, 148
MOTEN
  Laurinda, 135
MOULDEN
  Mary, 60
MOULTON
  Harriet, 132
  Rachael, 70
MOUNTS
  Lena, 49
MOWBRAY
  Katherine, 95
MOX
  Evelyn, 97
MOXLEY
  Esther, 94
  Winney, 72
MOXLY
  Maud, 27
MUCH
  Mamie, 144

MUDD
  Ethel, 21
MULHERON
  Helen, 24
MULHOLLAND
  Alice, 32
  Emma, 23
  Katie, 148
  Margaret, 73
  Nannie, 148
MULLEN
  Grace, 55
  Susan, 148
MULLINIX
  Nellie, 80
  Ruth, 95
MUMFORD
  Mary, 11
MUMMAW
  Geneva, 68
MUNDAY
  Armata, 81
  Bertha, 32
  Ouida, 56
MUNDLE
  Bettie, 88
MUNDY
  Hannah, 147
  Kate, 128
MUNOZ
  Harriet, 115
MUNSON
  Mary, 61
MURNANE
  Alice, 58
  Honora, 124
MURPHY
  Ellenora, 69
  Emma, 99
  Etta, 135
  Katie, 112
  Lizzie, 60

Margaret, 60
MURRAY
  Caroline, 129
  Carrie, 117
  Emma, 84
  Hattie, 128
  Janie, 124
  Margaret, 38
  Marie, 118
  Pearl, 43
  Rosa, 42
  Sarah, 120
  Stella, 116
  Virginia, 146
MURTAUGH
  Anna, 19
  Elizabeth, 124
  Mary, 111
  Rose, 40
  Winifred, 138
MUSE
  Fannie, 107
MUTERSBAUGH
  Alma, 56
MYERS
  Blanch, 44
  Catharine, 132
  Dorothy, 8
  Mary, 142
  S Bessie, 101

—N—

NAILOR
  Lena, 60
  Susan, 73
NALLS
  Ann, 10
NAPPER
  Anna, 75
NARRINGTON
  Louise, 63

POOLE
Daisy, 135
Edith, 37
Gracie, 113
Margaret, 115
Mary, 105
Rosa, 72
Ruth, 78
Vivian, 134
PORT
Edith, 106
PORTCH
Alice, 75
PORTER
Della, 79
Helen, 103
Ida, 80
Margaret, 69
Mary, 125
Nealy, 42
POSEY
Grisian, 48
Josephine, 91
Lulie, 10
Martha, 107
Mollie, 80
POSTON
Maude, 109
Sarah, 141
POTTER
Carrie, 116
Sarah, 13
POWELL
Alice, 54
Annie, 30
Carrie, 43
Ella, 1
Elsie, 86
Hazel, 36
Irma, 23
Louise, 128
Lucy, 55

Martha, 87
Mary, 23
Maud, 2
Ophelia, 20
Susan, 99
POWER
Mary, 110
Phoebe, 63
Veronica, 93
POWERS
Doris, 148
POYNER
Beatrice, 5
PRATHER
Lucy, 105
PRATT
Alice, 81
Mary, 73
PRICE
Fay, 101
Ida, 111
Madeline, 29
PRIDMORE
Martha, 61
Sarah, 132
PRIEST
Lottie, 130
PRIOR
Emma, 121
PROCTOR
Fannie, 94
Louise, 90
Maria, 83
PROSISE
Augusta, 65
PROVENZA
Rose, 101
PUGH
Bessie, 86
Laura, 112
Nannie, 109

PULLIN
Elizabeth, 63
PULMAN
Agnes, 100
Frances, 7
Gracie, 23
Irene, 115
Janet, 12
Jennie, 108
Nannie, 75
Sarah, 96
PULTZ
Nellie, 98
PUMPHREY
Ruth, 103
PURDUM
Blanche, 125
Frieda, 21
PUTNAM
Ann, 106
PUTT
Vera, 119
PYLES
Katherine, 43

—Q—

QUANDER
Alcinda, 64
Alice, 46
Catherine, 130
Elizabeth, 152
Emma, 60
Eunice, 85
Irene, 128
Minnie, 18
Susannah, 101
Susie, 65
QUEEN
Lucy, 19
QUICK
Hazel, 119

Ida, 62
S Christine, 38
QUIGG
Mary, 15
QUILTY
Frances, 90

—R—

RAGAN
Ella, 92
Ellen, 101
RALEIGH
Helen, 29
RALEY
Amanda, 142
RALSTON
Edith, 112
RAMSDELL
Myrtle, 5
RANDALL
Elsie, 8
Jennie, 52
Mary, 139
Sarah, 137
RANDOLPH
Hattie, 111
Margaret, 42
RANNEBERGER
Mabel, 3
RANSEL
Jemima, 138
RANSELL
Lizzie, 107
RASS
Mary, 153
RATCLIFFE
Jennie, 102
Maria, 31, 139
Marian, 139
Virginia, 46

RATHBURN
  Cora, 25
RATRIE
  Isabel, 47
RAUB
  Ida, 67
  Mary, 82
RAWLING
  Lillian, 54
RAY
  Lizzie, 92
RAYNOR
  Emma, 109
READE
  Mary, 21
READSHAW
  Alice, 70
  Mrs. L, 42
REAGAN
  Lillian, 87
  Margaret, 107
  Mary, 121
REARICK
  Helen, 119
RECTOR
  D Ann, 52
  Dorothy, 20
  Harriet, 88
  Hazel, 88
  Mary, 151
  Rosabelle, 93
  Sallie, 126
  Vera, 21
  Vivian, 124
REED
  Annie, 134
REEDY
  Mary, 8
REEVES
  Laura, 81
  Martha, 63

REGAL
  Minnie, 52
REICH
  Liley, 19
REID
  Anna, 40, 51
  Catharine, 134
  Edna, 96
  Elsie, 141
  Estelle, 40
  Fanny, 107
  Florence, 80,
    107
  Frances, 30,
    115
  Grace, 107
  Katie, 48
  Kitty, 128
  Lenora, 75
  Lula, 145
  M, 7, 45, 104,
    114, 128
  Margaret, 7,
    114
  Mary, 45, 128
  Rosa, 16
  Rose, 121
  Rowena, 38
  Sallie, 46
  Thedie, 51
  Virginia, 69
REIF
  Lottie, 65
REINBECK
  Della, 45
REMSBURG
  Pansy, 41
REST
  Eleanor, 87
REYNOLDS
  Carrie, 77
  Dora, 110

Elsie, 43
Florence, 128
Frances, 96
Ida, 4
Kate, 105
Lelia, 146
Marie, 79
RHIEL
  Catharine, 85
  Margaret, 12
RICE
  Frances, 89
  Hattie, 24
  Katherine, 98
  Marian, 45
  Mary, 61, 143
  Mattie, 91
  Nellie, 126
RICHARDS
  Mary, 11, 27,
    80
  Mildred, 61
  Nancy, 45
  Priscilla, 136
  Viola, 22
RICHARDSON
  Dorothy, 65
  Eliza, 52
  Elmira, 65
  Florence, 120
  H Virginia, 141
  Madge, 40
  Rose, 44
  Virginia, 63
RICHMOND
  Alice, 136
  Nancy, 112
RICKETTS
  Helen, 116
RICKS
  Eleanor, 152

RIDDLES
  Minnie, 125
RIDEOUT
  Grace, 8
RIDGELEY
  Rachael, 121
RIDGEWAY
  Edna, 44
  Laura, 66
RIELY
  Mary, 149
RIGG
  Beulah, 3
  Hattie, 49
  Irene, 9
  Maud, 117
  Susannah, 100
RIGGLES
  Mary, 131
  Naomi, 135
RIGHTER
  Emma, 31
RIKER
  Lottie, 146
RILEY
  Ellen, 117
  Jane, 54
  Jeanne, 11
  Jennie, 118
  Jessie, 97
  Kathleen, 50
  Lydia, 130
  Mary, 6, 62,
    132, 133
  Nora, 74
  Sarah, 50
RINKER
  Mary, 62
  Verna, 110
RISTON
  Ruth, 95

RITCHIE
  Jannie, 68
RITENOUR
  Annie, 145
RITZ
  Edith, 84
RIVERS
  Augustine, 39
RIVIERE
  Addie, 4
RIXEY
  Lillian, 149
ROACHE
  Ella, 19
ROANE
  Mary, 122
ROAT
  Barbara, 6
ROBERSON
  Belle, 153
  Diana, 2
  Ella, 2
  Fanny, 23
  Mary, 74
  Susannah, 101
  Virginia, 117
ROBERTS
  Ann, 7
  Esther, 45
  Margaret, 87
  Patricia, 86
  Ruby, 9
  Stella, 19
ROBERTSHAW
  Helen, 123
ROBERTSON
  Ella, 84
  Mary, 2
ROBEY
  Ada, 145
  Alice, 51
  Annie, 144

Appalonia, 116
Bessie, 94
Clara, 78
Effie, 73
Elsie, 11
Eva, 134
Frances, 21,
  116
Hattie, 98
Hazel, 34
Jennie, 36
Laura, 141
Luvine, 104
Malinda, 61
Millie, 63
Sarah, 104
ROBINSON
  Ada, 125
  Almira, 118
  Aloynsia, 60
  Bertha, 154
  Carrie, 68
  Catherine, 66
  Edna, 24
  Henrietta, 55
  Hilda, 96
  Janie, 65
  Jennie, 28
  Judy, 60
  Julia, 11, 117
  Katie, 66
  Lillian, 118
  Louisa, 17
  Lucy, 152
  Mamie, 100
  Marcia, 118
  Marie, 20
  Mary, 59
  May, 107
  Rose, 13
  Sally, 98, 105
  Susan, 117

Susie, 85
Sybilla, 53
Virginia, 4
ROBISON
  Jennie, 60
ROBY
  Alice, 52
  Artesha, 117
  Bertie, 27
  Ella, 116
  Levinia, 31
  Lillie, 62
  Margaret, 130
  Wesleyena, 18
ROCK
  Ida, 110
RODGERS
  Elizabeth, 88
ROESER
  Thekla, 28
  Thusnelda, 81
ROGERS
  Alice, 94
  Ann, 97, 152
  Annie, 97
  Birdie, 42
  Cora, 86
  Dora, 122
  Edith, 107
  Ella, 104
  Fanny, 48
  Maggie, 12, 33
  Mattie, 101
  Reba, 5
  Velma, 50
ROLLER
  Annie, 118
ROLLINS
  Britania, 28
  Edna, 31
ROPER
  Marie, 105

ROSE
  Lillie, 112
  Sarah, 18, 69
ROSENBERGER
  Elsie, 50
  Ethel, 130
ROSENHAMMER
  Theresa, 35
ROSS
  Elsie, 21
  Hanna, 29
ROTCHFORD
  Ida, 72
  Janapher, 38
  Katie, 136
  Roberta, 38
ROUFNER
  Irene, 74
ROURKE
  Maggie, 22
ROUSE
  Marguerite, 102
  Mary, 30
ROUSER
  Ola, 69
ROUZEE
  Mary, 141
ROW
  Annie, 60
  Dorothy, 80
  Edith, 118
  Susie, 21
ROWE
  Bernie, 109
  Julia, 25
ROWELL
  Annabel, 93
  Dorothy, 55
  Marguerite, 52
  Martha, 6
  Mary, 36

ROY
Delia, 14
Estelle, 119
Harriet, 135
Louisa, 128
Sarah, 17
ROYER
Blanche, 140
ROYSTON
Dorothy, 15
Lena, 99
RUCKER
Clara, 61
Lee, 123
RUCKET
Cora, 142
RUFFNER
Esther, 24
Mary, 150
RUKER
Carrie, 13
RUMMELS
Flora, 89
RUMSEY
Hannah, 14
RUNYON
Monteray, 81
RUPPERT
Amelia, 90
Margaret, 80
RUSH
Mable, 14
Mary, 33
RUSSEL
Carrie, 6
RUSSELL
Annie, 132
Ella, 128
Lyda, 110
Vashti, 14
Virginia, 14

RUST
Maggie, 134
RUTLEDGE
Louise, 52
RYAN
Genevieve, 13
Josephine, 154
Mabel, 33
Madeline, 42
Viola, 48
RYDER
Abbie, 76
RYER
Emma, 138

—S—

SABIN
Grace, 7
SACRISTE
Alice, 63
SAFFER
Annie, 31
Emma, 84
SAFFLE
Mary, 104
SAFFOLD
Ruth, 19
SAGAR
Emma, 61
SAGER
Geraldine, 47
SALSBURY
Annis, 129
SAMOY
Simone, 50
SAMPSON
Nettie, 82
SAMUEL
Mary, 97
SANBORN
Myrtle, 119

SANDERS
Adelaide, 4
Amy, 48
Margaret, 26
Martha, 18
Mary, 116
Maude, 41
Minnie, 140
Virgie, 116
SANFORD
Alberta, 113
Marcella, 135
Nettie, 104
SANGER
Bettie, 51
Lula, 76
SANSONE
Bernedeta, 29
SARTIVELL
Grace, 94
SASSCER
Helen, 120
SATTERFIELD
Audrey, 23
Sarah, 23
SAUERWEIN
Mildred, 103
SAULS
Lenore, 86
SAUM
Julia, 133
SAUNDERS
Bertha, 54
Carrie, 74
Catherine, 107
Effie, 59
Virgie, 25
SAUVEUR
Victoria, 122
SAVIDGE
Helen, 20

SAWYER
Lizzie, 23
SAYRE
Ollie, 76
SCHAFER
Ruth, 121
SCHALTZ
Anna, 115
SCHATZ
Hulda, 5
SCHEVING
Myrtle, 143
SCHILLER
Ophelia, 118
SCHLEIB
Barbara, 139
SCHLEY
Naomi, 121
SCHLICHTING
Amalia, 113
SCHMICK
Edith, 123
SCHMIDT
Bertha, 67
SCHNEIDER
Christine, 62
Katie, 109
Louise, 84
Pauline, 44
Wilhelmina, 57
SCHOFIELD
Catherine, 67
Edna, 4
Mamie, 73
SCHOOLEY
Annie, 122
SCHORTER
Mary, 8
SCHUERMAN
Martha, 8
SCHULTZ
Bessie, 29

SCHULTZE
Eva, 62
SCHULZ
Katherine, 18
SCHURTZ
Virginia, 118
SCOTT
Bernice, 42
Charlotte, 91
Clara, 5
Ethel, 114
Gracie, 59
Hannah, 100
Hyacinth, 70
Julia, 117
Kate, 60
Laures, 117
Lenora, 53
Margaret, 136
Minnie, 52, 65
Mome, 102
Norma, 24
Ruth, 73
Sarah, 113
Willins, 58
SEAL
Della, 147
Elizabeth, 100
SEALS
Eliza, 104
Fanny, 96
Lavenia, 136
Mary, 51
SEAMAN
Emma, 128
SEARS
Ethel, 77
SEAVER
May, 103
SEAY
Edna, 154

SEEF
Cora, 110
SEELER
Margaret, 140
SEIBERT
Mary, 27
SELVIN
Mary, 109
SELVY
Lucy, 71
SENNE
Hazel, 143
Helen, 8
SESSIONS
Maude, 36
SETTLEMYER
Irene, 24
SEWARD
Elanora, 104
SEWELL
Henrietta, 80
Marie, 105
Sarah, 77
SEXTON
Ida, 78
SEYMOUR
Violet, 150
SHACKLEFORD
Evelyn, 100
SHACKLETTE
Warwich, 70
SHAFER
Ida, 70
Margaret, 126
SHAFFER
Alberta, 121
SHANNON
Harriet, 84
SHARP
Catherine, 3
SHARPER
Annie, 73

Mary, 18, 77
Virginia, 71
SHARVEN
Nina, 75
SHAVER
Thelma, 23
SHAW
Florence, 73
Lydia, 78
Mattie, 62
Raydelle, 31
SHEA
Annie, 97
Nellie, 50
SHEAR
Addie, 83
Annie, 2
Caddie, 84
Gertrude, 118
SHEELS
Mae, 81
SHEETS
Anna, 7
Johny, 17
Mrs. N, 81
Nellie, 81
SHEID
Martena, 46
SHELDON
Alice, 122
SHELNITZ
Rose, 2
SHELTON
Delia, 87
Fannie, 130
Josie, 3
Mabel, 113
Martha, 17
Mora, 90
Queen, 146
Rosa, 62
Rose, 106

SHEPHERD
Alice, 133
Amelia, 133
Arlynne, 113
Bessie, 102
Eliza, 54
Georgia, 135
Gladys, 117
Katie, 129
Mary, 63, 107
Myrtle, 39
Nancy, 61, 89
Nettie, 68
Vivian, 23
Willie, 22
SHERIDAN
Florence, 57
SHERMAN
Elizabeth, 124
Elsie, 89
Fannie, 124
Grace, 114
Martha, 12
Mary, 118
SHERWOOD
Anna, 16
Annie, 75
Gladys, 41
Hattie, 46
Marianna, 150
Mary, 37
Rebecca, 16
SHIFFLETT
Annie, 32
Mary, 96
SHIMMEL
Ella, 137
SHIPLEY
Carrie, 96
Miriam, 114
SHIPMAN
Annie, 118

Carrie, 19, 92
Catherine, 39
Celia, 113, 148
Chainey, 70
Claudia, 24
Eliza, 19, 33
Elizabeth, 19
Elsie, 72
Emily, 2, 72,
   145
Emma, 106, 122
Evelyn, 64
Fannie, 127
Florence, 60
Grace, 46
Harriet, 85
Ida, 23, 108
Jane, 61
Janine, 42
Jennie, 11, 95
Josephine, 73
Judy, 46
Julia, 17, 95
Kate, 141
Keziah, 126
Lillian, 37, 148
Lottie, 77
Lucy, 30
Lydia, 53
Lyne, 152
Mabel, 70
Madge, 48
Maggie, 63
Mamie, 29
Margery, 62
Maria, 54
Mary, 2, 5, 16,
   70, 78, 100
Mattie, 91
Mildred, 13, 41
Mima, 132
Nettie, 105

Olive, 32
Pauline, 44
Rose, 54
Sallie, 124
Vallie, 53
Virginia, 118
Wilhelmina, 49
SMOOT
   Julia, 75
SMYTH
   Clara, 135
SNEEDON
   Frances, 90
SNIDER
   Alinda, 115
   Evalina, 89
   Laura, 111
   Lavenia, 20
   Sarah, 111
   Zadie, 99
SNOWDEN
   Elizabeth, 138
SNYDER
   Ada, 77
   Bessie, 130
   Daisy, 97
   Lillie, 26
   Malinda, 51
SONES
   Ruth, 5
SOPER
   Gertrude, 69
SORRELL
   Catherine, 80
SOULE
   Mary, 92
SOUTHERLAND
   Mary, 8
SPAIN
   Amanda, 148
SPALDING
   Mary, 86

SPARKS
   Blanche, 12
   Mary, 64
SPARROW
   Elizabeth, 54
   Susan, 127
   Wilhelmina, 34
SPAULDING
   Hilda, 5
   Mary, 72
SPEAKE
   Lavinia, 71
SPEER
   Almira, 93
   Carrie, 60
   Cecilia, 105
   E Ophelia, 117
   Elizabeth, 28
   Eunice, 150
   Eva, 147
   Georgiana, 24
   Harriet, 151
   Madeleine, 126
   Martha, 31
   Sarah, 26
SPENCER
   Dora, 43
   Dorothy, 117
   L Pauline, 58
SPICER
   Annie, 49
SPINDLE
   Agnes, 116
   Martha, 84
   Panola, 136
SPINKS
   Dorothy, 22
SPITTLE
   Rosa, 73
SPIVEY
   Ruby, 147

SPRAKER
   Norfa, 26
SPRIGG
   Matteele, 153
SPRINGMAN
   Ruth, 109
SPRINKLE
   Dorothy, 54
SPROUSE
   Mary, 150
STAATS
   Clara, 39
   Elsie, 54
   Nellie, 100
   Thelma, 78
STAFFORD
   Mary, 29
STAGE
   Catherine, 27
STAHL
   Emily, 21
STAHLMAN
   Carrie, 53
STALCUP
   Dorothy, 99
   Hazel, 117
STALEY
   Genevieve, 27
STALLING
   Helen, 114
STALLINGS
   Ethel, 47
   Sarah, 33
STAMP
   Ruth, 152
STANARD
   Ida, 11
STANDISH
   Olive, 43
STANTON
   Barbara, 11

STAPLES
  Emma, 117
STARK
  Etta, 8
STARR
  Sarah, 7
STEEL
  Allice, 79
  Jennie, 78
  Mary, 45
STEELE·
  Ann, 34
  Bessie, 144
  Effie, 53
  Frances, 19
  Gladys, 24
  Jane, 109
  Lawrence, 93
  Mary, 9, 98,
    110
  Sadie, 115
  Sarah, 90
  Viola, 123
STEERS
  Anna, 33
  Margaret, 36
  Mary, 140
STELL
  Alice, 46
STELY
  Katie, 16
STEPHEN
  Jean, 124
STEPHENS
  Ruth, 44
  Sarah, 23
STEPHENSON
  Arabella, 7
STEWARD
  Malessa, 65
STEWART
  Anna, 65

Fannie, 18
Frances, 126
Helen, 120
Isabella, 46
Jennie, 15
Leebertha, 149
Lillian, 98
Maria, 20
Mary, 42, 142
Minnie, 60
Rose, 67, 144
Rosetta, 144
Viola, 134
STILES
  Mary, 119
  Sarah, 131
  Viola, 144
STINE
  Irene, 30
STOBERT
  May, 95
STOCKETT
  Emma, 109
STODDARD
  Elizabeth, 14,
    53
  Mildred, 141
STOKES
  Annie, 1
  Mildred, 79
  Sarah, 131
  Winnie, 8
STONE
  Eudoxia, 1
  Fanny, 35
  Jennie, 113
  Jessie, 45
  Josephine, 144
  Lorena, 14
  Loretta, 93
  Margaret, 79
  Mary, 19

STONEBURNER
  Bessie, 7
STONESTREET
  Sallie, 86
STONNELL
  A B, 26
  Bessie, 12
  Ida, 14
  Margaret, 26
STORM
  Anna, 145
  Della, 46
  Fannie, 64
  Mariam, 114
STOTTS
  Carrie, 70
  Daisy, 85
  Sarah, 3
STOUT
  Alice, 65
  Catharine, 102
  Mary, 97, 102
STOY
  Dorothy, 10
STRATMEYER
  Everett, 54
STRAYER
  May, 43
STRETCH
  Edith, 146
STRIBLING
  Fannie, 133
STRICKLAND
  Pauline, 133
STROBLE
  Virginia, 16
STROMAN
  Emma, 131
STROTHER
  Catherine, 142
  Mary, 68, 138
  Priscilla, 73

STRUDER
  Emma, 101
  Josephine, 29
  Maggie, 118
  Margaret, 72
STRUZIK
  Lillian, 131
STUART
  Elizabeth, 40
  Ellen, 4
  Laura, 73
  Mary, 110
STUBBS
  Lutie, 86
STUDDS
  Annie, 49, 112
  Araminta, 30
  Gennetta, 24
  Harriet, 32
  Jeannette, 18
  Virginia, 91
STYLES
  Gracie, 63
  Mary, 152
SUDDEN
  Juliá, 102
SUIT
  Clara, 30
  Ethel, 41
SULLENS
  Ruth, 38
SULLIVAN
  Esie, 74
  Grace, 54, 128
  Mabel, 115
SUMMERALL
  Fannie, 115
SUMMERS
  Alice, 20
  Amelia, 36
  Bell, 65
  Luvenia, 100

Mary, 58, 75
Sally, 25
Sophia, 147
SUMNER
Charlotte, 38
Pearl, 43
SUTHERLAND
Amanda, 47
Emma, 77
George, 149
Lucy, 89
Mary, 135
SUTLER
Juanita, 140
SUTPHIN
Ann, 61
Gertrude, 148
Lola, 98
Ludie, 116
Mabel, 74
Olive, 119
Rachel, 32
SUTTON
Alice, 26
Ella, 83
Faith, 155
Mamie, 48
Mariana, 128
SWANN
Louisa, 126
SWART
E Gwyndolyn, 58
Edna, 2
Jane, 67
Mary, 2
SWARTZ
Pearl, 47
SWAYZE
Marie, 52
SWEENEY
Terry, 24

SWEENY
Gwinetta, 32
Leittie, 52
Sarah, 26
SWETNAM
Bettie, 61
Elizabeth, 48
Julia, 76
Nelle, 63
Roberta, 10
SWIFT
Ellen, 23
Margaret, 135
SWIMLEY
May, 95
SWINK
Margaret, 155
Martha, 3
SYLCURK
Helen, 128
SYLVESTER
Camilla, 25
Ida, 154
SYSSOCK
Fannie, 44

—T—

TAGGART
Martha, 1
TAIT
Mrs. O, 47
TALBERT
Carrie, 125
Hazel, 35
Margaret, 122
Sarah, 134
TALBOT
Harriett, 95
TALBOTT
Ada, 95
Nellie, 13

TALIAFERRO
Roberta, 143
TALIFERRO
Marion, 2
TANNER
Mary, 47
TANSELL
Mary, 32
TAPLET
Bessie, 86
TARBERT
Edith, 109
TARMAN
Virgie, 7
TATE
Adelaide, 51
Charlotte, 73
Pearl, 31
TAUGHINBAUGH
Anna, 67
TAULELLE
Rose, 80
TAVENNER
Mary, 45
TAYLOR
Abbie, 137
Alice, 136, 151
Alverta, 32
Amanda, 46
Annie, 115
Belle, 141
Betsey, 74
Blanche, 118, 119, 122
Della, 22
Dora, 42
Effie, 37
Elizabeth, 24, 35
Ella, 40
Elton, 146
Helen, 29

Julia, 42
Laura, 114, 128
Lillian, 55, 64
Louisa, 140
Lucinda, 16
Lucy, 26
Luella, 91
Mamie, 41
Margaret, 91
Martha, 144
Mary, 73, 126, 148
May, 10
Narcina, 13
Pansy, 135
Pauline, 49
Pearl, 75
Rachel, 83
Sarah, 49
Thelma, 67
Virginia, 114
TEBBS
Cecelia, 68
Harriet, 138
Martha, 71
Matilda, 3
TEMPLEMAN
Nellie, 118
TENNISON
Rebecca, 144
TERRELL
Beatrice, 91
Bessie, 120
Geneva, 71
Lucinda, 63
Mary, 64
Nettie, 142
Rebecca, 70
TERRETT
Eva, 119
Grace, 12
Hannah, 150

Jessie, 87
Lucy, 69
Nettie, 25
TERRY
  Emma, 144
  Lillian, 95
TESTERMAN
  Goldie, 105
TETLOW
  Ida, 62
THARP
  Alice, 135
THIERBACH
  Clara, 53
THOMAS
  Annie, 43
  Bertie, 74
  Bessie, 108
  Carrie, 24
  Cora, 133
  Esther, 21
  Eula, 7, 137
  Harriett, 65
  Hilda, 27
  Julia, 72
  Lillie, 70
  Lucretia, 63
  M Lois, 129
  Marion, 59
  Marjorie, 101
  Mary, 39, 87
  Odessa, 23
  Sally, 10
  Sarah, 33
  Verna, 49
  Virginia, 147
THOMPSON
  Alice, 48, 75,
    100, 111
  Alma, 140
  Anna, 31
  Annie, 63, 111

Barbara, 33
Beatrice, 93
Bertie, 108
Bettie, 15
Carrie, 79
Catherine, 122
Chloe, 20
Clara, 96, 138
Cordelia, 137
Dorothy, 49
Edith, 116
Edna, 41
Eliza, 68, 146
Elizabeth, 146
Ella, 18, 78
Elva, 122
Emma, 29
Estella, 148
Esther, 53
Ethel, 153
Eva, 114
Fedora, 10
Florence, 79
Frances, 56
Frank, 138, 139
Geneva, 136
Grace, 151
Hazel, 100
Helen, 12, 93
Ida, 31, 139
Julia, 135, 138
Katherine, 99
L, 8, 30, 138,
  139
Laura, 30
Lottie, 35
Louisa, 139
Mabel, 82
Maggie, 56
Margaret, 28,
  101
Martha, 22, 102

Mary, 58, 79,
  104, 128,
  129
Mattie, 93
Maud, 14
Minnie, 40, 88
Myrtle, 56
Nannie, 129
Olive, 66
Ona, 49
Rosa, 78
Rosie, 77
Ruth, 43, 107
Sallie, 42
Sarah, 31, 89
Susannah, 117
Thelma, 38
Virginia, 44
THOMSON
  Grace, 99
THORN
  Maggie, 27
THORNE
  Mary, 110
  Maud, 15
  Virginia, 112
THORNTON
  Ada, 142
  Caroline, 136
  Dulsey, 83
  Lucy, 38
  Mary, 145
THORTON
  Ethel, 99
THRIFT
  Lillie, 6
TIEFENTHALER
  Daisy, 54
TIFFANY
  Mary, 132
TILLETT
  Alice, 77

Daisey, 108
Fannie, 50
Lizzie, 106
Willella, 14
TILLEY
  Anita, 30
TILMAN
  Martha, 75
TINKHAM
  Nevada, 114
TINNER
  Caroline, 137
  Edith, 100
  Elizabeth, 6
  Elmira, 66, 84
  Emma, 104
  Frances, 26
  Louisa, 46
TINNEY
  Gladys, 87
TINSLEY
  Geneva, 75
TIPPETT
  Marion, 94
  Mary, 77
TITLOW
  Elizabeth, 63
TOBAN
  Lillie, 10
TOBIN
  Della, 126
  Elsie, 15
  Esther, 47
  Lola, 21
TORREYSON
  Annie, 89
TORRISON
  Mary, 141
TOWLES
  Mildred, 86
TOWN
  Hannah, 9

VAN HOESEN
  Dorothy, 149
VAN HORN
  Ellen, 128
VAN KANNER
  Effie, 94
VAN SICKLER
  Bessie, 120
  Margaret, 24
VAN VOORHIS
  Anna, 43
VAN VREAN
  Lillian, 92
VANDER VIES
  Marie, 82
VANDYCK
  Fannie, 145
  Lizzie, 142
  Roberta, 135
VANGENDER
  Bessie, 139
VASS
  Courtney, 53
  Ella, 36
  Rachel, 139
VAUGHAN
  Annabelle, 54
  Gertrude, 84
VEAL
  Florence, 114
VEALE
  Nannie, 77
VEITCH
  Georgia, 12
VENNEBUSH
  Cecelia, 141
VINCENT
  Virginia, 42
VIOLETT
  Mary, 57, 131
  Maud, 38
  Nellie, 148

VIOLLAND
  Adrienne, 77
VIRTS
  Esther, 87
VOLLAND
  Louise, 22
VOLTAIRE
  Mildred, 138
VON BRIESEN
  Carolyn, 92
VORHEES
  Mary, 127
VOSBURG
  Esther, 106
VOWLES
  Fannie, 61
  Garnett, 62
VROOM
  Elizabeth, 76

—W—

WADDELL
  Docia, 121
  Elizabeth, 35
  Mary, 11
  Viola, 25
WAFFOTT
  Laura, 135
WAGNER
  Addie, 16
WAGSTAFF
  Helen, 30
WAINE
  Sarah, 74
WAINES
  Edith, 86
WAINWRIGHT
  Frances, 115
  Mary, 123
WAKEFIELD
  Bessie, 144

  Oneita, 34
  Rita, 85
WAKEMAN
  Mollie, 15
WALCOTT
  Sara, 89
WALDVOGEL
  Lucy, 11
WALKER
  Alice, 26
  Annie, 52
  Clara, 19
  Edna, 131
  Elizabeth, 63,
    146
  Ella, 64
  Florence, 5, 56
  Jane, 28
  Jennie, 75
  Joanna, 98
  Julia, 134
  Kate, 40
  Laura, 25
  Lizzie, 52
  Lottie, 60
  Maggie, 144
  Margaret, 81
  Martha, 17
  Mary, 34, 50,
    86, 90
  Sarah, 88, 100
WALL
  Delia, 153
WALLACE
  Martha, 58
WALLER
  Ann, 140
  Fanny, 137
  Frances, 16
  Martha, 83
WALLOCH
  Ruth, 46

WALSH
  Alice, 113
  Leo, 66
WALSTENHOLME
  Margaret, 79
WALTERS
  Ella, 105
  Marian, 114
  Marietta, 33
  Martha, 122
  Maryon, 142
  Pearl, 145
  Regina, 31
  Sarah, 80
WALTHER
  Catherine, 92
WALTON
  Ann, 141
  Euphemia, 65
WALZEL
  Mary, 89
WANDSOR
  Alice, 125
WANZER
  Irene, 132
  Muriel, 116
WAPLE
  Annie, 83
  Minnie, 124
  Sarah, 114
WARD
  Elsie, 140
  Helen, 101
  Sara, 87
WARE
  Marjoria, 66
WARFIELD
  Bettie, 151
WARFORD
  Lillie, 85
WARNER
  Charlotte, 71

YOUNG
  Ada, 149
  Alberta, 17
  Alice, 68
  Carrie, 89
  Cora, 104
  Esther, 110
  Hattie, 36
  Julia, 98, 122
  Mary, 40
YOUNT
  Emma, 133

—Z—

ZAUGG
  Jeraldine, 110
ZEIGLER
  Violet, 127

ZINK
  Leoda, 89